The Trial *and* Triumph *of* Faith

The TRIAL *and* TRIUMPH *of* FAITH

Samuel Rutherford

THE BANNER OF TRUTH TRUST

THE BANNER OF TRUTH TRUST
3 Murrayfield Road, Edinburgh EH12 6EL, UK
P.O. Box 621, Carlisle, PA 17013, USA

★

First published 1645. Reprinted 1845 by the
Committee of the Free Church of Scotland
for the Publication of the Works of
Scottish Reformers and Divines

First Banner of Truth Edition 2001

ISBN 0 85151 806 0

Publisher's Preface

Samuel Rutherford (1600–61) is best remembered today for the soaring eloquence and pastoral wisdom of his *Letters.*[1] But he was not only a devotional writer. He was also a distinguished preacher, theologian and political thinker. All these aspects of his work appear in this book. Like the *Letters, The Trial and Triumph of Faith* shows the exalted devotion to Christ and the poetic gift that made his preaching so popular and successful. A visiting London merchant said that Rutherford's preaching showed him 'the loveliness of Christ'. The same feature shines out in *The Trial and Triumph of Faith*, originally published in 1645, as Rutherford expounds the incident of the woman of Canaan who came to Christ for the healing of her daughter, as recorded in Matthew 15 and Mark 7. Rutherford shows the overflowing of Christ's grace to the Gentiles. He also opens up the nature of prayer and of faith and the blessings promised to those who continue in them.

For the twenty-first-century reader who may not be familiar with Rutherford's writings, the following background information may be helpful. First, Rutherford, himself banished from his parish in 1636 for his opposition to Arminianism, used his preaching and writing to discuss theological errors and controversies current at the time of

[1] A selection of these is published by the Banner of Truth Trust: *Letters of Samuel Rutherford* (ISBN 0 85151 163 5, 208 pp. pbk., £2.50/$4.99).

writing. For example, in this book he deals at some length with the Antinomianism of men like Tobias Crisp, Robert Towne and Henry Denne. The terms and distinctions occurring in these discussions may seem academic, but such discussions of errors and misconceptions regarding faith and salvation are still of great value today. Old errors are constantly being revived in new guises by those who are unaware of the discussions of the past. Rutherford had pastoral objectives in view in refuting errors. He was often exceptionally attuned to the doubts and difficulties of ordinary Christians and a grasp of his arguments is of more than mere antiquarian interest.

Secondly, Rutherford was deeply interested in the struggle for further reformation in 'the three kingdoms' (England, Scotland and Ireland) and in ongoing attempts to limit the power of the king. At the time of the book's original publication Rutherford was in London serving as a commissioner to the Westminster Assembly, while the English Civil War was still being fought out. References to these contemporary affairs occur, both in the *Letter of Dedication* to Lady Jane Campbell (pp. 3–12) and in the course of the sermons, and might seem to distract from Rutherford's higher concern with the kingdom of God and salvation in Christ. We may better understand Rutherford and the occasionally violent imagery he uses if we remember that, in the conditions of the seventeenth century, these conflicts in church and state were literally life-or-death struggles. It is because the leaders of the time were prepared to risk their own lives[2] in resisting tyranny

[2] Rutherford himself would almost certainly have been put to death had he not been called, as he put it, to 'a superior Judge and judicatory'. As he lay dying, his book *Lex Rex* was burnt by the public hangman in Edinburgh and, by Archbishop Sharpe, at the gates of the college in St Andrews where he was Professor. For accounts of his life and influence see *The Scots Worthies* by John Howie and *Samuel Rutherford and His Friends* by Faith Cook, both published by the Banner of Truth Trust.

in church and state that we have inherited many of our rights and liberties, as well as the invaluable heritage of the writings of the time.

Finally, Rutherford's language and style are often highly poetic and figurative. This is how he describes Christ as the source of grace: 'Christ, for this cause especially, left the bosom of God, and was clothed with flesh and our nature, that he might be a mass, a sea, and boundless river of visible, living, and breathing grace, swelling up to the highest banks of not only the habitable world, but the sides also of the heaven of heavens, to over-water men and angels' (p. 11). Rutherford's lyrical language, though rooted in Scripture, is far removed from more prosaic ways of stating Christian truth.

Rutherford's ardent concern to commend Christ and faith in Him to the reader elevates *The Trial and Triumph of Faith* above any limited historical context and allows the book to speak powerfully to us today. He sees in the woman of Canaan an example of Christ's new creation, 'a flower planted and watered by Christ's own hand'. As he says of the passage he is expounding, 'To any seeking Jesus Christ, this text crieth, "Come and see."' But Rutherford also wishes to awaken believers to persevering prayer, 'to a fixed and resolved lying and dying at Christ's door, by continuing in prayer till the King come out and open, and answer the desire of the hungry and poor' (p. 24). Surely this call to persevering prayer is sorely needed at a time when the 'widespread prayerlessness'[3] of the evangelical church in America and Western Europe stands out.

June 2001

[3] D. A. Carson, *Call to Spiritual Reformation: Encouragement from Paul and His Prayers*, Grand Rapids: Baker Bok House, 1992.

TO THE RIGHT HONOURABLE

THE LADY JANE CAMPBELL,

VISCOUNTESS OF KENMURE; SISTER TO THE RIGHT NOBLE AND POTENT, THE MARQUIS OF ARGYLE,

GRACE AND PEACE.

MADAM,

I SHOULD complain of these much-disputing and over-writing times, if I were not thought to be as deep in the fault as those whom I accuse: but the truth is, while we endeavour to gain a grain-weight of truth, it is much if we lose not a talent-weight of goodness and Christian love. But, I am sure, though so much knowledge and light may conduce for our safe walking, in discerning the certain borders of divine truths from every false way; and suppose that searching into questions of the time were a useful and necessary evil only; yet the declining temper of the world's worst time, the old age of time, eternity now so near approaching, calleth for more necessary good things at our hands. It is unhappy, if, in the nick of the first breaking of the morning sky, the night-watch fall fast asleep, when he hath watched all the night. It is now near the morning-dawning of the resurrection. Oh, how blessed are we, if we shall care for our one necessary thing!

It is worthy our thoughts, that an angel, (never created, as I conceive) standing in his own land, "his right foot upon the sea, and his left foot on the earth," hath determined by oath, a controversy moved by scoffers, (2 Peter, iii. 3;) "yea, and with his hand lifted up to heaven, sware by him that liveth for ever and ever, who created heaven, and the things that are therein, and the earth, and things that therein are, and the sea, and things that are therein, that there should be time no longer." (Rev., x, 5, 6.) If eternity be concluded judicially by the oath of God, as a thing near to us, at the door, now about sixteen hundred years ago, it is high time to think of it; what we shall do, when the clay house of this tabernacle, which is but our summer house, that can have us but the fourth part of a year, shall be dissolved. Time is but a short trance;[1] we are carried quickly through it: our rose withereth, ere it come to its vigour: our piece of this short-breathing shadow, the inch, the half-cubit, the poor span-length of time, fleeth away as swiftly as a weaver's shuttle, (Job, vii, 6,) which leapeth over a thousand threads in a moment. How many hundred hours in one summer doth our breathing clay-post skip over, passing away as "the ships of desire, and as the eagle that hasteth to the prey." (Job, ix, 25, 26.) If death were as far from our knowledge, as graves and coffins (which to our eyes preach death) are near to our senses, even casting the smell of death upon our breath, so as we cannot but rub skins with corruption; we should not believe either prophets or apostles, when they say, "All flesh is grass," and, "It is appointed for all to die." Eternity is a great word, but the thing itself is greater: death, the point of our short line, teacheth us what we are, and what we shall be.

Should Christ, the condition of affairs we are now in, the excellency of free grace, be seen in all their own lustre and dye, we should learn much wisdom from these three. Christ speedeth little in conquer-

[1] A narrow covered passage.

ing of lovers: because we have not "seen his shape at any time," we look not upon Christ, but upon the accidents that are beside Christ; and therefore, few esteem Christ a rich pennyworth. But there is not a rose out of heaven, but there is a blot and thorn growing out of it, except that one only rose of Sharon, which blossometh out glory. Every leaf of the rose is a heaven, and serveth "for the healing of the nations;" every white and red in it, is incomparable glory; every act of breathing out its smell, from everlasting to everlasting, is spotless and unmixed happiness. Christ is the outset, the master-flower, the uncreated garland of heaven, the love and joy of men and angels. But the fountain-love, the fountain-delight, the fountain-joy of men and angels is more; for out of it floweth all the seas, springs, rivers, and floods of love, delight, and joy. Imagine all the rain and dew, seas, fountains, and floods, since the creation, were in one cloud, and these multiplied in measures, for number to many millions of millions, and then divided in drops of showers to an answerable number of men and angels;—this should be a created shower, and end in a certain period of time; and this huge cloud of so many rivers and drops, should dry up, and rain no more. But we cannot conceive so of Christ: for if we should imagine millions of men and angels to have a co-eternal dependent existence with Christ, and they eternally in the act of "receiving grace for grace out of his fulness," the flux and issue of grace should be eternal, as Christ is. For Christ cannot tire or weary from eternity to be Christ; and so, he must not, he cannot but be an infinite and eternal flowing sea, to diffuse and let out streams and floods of boundless grace Say that the rose were eternal; the sweet smell, the loveliness of greenness and colour must be eternal.

Oh, what a happiness, for a soul to lose its excellency in His transcendent glory! What a blessedness for the creature, to cast in his little all, in Christ's matchless all-sufficiency! Could all the streams retire into the fountain and first spring, they should be kept in a more sweet and firm possession of their being, in the bosom of their first cause, than in their borrowed channels that they now move in. Our neighbourhood, and retiring in, to dwell for ever and ever in the fountain-blessedness, Jesus Christ, with our borrowed goodness, is the firm and solid fruition of our eternal happy being. Christ is the sphere, the con-natural first spring and element of borrowed drops, and small pieces of created grace. The rose is surest in being, in beauty, on its own stalk and root: let life and sap be eternally in the stalk and root, and the rose keep its first union with the root, and it shall never wither, never cast its blossom nor greenness of beauty. It is violence for a gracious soul to be out of his stalk and root; union here is life and happiness; therefore the Church's last prayer in canonic Scripture is for union, (Rev., xxii, 20.) "Amen: Even so, come, Lord Jesus." It shall not be well till the Father, and Christ the prime heir, and all the weeping children, be under one roof in the palace royal. It is a sort of mystical lameness, that the head wanteth an arm or a finger; and it is a violent and forced condition, for arm and finger to be separated from the head. The saints are little pieces of mystical Christ, sick of love for union. The wife of youth, that wants her husband some years, and expects he shall return to her from over-sea lands, is often on the shore; every ship coming near shore is her new joy; her heart loves the wind that shall bring him home. She asks at every passenger news: "Oh! saw ye my husband? What is he doing? When shall he come? Is he shipped for a return?" Every ship that carrieth not her husband, is the breaking of her heart. What desires hath the Spirit and Bride to hear, when the husband Christ shall say to the mighty angels, "Make you ready for the journey; let us go down and divide the skies, and bow the heaven: I will gather my prisoners of hope unto me; I can want my Rachel and her weeping children no longer. Behold, I come quickly to judge the nations." The bride, the Lamb's wife, blesseth the feet of the messengers that preach such tidings, "Rejoice, O Zion, put on thy beautiful garments; thy King is coming." Yea, she loveth that quarter of the sky, that being rent asunder and cloven, shall yield to her Husband, when he shall put through his glorious hand, and shall come riding on the rainbow and clouds to receive her to himself.

The condition of the people of God in the three kingdoms calleth for this, that we now wisely consider what the Lord is doing. There is a language of the Lord's "fire in Zion," and "his furnace in Jerusalem," if we could understand the voice of the crying rod. The arrows of God flee beyond us, and beside us, but we see little of God in them: we sail, but we see not shore; we fight, but we have no victory. The efficacy of second causes is the whole burden of the business, and this burden we lay upon creatures, (and it is more than they can bear,) and not upon the Lord. God is crying lameness on creatures and multitude, that his eminency of working may be more seen. 2. Many are friends to the success of reformation, not to reformation. Men's faith goes along with the promises, until providence seem to them to belie the promise. Through light at a key-hole many see God in these confusions in the three kingdoms; but they fall away, because their joining with the cause, was violent kindness to Christ. It is not a friend's visit, to be driven to a friend's house to be dry in a shower, and then occasionally to visit wife and children. Christ hath too many occasional friends; but the ground of all is this, "I love Jesus Christ, but I have not the gift of burning quick for Christ." Oh, how securely should faith land us out of the gun-shot of the prevailing power of a black hour of darkness! Faith can make us able to be willing, for Christ, to go through a quarter of hell's pain. Lord, give us not leave to be mad with worldly wisdom. 3. When the temptation sleepeth, the madman is wise, the harlot is chaste; but when the vessel is pierced, out cometh that which is within, either wine or water: yet, if we should attentively lay our ears to hypocrites, we should hear, that their lute-strings do miserably jar; for hypocrisy is intelligible, and may be found out.

Would Parliaments begin at Christ, we should not fear that which certainly we have cause to fear; "One woe is past, and another woe cometh." The prophets in the three kingdoms have not repented of the superstition, will-worship, idolatry, persecution, profanity, formality, which made them "vile before the people;" and the judges and princes, who "turned judgment into gall and wormwood," are not humbled, because they were "a snare on Mizpah, and a net spread upon Tabor." No man repenteth, and "turneth from his evil way;" no man "smiteth on his thigh, saying, what have I done?" It is but black Popery (the name being changed, not the thing), to think the by-past sins of the land are bypast, and a sort of reformation for time to come is satisfactory to God, by the deed done.[1] Yea, the divisions in the church are a heavier plague than the raging sword. These same sins against the first and second Table; the reconciling of us and Babylon, pride, bribing, extortion, filthiness and intemperance unpunished, blood touching blood and not revenged, vanity of apparel, the professed way of salvation by all kinds of religions whatsoever; are now acted in another stage, by other persons, but they are the same sins.[2] If that Headship that flattering prelates took from Jesus Christ, and gave to the king, be yet taken from Christ, and given to men;—if Christ's crown be pulled off his head, no matter whose head it warm; it is taken from Christ both ways. I shall pray, that the fatness of the "flesh of Jacob, for this, do not wax lean," (Isa., xvii, 4,) and that the warfare of Britain be accomplished. But if the faithful watchmen know what hour of the night it is now, there is but small appearance, that it is near to the dawning of Britain's deliverance, or that our sky shall clear in haste. Would God the year 1645 were with child, to bring forth the salvation of Britain! It was once as incredible that the enemy should have entered "within the gates of Jerusalem." (Lam., iv, 12,) as it is now, that they can enter within the ports of London, Edinburgh, Dublin. I speak not this to encourage Cavaliers,[3] for certainly, God watcheth over them for vengeance; but that we go not on fur-

[1] Ex opere operato.—*Ruth.* [2] Alia scena, eadem fabula.—*Ruth.*

[3] Royalists, who persecuted the Presbyterians.

ther to break with Christ. The weakness of new heads, devising new religions, and multiplying gods; (for two sundry and contrary religions, argue interpretatively two sundry gods,) "according to the number of our cities," must come from rottenness of our hearts. Oh, if we could be instructed "before the decree," that is with child, of plagues to the sinners in "Zion, bring forth a man-child; and before the long shadows of the evening be stretched out on us!"

But of this theme no more. Grace is the proposition of this following treatise. When either grace is turned into painted, but rotten nature, as Arminians do, or into wantonness, as others do, the error to me is of a far other and higher elevation, than opinions touching church government. Tenacious adhering to Antinomian errors, with an obstinate and final persistance in them, both as touching faith to, and suitable practice of them, I shall think, cannot be fathered upon any of the regenerated; for it is an opinion not in the margin and borders, but in the page and body, and too near the centre and vital parts of the gospel. If any are offended, I desire to anger them with good will to grace; I shall strive and study the revenge only of love and compassion to their souls.

If some of these sermons came once to your Honour's ears; and now, to your eyes, it may be, with more English language, I having staid possibly till the last grapes were somewhat riper; I hope it shall be pardoned, that I am bold to borrow your name; which truly I should not have done, if I had not known of your practical knowledge of this noble and excellent theme, the Free Grace of God. I could add more of this; but I had rather commend grace, than gracious persons. I know that Jesus Christ, who perfumeth and flowereth heaven with his royal presence, and streweth the heaven of heavens to its utmost borders with glory, is commended that he was full of grace, a vessel filled to the lip. (Psalm xlv, 2; John, i, 16.) Yea, grace hath bought both our person and our service, (1 Pet., ii, 24, 25,) even as he that buyeth a captive, gives money not only for his person, but for all the motion, toil, and labour of his body, legs, and arms. And redeeming grace is so perfect, that Satan hath power possibly to bid, but not to buy any of the redeemed, no more than a merchant can buy another man's bought goods without his consent. All our happiness that groweth here on the banks of Time, is but thin sown, as very strawberries on the sea-sands. What good parts of nature we have without grace, are like a fair lily, but there is a worm at the root of it; it withereth from the root to the top. Gifts wither apace without grace: gifts neither break nor humble; grace can do both. Grace is so much the more precious and sweet, that though it be the result of sin, in the act of pardoning and curing sinful lameness; yet it hath no spring, but the bowels of God stirred and rolled within him only by spotless and holy goodness. Grace is of the king's house from heaven only; the matter, subject, or person it dwelleth in, contributed nothing for the creation of so noble a branch. Christ, for this cause especially, left the bosom of God, and was clothed with flesh and our nature, that he might be a mass, a sea, and boundless river of visible, living, and breathing grace, swelling up to the highest banks of not only the habitable world, but the sides also of the heaven of heavens, to over-water men and angels. So that Christ was, as it were, grace speaking, (Psalm xlv, 2 ; Luke, iv, 22 ;) grace sighing, weeping, crying out of horror, dying, withering for sinners, living again, (Heb., ii, 9; John, iii, 16; Rom., viii, 32, 33;) and is now glorified grace, dropping down, raining floods of grace on his members, (Eph., iv, 11–16; John, xiv, 7, 13, 16, 17). Christ now interceding for us at the right hand of God, is these sixteen hundred years the great apple tree dropping down apples of life; for there hath been harvest ever since Christ's ascension to heaven, and the grapes of heaven are ripe; all that falleth from the tree, leaves, apples, shadows, smell, blossoms, are but pieces of grace fallen down from Him who is the fulness of all, and hath filled all things. We shall never be blessed perfectly, till we all sit in an immediate union under the apple tree. This is a rare piece, by way of participation, of the divine nature. Christ passed an incomparable act of rich grace on the cross; and doth now act, and advocate for grace, and the applying of the grace of propitiation, in heaven, (1 John, ii, 1, 2); and by an act of grace, hath all the elect and ransomed ones engraven as a seal on his heart: and Christ being the fellow of God, (Zec., xiii, 7,) the man that standeth straight opposite to his eye, the first opening of the eye-lids of God is terminated upon the breast of Christ, and on the engravening of free grace. All the glory of the glorified is, that they are both in the lower and higher house, even when they are the Estates and Peers of heaven, the everlasting tenants and freeholders of grace; so that a soul can desire no fairer inheritance, than the patrimony, lot, and heritage of free grace. Now, to this grace commending your spirit, as an heir of grace, I rest,—Your Honour's at all obliged respectiveness in the grace of God. S. R.

CONTENTS.

SERMON I.

SERMON II.

SERMON III.

SERMON IV.

SERMON V.

SERMON VI.

SERMON VII.

SERMON VIII.

SERMON IX.

SERMON X.

SERMON XIV.

SERMON XV.

SERMON XVI.

SERMON XVII.

SERMON XVIII.

SERMON XIX.

SERMON XX.

SERMON XXIII.

SERMON XXIV.

Justification not eternal, 360. Faith is not only given for our joy and consolation; but also for our justification, both in our own soul and before God, 363. There is no warrant in Scripture for two reconciliations; one of man's reconciliation to God, and another of God's reconciliation to man, 366. Christ's merits, no cause, but an effect of God's eternal love, 366. What reconciliation is, 366. Joy without all sorrow for sin, no fruit of the kingdom of God, 367. The seeing of God, Heb., xii, 14, and the kingdom, 1 Cor., vi, John, iii, 3, not the kingdom of grace, but of glory, 368. All acts of blood and rough dealing in God to his own acts of mercy, 368.

SERMON XXV.

Omnipotency hath influence, on, 1st, Satan. 2nd, Diseases. 3rd, Stark death. 4th, On life itself. 5th, Mother-nothing. 6th, On all creatures, 371. Obediential power in the creation, what it is, 372. Omnipotency is (as it were) a servant to faith, 374. We worship a dependent God, 375. We have need of the Devil and other temptations for our humiliation, 377. Immediate mercies, are the sweetest mercies; cleared, 1st, In Christ. 2nd, Grace. 3rd, Glory. 4th, Comfort. 5th, The rarest of God's works, 378. The deceitfulness of our confidence, when God and the creature are joined in one work, 385.

SERMON XXVI.

Christ in four relations hath dominion over devils, 389. Satan goeth no where without a pass, 390. We often sign Satan's conditional pass, 391. A renewed will is a renewed man, 393. Eight positions concerning the will and affections, 393. A civil will is not a sanctified will, 393. The yielding of the soul to God, and to his light, a special note of a renewed will, 393. Affections sanctified, especially desires, 395. The less mixture in the affections, the stronger are their operations, 395. Mind and affections do reciprocally vitiate one another, 396. Spiritual desires seek natural things, spiritually: Carnal desires seek spiritual things, naturally, 396. God submitteth his liberality of grace, to the measure of a sanctified will, in four considerations, 397. Our affections, in their acts and comprehension, are far below spiritual objects, Christ and heaven, 397. More in Christ and heaven, than our faith can reach in this life, 398.

SERMON XXVII.

Satan not cast out of a land or a person, but by violence, both to Satan and the party; amplified in four considerations, 400. False peace known, 402. A roaring and a raging devil, is better than a calm and a sleeping devil, 402. God's way of hardening, as it is mysterious, so is it silent and invisible, 404.

THE

TRIAL AND TRIUMPH OF FAITH.[1]

SERMON I.

"*And from thence he arose, and went into the borders of Tyre and Sidon, and went into an house, and would that no man should know it: but he could not be hid.*"—MARK, vii, 24.

"*Then Jesus went from thence, and came into the coasts of Tyre and Sidon. And behold a woman of Canaan came out of the same coasts, and cried unto him, saying, Have mercy on me, O Lord, thou Son of David, for my daughter is grievously vexed with a devil.*"—MATTHEW, xv, 21, 22.

"*For a certain woman whose young (little) daughter had an unclean spirit, heard of him, and came, and fell at his feet: (The woman was a Greek, a Syrophenician by nation; and she besought him, that he would cast forth the devil out of her daughter.*"—MARK, vii, 25, 26.

THIS text being with child of free grace, holdeth forth to us a miracle of note: and because Christ is in the work in an eminent manner; and there is here also much of Christ's new creation, and a flower planted and watered by Christ's own hand, a strong faith in a tried woman; it requireth the bending of our heart to attention: for, to any seeking Jesus Christ, this text crieth, "Come and see." The words for their scope, drive at the wakening of believers in

[1] In the sermons and theological treatises of the seventeenth century, it was usual to introduce illustrations from the learned languages; and Rutherford, himself an accomplished scholar, has followed the general example. But as Latin, Greek, and Hebrew phrases, are unsuited to the taste of the present age, and would only interrupt the generality of our readers, the critical remarks of this kind are thrown into the form of foot-notes (which have Rutherford's name appended, to distinguish them from the occasional illustrations of the Editor,) so that the entire text of our author is preserved.

praying (when an answer is not given at the first,) to a fixed and resolved lying and dying at Christ's door, by continuing in prayer till the King come out and open, and answer the desire of the hungry and poor. 2. For the subject, they are a history of a rare miracle wrought by Christ, in casting forth a devil out of the daughter of a woman of Canaan: and for Christ to throw the devil out of a Canaanite, was very like the white banner of Christ's love displayed to the nations, and the King's royal standard set up to gather in the heathen under his colours. The parts of the miracle are,

I. The place where it was wrought. (Matt., xv, 21.)

II. The parties on whom; the mother and the possessed daughter: she is described by her nation.

III. The impulsive cause: she hearing, came, and prayed to Jesus for her little daughter: in which, there is a dialogue between Christ and the woman, containing, Firstly, Christ's trying of her, 1st, with no answer; 2nd, with a refusal; 3rd, with the reproach of a dog. Secondly, Her instancy of faith, 1st, in crying till the disciples interposed themselves; 2nd, her going on in adoring; 3rd, praying; 4th, arguing, by faith, with Christ, that she had some interest in Christ, though amongst the dogs; yet withal, (as grace hath no evil eye) not envying, because the morning market of Christ, and the high table, was the Jews' due, as the King's children, so she might be amongst the dogs, to eat the crumbs under Christ's table; knowing, that the very refuse of Christ, is more excellent than ten worlds.

IV. The miracle itself, wrought by the woman's faith: in which, we have, 1. Christ's heightening of her faith; 2. The granting of her desire; 3. The measure of Christ's bounty, "As thou wilt;" 4. The healing of her daughter.

Mark saith, that the woman came to Christ in a

house. Matthew seemeth to say, that she came to him in the way, as these words do make good, "Send her away, for she crieth after us." Augustine thinketh, that the woman first came to Christ while he was in the house, and desired to be hid, either because he did not (for offending the Jews) openly offer himself to the Gentiles, having forbidden his disciples to go to the Samaritans; or, because he would have his glory hid for a time; or rather, of purpose he did hide himself from the woman, that her faith might find him out: and then, refusing to answer the woman in the house, she still followeth him in the way, and crieth after him, as Matthew saith. For, 1. Christ's love is liberal, but yet it must be sued; and Christ, though he sell not his love for the penny-worth of our sweating and pains, yet we must dig low, for such a gold mine as Christ. 2. Christ's love is wise: He holdeth us knocking, till our desire be love-sick for him, and knoweth that delays raise and heighten the market and rate of Christ. We under-rate anything that is at our elbow. Should Christ throw himself in our bosom and lap, while we are in a morning sleep, he should not have the marrow and flower of our esteem. It is good there be some fire in us meeting with water, while we seek after Christ. 3. His love must not only lead the heart, but also draw. Violence in love is most taking, and delay of enjoying so lovely a thing as Christ, breedeth violence in our affections; and suspension of presence oileth the wheels of love, desire, joy: want of Christ is a wing to the soul.

Intepreters ask, what woman she was? Matthew saith, a Canaanite, not of any gracious blood; a Syrophenician; for Syrophenicia was in the border between Palestine and Syria, and it was now inhabited by the relics of the Canaanites; a Greek; not by birth, but because of the Greek tongue, and rites brought thither by Alexander, and the succeeding kings of Syria. All the Gentiles go under the name of Greeks in Scripture language, as, Rom., i, 14; Gal., iii, 28; 1 Cor., i, 22, 24: not because they are all Greeks by nation and blood; but, because conquest, language, and customs, stand for blood and birth. However, it standeth as no blemish in Christ's account-book, who was your father, whether an Amorite, or an Hittite, so ye come to him: he asketh not whose you are, so you be his; nor who is your father, so you will be his brother, and be of his house.

"*And from thence he arose, and went into the coasts of Tyre and Sidon.*" Mark, vii, 24. Christ wearied of Judea, had been grieved in spirit with the hypocrisy of the Pharisees, and the provocation of that stiff-necked people. He was chased away to the profane Pagans. The hardening of the Jews, maketh way to Christ's first and young love laid upon the Gentiles. Christ doth but draw aside a lap of the curtain of separation, and look through to one believing heathen: the King openeth one little window, and holdeth out his face, in one glimpse, to the woman of Canaan. So, Christ's works of deep Providence, are free mercy and pure justice interwoven, making one web. He departeth from the Jews, and setteth his face and heart on the Gentiles.

Consider the art of Providence here: 1st, The devil sometimes shapeth, and our wise Lord seweth; Babylon killeth, God maketh alive; sin, hell, and death, are made a chariot to carry on the Lord's excellent work. 2nd, The Providence of God hath two sides; one black and sad, another white and joyful. Heresy taketh strength, and is green before the sun; God's clearing of necessary and seasonable truths, is a fair side of that same providence. Adam's first sin, was the devil and hell digging a hole through the comely and beautiful frame of the creation of God; and that is the dark side of Providence: but the flower of Jesse springing up, to take away sin, and to paint out to men and angels the glory of a heaven, and a new world of free grace—that is a lightsome side of Providence. Christ scourged; Christ in a case, that he cannot command a cup of water; Christ dying, shamed, forsaken, is black: but Christ, in that same work redeeming the captives of hell, opening to sinners forfeited paradise, that is fair and white. Joseph, weeping in the prison for no fault, is foul and sad; but Joseph brought out to reign as half a king, to keep alive the Church of God in great famine, is joyful and glorious. The apostles whipped, imprisoned, killed all the day long, are sad and heavy: but sewed with this, that God causeth them always to triumph, and show the savour of the knowledge of Christ; and Paul triumphing in his iron chains, and exalting Christ in the gospel, through the court of bloody Nero,—maketh up a fair and comely contexture of divine Providence. 3rd, God, in all his works, now, when he raineth from heaven a sad shower of blood on the three kingdoms, hath his one foot on justice, that wrath may fill to the brim the cup of malignants, prelates, and papists; and his other foot on mercy, "to wash away the filth of the daughter of Zion, and to purge the blood of Jerusalem in the midst thereof, by the spirit of judgment, and by the spirit of burning." And this is God's way and ordinary path-road,

(Psalm xxv, 10.) And in one and the same motion, God can walk both to the east and to the west, and to the north and the south.

USE.—It is our fault, that we look upon God's ways and works by halves and pieces; and so, we see often nothing but the black side, and the dark part of the moon. We mistake all, when we look upon men's works by parts; a house in the building, lying in an hundred pieces; here timber, here a rafter, there a spar, there a stone; in another place, half a window, in another place, the side of a door: there is no beauty, no face of a house here. Have patience a little, and see them all by art compacted together in order, and you will see a fair building. When a painter draweth the half of a man; the one side of his head, one eye, the left arm, shoulder, and leg, and hath not drawn the other side, nor filled up with colours all the members, parts, limbs, in its full proportion, it is not like a man. So do we look on God's works by halves or parts; and we see him bleeding his people, scattering parliaments, chasing away nobles and prelates, as not willing they should have a finger in laying one stone of his house: yet do we not see, that in this dispensation, the other half of God's work makes it a fair piece. God is washing away the blood and filth of his church, removing those from the work who would cross it. In bloody wars, malignant soldiers ripping up women with child, waste, spoil, kill; yet are they but purging Zion's tin, brass, and lead, and such reprobate metal as themselves. Jesuits and false teachers are but God's snuffers, to occasion the clearing and snuffing of the lamps of the tabernacle, and make truth more naked and obvious.

SERMON II.

"*And he went into a house, and would that no man should know it.*"

THIS will, according to which, it is said, "he would that no man should know it," was his human will, according to which, the Lord Jesus was a man as we are, yet without sin; which was not always fulfilled. For his divine will, being backed with omnipotency, can never be resisted; it overcometh all, and can be resisted by none.

Consider what a Christ we have; one who, as God, hath a standing will that cannot fall. (Isa., xiv, 24.) "He doth all his pleasure." His pleasure and his work are commensurable. (Isa., xlvi, 10, 11; Psal. cxxxv, 6; Psal. cxv, 3.) Yet this Lord did stoop so low, as to take to himself man's will, to submit to God and law. And see how Christ, for our instruction, is content that God should break his will, and lay it below providence, (Matt., xxvi, 39.) Oh! so little and low as great Jesus Christ is! All is come to this, "O my Father, remove the cup; nevertheless, not as I will, but as thou wilt." Christ and his Father have but one will between them both: "I seek not mine own will, but the will of the Father that sent me." (John, v, 30.) "For even Christ pleased not himself." (Rom., xv, 3.) It is a sign of conformity with Christ, when we have a will so mortified, as it doth lie level with God's providence. Aaron's sons are killed, and that by God immediately from heaven with fire, a judgment very hell-like; (Lev., x, 3,) and Aaron held his peace. A will lying in the dust under God's feet, so as I can say, "Let his will, whose I am, enact to throw me in hell, he shall have my vote," is very like the mother-rule of all sanctified wills, even like Christ's pliable will. There is no iron sinew in Christ's will, it was easily broken; the tip of God's finger, with one touch, broke Christ's will: "Lo, I come to do thy will, O God." (Heb., x, 9.)

Oh, but there is a hard stone in our will: the stony heart is the stony will; hell cannot break the rock and the adamant, and the flint in our will: (1 Sam., viii, 19,) "Nay, but we will have a king," whether God will or no. God's will standeth in the people's way, bidding them return. They answer, "There is no hope, but we will walk after our own devices." (Jerem., xviii, 12.) Hell, vengeance, omnipotency, crossed Pharaoh's will, but it would neither bow nor break. "But the Lord hardened Pharaoh's heart, that he would not let the people go." (Exod., ix, 27.)

There be two things in our will, 1. The natural frame and constitution of it. 2. The goodness of it. The will of angels and of sinless Adam is not essentially good, for then, angels could never have turned devils; therefore, the constitution of the will needeth supervenient goodness, and confirming grace, even when will is at its best. Grace, grace now is the only oil to our wheels. Christ hath taken the castle, both in-works and out-works, when he hath taken the will, the proudest enemy that Christ hath out of hell. When Saul renders his will, he renders his weapon. This is mortification, when Christ runneth away with your will; as Christ was like a man that had not a man's will. So Saul, (Acts, ix, 6,) "trembling and astonished said, Lord, what wilt thou have me to do?" It is good when the Lord trampleth upon Ephraim's fair neck. (Hosea, x, 11.)

There is no goodness in our will now, but what it hath from grace; and to turn the will from evil to good, is no more nature's work, than we can turn the wind from the east to the west. When the wheels of the clock are broken and rusted, it cannot go. When the bird's wing is broken, it cannot fly. When there is a stone in the sprent and in-work of the lock, the key cannot open the door. Christ must oil the wheels of mis-ordered will, and heal them, and remove the stone, and infuse grace (which is wings to the bird): if not, the motions of will are all hell-ward.

"*But he could not be hid, for a certain woman,*" etc. Christ sometimes would be hid, because he hath a spirit above the people's windy air, and their hosanna. It is a spirit of straw, naughty and base, that is burnt up with that which hindered Themistocles to sleep.[1] "Honour me before the people," was cold comfort to Saul, when the prophet told him God had rejected him. But Christ desired not to be hid from this woman; he was seeking her, and yet he flieth from her. Christ, in this, is such a flier as would gladly have a pursuer.

2. Faith findeth Christ out when he is hid. "Verily thou art a God that hidest thyself." (Isa., xlv, 15.) But faith seeth God under his mask, and through the cloud; and, therefore, faith addeth, "O God of Israel, the Saviour!" Thou hidest thyself, O God, from Israel, but Israel findeth thee, (ver. 17,) "Israel shall be saved in the Lord, with an everlasting salvation." God casteth a cloud of anger about

1 Themistocles used to roam the streets of Athens at midnight, complaining, that the trophies of Marathon would not let him sleep.

himself, he maketh darkness his pavilion, and will not look out; yet Job seeth God, and findeth him out many hundred miles, (chap. xix, 26,) "Yet in my flesh shall I see God."

3. Reason, sense, nay, angels, seeing Christ between two thieves dying, and going out of this world, bleeding to death, naked, forsaken of friend and lover, they may wonder and say, "O Lord, what dost thou here?" Yet the faith of the thief found him there, as a king, who had the keys of Paradise; and he said in faith, "Lord, remember me when thou comest into thy kingdom." (Luke, xxiii, 42.)

4. Faith seeth him as a witness, and a record in heaven, as Job, (xvi, 19, 20,) even when God cleaveth his reins asunder, and poureth out his gall upon the ground, ver. 13. Believe then, that Christ gloometh, that he may kiss; that he cuts, that he may cure; that he maketh the living believer's grave before his eyes, and hath no mind to bury him alive. He breatheth the smoke and the heat of the furnace of hell on the soul, when peace, grace, and heaven is in his heart. He breaketh the hollow of Jacob's thigh, so as he must go halting all his days, and it is his purpose to bless him. Whereas we should walk by faith, we walk much, even in our spiritual walk, by feeling and sense; we have these errors in our faith, we make not the word of promise the rule of our faith, but only God's dispensation.

Now, God's dispensation is spotless, and innocent, and white, yet it is not Scripture to me; nor all that dispensation and providence seemeth to speak, the word of God. Ram-horns speak not taking of towns in an ordinary providence, as spear and shield and a host of fighting men do. "Killed all the day long, and estimated as sheep for the slaughter," speaketh not to me, that God's people are "more than conquerors through him that loved us." (Rom., viii, 36, 37.)

Our faith, in reference to dispensation, is to do two things: 1st. To believe in general, though dispensation be rough, stormy, black, yet Christ is fair, sweet, gracious; and, that hell and death are servants to God's dispensation toward the children of God. Abraham must kill Isaac; yet in Isaac, as in the promised seed, all the nations of the earth are blessed. Israel is foiled, and falleth before the men of Ai; yet Israel shall be saved by the Lord. Judah shall go into captivity, but the dead bones shall live again. Read the promise in general, engraved upon the dispensation of God. Garments are rolled in blood in Scotland and England. The wheels of Christ's chariot, in this reformation, go with a slow pace: the prince is averse to peace, many worthies are killed, a foreign nation cometh against us; yet all worketh for the best to those that love God. 2. Hope biddeth us to await the Lord's event. We see God's work, it cometh to our senses; but the event that God bringeth out of his work lieth under ground. Dispensation is as a woman travailing in birth, and crying out for pain; but she shall be delivered of two men-children,—Mercy to the people of God, Justice to Babylon. Wait on till the woman bring forth, though you see not the children.

2. We trust possession in our part, more than law, and the fidelity of the promise on God's part. Feeling is of more credit to us than faith; sense is surer to us than the word of faith. Many weak ones believe not life eternal, because they feel it not: heaven

is a thing unseen, and they find no consolation and comfort, and so, are disquieted. If we knew that believing is a bargaining and a buying, we should see the weakness of many. Should any buy a field of land, and refuse to tell down the money, except the party should lay all the ridges, acres, meadows, and mountains on the buyer's shoulders, that he might carry them home to his house, he should be incredulously unjust. If any should buy a ship, and think it no bargain at all, except he might carry away the ship on his back, should not this make him a ridiculous merchant? God's law of faith, Christ's concluded atonement, is better and surer than your feeling. All that sense and comfort saith, is not canonic Scripture; it is adultery to seek a sign, because we cannot rest on our husband's word.

SERMON III.

QUEST. But cannot Christ be hid? *Answ.* Not of himself. It is hard to hide a great fire, or to cast a covering upon sweet odours, that they smell not. Christ's name is as a sweet ointment poured out: he is a mountain of spices, and he is a strong savour of heaven, and of the higher paradise. You may hide the man, that he shall not see the sun: but you cannot cast a garment over the body of the sun, and hide day-light.

From which it appeareth, that Christ cannot be hid,

1. In his cause and truth. The gospel is scourged

and imprisoned, when the apostles are so served; yet it cometh to light, and filleth Jerusalem, and filleth all the world. What was done to hide Christ? When he and his gospel are buried under a great stone, yet his fame goeth abroad. Death is no covering to Christ. Papists burn all the books of Protestants; they kill and slay the witnesses. Antiochus and the persecuting emperors throw all the Bibles in the fire; but this truth cannot be hid, it triumpheth. As soon pull down Jesus from his royal seat at the right hand of God, as Babylon, prelates, papists, malignants, in these three kingdoms, can extinguish the people and truth of Christ.

2. Believers cannot hide and dissemble a good or an ill condition in the soul; the well-beloved is away, and the church's bed cannot keep her: all the watchmen, all the streets, all the daughters of Jerusalem, yea, heaven and Christ must hear of it: (Cant., iii, 1–3; v, 6–8.) Mary Magdalene's bed, and a morning sleep, and the company of angels and apostles, cannot dry her cheeks. "Woman, what ails thee?" saith the angel. "Oh," she weepeth, "Oh, what aileth me? They have taken away my Lord, and I know not where they have laid him. O apostles! where is he? O Sir, angel, tell me if you saw him? O grave! O death! Show me, is my Lord with you?" The love of Christ is no hypocrite. I grant, some can for a time put a fair face on it, when Christ is absent; but most of the saints look, as a bird fallen from the raven; as a lamb fallen out of the lion's mouth; as one too soon out of bed in the morning. Oh, sick of love! Oh, show him! I charge you tell him, watchmen, daughters of Jerusalem, that I am sick of love. Love is a paining, feverous, tormenting sickness: grace

cannot put on a laughing mask, when sweet Jesus is hidden; love hath no art to conceal sorrow. The countenance of David, (Psalm xlii, 5,) is sick; there is death in his face, when God is not the light of his countenance.

3. The joy of his presence cannot be hid: she cannot but tell and cry out, O fair, O white day! He is come again: "It was but a little that I passed from them, but I found him whom my soul loved." (Cant., iii, 4.) She numbered all the miles she had travelled while her Lord was absent: Joy will speak, it is not dumb: "The roof of thy mouth [is] like the best wine for my beloved, that goeth down sweetly, causing the lips of those that are asleep to speak." (Cant., vii, 9.) "Can the children of the bed-chamber mourn, as long as the bridegroom is with them?" (Matt., ix, 15.) *i. e.* They cannot choose but rejoice.

4. Grace in a sincere professor, and Christ, cannot be hid. There came a good fair breath, with a blast of a sweet west-wind of heaven, on Joseph of Arimathea: the time was ill, Christ was dead; and he can dissemble no longer. (Mark, xv, 43.) With much daring and boldness, he went unto Pilate with a petition: "I beseech you, my Lord Governor, let me but have this Jesus his dead body:" There was some fire of heaven in this bold profession. What would this be thought of, to see a noble and honourable Lord-Judge, with a dead and crucified man's body in his arms? But faith knoweth no blushing; grace cannot be ashamed. There was a strait charge laid on the apostles, "Preach no more in the name of Jesus." (Acts, iv, 18.) Peter and John boldly say, "We cannot but speak the things we have heard and seen." Lay as heavy weights as death, burning quick, sawing asunder, on the sincerity

of faith in the martyrs, it must up the mountain. David's grace was kept in, as with a muzzle put upon the mouths of beasts: (Ps. xxxix:) it was as coals of fire in his heart, and he behoved to speak even before the wicked: "I believed, therefore I spake." (Ps. cxvi, 10.)

5. When Jeremiah layeth unlawful bands on himself, to speak no more in the name of the Lord, there is a spirit of prophecy lying on him—he is not lord of his own choice. "But his word was in my heart, as a burning fire shut up in my bones; and I was weary with forbearing, and I could not stay." (Jer., xx, 9.) There is a majesty of grace on the conscience of the child of God, that must break out in holy duties: though temptation should hide Christ in his grace, tempted Joseph is overawed with this, "How can I then do this great wickedness, and sin against God?" (Gen., xxxix, 9.) This awful majesty of the grace of God's fear, causeth Joseph see nothing in harlotry, but pure, unmixed guiltiness against God. There is an overmastering apprehension of Christ's love, (2 Cor., v, 14,) that constraineth Paul to own the love of Christ, in dedicating himself to the service of the gospel. Though Paul would not have preached, yet he had a sum to pay; "I am debtor both to the Greeks and the Barbarians, both to the wise and the unwise." (Rom., i, 14.) Grace awed him, as a debt layeth fetters on an ingenuous mind; he cannot but relieve his free and honest mind in paying what he oweth.

6. God's desertion cannot so hide and over-cloud Christ, but against sense, the child of God must believe; yea, and pray in faith, "My God, my God, why hast thou forsaken me? O my God, I cry by day." (Psalm xxii, 1, 2.) Though sin over-cloud

Christ, and David fall in adultery and blood, there is a seed of Christ that must cast out blossoms; he cannot but repent and sorrow. God's decree of grace in the execution of it, may be broken in a link by some great sin; but Christ cannot but solder the chain, and raise the fallen sinner.

It shall be useful then for the saints, when the Spirit cometh in his stirrings and impetuous acts, to co-operate with him, and to answer his wind-blowing. It is good to hoist up sail, and make out, when a fair wind and a strong tide calleth. Sometimes grace maketh the heart as a hot iron; it is good then to smite with the hammer. When your spirit is docile, and there cometh a gale of Christ's sweet west-wind, and rusheth in with a warmness of heart, in a praying disposition to retire to a corner, and pour out the soul before the Lord; as we are to take Christ at his word, so are we to take Christ's Spirit at his work. He knocketh; knock thou with him. His fingers make a stirring upon the handles of the bar, and drop down pure myrrh;—let thy heart make a stirring with his fingers also. I grant, wind maketh sailing, and all the powers on earth cannot make wind; yet when God maketh wind, the seamen may draw sails, and launch forth. God preventeth in all these. The spirit beateth fire out of our flint, we are to lay to a match and receive; reach in the heart, under the stirrings of free grace; obey dispositions of grace, as God himself. When the sun riseth, the birds may sing, but their singing is no cause of the sun rising.

It is no truth of God that some teach, that the justified in Christ are of duty always tied to one and the same constant act of rejoicing, without any mixture of sadness and sorrow. For so they cannot, 1.

Obey and follow the various impressions of the Lord's absence and presence, of Christ's sea-ebbing and flowing, of his shining and smiling, and his lowring and frowning. 2. The faith of a justified condition doth not root out all affections; nay, not love, faith, desire, and joy: if there be sin remaining in the justified, there is place of sadness, for fear, for sorrow; for the scum of affections is removed by Christ, not the affections themselves. 3. Christ, for mere trial sometimes, for sin at other times, doth cover himself with a cloud, and withdraw the sense of his favour; and it is a cursed joy that is on foot, when the Lord hideth his face. The love of Christ must be sick and sad; I mean, the lover, when the beloved is under a cloud. It is not the new world with the regenerate man here; nor a land where there is nothing but all summer, all sun, neither night nor clouds, nor rain nor storm: that is the condition of the second Paradise, of the better Adam. 4. It is a just and an innocent sorrow, to be grieved at that which grieveth the Holy Spirit; and when the lion roareth, all the beasts of the field are afraid. Grace maketh not Job a stock, nor Christ a man who cannot weep.

"*And behold, a woman of Canaan*:" and "*A certain woman.*" (Matt., xv, Mark, vii.) Of the woman: 1. But one person of all Tyrus and Sidon came to him. 2. She was a Syrophenician by nation. 3. Her condition, She had a daughter vexed with a devil. 4. With an unclean devil. 5. The nearer occasion, She heard of him. 6. She adored. 7. She prayed: and so, way is made to the conference between Christ and her; and to the trial and miracle.

A CERTAIN WOMAN.—There is but one of all Tyrus and Sidon who came to Christ. 1. It beseemeth the mercy of the good Shepherd, to "leave ninety and nine sheep in the wilderness, and go after one which is lost." (Luke, xv, 4.) And when all is done, alas! he hath but one of a whole hundred. Christ hath not the tithe of mankind. He maketh a journey, till he is wearied and thirsty, through Samaria; yea, and wanteth his dinner, for one woman at that draught of his net, and thinketh he dineth like a king, and above, if he save one. (John, iv, 33, 34.) Oh, sweet husband's word! "I am married to you, and I will take you, one of a city, and two of a tribe, and I will bring you to Zion." (Jer., iii, 14.) Christ taketh sinners, not by dozens, not by thousands, (it is but once in all the word, (Acts, ii,) that three thousand are converted at once;) but by ones and twos. "Though Israel be as the sand of the sea, yet a remnant shall but be saved;" (Rom., ix, 27; Isa., x, 22;) the relics and refuse shall be saved only. 2. Common love scarce amounteth to grace, because grace is separative, and singleth out one of many; all graced persons are privileged persons; heaven is a house of chosen and privileged ones: there are no common stones in the New Jerusalem, but all precious stones; the "foundations sapphires, the windows agates and carbuncles, all the borders of pleasant stones." (Isa., liv, 11, 12.) 3. Christ's way lieth so, of two grinding at a mill, of two in the field together, of two in one bed, Christ will have but one: Christ often will not have both husband and wife, both father and son; but the one brother, Jacob, not Esau. Of a whole house, Christ cometh to the devil's fireside, and chooseth one, and draweth him out, and leaveth all the family to the devil. 4. Christ knoweth them well whom he chooseth: grace is a rare piece of the choice and the flower of the love of heaven: there be many common stones; not many pearls, not many diamonds and sapphires. The multitude be all Arminians from the womb; every heresy is a piece of the old Adam's wanton wit; thousands go to hell, black heretics and heterodox, as touching the doctrine of themselves; every man hath grace if you believe himself; every man taketh heaven for his home and heritage; dogs think to rest in Christ's bosom. Men naturally believe, though they be but up and down with Christ, yet Christ doth so bear them at good will, as to give grace and glory.

Objection 1. God's love is not infinite, if it be limited to a few. *Answer*. This should conclude, that there be an infinite number of men and angels, to whom God's love to salvation is betrothed in affection: but his love is infinite in its act, not in its object; the way of carrying on his love is infinite.

Object. 2. To ascribe God's not loving of men to God's disposition, heart, will, and pleasure, and not to our defects, is blasphemy. *Answ*. The Lord ascribeth his having mercy, and his hardening, to his own free-will, (Rom., ix, 18; Exod., xxxiii, 19;) and his love is as free as his mercy; and by this means, God's first love to us should arise from our love preventing his, contrary to his own word, (Deut., vii, 7; Eph., ii, 4, 5; Tit., iii, 3; 2 Tim., i, 9,) and man should be the first lover of the two. The creature then putteth the Lord in his debt, and giveth first to God, and God cannot but recompense. (Isa., xl, 13, 14; Rom., xi, 34, 35.) Now, it is no shame for us to live and die in the debt of Christ; the heaven of angels and men is an house of the debtors of Christ, eternally engaged to him, and shall stand in his debt-book ages without end.

Object. 3. Infinite goodness may as soon cease to be, as not be good to all, or withhold mercy from any. *Answ.* Every being of reprobate men and devils, is a fruit of God's goodness, but of free goodness; else God should cease to be, if he should turn his creatures to nothing; for he should cease to be good to things without himself, if these were all turned to their poor mother-nothing. 2. Mercy floweth not from God essentially, especially the mercy of conversion, remission of sins, eternal life, but of mere grace; for then God could not be God, and deny these favours to reprobates. Freedom of mercy and salvation is as infinitely sweet and admirable in God, as mercy and salvation itself.

Object. 4. But God is so essentially good to all, as he must communicate his goodness by way of justice, in order to free obedience; and that is life eternal, to those who freely believe and obey. *Answ.* But the great enemy of grace, Arminius, teaches us, that all the freedom of grace, (Rom., ix,) is resolved into the free pleasure of God, in which he freely, and without hire, purposed to reward faith, not the works of the law, with life eternal; whereas it was free to him to keep another order, if so it should seem good to him; and by this means, God is yet freely, and by an act of pure grace, not essentially good to all, even in communicating his goodness by way of justice: for what God doth by necessity of his nature and essence, that he cannot but do. But sure it is, by no necessity of nature doth the Lord reward works, faith, or any obedience in us, with the crown of life eternal: he may give heaven freely without one's obedience at all, as he giveth the first grace freely, (Ezek., xvi, 6–8; Rom., v, 10; Eph., ii, 3, 4.)

But this is surer, the fewer have grace, grace is the more grace, and the more like itself and free.

Object. 5. But I have a good heart to God. *Answ.* A quiet heart sleeping in a false peace, is a bad heart: most of sinners give their souls to the devil by theft; they think they are sailing to heaven, and know nothing till they shore, sleeping in the land of death. (Matt., vii, 21–23; Luke, xvi, 27, 28.)

Object. 6. Why, but God hath bestowed on me many favours and riches in this world. *Answ.* God's grace is not graven on gold. It should be but the logic of a beast, if the slaughter ox should say, "The master favoureth me more than any ox in the stall; I am free of the yoke that is upon the neck of others, and my pasture is fatter than their's."

Object. 7. The saints love me. *Ans.* The saints can mis-father their love, and love where God loveth not.

Object. 8. All the world loveth me. *Answ.* You are the liker to be a step-child of Jerusalem and of heaven; for, "The world loveth its own." (John, xv, 19.) Better it were to have the world a step-mother, than to be no other, but to lie in such a womb, and suck such breasts.

Object. 9. I believe life eternal. *Answ.* That faith is with child of heaven; but see it be not a false birth. Few or none come to age, and none clothed in white and crowned, but they were jealous of their faith, and feared their own ways. Natural men stand aloof from hell and wrath.

SERMON IV.

"The woman was a Greek, a Syrophenician by nation."

MUCH woe is denounced by the prophets against Tyrus and Sidon; yet sweet Jesus draweth aside the curtain, and openeth a window of the partition, and saveth this woman. Lo, here Christ "planting in the wilderness the cedar, the shittah tree, the myrtle, the oil tree," (Isa., xli, 19;) and here, Isa., lv, 13, is fulfilled, "And instead of the thorn (what better are Sidonians than thorns?) shall come up the fir tree, and instead of the briar, shall come up the myrtle tree; (and no praise to the ground, but to the good Husbandman:) and it shall be to the Lord for a name, for an everlasting sign, that shall not be cut off." Christ, then, can make and frame a fair heaven out of an ugly hell, and out of the knottiest timber he can make vessels of mercy, for service in the high palace of glory.

1. What are they all, who are now glorified? The fairest face that standeth before the throne of redeemed ones, was once inked and blackened with sin. You should not know Paul now, with a crown of a king on his head: he looketh not now like a "blasphemer, a persecutor, an injurious person." The woman that had once seven devils in her, is a Mary Magdalene far changed, and grace made the change. 2. Grace is a new world. (Heb., ii, 5.) The land of grace hath two summers in one year. "The inhabitants shall not say, I am sick; the people that dwell therein, shall be forgiven their iniquity." (Isa., xxxiii, 24.)

"Whosoever liveth, and believeth in me, shall never die." (John, xi, 26.) They are not mortal men that are in grace; there is neither sickness nor death in that land. 3. We say of such a physician, He hath cured diseases that never man could; he cured stark death: then you may commit your body to him, he is a tried physician. Christ hath made a rare copy, a curious sampler of mercy, of the apostle Paul; for in him he hath shown all "long-suffering, for a pattern to them that should hereafter believe in him to life eternal." (1 Tim., i, 16.) Heaven is a house full of miracles; yea, of spectacles and images of free grace. You may intrust your soul, with all its diseases, to Christ; he hath given many rare proofs of his tried art of grace; he hath made many black limbs of hell fair saints in heaven: such a man, such an artificer, threw down an old dungeon of clay, and made it up a fair palace of gold.

Object. But what am I, a lump of unrepenting guiltiness and sin, to such a vessel of mercy, as holy Paul, and repenting Mary Magdalene? *Ans.* Grace, as it is in God, and fitness to receive grace in us, is just alike to all. There was no more reason why Paul should obtain mercy, than why thou, or any other sinner like thee, should obtain mercy. There is a like reason for me to have noble and broad thoughts of the rich grace of Christ, as for Abraham, Moses, David, all the prophets and apostles to believe. There was no greater ransom given by Christ to buy faith and free grace for Noah, Job, and Daniel, to Moses and Samuel, than to poor and sinful me: it is one cause, one ransom, one free love. If there had a nobler and worthier Redeemer died for Moses and Paul, than for you and me; and another heaven, and a freer grace purchased to them, than to me, I should have been discouraged: grace is grace to thee, as to meek Moses: Christ is Christ to thee, as to believing Abraham. And further, The same grace that is here, is in heaven. 1. As faith that is freely given us, is the conquest of the new heir, Jesus Christ, (John, vi, 44; Phil., i, 29; Eph., i, 3,) so are all Christ's bracelets about our neck in heaven, and the garland of glory, the free grace of God. It is the same day-light when the sun breaketh forth out of the east, and at noon-day in the highest meridian. Though we change places when we die, we change not husbands. 2. We stand here by free grace. (Rom., v, 2.) Repentance and remission of sins are freely given here to Israel, by the exalted Prince Christ Jesus. (Acts, v, 31.) Our tears are bought with that common ransom; so the high inns of the royal court of heaven is a free and open house, and no bill put upon the inhabitants; neither fine, nor stent, nor excise, nor assessment, nor taxation; all is upon the royal charges of the Prince of the kings of the earth. There is no more hire, merit, wages, or fees there than here; the income of glory for eternity, and the life-rent of ages of blessedness, is all the good-will of Him who sitteth on the throne. Every apple of the tree of life is grace; every sip, every drop of the sea and river of life, is the purchase of the blood of the Lamb that is in the midst of them. 3. They be as poor without Christ who are there, as we are. Glory is grace, and their dependency for ages of ages is, that the Lamb which is in the midst of the throne, does feed them, and lead them unto living fountains of waters, and God wipeth away all tears from their eyes. (Rev., vii, 17.) Then they cannot walk there alone, but as the Lamb leadeth them; and if Christ were not there, or if he should take grace, glory, and all his own jewels and ornaments from Moses and Enoch, there should remain no more there but poor nature. As good angels do therefore not fall, because in Christ, the Head of angels, they are confirmed, (and if they lacked this confirming grace, they might yet fall, and become apostate devils,) so the glorified in heaven do therefore stand, and are confirmed in the inheritance, not by free-will there, more than here; but by immediate dependence of grace on the Lamb, whom they follow whithersoever he goeth. Grace, then, for kind, is as good as heaven. Glory, glory to our ransom-payer!

3. Her little daughter was vexed (she saith)[1] or grievously tormented with a devil. Then observe, that common punishments of sin, and sad afflictions do follow justified persons, as well as the wicked; for it was a sad burden to the mother, that the devil had such a dominion over her daughter; yet the text cleareth, that she was a justified person, as her instancy of praying, adoring, and great faith, even prevailing over Christ, under sad trials, do manifestly evidence. And we see the reasons that the Scripture allegeth, 1. That the gold of precious faith, and the upright metal therein, may be seen. (1 Pet., i, 7.) Afflictions are the servants and pursuivants of the accusing law, sent out to cause us lay hold, by faith, on peace made, and pardon purchased in Christ. The hot furnace is the workhouse of Christ; in that fire he taketh away the scum, the dross, the refuse of the true metal, that faith may be found unto praise, and honour, and glory, at the appearance of Jesus Christ. 2. Afflictions drive us

[1] *Kakos daimonizetai,* she is exceedingly devilled.—*Rutherford.*

to seek God, they being God's firemen; and his hired labourers, sent to break the clods, and to plough Christ's land, that he may sow heaven there; but Christ must bring new earth to the soil. In prosperity we come to God, but in a common way; as the grave man came to the theatre, only that he might go out again. But in trouble, the saints do more than come; they make a friendly visit when they come. Also, the prayers of the saints in prosperity, are but summer prayers, slow, lazy, and alas! too formal. In trouble, they rain out prayers, or cast them out in co-natural violence, as a fountain doth cast out waters. Both these are in one well expressed by the prophet: "Lord, in trouble they have visited thee; they pour out a prayer when thy chastening hand is on them."[1] (Isa., xxvi, 16.) 3. We must be made like Christ, in the cross and the crown, (2 Tim., ii, 12,) and conform to him. (Rom., viii, 29.) Christ the corner-stone: though there was no sin in him, yet before he was made the chief corner-stone, he was by death hammered. (Acts, iv, 10–12.) And much more, the strokes and smiting of the cross must knock down all the superfluity of naughtiness, and every height, till by smoothing and chipping, the child of God be made a stone, in breadth, length, proportion, smoothness, some way conform to the first copy, and to Christ the sampler-stone. There is a 4th reason, but it is a controverted one: The justified person may be afflicted for sin. Some teach that this is Popery, to affirm, that the justified bear the punishment of their sin;

[1] Vatabulus expoundeth *Malmad,* a murmuring, or prayer which trouble poureth out. The Chaldee paraphrast turneth it *silentium,* silence, because the conscience wakened is silent: it is a prophecy what God's fire doth effectuate, which you have, (Hos., v, 15,) "In their affliction, they will seek me early."

because, Christ only was wounded for our iniquity, and did bear, in his own body, our sins on the tree: therefore (say they) respect seemeth to be had (as one speaketh) to sin, not principally, but secondarily and occasionally; not as it offendeth God, who by that one sacrifice is for ever pacified, (Heb., x, 14; Matth., iii,) but as it offendeth and diseaseth the minds of the faithful: not that afflictions simply, properly, and immediately do ease, quiet, and cure the conscience, (for their natural effect is to deject and terrify, as appendices of the law;) but that they awaken and stir up our dulness, to a lively apprehension of Christ's righteousness. And so, while God, as a father, correcteth for sin, sin hath not properly with God the nature of sin, which is an offence of Divine justice, but is considered as a disease troubling his child; which in love, and in pity, he seeketh to make riddance of, in manner aforesaid, and not in anger and displeasure.

It is true, Papists hold, that when God forgiveth sin in David, he forgiveth not the punishment; for David is punished with the sword on his house for that same sin: but it is known, that this doctrine is a too-fall and pillar, to underprop the chamber in hell, which they call Purgatory: and that their meaning is, that punishment inflicted on a justified person, is a punishment satisfactory to the justice of God; that so, they may make the merits of the saints suffering, to ride up, as a collateral sharer with the high and noble blood of the killed Lamb of God, who only satisfactorily taketh away the sins of the world. This we disclaim; but, on the other hand, we hold, that there is another justice in God, than that legal and sin-revenging justice, which Christ's sufferings have expiated and fully satisfied, both in regard of God's acceptation, and of the intrinsical worth of the death of him who was God, the Prince of life. And this other justice, is also the justice of an offended father, correcting, though in mercy, (and so it is a mixed justice,) the sins of the saints as sins: 1. Because the sins of the saints are not only the offending of divine revenging justice, but also, a wrong done against this mixed justice, and against the mercy and kindness of God, (2 Sam., xii, 7–9; Exod., xx, 1, 2; Psalm lxxxi, 6, 7, 10, 11; and lxxviii, 11–13, 42, 53–56; Deut., xxxii, 11–18; Amos, iii, 2.) And therefore God doth punish, in his own, sins as sins.

2. Those who are not to perish with the world, are, for this cause, (because they eat and drink unworthily), sick, and punished with death. (1 Cor., xi, 30, 32, 33.) It is clearly against the text, that Mr. Towne saith, That a justified person, having the least measure of faith, cannot eat and drink unworthily; the smallest faith maketh them worthy; and so those who, in that text, did eat unworthily, did but dally with the gospel, and never actually put on Christ. But faith doth no more hinder a justified person to receive the Lord's supper unworthily, than it doth hinder him to commit adultery, or incest, or to kill; and whosoever should come to the Lord's table under these sins, without repenting, should eat and drink unworthily; and such a sin may a believer according to God's heart (as David was) commit. And there is great odds between being unworthy, and eating unworthily. All believers, of themselves, are unworthy of Christ and salvation, but being in Christ by faith, they are counted worthy; and yet they may eat and drink unworthily. But Mr. Towne's sense seemeth to carry, that a justified person cannot

sin, nor eat and drink unworthily, because faith maketh him worthy: and if so, the way of grace is a wanton merry way; the justified are freed from the law, and from any danger of sinning.

3. Nothing is more evident, than that David was punished according to the rule of that mixed and fatherly justice, which keeps a due proportion between the sin and the punishment. His sin was, to cut off Uriah's house out of Israel; God sendeth the sword against his house, all his days. He took another man's wife secretly, and did commit filthiness with her; the Lord took his wives, before the sun, and gave them to Absalom, who defiled his bed. (2 Sam., xii.) Here is justice, though, I grant, mixed with mercy; sword for sword, bed for bed. Eli honoured his sons more than God, and suffered them to profane priesthood and sacrifices; justice rooted out his sons from priesthood and sacrifice. Hezekiah, out of his pride, showed all his treasures, and all that was in his house, to the king of Babylon's messengers; and justice measured out the like to him: all that was in his house, and all his treasures, were carried away as a spoil to Babylon.

4. "Slay old and young—begin at my sanctuary." (Ezek., ix, 6.) "And behold thou shalt be dumb—because thou believest not my word." (Luke, i, 20.) The church of God, *in terminis*, saith so much: "The Lord is righteous, for I have rebelled against his commandment." (Lamen., i, 18,) "The yoke of my transgression is bound by his hand; they are wreathed, and come up upon my neck." (Verse 14.) "Wherefore doth a living man complain, a man for the punishment of his sin?" (Chap. iii, 39.) "Let us search and try our ways, and turn again to the Lord." (Verse 40.) "Who gave Jacob for a spoil, and Israel

to the robbers? Did not the Lord, against whom we have sinned?" (Isa., xlii, 24.) "I will bear the indignation of the Lord, because I have sinned." (Micah, vii, 9.) "For through the anger of the Lord it came to pass in Jerusalem, and Judah, until he had cast them out from his presence, that Zedekiah rebelled against the king of Babylon." (2 Kings, xxiv, 20.) It is not of weight that is brought, to take off the force of these pregnant scriptures. The church, consisting of mixed persons, good and bad, elect and reprobate, (say they,) is, according to the wicked party, punished in justice, but not the believing party. But I answer, all Judah, good and ill, Jeremiah, Daniel, and all the holy seed, were involved with the perverse and obstinate idolaters, in the same common calamity of a sad captivity. And it was not the ill figs, and stiff-necked idolaters, that did confess the Lord's righteousness, and their own rebellion against the Lord; nor did the wicked party enter into a trial of their ways, and acknowledge, that the unregenerate man only suffereth for his sins; nor did any of that side, with patience, hope, and silence, bear the indignation of the Lord: it was the true church, God's Jacob, the meek of the earth, that did thus stoop to God's correction; and yet these same were punished for their sins, as they acknowledge. (Lam., i, 18; Mic., vii, 9.)

5. This is also against the covenant, and threatenings thereof: "And if ye walk contrary to me, and will not hearken to me, I will bring seven times more plagues on you," etc. (Lev., xxvi, 21–40.) "If then (in their heavy afflictions) their uncircumcised hearts be humbled, and they then accept of the punishment of their iniquity," (verse 41,) "Then will I remember my covenant with Jacob." (Ver. 42.) "If

his children forsake my law, and walk not in my judgments," etc. (Psal. lxxxix, 30,) "Then will I visit their transgression with the rod, and their iniquity with stripes." (Ver. 32.) "Nevertheless, my loving-kindness will I not utterly take from him," etc. (Ver. 33.) Nothing is more evident, than that those who are in the covenant of grace, from whom God cannot remove the sure mercies of David, are visited for their iniquities, with temporal rods.

6. It is against God's anger and displeasure at the sins of his own children; for God is really angry at his own children's sins; and why then doth he not punish them for their sins? "The anger of the Lord was kindled against Moses." (Exod., iv, 14.) "Also the Lord was angry with me for your sake." (Deut., i, 37.) And the story showeth, because Moses sanctified not the Lord at the waters of Meribah, God would not suffer him to set his foot in the holy land. "God was angry with Solomon." (2 Chron., xi, 9.) "The Lord was very angry with Aaron." (Deut., i, 20.) The prophet Jehu said to Jehoshaphat, that good king, "There is wrath upon thee from the Lord." (2 Chron., xix, 2.) "For in my wrath I smote thee, but in my favour I have had mercy upon thee." (Isa., lx, 10.)

7. The contrary error is founded upon two other errors, That all afflictions are subservient officers and serjeants to the law; and so, they are signs of God's wrath, as is the law: And as believers are freed from the ruling power of the law, so also, from the rod. But this is false; for God's rod, of itself, is neither a sign of revenging justice, nor of free mercy; but it taketh its nature and specification from the intention and mind of God: all these externals fall alike to elect and reprobate. The repenting thief, and the blasphe-

ming thief are under the same rod of God; both die a violent death. Wicked Ahab, and good Josiah are both killed in war. The botches and agues threatened in the law, (Deut., xxviii, 60,) are upon Job, (chap. ii, ver. 7.) What maketh the same rod, to be a work of revenging justice, in the reprobate, and of justice mixed and tempered with mercy and fatherly kindness, in the other? Certainly, God's pleasure and wise intention, punishing for different ends, varieth the nature of the rods; so as an intention to take satisfactory vengeance on the reprobate, specifieth his rod, and maketh it punishment of black wrath, of salt and unmixed justice on him. And this intention, is an essential ingredient in satisfactory punishment. God writeth and engraveth upon the toothach of a reprobate, a parcel of hell; and he stampeth upon burning quick, racking and torturing, the engraving of heaven, of mercy and loving-kindness, in the believer. Bastard crosses, and lawfully begotten afflictions have the same father, but not the same mother. 2. If the patrons of this error could make God's rod as arbitrary, as they fancy the duties of the teaching and ruling law of God to be, they should cry down all crosses, and send all the justified persons to heaven with a pass, securing them from all affliction in the way to heaven; and so, Christ should bring his many children to glory, with dry faces and whole skins. Whereas Christ himself passed to heaven with the tear in his eye, and a bruised soul. The other error is, That Christ hath made a full atonement for sin, and fully satisfied justice for all that are justified in his blood; and therefore, they cannot be punished for sin themselves. But, 1. There is more in the conclusion than in the premises; *ergo*, the justified cannot suffer satisfactory punishment for sin, either in whole or in part. This is most true; no man's garments were ever dyed with one drop of red satisfactory vengeance for sin; Christ hath alone trode this winepress, and of all the nations, there were none with him. But yet it no ways followeth, that the regenerate do not suffer punishment for sin, according to the rule of another mixed and tempered justice. 2. If this argument from Christ's suffering have nerves, it shall conclude, that the elect, before they be justified, are never punished for sin, more than believing saints are; yea, that God is not displeased with Abraham's idolatry before his conversion, nor with Manasseh's blood, nor with Saul's persecution; because Christ paid justice for sins of elect persons committed before justification, as for sins committed after justification.

USE 1. We can fetch no conclusion of a bad condition from affliction. It is a part of tenderness of conscience in the regenerate, to be too applicatory of the law and of wrath: "I am afflicted above all others, therefore God is angry with me, and I am cast off by God." It is a bad consequence. There be some rules to be observed in affliction: 1. We are not either to over-argue or to under-argue, neither to faint nor despise. (Heb., xii.) Conscience is too quick-sighted after illumination, and too dull-sighted before. The reasons why we argue from afflictions to God's hatred are, 1. There is a conscience of a conscience in the believer; that is, even in an enlightened conscience, there is some ill conscience to deem ill of God. "For I said in my haste, I am cut off from before thine eyes." (Psal. xxxi, 22.) This is a hasty conscience; as we say, Such a one is a hasty man, and soon saddled, easily provoked to anger. This is a conscience soon provoked to anger. 2. We have not that love and charity to God, that we have to some friend. We have such a love to some dear friend, that all his blacks are white; his seeming injuries to us do not provoke us. We say, I can believe no evil of such a man; and we over-shoot ourselves in an over-charge and surfeit of charity, which proceedeth from an over-plus and dominion of love to a creature. We are in the other extremity to God and Jesus Christ. Sense of affliction cooleth our love, and we cannot extend charity so far to our Lord, as when we see he dealeth hardly with us, to keep the other ear without prejudice, free from the report that affliction, and the sense of affliction, maketh. 3. The flesh joineth with affliction against God: affliction whispereth wrath, justice, sin; and the flesh saith, That is very true; for flesh hateth God, and so, must slander his dispensation. Ahab could not but slander Micaiah: "He never prophesieth good (saith he) to me." Is not God's truth good? Surely, every word of prophecy is like gold seven times tried. The reason of the slander is given by himself —"I hate him." The other extremity is, that we under-argue in affliction; as 1. we say, It is not the Lord. The Philistines doubted whether God had sent the emerods on them, for keeping the ark captive, or if chance had done it. It is grace to father the cross right. 2. We look seldom spiritually on the cross: a carnal eye upon a cross is a plague. "God's anger set him on fire round about, and he knew it not; and it burned him, and he laid it not to heart." (Isa., xlii, 25.) It is strange, that God's fire should burn a man, and yet, he neither seeth nor feeleth fire. Why? There is something of God in the cross, that the carnal eye cannot see; because, as Zophar saith, "A fire not blown shall consume him." (Job, xx, 26.) Some make it (and not without reason) a fire that hath no noise of bellows or wind, to make it take fire, and to flame up. Some are burnt, and they neither hear nor see. There is a white powder, that burneth, and maketh no noise or sound. A dumb rod is twice a rod. We scarcely see what God is doing in this war; we are smitten of God in the dark. And so, wicked men never do come lawfully out of affliction; they see not God nor sin; and for that come they not out of prison by the king's keys, but they break the jail, and leap out of a window, the land is to see all the circumstances of this bloody war in these three kingdoms.

USE 2. We are to put a difference between God's afflicting one man, and a whole church. Now, God hath his fire in our Zion, and we wonder that wars have lain on Germany twenty-six years, and that for divers years the sword has been on us in these kingdoms. 1. There be many vessels to be melted: a fire for an afternoon, or a war for a morning of a day, or a week, cannot do it. Seven days' sickness of a dying child, putteth David to go softly and in sackcloth. Years are little enough to humble proud Scotland and England. God humbled Israel four hundred years and above, in Egypt, and kept them forty years in the wilderness; and Judah must lie smoking in the furnace seventy years. 2. One temple was forty-six years in building: God hath taken eighty years to reform England, and many years to reform Scotland, and the temple is not built yet: give to our Lord, time; hope, and wait on. 3. Babylon is a great cedar that cannot fall at the first stroke; it is not a work of one day or a year, to bring that princess, the lady of nations, from her throne of glory, to sit in the dust, and take the millstones and grind meal.

SERMON V.

"VEXED *with a devil;*" she is devilled, that is, fully possessed. The malice of the devil is a natural agent, and worketh as intently and bently as he can. As the fire putteth forth all its strength in burning; the sun heateth and enlighteneth as vehemently as it can; a millstone fallen from the sphere of the moon down to the earth, useth no moderation or abatement in its motion, the malice of hell being let loose, it worketh mischief by nature, not by will. Satan's possession is full: Peter saith to Ananias, "Why hath Satan filled thine heart to lie against the Holy Ghost?" (Acts, v, 3.) As there is a fulness of God, (Eph., iii, 19,) so there is a fulness of the devil, "being filled with all unrighteousness." (Rom., i, 29.) It is no wonder that cavaliers and malignants work as their father: the nature of the father is in the son; the manner of working is suitable to the nature of the worker; hell works like hell. "Behold thou hast spoken, and done evil as thou couldst." (Jer., iii, 5.) "They drew sin and iniquity, not with a rush or a thread, but with cords of vanity and with a cart rope." (Isa., v, 18.) "They do evil with both hands earnestly." (Mic., vii, 3.) All that malice and hell could do of cruelty to young and old, to women and sucking infants, hath been done in Ireland and England: the devil in his element is twice a devil; he is in his own when he formeth and actuateth bloody instruments, and he aboundeth in his own sphere. Satan's malice, by itself, is great, and a sinner's wrath is heavier than stones and sand; but when they are conjoined (as united force is stronger) who can stand before them? Christ's lambs have been preserved amidst devils and men since the creation, amongst wolves, by no human power and strength.

Observe, that all that came to Christ, have been forced through some one necessity or other; either a leprous body, blind eyes, a palsy, a bloody issue, a withered arm, or a dying son; and that some have been brought to Christ, at least, their parents or friends have come to Christ, through reason of bodily possession by the devil: but we read of none who came through reason of the devil's spiritual possessing of them, either by themselves or others. 1. There is much flesh and much nature in us, and so much sense and little spirit, and little of God: a blind eye will chase thee to Christ. a soul under the prince of darkness will not. 2. We are all body, and life, and time; but we are not all soul, and spirit, and eternity: heaven is far from being the master element in us. 3. Misplaced love is much. "Ye are of your father the devil," saith Christ to the Jews, (John, viii, 44.) Every child loveth the father. Why? And men love not the devil: doth not every wretch through nature's instinct abhor the devil? Is not this the mother-devotion of any wretch that knoweth nothing of God from the womb? "God save me from the devil and all his works; I have nothing to do with that foul spirit." It is true, there is a physical hatred of the devil, as he is a spirit, an angel, and a pursuivant of divine justice, inflicting evil of punishment on all men naturally; but there is in all men an inbred moral love of the devil, as he is a fallen spirit, tempting to sin: here every prisoner loveth this keeper; like loveth like; broken men and bankrupts flee together to woods and mountains; an outlaw loveth an outlaw; fowls of a feather flock together. The devil and sinful men are both broken men, and outlaws of heaven, and of one blood; wicked men are the children of the devil," (1 John, iii, 10); they have that natural relation of father and son; there is of the devil's seed in sinners. There is a spiritual concupiscence in devils to lust against God's image and glory; and Satan findeth his own seed in us by nature, to wit, concupiscence, a stem, a sprouting and child of the house of hell. It were good we knew our own misery: the man resolveth a prisoner has a sweet life, who loveth his own chains, because made of gold, and hateth them not because chains; and falleth to paint the walls of his dungeon, and to put up hangings in his prison, and will but over-gild with gold his iron fetters. Oh! are we not in love with our own dungeon of sin? And do we not bear a kind love to our father, the devil? We bring in provision for the flesh, and nourish the old man, as old as since Adam first sinned. Alas! we never saw our father in the face: we love the devil, as the devil fallen in sin; but we see him not as a devil, but only under the embroideries of golden and silken temptations: we sow to the flesh; we bring in our crop to the devil, but we know not our landlord; and because sense and flesh are nearer to us than God, we desire more the liberties of state, free commerce, and peace with the king, than Christ's liberties, the power and purity of the gospel, that we may negotiate with Heaven and have peace with God.

"*Unclean spirit.*"—This is the quality of this devil: an unclean devil. Now, whether he be called so, because he tempted the maid to some prodigious acts of uncleanness, or because, in general, he tempteth to uncleanness of sins; so as uncleanness is but a general epithet of all the devils, I profess my ignorance. However, all devils have this general name, "unclean spirits," because of their spiritual uncleanness. It is certain, devils are, 1. Black now, they being fallen in a smoky hell, and kept under the power and chains of darkness, and they are but lumps of black hell and darkness; whereas they were created fair angels. Truth is the fairest thing that is; obedience to God is truth. (John, iii, 21.) Sin is the most ugly and deformed thing in the world; and therefore sinners can have no communion with God, until they be washed. 2. Devils were once pure and clean spirits; their understandings were made clear to see God and his beauty; now, these fair spirits are darkened; for their fellow angels who sinned not, are yet seraphim and lamps of light; and these angels (saith Christ,) "Do always behold the face of my Father which is in heaven." (Matth., xviii, 10.)

Then, the more grace of Christ, the more clearness of saving knowledge and sound reason; grace maketh more solid wisdom than art or learning; by this, David excelled all his teachers, and the ancient ones. In Satan's fools the right principle of wisdom is extinguished. The prophet spoke it of statesmen, or rather state-fools, "Lo, they have rejected the word of the Lord, and what wisdom is in them?" (Jer., viii, 9.) As there be pollutions of the flesh, so are there pollutions of the mind and spirit, (2 Tim., iii, 8.) Men of corrupt minds are men of rotten minds; false opinions of God are rottenness in the understanding. "The spirit of a sound mind." (1 Tim., i, 7.) "Hold fast the form of sound words." (Ver. 13.) There are some words that come from a sick mind, as Tit., i, 13.

The apostle holdeth forth, that there be some sick of the faith, as there be some sound of the faith, (Prov., x, 7.) The Lord giveth sound wisdom its essence and being. Wisdom and the law of God is an abiding and a living thing that endureth to eternity; whereas indeed human wisdom, and false opinions of God, are passing away things; the lie liveth not a long age. Wisdom is a tree of life. "Let my heart be sound in thy statutes," (Psal. cxix, 80,) perfect, wanting nothing. A fool wanteth the best part of his heart. State wisdom, not lying level to Christ's ends, but commensurate with carnal projects, is but folly.

"*Hearing of him.*"—What had she heard? I. That Jesus was the Son of God, the Messiah of Israel, and could, and was willing to heal her daughter. Two things are here observable: 1. hearing of Christ, drew her to Christ. 2. It is good to border with Christ, and to be near-hand to him. There is a necessity that we hear of Christ, before we come to him. This is God's way: "Faith cometh by hearing." (Rom., x.) Christ is not in us from the womb; faith is not a flower that groweth out of such a sour and cold ground as nature; it is a stem and a birth of heaven.

II. None can come to Christ, except they hear a good report of him. How shall they believe in him of whom they have not heard? Those who come aright to Christ, must have noble, high, long, deep, and broad thoughts of Jesus, and know the gospel. Now, what is the gospel? nothing but a good report of Christ. You must hear a gospel-report of Christ, ere you come to him: ill principled thoughts of Christ keep many from him. "Strangers shall hear of thy great name, and of thy strong hand." (1 Kings, viii, 42.) Christ was to be heard by the deaf Gentiles: "In that day shall the deaf hear the words of the book." (Isa., xxix, 18.) We hear, and we hear not, because the Lord wakeneth not the ear, morning by morning, that we may hear as the learned. Many hear, but they have not the learned ear, nor the ear of such as have heard and learned of the Father. Many hear of Christ, a voice, and no more but a voice; they know not that prophecy, "Thine ears shall hear a word behind thee, saying, This is the way, walk ye in it." (Isa., xxx, 21,) There is another voice in our hearing; men do not hear, that they may hear. "Hear, ye deaf, and behold, ye blind, that ye may see:" (Isa., xlii, 18,) that is, hear that ye may hear, see that ye may see. The Lord giveth grace that he may give grace, and we are to receive grace that we may receive grace; grace is the only reward of grace.

III. We hear and we hear not; we see, but we have no reflex act upon our seeing. Many open their ears to Christ, but they hear not; they want a spiritual faculty of observing. "Seeing many things, but thou observest not; opening the ear, but he heareth not." (Isa., xlii, 22.)

IV. Many put Christ in an ear without a bottom, or in an ear with a hole in its bottom; we hear of Christ, (Heb., ii,) but we are as leaking and running out vessels. "Who among you will give ear to this, and hear for the time to come?" (Isa., xlii, 23.) Physicians give their three causes of deafness. 1. When there is carnosity on the ear-drum. This is extrinsical: the world is another lover, and the care of it; and that hindereth hearing. 2. When the organ of hearing is hurt and distempered, as a lame hand that cannot apprehend: now, when there be false fancies, and principles contrary to the gospel in the heart, the ear cannot hear. 3. When there is abundance of humours in the brain, and they raise a noise and tumult in the drum, and hinder sounds to be heard. When pride, and principles of sensuality and vain pleasures make a noise within, that neither Christ knocking, nor his voice without can be heard, men are deaf.

But why do we not hear and see Christ revealing himself in his ways and works? Reason would say, if hell and judgment were before our eyes, we should hear, and come to Christ. Suppose we saw with our eyes, for twenty or thirty years together, a great furnace of fire, of the quantity of the whole earth, and saw there, Cain, Judas, Ahithophel, Saul, and all the damned, as lumps of red fire, and they boiling, and leaping for pain, in a dungeon of everlasting brimstone; and the black and terrible devils, with long and sharp toothed whips of scorpions, lashing out scourges on them: and if we saw there our neighbours, brethren, sisters, yea, our dear children, wives, fathers and mothers, swimming and sinking in that black lake; and heard the yelling, shouting, crying of our young ones and fathers, blaspheming the spotless justice of God: —if we saw this, while we are living here on earth, we should not dare to offend the majesty of God; but should hear, come to Christ, and believe, and be saved. But the truth is, if we believe not Moses and the Prophets, neither should we believe for this; because we see with our eyes, and hear with our ears, even while we are in this life, daily, pieces and little parcels of hell; for we see and hear daily, some tumbling in their blood, thousands cut down of our brethren, children, fathers; malefactors hanged and quartered, death in every house. These, these be little hells, and little coals and sparkles of the great fire of hell, and certain documents to us, that there is a hell; yet we neither hear, nor come to Christ. Nay, suppose a preacher came from hell to the rich glutton's five brethren, (Luke, xvi,) and should bring with him all the lashes, and print of the whips of Satan's scorpions, on back and side, on thighs, arms, and legs; and though he should bring up to us, out of hell, ten thousand damned; and bring with him the fire, the red coals of the fury of God, every coal as great as a mountain, and offer them all to our eyes, and ears, and senses;—such is the power of our deafness and blindness, that we should not believe; for when many little hells work so little by length of time, this one great hell should never bring us to hear, and come to Christ. See how little we are affected with the blood of so many thousands of our own flesh in the three kingdoms![1] Alas! our senses are confined within time.

The other thing observable is, that it is good to be near the place where Christ is. It was an advantage, that the woman dwelt upon the borders of the land where Christ was. It is good for the poor to be a neighbour beside the rich; and for the thirsty to take up house, and dwell at the fountain; and for the sick to border with the physician. Oh! love the ground that Christ walketh on. To be born in Sion is an honour, "Because there the Lord dwelleth." (Psal. lxxxvii, 6.) It is a blessing to hear and see Christ, (Mat., xiii, 16.) We do not weigh, nor duly esteem what a favour it is, that Christ walketh in the midst of the golden candlesticks; that the voice of the turtle is heard in our land. It is ours, to build him a palace of silver.

[1] Alluding to the civil war which during this year, (1645,) was raging not only in England, but also in Scotland and Ireland.

For the sixth article, which is, her adoring of Christ, it shall be spoken of in another place. I hasten, therefore, to her prayer.

SERMON VI.

IN her prayer, as it is expressed by Matthew, we have, 1st, The manner of it: "she cried." 2nd, The compellation, or party to whom she prayeth: "O, Lord, thou Son of David." 3rd, The petition: "have mercy upon me." 4th, The reason: "for my daughter is vexed with a devil."

"She cried." The poor woman prayed (as we say) with good will,—with a bent affection. Why is crying used in praying? Had it not been more modesty to speak to this soul-redeeming Saviour, who heareth sometimes before we pray, than to cry out and shout?—for the disciples do after complain, that "she crieth so after them." Was Christ so difficult to be entreated? The reasons of crying are, 1st, Want cannot blush. The pinching necessity of the saints is not tied to the law of modesty. Hunger cannot be ashamed. "I mourn in my complaint, and make a noise," saith David, (Psal. lv, 2;) and Hezekiah, "Like a crane, or a swallow, so did I chatter; I did mourn as a dove," (Isa., xxxviii, 14). "I went mourning without the sun; I stood up, and I cried in the congregation." (Job, xxx, 28.) 2nd, Though God hear prayer, only as prayer offered in Christ, not, because very fervent; yet fervour is a heavenly ingredient in prayer. An arrow drawn with full strength hath a speedier issue; therefore, the prayers of the saints are expressed by crying in Scripture. "O my God, I cry by day, and thou hearest not." (Psal. xxii, 2.) "At noon will I pray, and cry aloud." (Psal. lv, 17.) "In my distress I cried to the Lord." (Psal. xviii, 6.) "Unto thee have I cried, O Lord." (Psal. lxxxviii, 13.) "Out of the depths have I cried." (Psal. cxxx, 1.) "Out of the belly of hell I cried." (Jon., ii, 2.) "Unto thee will I cry, O Lord, my rock." (Psal. xxviii, 1.) Yea, it goeth to somewhat more than crying: "I cry out of wrong, but am not heard." (Job, xix, 7.) "Also when I cry and shout, he shutteth out my prayer." (Lam., iii, 8.) He who may teach us all to pray, sweet Jesus, "In the days of his flesh offered up prayers and supplications, with strong crying and tears," (Heb., v, 7;) he prayed with war-shouts. 3rd, And these prayers are so prevalent, that God answereth them: "This poor man cried, and the Lord heard, and saved him from all his fears." (Psal. xxxiv, 6.) "My cry came before him, even to his ears." (Psal. xviii, 6.) The cry addeth wings to the prayer, as a speedy post sent to court upon life and death: "Our fathers cried unto thee, and were delivered." (Psal. xxii, 5.) "The righteous cry, and the Lord heareth." Psal. xxxiv, 17.) We all know the parable of the poor widow, and the unrighteous judge: if the oppressed be not delivered, Christ, and his Father, and heaven shall hear of it. Hence, 4th, Importunity in praying, "I will not let thee go (saith Jacob to his Lord) till thou bless me." So James calleth it, (chap. v, verse 16.) "Prayer possessed with a spirit," but a good spirit; prayer steeled with fervour of spirit;—so fervent, that David is like the post, who layeth by three horses as breathless; his heart, his throat, his eyes: "I am weary of my crying, my throat is dried, mine eyes fail, while I wait for my God." (Psal. lxix, 3.) 5th, There is violence offered to God in fervent prayer. (Exod., xxii, 10.) Moses is answered, when he is wrestling with God by prayer for the people, "Now, therefore, let me alone, that my anger may wax hot against them:" "Let me alone," is a word of putting violent hands on any. There be bones and sinews in such prayers; by them the King is held in his galleries, (Cant., vii, 5).

Object. 1. But if so be that prayers must be fervent, even to vocal crying and shouting, then I cannot pray, who am often so confounded, that I cannot speak one word. *Ans.* So was the servant of God, in a spiritual kind of praying, in uttering Psal. lxxvii, when he saith, verse 4, "Thou holdest mine eyes waking; I am so troubled, that I cannot speak." Yea, groaning goeth for praying to God: "The Lord looked down from heaven, to hear the groaning of the prisoner." (Psal. cii, 20.) "The Spirit intercedeth for us with sighs that none can speak." (Rom., viii, 26.) Faith doth sigh prayers to heaven; Christ receiveth sighs in his censer, for prayer. Words are but the body, the garment, the outside of prayer; sighs are nearer the heart-work. A dumb beggar getteth an alms at Christ's gates, even by making signs, when his tongue cannot plead for him; and the rather, because he is dumb.

Object. 2. I have not so much as a voice to utter to God; and Christ saith, "Cause me hear thy voice." (Cant., ii, 14.) *Ans.* Yea, but some other thing hath a voice beside the tongue: "The Lord has heard the voice of my weeping." (Psalm vi, 8.) Tears have a tongue, and grammar, and language, that our

Father knoweth. Babes have no prayers for the breast, but weeping; the mother can read hunger in weeping.

Object. 3. But I am often so, as I cannot weep: weeping is peculiar to a man as laughing is, and spiritual weeping is peculiar to the renewed man. *Ans.* Vehemency of affection doth often move weeping, so as it is but spilt weeping that we can attain: hence, Hezekiah can but "chatter as a crane, and a swallow, and moan as a dove," (Isa., xxxviii, 14). Sorrow keepeth not always the road-way; weeping is but the scabbard of sorrow, and there is often more sorrow where there is little or no weeping; there is most of fire, where there is least smoke.

Object. 4. But I have neither weeping one way or other, ordinary nor marred. *Answ.* Looking up to heaven, lifting up of the eyes, goeth for prayer also in God's books. "My prayer will I direct to thee, and I will look up." (Psal. v, 3.) "Mine eyes fail with looking upward," (Psal. lxix, 3). Because, 1st, Prayer is a pouring out of the soul to God, and faith will come out at the eye, in lieu of another door: often affections break out at the window, when the door is closed; as smoke venteth at the window, when the chimney refuseth passage. Stephen looked up to heaven, (Acts, vii, 55). He sent a post; a greedy, pitiful, and hungry look up to Christ, out at the window, at the nearest passage, to tell that a poor friend was coming up to him. 2nd, I would wish no more, if I were in hell, but to send a long look up to heaven. There be many love-looks of the saints, lying up before the throne, in the bosom of Christ. The twinkling of thy eyes in prayer, are not lost to Christ; else Stephen's look,

David's look should not be registered so many hundred years in Christ's written Testament.

Object. 5. Alas! I have no eyes to look up. The publican, (Luke, xviii,) looked down to the earth. And what senses spiritual have I to send after Christ? *Ans.* There is life going in and out at thy nostrils. Breathing is praying, and is taken of our hand, as crying in prayer. "Thou hast heard my voice; hide not thy ear at my breathing, at my cry." (Lam., iii, 56.)

Object. 6. I have but a hard heart to offer to God in prayer; and what can I say then, wanting all praying disposition? *Ans.* 1st, Therefore pray, that you may pray. 2nd, The very aspect, and naked presence of a dead spirit, when there is a little vocal praying, is acceptable to God; or, if an overwhelmed heart refuseth to come, it is best to go and tell Christ, and request him to come, and fetch the heart himself. 3rd, Little of day-light cometh before the sun; the best half of it is under ground. "We ourselves groan within ourselves." (Rom., viii, 23.) All is here transacted in our own heart. The soul crieth, Oh! when will my father come, and fetch his children? When shall the spouse lie in her husband's bosom? 4th, If Christ's eye but look on a hard heart, it will melt it. 5th, I show here the smallest of prayer in which the life and essence of prayer may breathe and live. Now, prayer being a pouring out of the soul to God, much of the affections of love, desire, longing, joy, faith, sorrow, fear, boldness, comes along with prayer out to God, and the heart is put in Christ's bosom. And it is neither up nor down to the essence of sincere praying, whether the soul come out in words, in groans, or in long looks, or in sighing, or in pouring out tears to God, (Job, xvi, 20,) or in breathing.

Object. 7. What shall be done with half-praying, and words without sense? *Ans.* This is the woman of Canaan's case: Piscator observeth an ellipsis with words, of the particle (*gar*), or because, or for: "Have mercy on me, my daughter is vexed:" she should have said, "*because* my daughter is vexed:" but the mind is hasty, that she lets slip words. So are broken prayers set down in Scripture, as prayers. "I love, because the Lord hath heard my voice." (Psal. cxvi, 1.) There is nothing in the Hebrew but one word, (*Ahabti*) I love; but he showeth not whom he loveth. It is a broken word, because, as Ambrose saith, he loved the most desirable thing. I have love, (he would say) but its centre and bed is only God. "My soul is sore vexed, but thou, O Lord, how long?" (Psal. vi, 3.) That is a broken speech, also. "For my love they were mine enemies."[1] (Psal. cix, 4.) The reasons of broken prayers are often, 1st, The hastiness of the affections; not the hastiness always of unbelief, (Isa., xxviii, 16,) but often of faith, (2 Pet., iii, 10). Love and longing for Christ have eagle's wings; and love flieth, when words do but creep as a snail. 2nd, It cometh from a delique in the affections (they are broken as a too high-bended bow) that there is a swooning and delique of words. Every part of a supplication to a prince, is not a supplication; a poor man out of fear may speak nonsense, and broken words that cannot be understood by the prince; but nonsense in prayer, when sorrow, blackness, and a dark overwhelmed spirit dictateth words, are well known in, and have a good sense to God. Therefore, to speak morally,

[1] In the Hebrew it is *vaani tephilla*, (at ego oratio); but I—prayer; or, I was all prayer; as if I, in soul and body, had been made of prayer.—*Rutherford.*

prayer being God's fire, as every part of fire is fire; so here, every broken parcel of prayer is prayer. So the forlorn son forgot the half of his prayers; he resolved to say, "Make me as one of thy hired servants;" (Luke, xv, 19,) but (verse 21,) he prayeth no such thing; and yet, "his father fell on his neck, and kissed him." A plant is a tree in the potency; an infant, a man; seeds of saving grace are saving grace; prayer is often in the bowels and womb of a sigh; though it come not out, yet God heareth it as a prayer. "And he that searcheth the hearts, knoweth what is the mind of the Spirit, because he maketh intercession for the saints according to the will of God." (Rom., viii, 27.) "Lord, thou hast heard the desire of the humble." (Psal. x, 17.) Desires have no sound with men, so as they come to the ear; but with God, they have a sound, as prayers have. Then when others cannot know what a groan meaneth, God knoweth what is under the lap of a sigh, because his Spirit made the sigh: he first made the prayer, as an intercessor, and then, as God he heareth it; he is within praying, and without hearing.

Object. 8. But, are all my cryings in prayer, works of the Spirit? *Ans.* The flesh may come in and join in prayer, and some things may be said in haste, not in faith; as in that prayer, "Hath God forgotten to be gracious?" (Psal. lxxvii, 9.) Nor is that of Jeremiah to be put in Christ's golden censer, to be presented to the Father: "Wilt thou be altogether to me as a liar, and as waters that fail?" (Jer., xv, 18.) Nor that of Job, (xiii, 24,) "Wherefore holdest thou me for thine enemy?" Christ washeth sinners in his blood, but he washeth not sin: he advocateth for the man that prayeth to have him accepted, but not for the upstarts and boilings of corruption and the flesh that are mixed with our prayer, to have them made white. Christ rejecteth these things in prayer that are essentially ill; but he washeth the prayer, and causeth the Father accept it. There be so many other things that are a pouring out of the soul in prayer; as groaning, sighing, looking up to heaven, breathing, weeping; that it cannot be imagined, how far short printed and read prayers come of vehement praying: for you cannot put sighs, groans, tears, breathing, and such heart-messengers down in a printed book; nor can paper and ink lay your heart, in all its sweet affections, out before God. The service-book then must be toothless and spiritless talk.

SERMON VII.

SON of David; "*O Lord, thou Son of David!*" In this compellation, consider why Christ is called the Son of David, never the son of Adam, never the son of Abraham. It is true he is called frequently the Son of man; but never when any prayeth to him: and he is reckoned, in his genealogy, David's son, Abraham's son, the Son of Adam; but the Son of David is his ordinary style, when prayers are directed to him in the days of his flesh. The reasons are 1st. Christ had a special relation to Abraham, being his seed; but more special to David, because the covenant was in a special manner established with David, as a king, and the first king in whose hand the

Church, the feeding thereof as God's own flock, was, as God's deposit and pawn laid down. The Lord established the Covenant of Grace with David, and his son Solomon, who was to build him an house; and promised to him an eternal kingdom, and grace, and perseverance in grace, and that by a sure covenant, "the sure mercies of David." (Isa., lv, 3; 2 Sam., vii, 8–16; 1 Chron., xxii, 9, 10; 2 Sam., xxiii, 5.) "Yet hath he made with me an everlasting covenant, ordered in all things and sure, for [this is] all my salvation and all my desire. "I have made a covenant with my chosen, I have sworn unto David my servant." (Ps. lxxxix, 3, 4.) "Thy seed will I establish for ever, and build up thy throne to all generations." (Ver. 21–37.) Gabriel the angel speaketh the same to Zacharias. (Luke, i, 32, 33; so, v, 68, 69; Acts, xiii, 34–37; and ii, 30.) Now, it was necessary, that Christ the Messiah should lineally descend of a king: Abraham was not a king; Adam was not formally a king by covenant, as David was. 2nd, Christ changeth names with David, as he never did with any man. Christ is never called Abraham; but, "David my servant shall be a prince among them." (Ezek., xxxiv, 23, 24.) "They shall seek the Lord their God, and David their king." (Hos., iii, 5.) 3rd, David entered to a typical throne against the heart of Jew and Gentile, (Psalm ii, 1, 2,) and so did Christ, (Acts, iv, 25, 26;) and did feed the people of God in the midst of many enemies; (Psalm cx, 1, 2;) and so did Christ. (Acts, ii, 34–36.) Not so Abraham; he was a befriended man in a strange land.

That which I aim at is this: By the received divinity of the Jews, and of the Gentiles who knew God, Christ was a King by the covenant of grace, and the special party of the new covenant, as was David. This may be made more evident, if we enquire a little in the covenant: 1. What it is. 2. Who be the parties. 3. What promises. 4. What conditions. 5. What properties. 6. Some uses, with all brevity. The covenant is here a joint and mutual bargain between two, according to which, they promise freely such and such things each to other: hence God and man made up a solemn bargain in Christ. 2. They both consent. Christ forced not his spouse to marry against her will, nor was God forced to make a covenant. Love and grace was that which led Christ's hand at the pen, in signing the covenant with his blood. 3. As a cluster of stars maketh a constellation, a body of branches a tree, so a mass of promises concurreth in this covenant. Wherever Christ is, clusters of divine promises grow out of him, as the motes, rays, and beams from the sun, and a family (as it were), and a society of branches out of a tree. 4. There is here giving and receiving. Christ offereth and giveth such and such favours; we receive all by believing, except the grace of faith, which cannot be received by faith, but by free favour and grace, without us, in God. Grace, first and last, was all our happiness. If there had not been a Saviour (to borrow that expression), made all of grace, grace itself, we could never have had dealing with God.

2. The parties of the covenant are God and man. Oh, how sweet! that such a potter, and such a former of all things, should come in terms of bargaining with such clay, as is guilty before him! Now, the parties here, on the one part, is GOD; on the other, the Mediator, Christ, and the children that the Lord gave him. Observe, 1. In the covenant of nature and

works, God and his friend Adam were parties contracting; and in the second covenant, God, and his fellow, Christ, and all his, are parties. A covenant of peace cannot be between an enemy and an enemy, as they are such; those who were enemies, must lay down wrath, ere they can enter into covenant. Contraries, as contraries, cannot be united. God being the sole author of this covenant, did lay aside enmity first. Love must first send out love, as fire must cast out heat. It is true, this covenant is made with sinners, (as God made the covenant of nature with Adam, yet righteous,) but an union covenant-wise could never have been, except God had in a manner bowed to us, and grace proved out of measure gracious.

Christ is the party here; so, Christ hath a sevenfold relation. 1. As he is more than a creature, he is the Covenant itself. 2. As he dealeth between the parties, he is the Messenger of the covenant. 3. As he saw and heard, and testifieth all, he is the Witness of the covenant. 4. As he undertaketh for the parties at variance, he is the Surety of the covenant. 5. As he standeth between the contrary parties, he is the Mediator of the covenant. 6. As he signeth the covenant, and closeth all the articles, he is the Testator of the covenant. 7. As he is a side, or the half of the covenant, he is the Party contracting in the covenant.

For the first: "I gave thee for a covenant of the people, for a light of the Gentiles." (Isa., xlii, 6.) "I will preserve thee, and give thee for a covenant of the people." (Isa., xlix, 8.) Christ, God and man, is all the covenant: 1. Because he is given to fulfil the covenant on both sides. 2. He is the covenant in the abstract; he is very peace and reconciliation itself, "And this man shall be the peace, when the Assyrian shall come into our land." (Mic., v, 5.) As fire is hot for itself, and all things hot for it, and by participation, so thou art in so far in covenant with Christ, as thou hast any thing of Christ. Want Christ, and want peace and the covenant.

2. "The Lord whom ye seek, shall suddenly come to his temple, even the Messenger or Angel of the covenant, whom ye delight in." (Mal., iii, 2.) Christ travelleth with tidings between the parties. 1. He reporteth of God to us, "That it is his Father's will that we be saved." (John, vi, 39.) 2. Christ reporteth of himself, for it setteth Christ to be a broker for Christ; and Wisdom to cry in the streets, Who will have me? (Prov., i, 20–22; and ix, 1–5.) It became the Lord Jesus to praise himself, "I am that Bread of life: I am the Light of the world;" (John, vi, 48; and viii, 12.) "I am the door." (x, 9.) And "I am the good Shepherd." (Ver. 11.) 3. He praiseth his Father, "My Father is the good husbandman." (John, xv.) 4. He suiteth us in marriage, and commendeth his Father, and our father-in-law. You marry me, dear souls; Oh, but my Father is a great person: "In my Father's house are many dwelling-places." (John, xiv, 2.) 5. He commendeth us to the Father: a messenger making peace will do all this, "They have received thy words, and have known surely that I came out from thee, and they have believed that thou didst send me." (John, xvii, 18.) "O righteous Father, the world hath not known thee, but I have known thee, and these have known that thou hast sent me." (Ver. 25.) Ministers cannot speak of Christ and his Father, as he can do himself. Oh, come! hear Christ speak of Christ, and of his Father.

and of heaven, for he saw all. O sweet believer! Christ giveth thee a good report in heaven; the Father and the Son are speaking of thee behind backs. A good report in heaven is of much esteem; Christ spake more good of thee than thou art all worth. He telleth over again Ephraim's prayers behind his back. (Jer., xxx, 18.) Oh, woe to thee! Christ is telling black tidings of thee in heaven: Such a man will not believe in me; he hateth me, and my cause and my people. Christ cannot lie of any man.

3. Christ is an eye-witness of the covenant, and heard and saw all. The whole covenant was a bloody act, acted upon his person, "Behold I have given him for a witness to the people." (Isa., lv, 4.) "The faithful Witness," (Rev., i, 5,) "The Amen, the faithful and true Witness." (iii, 14.) The covenant saith, 1. "The Son of Man came to seek and to save the lost;" (Luke, xix, 10). Amen, saith Christ, I can witness that to be true. 2. Christ died and rose again, for sinners. Amen, saith the Witness, "I was dead, and behold I live for evermore. Amen." (John, i, 18.) Christ putteth his seal to that: "This is a true and faithful saying, that Christ Jesus came into the world to die for sinners." I can swear that is true, saith Christ. 3. The world shall have an end, (saith the covenant,) and time shall be no more. "By him who liveth for ever and ever, who created heaven and earth," saith this angel witness, (Rev., x, 6,) that is most true; "Time shall be no more." It is a controversy to the world, if eternity be coming. Christ endeth the controversy with an oath. 4. Christ shall judge the world, and all shall bow to me: This Amen of God saith, That is true, "For it is written, As I live, saith the Lord, every knee shall bow to me."

(Rom., xiv, 11.) The covenant of works had a promise: but because it was, 1. Conditional; 2. To be broken and done away; it had no oath of God, as this hath. O doubting soul! thou sayest that thy salvation is not sure. Why? And it is a sworn article of the covenant; thou hast Christ's great oath on it. Alas! God loveth not me. Hast thou the Son? Thou hast a true testimony it is not so; and "A faithful witness will not lie." (Prov., xiv, 5.) Christ has cause to remember that thou art saved; he beareth the marks of it in his body. Atheist! thou sayest, Who knoweth there is a heaven and a hell? Why, the witness of the covenant saith, I was in both, and saw both.

4. "Christ is the surety of the better covenant;" (Heb., vii, 22;) and in this, the Father is surety for Christ. If he undertake for David and Hezekiah, (Psalm cxix, 122; Isa., xxxviii, 14,) far more for his own Son. God hath given his word for Christ that he shall do the work, "Behold my righteous servant shall deal prudently;" (Isa., lii, 13,) and "Behold the Lord God will help me:" (Isa., l, 9:) And again, the Son is surety to the Father, and the great undertaker, that God shall fulfil his part of the covenant; that the Father shall give a kingdom to his flock, (Luke, xii, 32; John, vi, 37–39). 1. Christ, as surety for us, hath paid a ransom for us; 2. Giveth a new heart to his fellow-confederates; 3. And is engaged "to lose none of them," (John, xvii, 12,) "but raise them up at the last day." (John, vi, 39.) If we could surrender ourselves to Christ's undertaking, and get once a word that he is become good to the Father for us, all were well. Woe to him who is that loose man, as he has not Christ under an act and bond of surety,

that he shall keep him to the day of God! We make loose bargains in the behalf of our souls.

5. As Christ standeth between the two parties, he is the great Lord Mediator of the new covenant, (Heb., xii, 24), 1. Substantially. Our text calleth him, Lord, the Son of David. By condition of nature, he hath something of God, as being true God, and something of man, as sharing with us. Hence is he mediator by office, and layeth his hands on both parties, as a day's-man doth: (Job, ix, 33). In which, he hath a threefold relation: 1. Of a friend to both; he hath God's heart for man, to be gracious, and satisfy mercy; and a man's heart for God to satisfy justice. 2. Of a reconciler, to make two one; to bring down God to a treaty of peace; to take him off law, and high demands of law, which sought personal satisfaction of us; and in his body, to bring us up to God by a ransom paid, and by giving us faith, to draw near to his Father. So he may say, Sister and spouse, come up now to my Father, and your Father; to my God, and your God; and Father; come down to my brethren, my kindred, and flesh. 3. He is a common servant to both: God's servant, in a hard piece of service as ever was, "Behold my servant," (Isa., lii, 13; xlii, 1,) and "My righteous servant:" (Isa., liii, 11:) Yea, and our servant, "He came not to be served, but to serve, and give his life a ransom for many." (Matt., xx, 28.) Alas! both parties did smite him: "It pleased the Lord to bruise him." (Isa., liii, 10.) "God spared not his own Son," (Rom., viii, 32;) and the other party, his own, smote him: "This is the heir; come, let us kill him, (say they,) and seize on the inheritance." (Matt., xxi, 38.) This was cold encouragement to sweet Jesus. If it had been referred

to us, for shame, we could not have asked God to be a suffering Mediator for us. There is more love in Christ, than angels and men could fathom in their conceptions.

6. The covenant is the testament of our dead friend, Jesus; he died to confirm the testament. (Heb., ix, 16, 17.) Every blood could not seal the covenant. Christ's blood, as dying, sealed the everlasting covenant. (Heb., xiii, 20.) It both expiated the sins of the covenanters, and also, brought back the great Shepherd of the sheep from death: for, Christ having once paid blood, and died, it was free to the surety to come out of prison, when he had paid the sum.

7. The seventh relation of Christ maketh way to the parties. And here, Christ cometh under a double consideration; one as God; so he is one with the Father and Spirit, and the Lord and the author of the covenant. 2. As Mediator; and so, he is on our side of the covenant. Then is the covenant made with Christ, and all his heirs and assignees, principally with Christ, and with Abraham's nature in him; but personally, with believers. 1. The Scripture saith so, "The promise (or covenant), is made to Abraham and to his seed: he saith not, And to seeds, as of many, but as of one: And to thy seed, which is Christ." (Gal., iii, 16.) I grant, Beza, Piscator, and many, expound Christ, for mystical Christ; for, (say they,) it cannot be meant of Christ personally, for so it should fight with the scope of Paul, who proveth the promise of life eternal to be made to all believers. 2. It should follow, that life eternal is given to Christ only. But, with leave, this is not sure; for the truth is, the promise is neither made to Christ's person singly considered, nor to Christ mystical: for, 1. The promise is

made to Christ, in whom the covenant was confirmed. (Ver. 17.) 2. In whom the nations were blessed. (Ver. 14.) 3. In whom we "receive the promise of the Spirit through faith." (Ver. 14.) Who was "made a curse for us." (Ver. 13.) Now, not any of these can agree with Christ mystical. Christ mystical did not confirm the covenant, nor give the Spirit, nor was he made a curse; but Christ mediator, is he to whom the promises are made, and in him, to all his heirs and kindred, not simply in his person, but as a public person and Mediator.

1. Because the Scripture saith, "to Abraham, and to his seed;" that is, Christ, was the covenant made; and these words of the covenant, "He shall cry to me, Thou art my Father, my God," (Psalm lxxxix, 26,) are expounded. And again, "I will be to him a Father, and he shall be to me a Son;" (Heb., i, 5,) and, "Go to my brethren, and say to them, I ascend unto my Father and your Father, to my God, and to your God." (John, xx, 17.) So, Christ the heir of all things, and the second heirs under him, are all but one confederate family. 2. The covenant made with David and his seed, and the fathers, is fulfilled to Christ and his seed. "As concerning that, he raised him up from the dead, no more to see corruption, he said, on this wise, I will give you the sure mercies of David." (Acts, xiii, 34, 35.) 3. As the covenant of nature and works was made with Adam and all his, and there were not two covenants; so here, the better covenant coming in place of the former, is made with the second Adam and his children. (Rom., v, 18, 19; 1 Cor., 15, 20, etc.) 4. All that serveth to make a covenant are here; 1. God demandeth of his Son, that he lay down his life; and

for his labour he promiseth, "that he shall see his seed, and God shall give him many children," (Isa., liii, 10.) 2. The Son consenteth to lay down his life, and saith, "Here am I to do thy will; thou hast given me a body." This is the formality of a covenant, when Christ consenteth to the condition. Now, this covenant was manifested in time, between the Father and the Son, but it was transacted from eternity. This is comfortable, that the Father and Christ transacted a bargain from eternity, concerning thee, by name. There was communing between the Father and Son, concerning thy heaven: Father, what shall be given to thy justice, to ransom such a one, John, Anna, etc.? And Christ, from eternity, did bind for such a person, that he shall believe in time. The redemption of sinners is not a work of yesterday, or a business of chance; it was well advised, and in infinite wisdom contrived: therefore put not Christ to be challenged of his engagement, by refusing the Gospel. When thou believest, thou makest Christ's word good; he that believeth not, maketh God a liar, though in another sense; and for aught he knoweth, even in this, that he frustrateth Christ's undertaking in the covenant. Men believe the Gospel to be a cunningly devised fable. (2 Pet., i, 16.) The Father and Christ are both in this business; heaven, hell, justice, mercy, souls, and deep wisdom, are all in this rare piece: and yet, men think more of a farm and an ox, (Luke, xiv, 18, 19,) and of a pin in the state, or a straw, or of the bones of a crazy livelihood, or a house.

3. Touching the promises, 1. There is no good thing, but it is ours by free promise, and not by simple donation only. This covenant turns over heaven,

earth, sea, land, bread, garments, sleep, the world, life, death, into free grace; yea, it maketh sin and crosses, golden sins, and crosses by accident, through the acts of supernatural providence towards us, (1 Cor., iii, 21; Rom., viii, 28,) working on, and, about our sins. 2. All good cometh to us now, not immediately, but through the hands of a free Redeemer; and though he be a man who redeemed us, yet because he is God, there is more of God, and heaven, and free love, in all our good things, than if we received them immediately from God; as ravens have their food from God, without a mediator, and devils have their being only by creature-right, not by covenant-right.

Now, for the promises; they flow from God to us, but all along they fall first on Christ. They are of two sorts, 1st. Some only given to Christ, not to us; as the name above all names to be adored, and set at the right hand of God, is properly promised to Christ. Angels share not with him in this chair. (Phil., ii, 9, 10; Heb., i, 5, 13.) There is promised to Christ, 'a seed, a willing people, the ends of the earth for his inheritance.' (Isa., liii, 10; Psal. cx, 2; and ii, 8, 9.) Christ's locks and his hair are bushy and thick, (Cant., v, 11). He is not bald, nor grey-haired; but he hath "a seed like the stars for multitude, that no man can number;" (Rev., vii, 9;) but all those hairs grow out of a head of gold, and his offspring of children is as numerous as the dew of the morning dawning, (Psal. cx, 3; Mich., v, 7,) though the devil's locks be more numerous. But it is woeful, that Christ and his children, standing upon Mount Sion, being a huge army, and a pleasant sight, yet thou art none of that numerous house. All round about thee are graced of him, and thou livest and diest in the house;

but lay not in the womb of the morning, and shall not abide in the house with the sons.

But there be other promises which go along with Christ and his seed; and these of two sorts, general and special. General, the mother-promise, "I will be your God," is made both to Christ, "He shall cry to me, Thou art my Father, my God;" (Psal. lxxxix, 26,) and to us, "I will be your God." (John, xx, 17; Psal. xxii, 1.) How sweet is it, that Christ, having God to his Father by eternal birth-right, would take a new covenant-right to God for our cause! Oh! what an honour it is to be within the covenant with the first Heir!

Quest. But why are all the promises inclosed in this one, "I will be your God"? *Ans.* 1. Because, as Christ hath covenant-right to the promises by this mother-right, that God is his God by covenant, so we first must have God under the relation of a God made ours in a covenant, a Father, a Husband; and then, by law, all his are ours.

2. Christ God is more than grace, pardon, holiness—than created glory, as the husband is more excellent than his marriage-robe, bracelets, rings; and we are to lay our love and faith principally upon the Father and the Son, more than all created graces. The well and fountain of life is of more excellency than the streams; and the tree of life, than the apples of the tree of life. Christ himself, the objective happiness, is far above a created and formal beatitude, which issueth from him, as the whole is more excellent than the part, the cause than the effect.

Special promises are made first to Christ, and then by proportion to us; and they are these,—1. God promiseth to grace his Son above his fellows, that he may die and suffer, and merit to us grace answerable to this,—"A new heart, and a new spirit," (Jer. xxxii, 39; Ezek., xxxvi, 26, 27.) "For out of his fulness we receive, and grace for grace," (John, i, 16.) 2. Justification is promised to Christ, not personal, as if he needed a pardon for sin, but of his cause. There is a cautionary, or surety-righteousness, due to the surety, when he hath paid the debts of the broken man, and cometh out of prison free by law: so he came out of the grave for our righteousness, but having first the righteousness of his cause, in his own person. "He is near that justifieth me," saith Christ; "who shall contend with me?" (Isa., l, 8.) "Justified in the Spirit." (1 Tim., iii, 16.) So have we justification of our persons, and remission in his blood, (Eph., i, 7;) and that by covenant, (Jer., xxxi, 32, 33). 3. Victory and dominion are promised to Christ, (Psal. cx, 1, 2; Psal. lxxxix, 21, etc.). He must reign, till he hath put all his enemies under his feet; (1 Cor., xv, 25,) and victory over all our enemies is promised to us, (John, xvi, 33, and xiv, 30; Rom., vi, 14, 15; Gal., iii, 13; Col., ii, 14, 15.) 4. The kingdom and glory is sought by Christ, (John, xvii, 5,) from his Father; then he had a word of promise from his Father for it, (Phil., ii, 9, 10,) and we have that also. (Luke, xii, 32; John, xvii, 24; John, xiv, 1–3.) 5. Christ had a word of promise, when he went down to the grave, as some favourite by law goeth to prison, but hath in his bosom from his prince, a bill of grace, that within three days he shall come out, to enjoy all his wonted honours and court, (Psal. xvi, 10, 11:) so have we the like, (John, xi, 26, and vi, 38, 39.)

SERMON VIII.

THE condition of the covenant is faith; holiness and sanctification is the condition of covenanters, (Gal., iv, 21–24; Rom., x, 4–7). *This do*, was the condition of the covenant of works. *This believe*, is the condition of this covenant; because faith sendeth a person out of himself, and taketh him off his own bottom, that in Christ he may have his righteousness: works is a more selfish condition, and giveth therefore less glory to God. Faith holdeth forth God in Christ, in the most lively and lovely properties of free grace, mercy, love transcendent; hence a believer, as such, cannot possibly glory in himself; all that faith hath, is by way of receiving and begging-wise.

Object. 1. But some teach, that this covenant hath no condition at all; so Dr. Crispe and other libertines: For this is an everlasting covenant; man is not now so confirmed in grace, but he may fail in believing; and so soon as the condition faileth, the covenant faileth, as we see in the first covenant. *Answ.* 1. That we have no confirming grace to establish us to the day of Christ, is to teach with some Familists, that there is no grace in sound believers, different in kind and nature from that grace which is in many hypocrites. Yea, but the pure in spirit are blessed and shall see God; hypocrites are not so. And what else is this but the king's road-way to the apostacy of the saints, if believers have not Christ for their undertaker, to bring them to glory,—to intercede for them? (Heb., ii, 10; Luke, xxii, 32, 33.) 2. And though they believe not at the first hour, yet this gospel-covenant is not frustrated, even if poor souls believe at the eleventh hour. The former covenant leaveth sinners for the first breach without remedy, or hope of life, by the tenor of the law; not so this covenant. Christ knocketh till his locks be wet with night rain.

Object. 2. "I will put my law in your inward parts," is no condition to be performed by us, but by God only; and so all the tie lieth upon God: if God do not this as he promiseth, (Jer., xxxi,) must not the fault or failing be his, who is tied in a covenant to perform his part, and doth it not? Now, this God promiseth, (Jerem., xxxi; Heb., viii, 10; Ezek., xxxvi, 26, 27.) *Ans.* Either doth God promise to give us faith, and to cause us to walk in his ways, (Ezek., xxxvi, 26, 27,) and to "circumcise our hearts to love the Lord," (Deut., xxx, 6,) which Arminians deny, contrary to the clear day-light of Scripture; or then, whenever we sin, who are under the covenant of grace, by committing and acting works of the flesh, and omitting to believe, pray, praise, humble our souls for sin, God is to be blamed, who worketh not in us by his efficacious grace to will and to do, as he hath promised; (Phil., ii, 13; Ezek., xxxvi, 26, 27;) and the regenerate cannot sin at all, because it is the Lord's fault (God avert blasphemy) that we sin; for without his giving of a new heart, and his efficacious moving us to walk in his way, to which God is tied by covenant, (Ezek., xxxvi, 27; Deut., xxx, 6,) we cannot choose but sin. Hence they teach, we are not obliged to pray, nor do we sin in not believing, in not praying, when the breath of the wind of the Holy Ghost doth not blow, and stir us to those holy duties. Hence also it is taught, that none are exhorted to believe, but such whom we know to be the elect of God, or to have his Spirit in them effectually working.

Object. 3. To do any thing in conscience to a commandment, is to be under the law, and contrary to the covenant of grace. *Ans.* The law of grace or gospel hath commandments, as "Let not sin reign therefore in your mortal bodies." (Rom., vi, 12.) And this is backed with a reason taken from the promise of grace, "For sin shall not have dominion over you; for you are not under the law, but under grace;" (ver. 14,) so "Work out," etc., (Phil., ii, 12.) for, "It is God who worketh in you." (ver. 13.) Though we have no physical dominion over the assisting grace of God, so as I can forcibly command the wind of the Spirit to blow when I please; yet have we a certain moral dominion, by virtue of an evangelic promise. So, as faith is to have influence in all acts of sanctification, and to look to the promise of assistance, which He who cannot lie hath promised, though he be not tied to my time and manner of working; yet do I sin in not praying, and in not believing, even when his wind bloweth not: God's liberty and freedom of grace, doth not destroy the law of either works or grace, and free me from my duty.

Object. 4. Believing and obedience of faith is but a consequent of the covenant, not an antecedent; so I must believe upon other grounds, but not in way of the condition of the covenant, for in that tenor, I am to do nothing. *Ans.* The apostle, (Rom., x,) expressly distinguisheth between the righteousness of the law, (verse 5,) which requireth Doing as a condition, and the righteousness of faith, (verse 6,) which requireth Believing, (verse 10.) And "We, through the Spirit, wait for the hope of righteousness through faith." (Gal. v, 5.) Nor can any have claim to the covenant but such as believe.

Object. 5. The covenant is God's love to man, to take him to himself, and that before the children do good or ill; and to him that worketh, is the reward not reckoned of grace, but of debt. *Ans.* The covenant is a fruit and effect of God's love, but it is not formally God's love; for because God loved Israel, therefore did he enter into covenant with them, (Deut., vii, 7, 8; Ezek., xvi, 8,) and Arminians expound that of Jacob's embracing of the covenant by faith, and of Esau's rejecting it through unbelief; whereas Paul speaketh of Jacob and Esau, as they lay stated in the eye and view of God from eternity, ere they were born, and had as yet neither done good nor ill. Now, the covenant of grace, or gospel manifested to Jacob and Esau, is not eternal, but proposed to them after they are born, and when the offer of Christ in the gospel is made; and how could Esau, before he was born, refuse the gospel, except you say, he did evil before he did evil?—which is nonsense. 2. Paul saith plainly, "To him that believeth is the work reckoned."

Object. 6. Our act of believing is a work, and no work can be a condition of the covenant of grace; yea, Christ alone justifieth. Faith is not Christ, nor any partner with him in the work; yea, we are justified before we believe, and faith only serveth for the manifestation of justification to our conscience; for we believe no lie, when we believe we are justified, but a truth. Then it must be true, that we are justified before we believe.

Ans. 1. Christ alone, as the meritorious cause, justifieth, and his imputed righteousness as the formal cause; and this way Christ alone justifieth the patriarchs, prophets, apostles, and all believers ere they be born; but this is but the fountain, ready to wash.

But believe it, Christ washeth not till we be foul, he clotheth us not till we be naked, he giveth not eye-salve till we be blind, nor gold till we be poor, nor is his name our righteousness till we be sinners. 1. Men not born cannot be the object of actual righteousness: the unborn child needeth no actual application of Christ's eye-salve, of his gold and righteousness. Now, justification is a real favour applied to us in time, just as sanctification in the new birth: "And such were some of you; but ye are washed, but ye are sanctified, but ye are justified;" (1 Cor., vi, 11). Then they were sometimes not washed. 2. Poverty putteth beauty, worth, and a high price on Christ; sense of sin saith, "Oh, what can I give for precious Jesus Christ?" But his Father cannot sell him.

2. Yet is faith a palsy-hand under Christ to receive him, (John, i, 11). It is an evangelical act, and not a mere passion, but of grace deputed to be a receiver—a certain inn-keeper to lodge Christ; and so, Christ alone doth not justify us, being mere patients; this is not to put faith in the chair and throne of estate with Christ: faith giveth glory to Christ, and taketh grace as an alms, but taketh no glory from him: "But he was strong in the faith, giving glory to God," (Rom., iv, 20). We cannot be justified before we believe. 1. We are damned before we believe; "He that believeth not is condemned already," (John, iii). 2. "He that is justified is glorified,' (Rom., viii, 30,) "and saved," (Mark, xvi, 16). 3. We are born, and by nature the sons of wrath, (Eph., ii, 3). We ourselves were sometime disobedient, etc., but he hath saved us, that being justified by his grace, we should be made heirs according to the hope of eternal life. Paul maketh clearly two different times

and states of the saints; "When we were in the flesh, and the motions of sins which were by the law, did work in our members, to bring forth fruit unto death," then our first husband, the law, was living, and we under a mother and father that begat children to death, and so we were unjustified; but now, we are delivered from the law;" (Rom., vii, 5, 6). "Ye are not under the law, but under grace;" (Rom., vi, 14;) when Christ, our second husband, marrieth the widow freed from her first husband, the law. Then are we under grace, and justified; and then, new Lord, new law. 4. By faith we are only united to Christ, possessed of him, Christ dwelling in us, (Eph., iii, 17). Living in him by faith, (John, xi, 26; Gal., ii, 20). Receiving Christ, (John, i, 11.) Having Christ, (1 John, v, 12). Married to Christ, (Eph., v, 32). Eating and drinking Christ by faith, (John, vi, 35, 47, 45). Coming to him as to a living stone, (1 Pet., ii, 4). Abiding in him, as branches in the tree, (John, xv, 4, 5). Now, if we were justified before we believe, we should have an union by the vital act of faith before we be justified; and so we should live before we live, and be new creatures, while we are yet in the state of sin, and heirs of wrath. 5. This justification without faith, casteth loose the covenant, "I will be your God."

But here a condition—God is not bound and we free; therefore this is the other part, "and ye shall be my people." Now, it is taught by libertines, that there can be no closing with Christ, in a promise that hath a qualification or condition expressed; and that conditional promises are legal. It is true, if the word "condition" be taken in a wrong sense, the promises are not conditional. For, 1st, Arminians take a condition for a free act, which we absolutely may perform or not perform by free will, not acted by the predetermining grace of Christ; so jurists take the word: but this maketh men lords of heaven and hell, and putteth the keys of life and death over to absolute contingency. 2nd. Conditions have a Popish sense, for doing that which, by some merit, moveth God to give to men wages for work, and so, promises are not conditional: but libertines deny all conditions. But taking condition, for any qualification wrought in us by the power of the saving grace of God; Christ promiseth soul-ease, but upon a condition, which, I grant, his grace worketh, that the soul be sin-sick for Christ; and he offereth "wine and milk," (Isa., lv, 1;) "And the water of life freely," (Rev., xxii, 17,) upon condition that you buy without money: no purse is Christ's grace-market, no hire and sense of wretchedness is a hire for Christ. And the truth is, it is an improper condition, if a father promise lands to a son, so he will pay him a thousand crowns for the lands; and if the Father of free grace can only, and doth give him the thousand crowns also: the payment is most improperly a hire or a condition, and we may well say, the whole bargain is pure grace; for both wages and work is free grace. But the ground of libertines is fleshly laziness, and to sin, because grace aboundeth; for they print it, that all the activity of a believer is to sin. So, to believe must be sin; to run the ways of God's commandments with a heart enlarged by grace, must be no action of grace, but an action of the flesh.

6. Paul, in the Epistle to the Romans, to the Galatians, taketh for granted, that justification is a work done in time, transient on us, not an immanent and

eternal action remaining, either in God from eternity, or performed by Christ on the cross, before we believe; and so, never taketh on him to prove, that we are justified before we either do the works of the law, or believe in Jesus Christ; but that we are justified by faith, which certainly is an act performed by a regenerate person; for a new creature only can perform the works of the new creature, and faith is not the naked manifestation of our justification, so as we are justified before we have faith. Satisfaction is indeed given to justice, by Christ on the cross, for all our sins, before we believe, and before any justified person who lived these fifteen hundred years was born: but, alas! that is not justification, but only the meritorious cause of it—that is, as if one should say, This wall is white since the creation of the world, though this very day only it was whitened, because whiteness was in the world since the creation. Justification is a forensical sentence in time pronounced in the gospel, and applied to me now, and never till the instant now that I believe. It is not formally an act of the understanding, to know a truth concerning myself; but it is an heart-adherence of the affections to Christ, as the Saviour of sinners, at the presence of which, a sentence of free absolution is pronounced. Suppose the prince have it in his mind to pardon twenty malefactors: his grace is the cause why they are pardoned; yet are they never in law pardoned, so as they can in law plead immunity, till they can produce their prince's royal sealed pardon.

5. The properties of the covenant I call, 1st. The freedom of it, consisting in persons. 2nd. Causes. 3rd. Time. 4th. Manner of dispensation. 1. Men, and not condemned angels, are capable of this cove-

nant. 2. Amongst men, some nations, not others, (Psalm cxlvii, 19, 20.) 3. So many, not any other. 4. The father, not the son; the poor, not always kings; the fool, not the wise man; the husband, not the wife; not these who were bidden to the supper, but beggars, halt, withered, lame. 2. Causes in the first covenant: there was grace, not deserving, and therefore, now, as the law is propounded, it is a pursuivant of grace, and the gospel's servant, to stand at Christ's and the believer's back, as an attending servant. 2. Yea, "Mercy unto thousands," towards those who have but evangelic love to Christ, cometh into the law, Christ having (in a sort) married the two covenants. 3. "I am the Lord thy God," (Exod., xx,) is grace standing at the entry of the door, to those that are under the law, to bring them out; but in the gospel, all is unmixed grace: 1. Not personal obedience is my heaven; but I stand still, and another doth all that may merit glory. Christ saith, "Do ye but stand still; behold me, and see, friends, my garments rolled in blood: I bind for you, only consent; put your hand to the pen, but I am the only undertaker to fight it out for you." 3. For time: the first breach of the law is wrath, and no place by law for repentance; but here come to Christ who will, and when you will, after thou hast played the harlot with many lovers. Bring hell, and sins red as scarlet and crimson; come and be washen: come at the eleventh hour, and welcome; fall, and rise again in Christ; run away, and come home again, and repent. 4. The manner is, 1. That so much as would have bought ten thousand worlds of men and devils, was given for so many only; an infinite overplus of love, so as (I may say) Christ did, more than love us. Egypt and Ethiopia were not given for our ransom. 2. A sure and eternal covenant, bottomed upon infinite love. Why may not the link be broken, and the sheep plucked out of his hand? Why, the Father that gave them to me, is greater than all. Where dwelleth he? In what heaven? Who is stronger than the Father? The covenant with night and day is natural, and cannot fail; confirming grace in the second Adam is more con-natural. 3. Well ordered: Christ keeping his place, the Father his place, faith its place, the sinner his place.

USE 1. All without this covenant are miserable; Christ undertaketh not for them: the Lord dealeth with them by law: read Deut., xxviii, Lev., xxvi, Job, xx, and xviii, 27. They have bread, but it is not sure; not so the believer: "His bread shall be given him, his waters shall be sure." (Isa., xxxiii, 16.) The believer has all by the free holding of grace; his bread by covenant, his sleep by promise, safety from the sword to lie down, and no man shall make him afraid by covenant; his land is tilled by the covenant of grace, (Ezek., xxxvi, 34). The man not in this covenant hath all by tenor of the condemning law; the weapon of steel shall go through bones and liver, by virtue of the curses of the law.

USE 2. Men never try their standing, whether they be under the first husband, the law, or if they be married to the better husband, Christ, and under grace. Where art thou, O sinner? in Christ or no? They live at random, and by chance, not knowing that the two covenants have influence on eternity: a man is judged according to his state, rather than his actions.

USE 3. No state so stable and sure as the covenant of grace. Christ is surety for the believer, that he fall not away. Christ's honour is engaged, he shall not have shame of his tutory: "I know I shall not be ashamed," saith Christ; (Isa., l, 7). It is his honour to raise me when I fall.

USE 4. We may use arguments of faith, challenging God, "Turn thou me, and I shall be turned." (Jer., xxxi, 18.) Why? "For thou art the Lord my God." The covenant is faith's Magna Charta, the grand mother-promise; all prayers must be bottomed on this, "Do not abhor us," (Jer., xiv, 21). Why? "Art not thou he, the Lord God?" (Verse 22). "Remember not our iniquity for ever; behold, see, we beseech thee, (Isa., lxiv, 9). Why? We are all thy people." Every one doth for its own; the prince for his own people, the father for his own children; yea, the dam for her own young ones, the shepherd for his own sheep; and God for his own in covenant with him. An offensive and defensive covenant of peace and war taketh in the believer, and all that serveth him: the stones of the field; (Job, v, 23;) and in covenant with the horse thou ridest on, that it shall not cast thee, and crush thee; in covenant with the sword, with the cannon and musket, with the spear and bow; yea, with death, as a boat to carry thee over the water to thy Father's land. So the covenant, "I will bless them that bless thee, and curse them that curse thee; I have created the waster to destroy," (Isa., liv, 16). Creation is a work of omnipotency only, no creature can do it. Then fire cannot consume, water cannot drown the saints, except by a dispensation of the Lord.

USE 5. Christ is not fastened as a loose nail, or as a broken or rotten wedge in the covenant. He is there as a nail in a sure place, (Zach., x, 4, Isa., xxii, 23). Hang all the vessels of the Father's house on Christ.

He cannot break. O sweet! we are given to the surety of the covenant, (John, xvii, 3). Son, answer for him; thy life for his life, thy glory for his glory; and render account of him, when the kingdom shall be given up to the Father. Adam was surety in the first covenant, and so it fell out. Free-will holdeth all sure in the Arminian covenant.

USE 6. In desertion, to swim upon the covenant, keepeth from sinking; so Christ, in his sad and black hour, "My God, my God, why hast thou forsaken me?"

SERMON IX.

"O LORD, *thou Son of David.*" The one word "O Lord," holdeth forth Christ's Godhead; the other, "Son of David," holdeth forth his manhood. Here is the perfection of our Mediator, in that he is the substantial covenant, and Emmanuel, God with us, or God us, in a personal union; the substantial marriage and alliance between the two houses of heaven and earth; God and clay. 2. "He is not ashamed to call them brethren," (Heb., ii, 11). And why would he take part of flesh and blood, but because he would be a child of our house? (Verse 14.) 3. He would be of blood to us: not only come to the sick, and to our bed-side, but would lie down and be sick, taking on him sick clay, and be, in that condition of clay, a worm and not a man, that he might pay our debts; and would borrow a man's heart and bowels to sigh for us, man's eyes to weep for us, his spouse's body, legs, and arms, to be pierced for us; our earth, our breath, our life, and soul, that he might breathe out his life for us; a man's tongue and soul to pray for us: and yet, he would remain God, that he might perfume the obedience of a High Priest with heaven, and give to justice blood that chambered in the veins and body of God, in whom God had a personal lodging.

Use 1. Oh, what love! Christ would not intrust our redemption to angels, to millions of angels; but he would come himself, and in person suffer; he would not give a low and a base price for us clay. He would buy us with a great ransom, so as he might over-buy us, and none could over-bid him in his market for souls. If there had been millions of more believers, and many heavens, without any new bargain his blood should have bought them all, and all these many heavens should have smelled one rose of life; Christ should have been one and the same tree of life in them all. Oh, we under-bid, and undervalue that Prince of love, who did overvalue us; we will not sell all we have to buy him; he sold all he had, and himself too, to buy us.

Use 2. What an incomparable thing must the Mediator God-man be? There is no fair creature, no excellent one, but there is a piece of nothing, and creature baseness and creature vanity in it; even a thing of blood, to the mother-nothing of the creation of God. There is no rose, but it hath a briar growing out of it, except the rose of Sharon, that flower of the field, not planted with hands; the Son without a father, "and who shall declare his generation?" A rose that should smell, and cast out odours for a mile of earth, or for ten miles, could draw to it many beholders; but if it should smell for the bounds of the half of the earth, it should be more admirable. The flower that sprang out of the root of Jesse, spreads his beauty, and the odours of his myrrh through heaven and earth. Could the darkness of hell stand and look on the face of the sun, blackness of darkness should be better seen. But convene all the little pieces of the creation; summon before Christ, fair angels, all the troops of the sinless glorified spirits; the broad skies, fair heavens, lightsome stars; all the delicious roses, flowers, gardens, meadows, forests, seas, mountains, birds; all the excellent sons of Adam, as they should have been in the world of innocency, and let them all stand in their highest excellency before Jesus Christ; the matchless and transcendent glory of that great ALL should turn the worlds all into pure nothing. What wonder, then, that this same Lord Jesus be the delight, and heaven of all in it? The Lamb hath his throne in the midst thereof. (Rev., vii, 17). "And they shall see his face," (Rev., xxii, 4.) They do nothing else, but stare, gaze, and behold his face for ages, and are never satisfied with beholding: suppose they could wear out their eyes at the eye-holes in beholding God, they should still desire to see more. To see Him face to face, hath a great deal more in it, than is expressed; words are short garments to the thing itself. Your now sinful face to his holy face, your piece clay face to his uncreated soul-delighting face, is admirable. We do not praise Christ, and hold out his virtues to men and angels. The creatures, as the heaven, sun, moon, are God's debtors, and they owe him glory: but men, who have understanding and tongues, are God's factors and chamberlains, to gather in the rent of glory and praise to God. The heavens do indeed "declare the glory of God," (Psalm xix, 1,) but they are but dumb musicians; they are the harp, which of itself can make no music: the creatures borrow man's mouth and tongue, to speak what they have been thinking of God, and his excellency, these five thousand years. Now, all the glory of God, and the glory of the creatures, are made new by Christ, (Rev., xxi, 5,) and made friends with God. (Col., i, 20,) and are in a special manner in the Mediator Christ; he is, "the irradiation or brightness of the glory,[1] and the character or express image of his person," (Heb., i, 3). All creatures, by Adam's sin, lost their golden lustre, and are now vanity-sick, like a woman travailing in birth, (Rom., viii, 22). All the creatures by sin, did less objectively glorify God, than they should have done, if sin had never been in the world; and so, they were at a sort of variance and division with God. "And it pleased the Father in Christ, to make friendship between God and all things,"[2] (Col., i, 20,) that is to confirm angels, to reconcile man, to restore the creatures to be more illustrious objects of his glory. Now, the income of the rents of glory is more due to Christ, and the debt the greater, in that Christ hath made all things new; and why should we not, in the name of sun, moon, earth, heaven, which are all loosed from the arrestment of vanity by Christ, and in the name of angels and of saints redeemed, hold forth the praises and the glory of God in Christ? Pay, pay what you owe to Christ, O, all creatures! but especially, you redeemed ones.

USE 3. If Christ the Mediator be so excellent a person, we are to seek our life the gospel-way in Christ. We often conceive legal or law thoughts of Christ, when we conceive the Father just, severe, and Christ

[1] Apaugasma tes doxes. [2] Apokatallaxai ta panta.

his Son to be more meek and merciful; but the text calleth him Lord, and so, that same God with the Father; nor hath Christ more of law, by dying to satisfy the law, nor is he more merciful than the Father, because he and the Father are one. There are not two infinite wills, two infinite mercies, one in the Father, another in the Son; but one will, one mercy in both; and we owe alike love and honour to both, though there be an order in loving God, and serving him through Christ.

Use 4. Infinite love, and infinite majesty, concur both in Christ. Love and majesty in men, are often contrary to one another, and the one lesseneth the other; in Christ, the infinite God breatheth love in our flesh. 1. If we see but little of Christ, we know not well the gospel spirit. We rest much on duties, to go civil saints to heaven; but the truth is, there be no moral men and civilians in heaven, they be all deep in Christ who are there. We are strangers to Christ and believing. 2. The spirit of a redeemed one can hardly hate a redeemed one, or be bitter against them; Christ in one saint, cannot be cruel to Christ in another saint. 3. Christ cannot lose his love, or cast it away: the love of Christ is much for conquering hearts; "his chariot is bottomed and paved with love." Duties bottomed on Christ's love, are spiritual. As the Father accepteth not duties, but in Christ, so cannot we perform them aright, when the principal and fountain-cause is not the love of Christ. (John, xxi, 15.)

Use 5. The Ancient of Days, the Father of Ages, taketh a style from his new house, the Son of Man: he hath an old house, from whence he is named, the Son of God. He must affect us, and his delight be with the sons of men, when he taketh a name from us: we should affect him, and affect a communion with him, and strive to have Christ's new name, as he taketh our new name, the Son of Man, of David.

"*Son of David, have mercy upon me.*" The second article of her prayer is conceived under the name of mercy.—Why? God's mercy is a spiritual favour: deliverance to her daughter is but a temporary favour that may befall a reprobate. The devil may be cast out of the daughter's body, and not out of the mother's soul. Yea, but to the believer, all temporal favours are spiritualised, and watered with mercy.

1. They are given as dipped in Christ's bowels, and mercy, wrapt about the temporary favour. Jesus cured the leper. (Mark, i, 41.) But how? "Jesus, moved with compassion, put forth his hand and touched him." So is the building of the temple given, but oiled with mercies, "Therefore, thus saith the Lord, I am returned to Jerusalem with mercies; my house shall be builded in it." (Zach., i, 16.) Epaphroditus recovered health, but with it some of God's heart and bowels also, "For indeed he was sick, near to death, but God had mercy on him." (Phil., ii, 27.)

2. The ground of it is God's mercy; the two blind men, put this in their bill: they cry, "Have mercy on us, O Lord, thou Son of David." (Matt., xx, 30.) They will not have seeing eyes, but under the notion of mercy. David, pained with sore sickness, as some think, or under some other rod of God, desireth to be healed upon this ground, "Have mercy upon me, O Lord, for I am weak." (Psalm vi, 2.)

3. Faith looketh to temporal favours, as faith, with

a spiritual eye, as Christ and his merits goeth about them. "By faith, Joseph, when he died, made mention of the children of Israel's departure:" (Heb., xi, 22,) "By faith, Moses, come to age, refused to be called the son of Pharaoh's daughter." (Ver. 24.)—Why? and that was but a civil honour: Moses' faith looked at it in a spiritual manner.

4. That same ground that moveth God to give Christ, is enough to move him to give all other things with Christ. As by what right? even by the right of a son. A father giveth the inheritance to his son; by that same, he giveth him food, raiment, protection, physic. There are not two patents here, but by one and the same covenant. The Lord giveth to his people remission of sins. (Ezek., xxxvi, 25, 26.) And "He multiplieth the fruit of the trees, and removeth the famine." (Ver. 30.) In the same spiritual capacity of sons, we pray, that our Father would forgive us our sins, and give us our daily bread. Get Christ first, the great ship, and then all other things: the cock-boat saileth after him, with the same motion and wind; they be not two tides and two winds that carry on the ship and the boat. Christ, enjoyed by faith, traileth after him death, life, the world, things present, and things to come. If God give you Christ, in the same charter all things are yours, "because ye are Christ's, and Christ God's." (1 Cor., iii, 23.) Christ watereth with his blessing all things. If all that a saint hath be blessed, and every thing (to speak so), mercied and christianed, even his basket and his dough, (Deut., xxviii, 5,) his inheritance must be blessed: much more, all Christ's inheritance must be blessed; because he is the seed, the spring, and abstract of blessings. Now, Christ "is appointed the heir of all things." (Heb.,

i, 2.) Then he is the heir of a draught of water, of brown bread, of a straw bed on the earth, and hard stones to be the pillow. To the saints, to the children of God, hell (to speak so), is heavened, sorrow joyed, poverty riched, death enlivened, dust and the grave animated and quickened with life and resurrection. God save me from a draught of water without Christ! Peace and deliverance from the sword, without Christ and the gospel, are linked and chained to the curse of God. Alas! if men have the single creature, they make no account how other things go. Give us peace upon any terms, say they. You may have the earth, peace, and the creature, and the devil to salt them to you with the curse of God. Judas had the bag at his girdle, but withal, the devil in his heart. The creature wanteth life and blood without Christ.
2. All mercy—that is, graced mercy, is to be sought in Jesus Christ; every mercy is mercy, because it is in Christ; every stream is water, because it is of the element of water. Every thing in its own element and nature is most copious. Water is nowhere so abundant as in the sea; so in Christ the great treasure of heaven, there is fulness, (John, i, 16). But (Col., i, 19,) there is a fulness[1] in Christ. But 2. A fulness, that fulness, that all-fulness.[2] And 3. That all-fulness is not in Christ, as a stranger in an inn, coming in, and going out; "but it pleased the Father that it should dwell and remain in him." The grace and mercy that is in Christ must be sought, and no other, upon these grounds: 1. It is a special choice mercy that is in Christ. For, 1. No person could serve God's ends in such a way as Christ did, being so complete as he is. God, out of the depth of his wisdom,

[1] Pleroma.—*Rutherford.* [2] Pan to Pleroma.—*Rutherford.*

found out such a Mediator, and so graced. Isaac should have been undutiful, if he had refused a wife of his father's choosing, for both out of love and much wisdom he choosed her. Now, when God, out of infinite love and deep wisdom, hath chosen to us an husband, an head, such a head, such a captain and leader, in whom there is such fulness, shall we refuse him, and shall we not seek the best things in him? Now, Christ is a husband of God's choosing, "Behold my chosen one in whom my soul delighteth." (Isa., xlii, 1.) 2. It is not from God that we now receive mercy immediately, but from Christ, God in the Mediator. Though grace and mercy be every way free, yet now mercy is a flower that groweth in our land, in him who is our blood-friend: so now, we have mercy by nature, as well as by good will; we must have it by an act of the man Christ's will; and when our writs are waxen old, why seek we not that which God hath laid by for us? Grace is more con-natural to us now, in that it is in the bosom of our brother, and ours by derivation. 3. There is a difference between mercy and purchased mercy; it is paid-for mercy that we receive, and so, more excellent than angel mercy. As some waters that run through metals have a more excellent virtue than those that spring from pure earth, mercy is so much the more desirable, that it is a river issuing through that more than golden and precious Redeemer; and so, to us it is twice mercy, to the angels it is but once mercy. Even as the bee gathers sweetness out of various and divers flowers, yet it is so composed, that the liquor resulting out of them all, hath not any particular taste from the sundry flowers, the violet, the pink, the rose, the woodbine, the clover, but it tastes of honey only;—so all we have meeting in Christ, wife, children, houses, lands, honour, to the saints have not their own natural taste, but out of all there is in them a spiritual resultance of some heavenly composure of Christ's sweetness, and are so sprinkled, and dipt in grace and mercy, that as fresh rivers do borrow a new taste from the sea, when they flow into its bosom, so all earthly favours borrow a new smell and relish from the fountain Christ. What do they say, then, that teach, that a man may have all graces, yea, and poverty of spirit, and yet want Christ; as if these could be separated? He that believeth hath the Son: Grace and Christ cannot be separated. (Eph., i, 2; Gal., i, 3; John, i, 16.) These byways sunder souls and the foundation Christ.

SERMON X.

"MY *daughter is grievously vexed with a devil.*" Children, especially to mothers, whose affections are more weak and soft, are taking lovers, especially being parts and substantial shadows of ourself; yet four things are considerable in us to them. 1. So to hold, as we are willingly to let go; love them as creatures only: often the child is the mother's daughter, and the mother's god. 2. We are to strive to have them freed from under the power of the devil, as this woman doth; for they come into the world fuel for hell. Parents make more account, all their life, to make gold, rather than grace, their children's patrimony and legacy. 3. Look at them as May flowers;

as born to come and appear for a space in the element of death: so they sport, laugh, run, eat, drink, and glisten like comets in the air, or flying meteors in the sphere of the clouds, and often go down to the grave before their parents. 4. Beware of selfishness, for children are ourself, and their sins white and innocent sins to us. Eli honoured his sons more than God, and God put a mark of wrath on his house.

"*My daughter:*"—Observe the rise of this passage of providence. 1. Christ, wearied of Judea, came to the borders of Tyre and Sidon. 2. He went to a house to hide himself from her. 3. She heard of Christ. 4. The hard condition her daughter was in, tormented with a devil; upon this, God driveth her to Christ. 5. Christ is hereby declared to be the Saviour of the Gentiles. 6. An illustrious miracle is wrought. See a wise consociation of many acts of providence, as one cluster of passages of the art of wise omnipotency;—as many herbs and various sorts of flowers make up one pleasant and well-smelled meadow; many roses, lilies, and the like, one sweet-smelling garden. In which, those practical considerations may have our thoughts for rules:

Rule 1. Go not before God and providence, but follow him. Prescription of such and such means to God, and no other, is to stint omnipotency, and to limit the Holy One of Israel. The true God tied to a forbidden image, to receive glory, is made an idol; so to fetter God to this mean, as if not free to work by other means, is idolatrous.

2. The book of providence is full, both page and margin: God hath been adding to it sundry new editions; and like children, we are in love with the golden covering, the ribbons, filleting, and the pictures

in the frontispiece, but understand little of the argument of providence. "Whoso is wise, and will observe these things, even they shall understand the loving kindness of the Lord." (Psalm cvii, 43.) "I said (said Elihu) days (things of providence) shall speak, and multitude of years should teach wisdom." (Job, xxxii, 7.) God is worthy to be chronicled.

3. God hath not laid his God-head and omnipotency in pawn, in the power of means, so as God useth means, because they are efficacious; but because he useth them, they are efficacious. A ram's horn is as near of blood to cause the walls of Jericho to fall in God's hand, as engines of war; a straw is a spear to omnipotency.

4. His ways are often contrary to our judgment: we lie and wait the way to see God come upon the tops of the mountains; but we are deceived—he cometh the lower way through the valleys. We thought omnipotence must change the king's heart, ere such brambles as prelates be thrown over the hedge: but our king is himself, and Omnipotence taketh another way. The disciples thought that Christ would make them kings, and restore the kingdom—Christ is dead and buried, and he goeth another low way, through death's belly, to make them kings and priests to God. Christ goeth away, there be great endeavours, and running through streets, cities, walls: "O streets, saw you him? O broad ways, saw you him whom my soul loveth? O dear watchmen, where is he?" But they are all dumb; Christ taketh a lower way! "It was but a little that I passed from them, but I found him whom my soul loveth." (Cant., iii, 4.)

5. Slander not God's ways of providence, with the

reproach of confusion and disorder: to God all his works are good, very good, as were the works of creation. There is a long chain and concatenation of God's ways, counsels, decrees, actions, events, judgments, mercies; and there is white and black, good and evil, crooked and straight, interwoven in this web; and the links of this chain, partly gold, partly brass, iron, and clay, and the threads of his dispensation, go along through the patriarchs' days, Adam, Enoch, Noah, Abraham, Isaac, and are spun through the ages of Moses, and the church in Egypt, and the wilderness, and come through the times of the kings of Israel and Judah, and the captivities of the church, and descend along through the generations of prophets, Christ, the apostles, persecuting emperors, and martyrdoms of the witnesses of Jesus, slain by the woman drunken with the blood of the saints, till the end of the thread and last link of the chain be tied to the very day of the marriage of the Lamb. Now, in this long contexture of divine providence you see, 1. Not one thread broken. "My Father worketh hitherto, and I work," (saith Christ). Providence hath no vacancy, but causes, events, actions, ways, are all bordered one upon another, by the wisdom of providence, so that links are chained and fettered to links, not by hazard or chance. 2. Though this web be woven of threads of divers colours, black and white, comfortable and sad passages of God's providence, yet all maketh a fair order in this long way. Jacob weepeth for his dead child Joseph; Joseph rejoiceth to come out of the prison to reign: David danceth with all his might before the ark; David weepeth sore for Absalom his son's miserable death: Job washeth his steps with butter, and the candle of the Almighty shineth on his head; and Job defileth his horn in the dust, and lieth on ashes, and mourneth. All is beauty and order to God.

6. Put the frame of the spirit in *equilibrio*, in a composed, stayed, indifferent serenity of mind, looking to both sides, black and white, of God's providence. So, holy David was above his cross. "If I shall find favour in the eyes of the Lord, he will bring me again, and show me both the ark and his habitation; but if he thus say, 'I have no delight in thee,' behold, here am I; let him do to me as seemeth good." (2 Sam., xv, 25, 26.) He putteth his soul upon God's two *ifs*—if he save, it is good; if he destroy, it is good. Make sure this general: Christ is mine; at that anchor, in this harbour my vessel must ride. Whatever wind blow in externals, Christ died for me. If I live, it is in Christ; if I die, it is to Christ; if I ride with princes on horses, it is good; if I go on foot with servants, it is good. If Christ hide his face and frown, it is Christ, it is good; if it be full moon, and he overshadow the soul with rays and beams of love and light, it is also Christ, it is also good.

7. In all things bless Christ. Let thy desires be low. "Seekest thou great things for thyself?" (Jer., xlv, 5.) "Seek them not," saith Jeremiah to Baruch. It is easier to add to desires, than to subtract: better the heart ascend from a salad of herbs to wines, than compel thy spirit to descend and weep.

8. Faith's speculations to the worst and hardest, in point of resolution, are sweet. Job putteth on a conclusion of faith, from black premises. Suppose the devil and hell form the principle, faith can make a conclusion of gold and of heaven. What if God should kill me? What though it were so? Yet I will trust

in God, (Job, xiii. 15). What if he throw me into hell? It were well resolved; I would out of the pit of devils cry, "Hallelujah, praise the Lord in his justice." What if the enemy in war prevail over me? What if I were brought from scarlet, to embrace the dunghill? Faith can shape what providence possibly may never sew. What if I be brought to the wheel, to the rack, to burning quick?

9. There is a mystery of providence, that we see not; we know not what God is doing with us, when he is binding us: as the sheep hath no notion of death in its fancy, even when the knife is at its throat, so are we.

10. Providence walketh long in uncertainties; his way that ruleth the world, is in the clouds. Peace is within a step, yet cometh not full victory and deliverance near: and the enemy is well nigh subdued, and the Lord turneth the scales, and layeth us low again. Life is within the eighth part of a span to Ahab; yet God so timeth and placeth vengeance, that the arrow of God must pitch on no place, but between the joints of the harness, and Ahab is killed.

11. We are, with all silence and quietness of spirit, to submit to God's ways, not to fret. Believing can ease us, disputing cannot.

12. It is easier to see what is inflicted on us, than to see who inflicteth it. Evil cometh, and we look no higher than the creature, as if the world created itself. So is this, when we dream that the creature moveth, and is not moved of God.

13. This is to be observed, that God ascendeth in all his course, and providence never goeth down the mount. When Joseph goes down to the pit, to the prison, God in his course of providence is going up.

and advancing the frame of beautiful providence; for Joseph's going down and his fall, is a higher step to God's exalting of Joseph, and saving his church. Judah's falling into captivity, is not God's falling, but his advancing of the work, to do them good in the latter end. Reformation goeth down when obstructions and lets come in the way; but God worketh on. Second causes move backward and miscarry, when omnipotency carrieth on the Lord's work.

SERMON XI.

"*But he answered her not a word: And his disciples came and besought him, saying, Send her away, for she crieth after us. But he answered and said, I am not sent, but unto the lost sheep of the house of Israel. Then came she and worshipped him, saying, Lord, help me.*"—MATTHEW, XV, 23–25.

WE now enter into the dialogue between the woman and Christ. The first trial is, The woman crieth, but Christ answereth not a word. I show first, Wherein the temptation standeth. 2nd, The reasons of it; and in what cases Christ answereth not. 3rd, Bring the uses.

For the first,—God's temptations, and Satan's, and the flesh's agree in this, that all temptations are of one colour, viz., white, and seeming good. Even when the skin of temptation is black as hell, yet there is white in it; as "curse God and die," that thou mayest be hidden in the grave from misery. The reason is, temptation were not temptation, if it had not a taking power to break in upon reason. This is clear in Satan's temptations: he knows man is a fallen and broken creature like himself; yet that there is reason left, and that must have a fair object. The first black apple must be good to the eye, so the devil suiteth a wife ever in his whites; though, if you should wash the devil and the lie, the bones are always black. Now, this woman seeth that which she looked not for, and the affections must be stirred. Is this the Lord, the hearer of prayers? 2nd, Is this he that biddeth us pray, and promiseth to hear? 3rd, Is this the meek Lamb of God, of whom it is said, "He shall carry the lambs in his bosom;" and "A bruised reed he shall not break, a smoking flax he shall not quench"? He answereth me not one word; yea, he denieth me to be his; as it is hereafter, he reproacheth me with the name of a dog. Nature would say, I repent that ever I came to him; let my daughter suffer twenty, one hundred, a legion of devils; I have done with Christ; I come no more to him; especially, supposing what was true, that she had a great faith, and faith cannot be but loving and kind to Christ. "What? my heart saddened and broken; my daughter vexed with a devil! But oh, alas, my Saviour answereth not one word! Sweet Jesus rejecteth me; how can I stand under so many hells? He cureth all that come unto him: I am the first that ever this King sent away with a sad heart. He casteth none away that cometh, he welcometh all; only he will not look on me, poor and miserable. Oh, what can I now do?"

You may know a mother's heart to her tormented child, and a believer's bowels to a Saviour; here is a burden above a load. But why answereth he all sinners, but not one word to me? *Ans.* 1. Few or none are tempted, but the upshot of the temptation is, to beget big apprehensions of the temptation. Never was man in the condition I am in. Christ answereth the devils when they cry; he will not give me one look, one cast of his eye, not one half word. The temptation must represent Christ as a nonsuch for rough dealing, and the tempted a nonsuch for misery. Elias must say, "I, even I only, am left alone, and they seek my life," (1 Kings, xix, 10). "Our fathers trusted in thee, they trusted in thee, and were delivered." (Psal. xxii, 4.) But I am nobody: "But I am a worm and no man." (Ver. 6.) "O passers by, hear, behold, and see if there be any sorrow like unto my sorrow!" etc. (Lam., i, 12.) "We are made a theatre, a spectacle to men and angels." (1 Cor., iv, 9.) The temptation must put on the face of hell to drive at this, to cause the child of God put himself out of the kalendar and society of God's children. Hence that—"No, there was never a soul since the world was, like me,—I am alone." 1. Christ once, first or last, must be no Christ, and God not God, to the tempted, "Hath he forgotten to be gracious?" (Psal. lxxvii, 9.) A forgetting God, a changed God is not God; stick by this principle; yet he is Christ, and my Christ too.

2 It is said, he answered her not a word; but it is not said, he heard not one word: these two differ much. Christ often heareth when he doth not answer; his not answering is an answer, and speaks thus, Pray on, go on, and cry; for the Lord holdeth his door fast bolted, not to keep out, but that you may knock and knock. Prayer is to God, worship; to us, often, it

is but a servant upon mere necessity sent on a business. The father will cause his child say over again, what he once heard him say, because he delighteth to hear him speak; so God heareth and layeth by him an answer for Ephraim: "I have heard Ephraim bemoaning himself," (Jer., xxxi, 18 ;) but Ephraim heard not, knew not, that God told all Ephraim's prayer over again behind his back. 3. No answer from Christ is hell to a believer, but to kiss and embrace hell, because it is Christ's hell, is a work of much acceptance;—when you say, I will pray, and die praying, though I be never heard, because praying is my duty, and God's glory, let me die in a duty that glorifieth him. 4. Wrestling addeth strength to arms and body; praying, and praying again, strengtheneth faith; customary running lengtheneth the breath; by much praying faith is well breathed; Jacob is stronger in the morning, when he hath prayed a whole night, than at bed-time, "The angel said, Let me go, for the day breaketh: And he said, I will not let thee go till thou bless me." (Gen., xxxii, 26.) Then in the dawning he hath prayed harder, and used his arms with greater violence than before; by this, hunger groweth fatter, sense stronger; it is here, "eat and be hungry; pray, and desire more strongly to pray."

3. Reasons of God's not hearing prayer, are, 1. Superstitious and false worship. "Moab wearied of his high places, comes to his sanctuary to pray, but prevaileth not." (Isa., xvi, 12.) Wild-fire cannot roast raw flesh. 2. God hears not sinners, (John, ix, 31.) "Let his prayer be sin." (Psal. cix, 7.) Yea, the prayers of Britain are not heard, nor their solemn fasts accepted, "For iniquity hath separated between God and us," (Isa., lix, 2). 3. God heareth

not, when there is a heart-love to vanity, (Psal. lxvi, 18; Job, xxxv, 45). 4. God heareth not malignants, nor us, when many are heart-enemies to the cause, (Psalm xviii, 41). 5. He heareth not bloody men, (Isaiah, i, 15). Now for the saints, sense maketh non-answering a merciful judgment; it is here as in riches; he is rich who thinketh himself rich, and desireth no more: so, not to be answered is a plague; but to find you are not answered, and be sad for it, hath much of Christ. The saints are heavier, because God answereth not, than because the mercy is denied.

Quest.—How shall we know we are answered? *Ans.* Hannah knew it, by peace after prayer. 2. Paul knew it, by receiving new supply to bear the want of that he sought in prayer; he is answered that is more heavenly after prayer. 3. Liberty and boldness of faith, is a sign of an answered prayer. The Intercessor at the right hand of God cannot lose his own work; his Spirit groaneth in the saints. Doth not my head accept what I set my heart on work to do? (Rom., viii, 23, 26, 27, compared with Rev., viii, 3.) 4. We are heard and answered of God, when we are not heard and answered of God. I pray for a temporal favour—victory to God's people in this battle; they lose the day. Yet I am heard and answered, because I prayed for that victory, not under the notion of victory, but as linked with mercy to the church, and the honour of Christ. So, the formal object of my prayers, was a spiritual mercy to the church, and the honour of Jesus Christ. Now, the Lord, by the loss of the day, hath shown mercy to his people in humbling them, and glorifieth his Son, in preserving a fallen people. So he heareth that which is spiritual in my prayers; he is not to hear the errors of them. Christ putteth not dross in his censer of gold. 5. We are heard, whenever we ask in faith; but let faith reach no further than God's will. When we make God's will our rule, he will do his own will; if he do not my will, it is to be noted, that the creature's will, divided from God's will, in things not necessary for salvation and God's glory, is no part of God's will, and no asking of faith. Therefore, faith frequently, in the Psalms, prayeth, and answereth, "Attend unto me, and hear me." (Psal. vi, ver. 4, compared with ver. 9. Psal. lv, 2.) "God shall hear and afflict them." (Ver. 19.) "Be merciful unto me, O God," etc. (Psal. lvii, 1.) "He shall send from heaven, and save me from the reproach of him that would swallow me up." (Ver. 3.) "Deliver me from mine enemies, O my God." (Psal. lix, 1.) "Deliver me from the workers of iniquity." (Ver. 2.) "The God of mercy shall prevent me, God shall let me see my desire upon mine enemies." (Ver. 10.) "O God, thou hast cast us off, thou hast scattered us," etc. (Psal. lx, 1.) But in the end, "Through God shall we do valiantly." (Ver. 12.) The prophesying of faith is not dead with the prophets. Faith seeth afar off as yet. To see things that God shall do, either by himself or by angels, is an act of prophecy, and differeth not in nature from the prophetical light of the prophets. Now, the light of faith seeth as yet the same, viz., that Christ shall raise the dead, and send his angels to gather in his wheat into his barn. Especially hope of glory is prophetical. 6. Patience to wait on, till the vision speak, is an answer. 7. Some letters require no answer, but are mere expressions of the desires of the friend. The general prayers of the saints, that the Lord would gather in his elect, that Christ would come and marry the bride, and consummate the nuptials, do refer to a real answer, when our husband, the King, shall come in person at his second appearance.

USE 1.—You take it hard, that you are not answered, and that Christ's door is not opened at your first knock. David must knock, "O my God, I cry by day, and thou hearest not, and in the night season I am not silent." (Psal. xxii, 2.) The Lord's church, "And when I cry and shout, he shutteth out my prayer." (Lam., iii, 8.) Sweet Jesus, the heir of all, prayed with tears and strong cries, once, "O my Father," again, "O my Father," and the third time, "O my Father," ere he was heard. Wait on, die praying, faint not.

USE 2.—It is good to have the heart stored with sweet principles of Christ, when he heareth not at the first. It is Christ, he will answer. It is but Christ's outside that is unkind.

SERMON XII.

And his disciples came and besought Him, saying, Send her away," etc.

IN the disciples we see little tenderness: no more but "send her away, she troubleth us with crying." Forsooth, they were sore slain, that their dainty ears were pained with the crying of a poor woman! Why, they say not, 'Dear Master, her little daughter is tormented with the devil, and thou, her Saviour, answereth her not one word; she cannot but break her heart; we pray thee, Master, heal her daughter.'

DOCTRINE.—Natural men, or Christ's disciples, in so far as there is flesh in them, understand not the mystery of sorrow, and fervour of affection in the saints, crying to God in desertion, and not heard. 1. Natural men jeer at Christ deserted: "He trusted in the Lord, let him deliver him." (Psal. xxii, 8.) Heavy was the spirit of the weeping Church, a captive woman at the rivers of Babylon; yet, see, they mock them: 'Sing us one of the songs of Sion.' 2. Even the saints, in so far as they are unrenewed, are strangers to inward conflicts of souls praying, and not answered of God. The fainting and swooning Church is pained; "O dear watchmen, saw you my husband?" (Cant., v, 6, 7.) Heavy was her spirit, but what then? "The watchmen, that went about the city, found me, they smote me, they wounded me; the keepers of the walls took away my veil from me." (Ver. 7.) Instead of binding up her wounds, they returned to her buffets, and pulled her hair down about her ears. And the daughters of Jerusalem say to the sick sighing Church pained for the want of her Lord, "What is thy beloved more than another beloved?" etc. (Ver. 9.) Whereof is thy Christ made? of gold? or is thy beloved more precious than all beloveds in the world? Troubled Hannah grieved in spirit, to Eli, is a drunken woman. The angels find Mary Magdalene weeping, they leave her weeping, they give her a doctrinal comfort; "Woman, why weepest thou? He is not here, He is risen again." 1. If a string in the conscience be broken, the apostles that were with Magdalene cannot tie a knot on it again. If there be a rent in the heart, so as the two sides of the soul of the woman rend asunder, she, poor woman, still weepeth: "Oh, why speak you, O angels, to comfort me? They have taken away my Lord: Angels, what are you to me?" And, indeed, they cannot sew up the woman's rent heart. This is the Lord's prerogative, "I create the fruit of the lips, peace." (Isa., lvii, 19.) I know no creator but one, and I know no peace-creator but one. Peace of conscience is grace; grace is made of pure nothing, and not made of nature. Pastors may speak of peace, but God speaketh peace to his people. (Psal. lxxxv, 8.) 2. There be some acts of nature, in which men have no hand: to bring bread out of the earth, and vines, men have a hand; but in raising winds, in giving rain, neither king, armies of men, nor acts of Parliament have any influence. The tempering of the wheels and motions of a distempered conscience is so high and supernatural a work, that Christ behoved to have the Spirit of the Lord on him above his fellows, and must be sent with a special commission to apply the sweet hands, the soft merciful fingers of the Mediator, with the art of heaven, that I (saith he) should, as a chirurgeon, bind up with splints and bands the broken in heart, and comfort the mourners in Sion. (Isa., lxi, 1.) There must, 3rd, be some immediate action of Omnipotency, especially when he sets a host of terrors in battle array against the soul, as is evident in Saul, in Job, "His archers compass me round about;" (xvi, 13,) that is, no less than the soul is like a man, beset by enemies round about, so as there is no help in the creature, but he must die in the midst of them. "The terrors of God do set themselves in array against me." (Job, vi, 4.) Only, the Lord of Hosts, by an immediate action, raiseth these soldiers, the terrors of God; he only can calm them.

USE 1. What wonder, then, that ministers, the

Word, comforts, promises, angels, prophets, apostles, cannot bind up a broken heart? Friends cannot, till a good word come from God. It is easy for us on the shore, to cry to those tossed on the sea between death and life, "Sail thus and thus." It is nothing to speak good words to the sick; yet angels have not skill of experience in this. The afflicted in mind are like infants that cannot tell their disease; they apprehend hell, and it is real hell to them. Many ministers are but horse-physicians in this disease; wine and music are vain remedies, there is need of a Creator of peace. "She is frantic (say they), and it is but a fit of a natural melancholy and distraction."

Use 2. The disciples are physicians of no value to a soul crying, and not heard of Christ. Oh! Moses is a meek man, David a sweet singer, Job and his experience profitable, the apostles God's instruments, the Virgin Mary is full of grace, the glorified desire the church to be delivered; but they are all nothing to Jesus Christ. There is more in a piece of a corner of Christ's heart (to speak so) than in millions of worlds of angels and created comforts, when the conscience hath gotten a back-throw with the hand of the Almighty.

Ver. 24. "*But he answered and said, I am not sent but for the lost sheep of the house of Israel.*"

In this answer, two things are to be observed, 1. The temptation coming from Christ, denying he had any thing to do with this woman: "I am not sent for her." 2. The matter of the temptation, containing Christ's, 1. Sending, 2. To whom, To the House of Israel. 3. Under what notion; The sheep of the House of Israel. 4. What sort of sheep; The lost sheep. In the temptation, consider, 1. Who tempteth;

2. The nature of the temptation. For the former, it is Christ who tempteth. Hence these positions:

1. Pos. God tempteth no man to sin. "Let no man say when he is tempted, I am tempted of God, for God cannot be tempted, neither tempteth he any;" (James i, 13;) "but every man is tempted when he is drawn away of his own lust:" (ver. 14.) God doth try, rather than tempt. 1. God cannot command sin. 2. He cannot actuate the crooked faculties to sin, as he that spurreth a horse, putteth the horse to actual motion; but the dislocated leg of the horse, putteth in act the halting power of the horse. 3. He cannot infuse sinful habits, which are as weights of iron and lead, to incline the soul to sin. 4. He cannot approve sin. Satan never tempteth, but upon practical knowledge, either that the wheels may run down the mount, as he tempted Eve, and upon that false persuasion tempted Christ to sin; or then, he knoweth sin hath oiled the wheels and inclinations, and so he casteth in fire-brands, knowing that there is powder and fire-wood within us, in our concupiscence. He should not offer to be a father to the brood of hell, if he knew not that a seed and mother were within us. Except Christ by grace cast water on our lusts, and cool the furnace, we conceive flames easily.

2. Pos. Neither devils, nor men, nor our heart, may, without sin, tempt or try the creature, by putting it to do that which may prove sin, upon any intention to try, whether that creature shall obey God or not. Had Abraham commanded Isaac to kill Jacob his son, to try whether Isaac loved God or no, it had been a sinful tempting of him. A creature cannot put his fellow-creature upon the margin and border

of death (such as all sin is) to try if the creature hath a good head that cannot be giddy. God may try duties by events: he is the Potter, we the clay; but clay is limited to try events upon clay by duties only, and not duties by events.

3. Pos. Wanton and vain reason would say, Why did the wise Lord create such a tree of knowledge, the tasting whereof was the second death by law, and that in Eve's eye? Why did not God fortify the first besieged castle, Eve's will and mind, with grace, that the day should not have been the devil's? But, O vain man, is the potter holden to make a vessel of earth as strong as a vessel of iron or brass, that though it fall by no fault of the maker, it shall not be broken? We may say to superiors of clay, yea to angels, Who art thou that commandest? And, besides, we may say, What dost thou? and Why dost thou? and, What commandest thou, another gospel, or no? and we may take their will with a reserve. But we may know of God, who he is, that he is Jehovah; but we are not to enquire, Lord, why dost thou this? or, Lord, what is it that thou commandest? The agent here warrants the action, and all its motives. God infuseth wisdom and goodness in all his ways, because they are his ways. Goodness is a stranger to what angels and men do, except there be a safer law for their doing, than their person. God must have absolute obedience, though he seeketh no blind obedience; men's actions must be warranted, not only from the wisdom of the doer, but also from the nature of the deed. God's actions have all, and abundance of goodness in them, from the Lord. It is enough to me what I suffer (I mean, it ought to be enough), if ten hells for one sin, if the absolute

Former of all things do it. We love to put law on God; whereas, to examine mens' commandments, is religion; we take them upon trust: and to examine God's ways is arrogancy; yet we must judge God. We see, in permitting sin in bloods, in confusion, in the fall of Adam, more fairness, beauty, and glory in Christ Jesus, and his new heaven, than we can see of blackness of hell, of sin, in devils and in sin: Possibly it should have been lawful to the creature, and to angels to permit sin; so they could and would from thence raise a gospel, a heaven of free-grace.

Now for temptations from God; we are to consider that they are all reason, all wisdom, all goodness.

1. Pos. Christ saith to the disciples of her (it had been some comfort if he had given herself but one word), I am not sent for this woman, nor for any of her blood and kindred; she is a Gentile, I am sent primarily for Jews. Hence, Christ may, in words, and to the apprehension of weak ones, say, I am not thy Saviour; thou art not any of my redeemed ones. Christ may give rough answers, when he hath a good mind. He put a hard word upon the nobleman, that came to him for his dying son: "Ye (and all your nation) will not believe, except ye see signs and wonders." (John, iv.) Never any man saw and apprehended harder things of God than Jeremiah: "Wilt thou be altogether to me as a liar, and as waters that fail?" (Jer., xv, 18.)

2. Pos. How often do the promises of the gospel lie at a distance to us, and we have four doubts touching them: 1. They are not mine. In dispensation, God dealeth otherwise with me than with the rest. So David, "Our fathers trusted in thee, they trusted in thee, and thou deliveredst them;" (Psal.

xxii, 4:) and why should he not deliver thee also? Alas, it is not so: But I am a worm and no man, (ver. 6). So Isaiah, xlix, 13, "Sing, O heavens; be joyful, O earth, and break forth into singing, O mountains." What is the matter, that the skies and stars are bidden sing psalms?—"For God hath comforted his people, and will have mercy upon his afflicted." Yea, but no mercy for me; "But Sion said, The Lord hath forsaken me, and my God hath forgotten me:" (ver. 14). Whoever find mercy, God's dispensation saith, I shall find none. 2. For unworthiness and sin, I am incapable of mercy: The forlorn son dare not believe his father will make him a son in his house. Why? there is all his reason: "Father, I have sinned against heaven, and in thy sight, and am no more worthy to be called thy son; make me as one of thy hired servants." (Luke, xv, 18, 19.) Such was Peter's reasoning; "Lord, depart from me, for I am a sinful man." 3. I know not how the promises shall be made good to me: but Joseph had a word, that the sun, moon, and the eleven stars should honour him. But how that could be performed he saw not, when he was sold as a slave, and that was far from honour; yet was he to believe his dream should be fulfilled. And so Abraham did adhere to the promise, when God commanded the son of promise to be killed, "Accounting that God was able to raise him up, even from the dead." (Heb., xi, 19.) 4. I see not the time of the fulfilling the promise; yet "Though the vision tarry, wait for it, because it will surely come and not tarry." (Hab., ii, 3.) We are to remember, God can trail his promise, in our seeming, through hell, and the devil's black hands, (as he led Christ through death, the curse, and hell,) and yet fulfill it. When Christ is under a stone, and buried, the gospel seems to be buried.

3. Pos. Christ is on both sides: he holdeth up, and throweth down, in one and the same act; he denieth the woman to be his, and is on her side to grace her, to believe that he is her's. Christ putteth his child away, and he desireth that his child should not be put away from him; he is for Jacob in his wrestling, and as if he were against him, saith, 'Let me alone.' Christ here doth both hold and draw, oppose and defend at once.

"*I am not sent:*" He doth not here deny the interest of the Gentiles in the Messiah; but his meaning is, I am not first and principally sent, 2. in the flesh, and personally as man for the Gentiles, to preach the gospel to them, and to work miracles for them; but principally, as the minister of circumcision, to the Jews. Therefore, (Matt., x,) he forbiddeth his disciples to go to the Samaritans, but rather, to preach to the house of Israel. First, then, a word of Christ's sending which includeth these three—

1. Designation.
2. Qualification.
3. Special Commission.

1. The designation was an act of divine and voluntary dispensation, according to which, the second person of the Trinity, the Son of God, not the Father, not the Holy Ghost, was designed, and set apart to take on him our nature, place, and the office of the Mediator to redeem us, in his own person. The Son was fittest to be the first and original sampler of sons; the Son by natural generation, was the most apt person to be the perfect mould and pattern of all the sons by the adoption of grace. (Gal., iv, 4.) The

substantial power of God is in the Holy Ghost; the personal rise and fountain of all the excellencies of God, was in the Father; and so, though there was no unfitness in either to be our King, Priest and Prophet, yet the love, grace, mercy, righteousness of God, and his infinite wisdom, dwelleth in the Son. Oh, what a bargain of love, that (to borrow the word) the lot of matchless love and free grace fell upon the Son: 'Son, my only-begotten Son, thou must go down, empty thyself, and leave heaven, and go and bring up the fallen sons out of hell.' Mankind, like a precious ring of glory, fell off the finger of God, being his image, and was broken: the Son must stoop down, though it pain his back, to lift up the broken jewel, and mend, and restore it again, and set it as a seal on the heart of God. This was the rise of the covenant from eternity, that Christ gave his word as the prime Son, that all the derived sons should put their hands and hearts to the pen, and sign and subscribe the covenant of grace: the writs, evidences, and charters of our salvation were concluded, and passed the sign and seal of the blessed Trinity in heaven from eternity. The gospel is not a yesterday's fable; it is an old counsel of infinite wisdom.

2. The Son was qualified, 1. With a passive aptitude (to speak so) to be a man, that he might suffer 2. He was graced with all active endowments to be a mediator. 1. The ground-work of all, was the grace of union, the Godhead dwelling bodily in him. 2. The sea of infused graces above all his fellows; to say nothing of what he learned by experience: being a Son put to school, he learned his lesson of obedience with many stripes, though an innocent child, (Heb., xii, 8). Hence he came loaded with grace and blessings for all the cursed sons.

3. All was nothing, except this Ambassador of heaven had also a commission for us; but he brought two writs, two books from heaven. 1. He came as a flying angel, with the everlasting gospel, to preach to the nations: 2. The Book of Life also. In the former, were three acts of law; so Christ is our Saviour both by nature and by a positive law. Christ and grace are law: 1. Because of his place and birth, being our *Goel*[1] and nearest kinsman, he was more kind than any other here to redeem the sold inheritance. Christ's nature in the womb was grace; it is nothing but nature, and that bad enough, for us to be born. Christ's mother's womb was grace: it was grace that the Son should be conceived and born, and by this he had law to us. 2. Christ's act of dying was a special law: "This commandment received I of my Father, that I should lay down my life." (John, x, 18.) 3. By his death and resurrection he is made a Prince by law, and hath law and authority to forgive sins, (Acts, v, 31; Matt., ix, 6); and power to give life eternal, (John, xvii, 2,)—and rule all by a new law in his new kingdom. (Matt., xxviii, 8.) Our heaven now, is by law and a special commission; but the gospel is a general: he brought all God's secrets from heaven; and in his special commission, Christ hath, as it were, private instructions: Save such and such persons, not any other, not all Israel, but the lost sheep; not the goats. There is a great mystery, how there be no double-dealing in the gospel, and two contrary wills in God.

Use 1. He offereth, in the gospel, life to all, so they believe; and God mindeth to work faith, and intendeth to bestow life on a few only; like a king's

[1] A name among the Hebrews for the person next in succession.

son coming to a prison of condemned men, with offered pardons to all, upon condition they accept of them; but yet he singleth out some, and persuadeth them to lay hold on the Father's grace; and by the head taketh them out, and leaveth all the rest to justice. Yet is it no greater mystery than this, "Many are called, but few are chosen." So Christ's sending with his commission, cometh under a two-fold notion: one is, in the intention of the Evangel; the other is, in the intention of him who proposeth the Evangel to men,—I mean, God's intention to give faith and effectual grace. The former is nothing but God's moral complacency of grace, revealing an obligation that all are to believe if they would be saved; and upon their own peril be it, if they refuse Christ. This is the heart and mind of Christ to persons, revealing two things: 1. Men's duty; 2. God's grace to give life eternal to believers. But the latter is not a moral will in God only, but a real physical will, (to speak so,) according to the which, Christ effectually, strongly layeth bands of love, cords of sweet enforcing grace, to persuade the soul to take Jesus Christ. Christ cometh to the mind under a higher apprehension, with his rainy and wet hair, knocking, and again knocking, to show his face in such soul-redeeming beauty and excellency, as the soul must be taken captive, subdued, and overcome with the love of Christ; as the spouse is so wrought on with the beauty, grace, riches, endowments of excellency, words of love of such an husband, that she is forced to say, 'I have no power, neither heart nor hand to refuse you.' Now, the former notion of the gospel is enough to lay the obligation of believing on all; so as though the gospel reveal not God's purpose of election, (that is only and formally revealed in, and by God's efficacious working of faith, called the inward calling,) yet it saith this to all, 'You are all to believe no less, than if there were not any reprobated persons amongst you.' If, therefore, any despairing ones, as Cain, yea, and many weak ones, refuse to believe, on this ground, Why should I believe? the gospel hath excepted me, it belongeth not to me, I am a reprobate,—they are deluded, for the gospel formally revealeth neither the Lord's decree of election nor reprobation. The embracing of the gospel, and the final rejection thereof, can speak to both these; but that is neither the gospel voice, nor the gospel spirit, that revealeth any such bad tidings. It is true, Satan may speak so, but Christ cometh once with good tidings to all, elect and reprobate. Men do here buy a plea against Christ, and force a quarrel upon him. The believer breaketh first with Christ, before ever Christ breaketh with him. Bad tidings are too soon true. I doubt if reprobation be so far forth revealed to any, even to those that sin against the Holy Ghost, as they are to believe their own impossibility to be saved; for though a man knew himself to be over score and past all remedy, he is obliged to believe the power of infinite mercy to save him, and to hang by that thread, in humility and adherence to Christ.

2. If Christ be sent for lost Israel, and say in the gospel, 'Who will go with me?' and say to thee, 'My Father the King sent me, his own Son, to bring thee up to his house,' why, but thou shouldst go? When old Jacob saw the chariots and messengers that Prince Joseph, his own son, yet living, had sent to fetch him, "His heart failed for joy." Seest thou the chariot of Pharaoh paved with love? make, then, for the journey.

The home we have here is a taking lover; why, but thou mayest say, I cannot stay here, the king hath sent for me.

SERMON XIII.

"OF ISRAEL." It was then a privileged mercy, that Christ was sent to the Jews. 1. The Jew is the elder brother, and the native heir of Christ. Christ is of their blood and house. (Rom., i, 2, 3, and ix, 3.) They were Christ's first bride. Alas! they killed their husband. There is a born Jew in heaven, in soul and body: it is sweet to have any relation to Christ. 2. The catholic covenant of grace made with the great sister, the Church Universal, was first laid down in pawn in their hand; they put their hand first to the contract, in subscribing the marriage contract, (Jerem., ii, iii). Israel was holy to the Lord, and the first fruits of his increase. Oh, sweet! the fallen race of mankind was Christ's corn-field, and his wheat. The Jews were the first sheaf of the field, (Deut., vii, 6). They got Christ's young love, and, (to speak so,) the first handsel of free grace in a church-way. 3. Christ, in the Jewish flesh, (yet not excluding Ruth, Rahab, and other Gentiles of the blood-royal,) acted the whole gospel. A born Jew redeemed the lost world, offered a sacrifice to God for sinners: a born Jew is heir of all things, is exalted a prince to guide and rule all, and shall judge men and angels. 4. The Lord Christ, in the flesh, was first offered to them; they had the first gospel-love, (Matt., x, 5, 6; Acts, xiii, 46). 5. The oracles of God were committed to them, (Romans, iii, 1; ix, 4); the testator Christ's written will, was in their keeping. 6. God was their first crowned King. He gave Ethiopia, and Egypt, and Zeba, a ransom for them, and was their lawgiver. 7. Every male child among the Jews did bear somewhat of Christ in his flesh, (Col., ii, 11,) when all the world was without Christ. 8. Their land was Christ's by a special typical right. God saith of it, "It is my land." Christ was their sovereign landlord, and they the great King's freeholders. 9. The Lord never dwelt in a house made with hands, in a temple, as amongst them, having special respect to the true Temple, Jesus Christ, (John, ii, 19).

Use 1. Let us pray our elder sister home to Christ. They said, "We have a little sister, and she hath no breasts; what shall we do for our sister in the day that she shall be spoken for?" (Cant., viii.) Now, we have a greater sister, what shall we, the Gentiles, do for her? There is a day when "ten men shall take hold, out of all nations, of the skirt of a Jew, saying, We will go with you; we have heard that God is with you." (Zech., viii, 23.)

Use 2. It is the happiness of our land, that we have a three-fold relation to Christ,—I mean these two nations—that we have avowed the Lord by a national testimony;[1] and the nations are public martyrs and witnesses of Christ, in that they are made a field of blood, for no other quarrel, but because they desire to stand for Christ's truth against Antichrist. Surely in the intention of Papists, now in arms against us, there is no cause of war but this only. 2. That we have sworn that the Lord shall be our God in a solemn cove-

[1] The Solemn League and Covenant, which was subscribed by England in 1643.

nant. 3. That we are honoured to build the Temple of the Lord, and reform religion. Oh, that we could see our debt and be thankful!

USE 3. The Jews had the morning market of Christ, and they would not pay the rent of the vineyard to the Lord thereof. We have the afternoon of Christ; and know we what a mercy it is, that "our Beloved feedeth amongst the lilies, till the day break, and the shadows fly away;" and that "the voice of the turtle is heard in our land"? God, for our abuse of the gospel, hath sent among us the bloody pursuivants, and officers of his wrath, men skilful to destroy; God is now in three kingdoms, arresting the carcases of men. We are owing much to God; he will now have husbands and sons from us, and legs and arms of wounded and slain men from us, for that rent we owe to the Lord of the vineyard,—for our contempt of the gospel.

"Sheep,"—first a word of sheep, then of "*lost sheep*." I take no other reasons why the redeemed of the Lord are called sheep, than are obvious in Scripture. 1. The sheep are passive creatures, and can do little for themselves; so can believers in the work of their salvation: as,

1. They have not of themselves more knowledge of the saving way than sheep, and so cannot walk, but as they are taught and led. "Teach me, O Lord." (Psalm cxix, 33.) "Lead me in thy truth." (Psalm xxv, 5.) Like a blind man holding out his hand to his guide, so they: "Lord, lead me in thy righteousness." (Psalm v, 8.) It is not common leading, but the leading of children learning to go by a hold. "When Ephraim was a child, I loved him." (Hosea, xi, 1.) "I taught Ephraim also to go, taking them

by their arms;" but Ephraim, like a child, knew not his leader: "But they know not," saith the Lord, "that I healed them." (Ver. 3.) 3. Leading may suppose some willingness; but we must be drawn: "No man can come to me, except the Father draw him," (John, vi, 44). "Draw me, we will run after thee." (Cant., i, 4.) 4. There is a word of special grace, which is more than teaching, leading, drawing; and that is, Leaning: "Who is this that cometh up from the wilderness, leaning upon her Beloved?" (Cant., viii, 5.) 5. There is a word yet more, and that is Bearing: when the good shepherd hath found the lost sheep, "He layeth it on his shoulders with joy." (Luke, xv, 5.) "Hearken to me, C house of Jacob, and all the remnant of the house of Israel, which are born (by me) from the belly and carried from the grey hairs:" (Isa., xlvi, 3:) So also, "God beareth them on eagles' wings." (Deut., xxxii, 11.) Grace, grace is a noble guide and tutor.

2. The life of sheep, is the most dependent life in the world: no such dependent creatures as sheep: all their happiness is the goodness, care, and wisdom of their shepherd; wolves, lions, leopards, need none to watch over them. Briers and thorns grow alone; the vine tree, the noble vine, is a tender thing, must be supported. Christ must bear the weak and lambs in his bosom. (Isa., xl, 11.) The shepherd's bosom and his legs, are the legs of the weak lamb. Even the habit of grace is a creature, and no independent thing; and so, in its creation, in its preservation, it dependeth on Christ: grace is as the new born bird; its life is the heat and warmness of the body, and wings of the dam. It is like a chariot; though it have four wheels, yet it moveth only, as drawn by the strength of horses without it. It is a plough

of timber only, without iron and steel that breaketh up no earth. The new seed of God acteth, as acted by God: hence repenting Ephraim, "Turn thou me and I shall be turned." (Jer., xxxi, 18.) Renewed David is often at this: "Quicken me, quicken me:" the swooning Church; "Stay me with flagons, and comfort me with apples." (Cant., ii.)

3. Sheep are docile creatures. "My sheep hear my voice; I know them, and they follow me." (John, x, 27.) There is a controversy with Papists, how we know Scripture to be the word of God. There are two things here considerable; one within, and another without. How knoweth the lamb its mother amongst a thousand of the flock? Natural instinct teacheth it. From what teacher or art is it, that the swallow buildeth its clay house and nest, and every bee knoweth its own cell and waxen house? So the instinct of grace knoweth the voice of the Beloved amongst many voices, (Cant., ii, 8). And this discerning power is in the subject. There is another power in the object. Of many thousand millions of men, since the creation, not one, in figure and shape, is altogether like another; some visible difference there is: amongst many voices, no voice like man's tongue: amongst millions of divers tongues of men, every voice hath an audible difference printed on it, by which it is discerned from all other. To the new creature, there is in Christ's word some character, some sound of heaven, that is in no voice in the world, but in his only: in Christ represented to a believer's eye of faith, there is a shape, and a stamp of divine majesty: no man knoweth it but the believer; and in heaven and earth Christ hath not a marrow like himself. Suppose there were an hundred counterfeit moons, or fancied suns in the heaven; a natural

eye can discern the true moon, and the natural sun from them all. The eye knoweth white, not to be black nor green. Christ offered to the eye of faith, stampeth on faith's eye, little images of Christ, that the soul dare go to death and to hell with it, that this, this only was Christ, and none other but he only.

4. Sheep are simple: fancy leadeth them much, therefore they are straying creatures. (Isa., liii, 6; Psalm cxix, 176; 1 Peter, ii, 25.) There is nothing of the notion of death, or of another life in the fancy of sheep; a mouthful of green grass carrieth the sheep on upon a pit, and the mouth and teeth of lions and wolves. Fancy is often the guide of weak believers, rather than faith: little care we by nature, what we shall be in the next generation. Fancy and nature cannot out-see time, nor see over or beyond death. Fair green-like hopes of gain, are to us hopes of real good: we think we see two moons in one heaven. There is a way good-seeming that deceiveth us; but black death is the night lodging of it. Alas! we are journeying, and know not our night-inns, and where we shall lodge when the sun is going down: poor soul! where shall you be all night?

1. If believers be such dependent creatures, what do libertines and Antinomians teach us?—that the soul need not go out to Christ, for fresh supply, but is acted by the spirit inhabiting and dwelling in us: also, that it is the way of the law, not of the gospel, that we act in the strength of Christ. Both these are against the gospel: 1. We are commanded to pray, even the sons who in faith call God, "Our Father which is in heaven; lead us not into temptation;" which God doth no other way, than by giving us new supply of grace to actual resistance. And Christ will

have us to pray, "Lord, increase our faith." The virgins in love with Christ, pray "draw us." Paul prayeth, that the God of peace would sanctify the Thessalonians wholly; (1 Thess., v, 23;) and for this, he boweth his knee, that the believing Ephesians may be strengthened, "according to the riches of his glory, with might by his Spirit in the inner man, that Christ may dwell in their hearts by faith; and that, with all the saints, they may be able to comprehend the transcendent love of God in Christ," (Eph., iii, 15–19.) And that author, "That the God of peace may make the saints perfect in every good work, to do his will, working in them that which is well pleasing in his sight." (Heb., xiii, 20, 21.) 2. It is against Christ's intercession, whose it is to keep the faith of the saints from falling, (Luke, xxii, 32,) and who "finisheth our faith," (Heb., xii, 2,) "confirmeth us to the end," (1 Cor., i, 8,) advocateth for new grace, (1 John, ii, 1, 2,) "appeareth in the presence of God for us," (Heb., ix, 24). 3. This cannot stand with the promise of perseverance, made in the covenant of grace, (Jer., xxxii, 40, 41; Isa., lix, 21–24; Ezek., xxxvi, 27; John, vi, 39, 40; and iv, 13, 14). Nor, 4. with the faith of persuasion of perseverance, (Rom., viii, 38, 39; Jude, 24, 25; Psalm xxiii, 6; 2 Tim., iv, 18). And 5. This must infer, either that the regenerate do not, and cannot sin, by not believing and persevering in faith, and perfecting holiness in the fear of God, (which is blasphemy); or that the saints may finally fall from grace; or that the use of grace, and willing and doing in the saints, is not of, or from confirming and assisting grace. 6. This putteth our stock of grace in our own hand; as if Christ did literally only reveal to us the way to heaven, and leave it to our own free will, to guide well or ill.

USE 1.—And so, we are to thank Christ for beginning in the spirit, and to thank ourselves that we go on, and grow in grace, or end not in the flesh? Nay, but Christ's dispensation, in whose grace we are strong, (Eph., vi, 10,) and "can do all things," (Phil., iv, 13,) is nothing but one continued act of free grace, or a long cord or chain of dependency on Christ: yea, grace is glory on the wheels; it is glory like wheat in the blade, in the way in the flux and tendency to the ear and harvest, depending on the continued aspect of the summer Sun of Righteousness. The new creature is the iron in the fire of heaven in the moulding and framing, and under the hammer and tools of Christ, and a rose in the opening, before it cast out its leaves. And in this, we are to have these considerations:

1. Faith is leisurely to look to Christ, in bringing his work out of the mould, and taking the new ship off the stocks as a perfected vessel. We conceive erroneously that faith only eyeth Christ as pardoning; and that it hath no eye, no activity and influence on our own gracious acts wrought in us by Christ. But faith is an agent, as it is a patient, and joineth with Christ and with free will, to an active purifying of the heart: it believeth heaven, and worketh heaven.

2. We often go on, imagining that we are in a way of backsliding. Deserted souls, not conscious of the reflex acts of believing and longing for Christ, think themselves apostates, when they are advancing in their way. In great water-works, where there be a great multitude of wheels, the standing of some five or six is the advancing of the work in other twenty, or forty wheels. In desertion, some wheels are at a stand, and move not; as often acts of feeling, joy, self-delight in the

actual beholding of Christ, are at a stand; and then it is thus:—"I said, I am cast out of his sight;" yet other wheels are moving, as 1. Humble and base thoughts of himself. 2. Broad and large thoughts of Christ, and his grace. 3. Hunger and longing for Christ. 4. Self-diffidence is much. 5. Care and love-sickness: "Saw you him whom my soul loveth?" is vehement. 6. Sense of sin, and of wants and spiritual poverty, increaseth now. 7. Sense of the misery of the combat, is much more than before: "O miserable man that I am!" 8. Believing under hope, and against hope, is strongest now. 9. There is more tenderness and humble fear now than before. 10. A stronger resolution to entertain Christ more kindly, when he shall return again in his fulness of presence. 11. Sorrow, that remembering, he said, "My head is full of dew, and my locks with the drops of the night," (Cant., v, 6,) yet the sleeping soul kept him at the door.

3. We are to adore that dispensation, which will have us not stepping one foot to heaven, but upon grace, and upon grace's charges. He could make saints to be sinless angels: but what haste? We should then, not yet being habituated with glory, nor confirmed in heaven, think little of Christ.

USE 2.—If we be so dependent on Christ, we have not ended with all law-directions: the law standeth us yet in good use; I mean, when Christ hath made us and the law friends, and hath removed the curse, and made the believer say, "O how love I thy law!"

Object. 1.—Can you (saith M. Towne) "separate the directing or commanding power of the law, from the condemning power of the law? Can the law speak to any but to those who are under the law? Is it law at all if it condemn not?"

Ans. Actual condemnation may well be separated from the law; as a lion is a lion, and yet being chained, cannot actually devour. To condemn, may well be removed from the law; it could not condemn Adam, before sin entered in the world; it cannot condemn the holy, elect, and sinless angels; yet it had, and hath a commanding and obliging power to command and direct both: to condemn, is accidental to the law, as the state of sin is accidental to man. 2. The law may speak by way of direction to believers, but cannot speak to them by way of actual condemnation, because Christ hath removed the curse.

Object. 2. Holiness, and walking in the way of holiness, contributeth not one jot to salvation, as causes, or as the way thereto—Christ hath done that perfectly.

Ans. I pray you consider three things here: 1. The will of God to save; yea, and to justify the ungodly. 2. The law-right to righteousness and salvation. 3. Actual salvation. 1. Christ's merits are neither cause, nor motive, nor condition moving God to will, to choose, or ordain persons for glory: this is an act of eternal election to glory, which is not from Christ's merits; nor doth any external work or condition, either good or evil, in Jacob or Esau, or in the surety Christ, move God to such an act of free liberty. Libertines are ignorant in so speaking; yea, faith is no condition, cause, or motive of such a will. 2. Christ's merits, not faith, not holiness in us, must be the cause of our law-right to righteousness and glory: Christ alone gave the price of redemption for us; no garments were rolled in blood, for a patent and right to heaven, but his only; he alone trod the wine-press of God's wrath. In these two notions, works of holiness have no footing in the work. But 3, As touching actual salvation, the way to it is holiness, without which none can see God. It is expressly commanded, "Be ye holy, as I am holy," (1 Pet., i, 19, 20). "But being now made free from sin, and become servants to God, ye have your fruit unto holiness, and the end life everlasting," (Rom., vi, 22). "If ye do these things ye shall never fall, for so an entrance shall be ministered unto you abundantly, unto the everlasting kingdom of our Lord and Saviour Jesus Christ," (2 Pet., i, 10). "To him that overcometh I will give to eat of the tree of life, which is in the midst of the paradise of God," (Rev., ii, 7). "To him that overcometh will I grant to sit with me in my throne, even as I also overcame, and am set down with my Father on his throne." (Rev., iii, 21.) They answer, "Overcoming is by faith." But I reply; faith, to libertines, is but a believing that Christ hath overcome in their person and place; for faith is no more to them a condition or way to salvation, than good works: For faith (say they) is not Christ; Christ only is the way to heaven. But this were a vain promise, if overcoming were not, 1. A duty required of us in time, upon the performance whereof, we have an entrance made to life eternal. 2. If overcoming be but only believing, and so an act of the soul only, those to whom the promise is made, are to do no more, but believe Christ hath overcome the persecuting world for them, and yield; and in profession deny the faith, and accept of conditions of life, and so be foiled, and yet claim right to the promise, contrary to the intent of Christ, who commendeth Pergamus for not denying the faith. (Rev., ii, 13.) Now, in all this, as the walking in the way to a fair palace to dwell in it, in honour and happiness, cannot be the price, the ransom, the sum given to buy right to that place, and to the honour and happiness thereof; so neither can our walking in the way to glory, be the price of glory.

Object. 3. But we are saved by Christ's merits before we can do any good works; then good works come not, to perfect and make up salvation.

Ans. So are we, in regard to right of purchase, saved before we believe; yet that hindereth not, but faith is a way to salvation. 2. This concludeth, that good works are no cause, or way, or mean of obtaining the right of purchase to redemption, which we yield; but not, that we are actually saved without walking in the way, called the "way of holiness, which the unclean shall not pass over." (Isa., xxxv, 8.)

Object. 4. We are to do good works, from the principle of the love of Christ constraining us, not from the law commanding, or directing us.

Ans. 1. These are no way contrary: the regenerate, from both principles, are to walk in love and holiness as Christ did. The law directing is not abolished by grace, or by love to Christ, and this is no other than the reasoning of old libertines. Paul said, "Now we are delivered from the law." (Rom., vii, 6.) O, then, said libertines, "we may sin, and fleshly walking shall not prejudge salvation, nor condemn us." "What shall we say then? Is the law sin? God forbid;" (ver. 7;) and "Where sin abounded, grace did much more abound." (Rom., v, 20.) Then said the libertine, "What shall we then say? shall we continue in sin, that grace may abound? God forbid." (Rom., vi, 1, 2.) Then the law commandeth and directeth not to sin; and Christ and grace being friends, speak with the same mouth, "God forbid that we sin." We are not so freed from the commanding power of the law, as that we sin not. When we do what is contrary to God's law, we are so far under the law, as not to sin, because the rule of the law is removed; nay, the law backs a man till he come to Christ and to glory; and Christ backs the law, and saith, The law forbiddeth you sin; I say, Amen. Grace saith, Sin not; and Christ also layeth new bands of love, and obligation to thankfulness on us, not to sin, but removeth not the ancient bounds. Grace and condemnation are opposite, but not grace and the commanding power of the law.

Object. 5. The law is a letter of death and bondage, and can never convert the soul—only the gospel doth that; for in the gospel, grace is given to obey what is commanded: Therefore, your law-preachers lead men from the foundation, Christ.

Ans. 1. The letter of the law, without the spirit of Christ, cannot convert any, nor can the letter of the gospel, or gospel threatenings without the spirit of grace, convert any. Both law and gospel, separated from the spirit, are alike in this; and neither law nor gospel, according to this reasoning, should be preached. Antinomians do in downright terms teach this: for they say, 1. That the due searching and knowledge of the Scriptures, is not a safe and sure way of searching and finding Christ: The word saith the contrary, (Ps. xix, 7–9; Acts, x, 43; Rom., iii, 21; John, v, 39; Luke, i, 70, 71). 2. To do any thing by virtue of a commandment, is a law-way, not a gospel obedience: this is contrary to Ps. cxix, 6, 11, 43, 44; and 2 Pet., i, 19, 20; 2 Tim., iii, 16. 3. All verbal covenants, and the word written, is but a covenant of works, and taketh men off from Christ; and the whole letter of the Scripture holdeth forth a covenant of works. All doctrines, revelations, and spirits, are to be tried by Christ, rather than by the Word. Those that go from the sun, must at length walk in darkness. Anabaptists of old, said, the covenant of grace was written in the inward parts, and in the heart, and therefore, there was no need of word or ministry: but when Satan knocketh, his knock is dumb and speechless; he bringeth not the word, and speaketh not according to the law and testimony, because he is a dumb devil: Christ bringeth the word with him. To all these, we can say no other, than that they condemn the Scriptures and the preaching of the Word; because nothing can avail us to salvation without the Spirit. This is, 1. To condemn the wisdom of our Lord, who hath appointed, that faith should come by hearing, and that the things that are written, are written, "that we in believing might have eternal life," (John, xx, 31). 2. It is to fetter the free operation of the Spirit, whose wind bloweth when he listeth, to the preaching of the Word. 3. Yea, to make Christ's death, resurrection, ascension, and intercession at the right hand of God, which all must be the marrow of the evangel, things merely legal, and things belonging to the covenant of works; because all those, without the grace of the Spirit, are merely fruitless to many thousands.

Object. 6. But repentance in the New Testament, is nothing else but the change of the mind, and to be of another mind, than to seek righteousness by the works of the law; even to seek it in Christ alone: and mortification, is but the apprehension of sin slain by Christ, and so, repentance is a part of faith, though repentance in the Old Testament was to bewail sin, and forsake it.

Ans. But this is to dally with Christ. All mortification and dominion over our lusts, that fighteth against mercy and justice, and the duties of the second Table, must be, by this means, an act of faith, and the new light of Christ in the mind, believing our righteousness to be in Christ; and so, an act of internal worship belonging to the first Table. Then, as the Scripture saith, the sinner is justified by faith, apprehending Christ's righteousness; so might we well say, that we are justified by repentance and by mortification. 2. That repentance layeth hold on Christ's righteousness. 3. That as to believe only, without works, doth justify and save; so to repent only (that is, to change the mind, and apprehend righteousness, not in works, but in Christ) without all holiness and forsaking of sin, should save us. But this is, to acquit men from all duties of the second Table, yea, and of all the first Table; loving of God, praying, praising, hearing, etc., except only we are to believe: This is clearly the way of the old Gnostics, who placed all holiness in mere knowledge and apprehension of God's will, without love or obedience. Repentance is sorrow according to God, (1 Cor., vii, 9, 10; James, iv, 9,) and eschewing evil, and doing good, (1 Pet., iii, 11,) and the "crucifying of the old man, and the lusts thereof, as fornication, uncleanness, inordinate affection, evil concupiscence, covetousness," (Col., iii, 5). And these are commanded in the New Testament, as the very lesson of the grace of God, (Tit., ii, 11). It is true, in the Old Testament, the people were under tutors and bondage; but that was in regard of the carnal commandment of ceremonies, the cognisance of our bloody demerit held forth in bloody sacrifices. 2. In regard, less of Christ and the sweetness of the gospel was then known, and the law chased harder the guilty to Christ. But 1. Servile obedience, through apprehension of legal terrors, was never commanded in the spiritual law of God to the Jews, more than to us. 2. The Jews were not justified by the works of the law more than we; but by faith in Christ, as well as we, (Acts, xv, 11, Acts, x, 42, 43, Heb., xi, 1 Cor., x, 1–3). Yea, we are justified as David and Abraham were, (Rom. iv, 3–8). Yea, the Jews' seeking of righteousness by the works of the law, is a stumbling at the stone laid in Zion, (Rom., ix, 31–33). Yea, it is blasphemy to say, repentance in the Old Testament was a sorrow for sin, and a forsaking of it; as if under the New Testament, we were licensed to sin, and turn grace into wantonness.

SERMON XIV.

"LOST *sheep*." Lost, is either understood of the common condition of all men, and so, because all are the heirs of wrath, (Eph., ii). "All have sinned, and come short of the glory of God," (Rom., iii, 23,) and so are lost. But the Scripture entitleth men by that which they are in their own esteem; as "I am not come to call the righteous, but sinners to repentance," (Matt., ix, 13). This may seem to hold forth, that there be some sinners, and some not sinners, but righteous; whereas none are righteous that sinneth not, (Rom., iii, 10). But God giveth to men the title which they give themselves, and so, lost here, is such as are lost in their own esteem; for Christ's intention in coming in the flesh and dying, is to seek and to save the lost, (Luke, xix, 10). In this sense, (Matt., ix, 13, and 1 Tim., i, 15,) Christ came to save sinners, otherwise all the house of Israel are lost. "My people have been lost sheep," (Jer., l, 6). "Neither have ye sought that which was lost," (Ezek., iii, 4). Nor is this to be meant of the lost considered, as redemption is purchased, in this notion, Christ died for his enemies, (Rom., v, 10,) the just for the unjust, (1 Peter, iii, 18,) and so, for the lost: But we are here led to this, that those at whose salvation Christ hath a special aim, and whom he actually converteth, are first sinners, and lost in their own eyes; as is clear, Matt., ix, 13, 1 Tim., i, 15, Luke, xix, 10. It is one thing to be lost, and a sinner, and another thing to be self-lost; as many are loaded who are not weary, and yet none are weary, but they be loaded. 1. All that Christ converteth are self-sinners too, but Christ converteth not all sinners. Hence, Christ actually calleth and saveth but those who are such and so prepared; now there is a preparation of order, and a preparation of deserving. I cannot say, there are preparations in the converted, by way of deserving. Christ calleth not sinners because, or for, that they are sinners in their own sense, for he hath mercy on whom he will. 2. Nor are there preparations in the converted, to which conversion is promised as a free reward of grace, which may be called moral preparations—there is no such promise in the word as this: "Whosoever are wearied and lost in their own eyes, they shall be converted." Yea, 3. It is hard to affirm, that all who are prepared with these preparations of order, are infallibly converted: it is likely Judas and Cain reputed themselves sinners, and had some law-work in their heart, and yet were never converted. But God's ordinary way, is to bring men unto Christ, being first self-lost and self-condemned, and that, upon these grounds that proveth God's way of working to be successive. 1. Because conversion is a rational work, and the gospel is a moral instrument of conversion, therefore Christ here openeth a vein, ere he give physic; he first cutteth, and then cureth; for though in the moment of formal conversion, men be patients, and can neither prevent Christ, nor co-operate with Christ, yet the whole work about conversion is not done in a moment; for men are not converted as the lilies grow, which do not labour nor spin. There be some pangs in the new birth. Nor are men converted, as Simon carried Christ's cross, altogether against their will: they do hear and read the word freely. Nor are men converted beside their knowledge, as Caiaphas prophesied; nor are we to think with enthusiasts, that God doth all with one immediate rapt, as the sun in its rise enlighteneth the air. The gospel worketh morally, as doth the law. Reasons work not in a moment, as fire-flaughts in the air: Christ putteth souls to weigh the bargain, to consider the field and the pearl, and then buy it. 2. Christ's saving and calling the lost, is a new generation as well as a creation. A child is not born in one day; saving grace is not physic that worketh the cure, while the sick man is sleeping: Christ casteth the metal in the fire, ere he form the vessel of mercy; he must cast down the old work, ere he lay the new foundation. 3. Conversion is a gospel blessing, and so, must be wrought in a way suitable to the scope of the gospel. Now, the special intent of the gospel is to bring men to put a high and rich price upon Christ, and this is one gospel-offer: What thinkest thou of so excellent a one as Christ? What wouldst thou part with? What wouldst thou do or suffer for Christ? Now, men cannot prize Christ, who have not found the terrors of the law: so Paul, finding himself the chief of sinners, and in that case saved, (1 Tim., i, 15,) must hug and embrace Christ, and burst out in a Psalm (v, 17,) "Now, to the King eternal, immortal, invisible, the only wise God, be honour and glory for ever and ever, Amen." A sight of the gallows, of the axe, raiseth in the condemned man's heart, high thoughts of the grace of a pardoning prince: to be a tenant of free grace, is so sweet a free-holding, that it must put a high rate on free grace. 4. The clay organs, and faculties of the soul working by them, cannot bear the too great violence of legal terrors; for, in reviving the spirit, "If he should let out all his wrath, the souls should fail that he has made," (Isa., lvii, 16). Nor can they bear that God let out all his strength of love in one moment. Rough or violent dealing would break crystal glasses; Christ would break the needle when he seweth the heart to himself, if he should put forth all his strength; too swift motion of wheels may break the mill: Christ must drive softly, for a sight of the fourth part of the fire of hell, and a sight of one chamber or one window of heaven, is enough at once.

1. It is not enough to be fitted for the physic, and not for the physician. The weary and laden are fit to be eased; but not fitted for Christ the Physician, except they come to him and believe. Faith is a thing very suitable for Christ: "Ho, every one that thirsteth, come ye to the waters, and he that hath no money,

come, buy and eat," (Isaiah, lv, 1). It is true, in regard of all good deserving moving God to have mercy on one rather than another. Jerusalem and all converted are lying in their blood, and no eye pitying them, (Ezek., xvi, 6, 8); and therefore are none discouraged to come because of their wretched estate: that is to say, we cannot come, we have no money; but Christ invited those who have no money; and though Christ seem to exclude the woman from mercy, yet Christ, in wisdom, holdeth forth the promise here in that latitude of free grace—while as he saith, he came for the lost sheep; that there is room for the woman, and all believing Gentiles, to come in, and lay hold on the covenant. Sense of wretchedness and unbelief representeth Christ as too narrow, and contracteth and abridgeth the promises, as if there were no place for thee, because thou art thus and thus sinful.

Object. 1. The King putteth forth a general proclamation to all thieves: Oh! saith one, but he may mean others, but not me. Why, he means thieves in general; he excepteth none: why shouldst thou say, Not me? Christ belongeth to sinners as sinners; he receiveth sinners as sinners, yea, he ascended on high, to give gifts to the rebellious; therefore there is no qualification required in men that believe in Christ; no, nor doth unbelief debar a man from Christ; it only excludeth him from the experimental knowledge that Christ is his.

Ans. 1. It is true, the gospel excepteth no man from pardon, and all that hear the gospel are to be wearied and laden, and to receive Christ by faith, as if God intended to save them. But the promises of the gospel are not simply universal, as if God intended and purposed, that all and every one should be actually redeemed and saved in Christ, as Arminians teach; and so God excepteth in his own hidden decree, not a few: though he reveal not in the gospel who they are, yet he revealeth in the gospel the general, that "many are called, but few are chosen:" And I grant, there is no ground for any one man not to believe upon this ground, because some are reprobated from eternity, and it may be I am one of those, for the contrary is a sure logic; many are chosen to life eternal; and it may be that I am one of those. 2. It is most untrue, that Christ belongeth to sinners as sinners, for then, Christ should belong to all unbelievers, how obstinate soever, even to those that sin against the Holy Ghost. Nay, Christ belongeth only to sinners elected to glory, as elected to glory in regard of God's gracious purpose, and He belongeth only to believing sinners, as believing, in regard of actual union with Christ, (Eph., iii, 17, Gal., ii, 20). 3. It is false that sinners, as sinners, do receive Christ, for so, Judas and all sinners should receive Christ: now the Scripture showeth, that believers only receive him, (John, i, 12, Gal., ii, 20, Eph., iii, 17). 4. It is false, that sinners, as sinners, believe in Christ. This way of libertines is a broad way for sorcerers, thieves, murderers, parricides, idolaters, remaining in that damnable state, to believe; whereas sinners, as such, sinners thus and thus qualified, are to believe; that is, humbled, wearied, and self-condemned sinners only, are to believe, and come to Christ. It is true, all sinners are obliged to believe, but to believe after the order of free grace; that is, that they be first self-lost and sick, and then be saved by the physician.

I cannot but here mention some damnable errors of libertines, contrary to this truth of Christ; as this,

That the Spirit acts most in the saints when they endeavour least. 1. It may be by accident, and through our abuse, who confide in our endeavours and works, that grace and the Spirit will not flatter merits, which are too natural to us;—that God hinder a sweating wrestler who hath spent nights in prayer, and is careful in all means, and abundant in the work of the Lord. See and understand, that free-grace, not our endeavours, leadeth us on to heaven. Better it is I be conscious to myself that I am Christ's debtor, not debtor to myself. 2. That we see *self* to be wretched, and that *self* loveth to share and to divide the glory with free-grace. 3. That Christ reserveth the flowing of his tide, and the blowing of his wind, to his own free-grace, (John, iii, 8;) and that grace, in its filling the sails, is not in the seaman's power. But this error is the daughter of another more damnable; that is, That the activity and efficacy of Christ's death, is to kill all activity of graces in his members, that Christ may be all in all. This I take to be the marrow of fleshly libertinism, that not only the regenerate cannot sin, but they ought to sin, that grace may abound; and that Christ died for this end, that we should live in sin; the contrary of which is said, "That Christ died that he might destroy the works of the devil, that is, sin. (1 John, iii, 8.) Now, the not stirring up of the grace of Christ in us, is a grievous sin, (1 Tim., iv, 14; 1 Cor., xv, 10). "Yea, he bare our sins on the tree, that we, being dead to our sins, should live unto righteousness." (1 Peter, ii, 24.) "That we should walk in newness of life." (Rom., vi, 4.) And Gal., i, 4, "Christ gave himself for us, that he might deliver us from this present evil world, according to the will of God and our

Father." And 1 Pet., i, 18, "We are not redeemed from our vain conversation, received by tradition from our fathers, by any corruptible thing." This maketh good that which is the upshot of all the Antinomian doctrine, that Christ is so our sanctification, that there is neither law nor gospel which requireth of us that we be holy. Hence their fifth error,—"Here is a great stir about graces, and looking to hearts, but give me Christ; I seek not for graces, nor promises, nor sanctification; tell me not of meditation and duties, but tell me of Christ." So Christ hath not only suffered for us all that he should suffer, so as it is sacrilege to add to his sufferings our own; and the like sacrilege it is for us to be holy, and to add any of our active holiness to his active obedience. So Mr. Towne saith. "All our obedience, as it is the work of the Spirit, it is passive, and truly called the fruit of the Spirit, (Gal., v, 22;) and so, it is an entire work, and undefiled, every way corresponding to the mind of the efficient and Author, which is the law and rule he worketh by. But as it is actively our obedience, so it is very imperfect and polluted; yea, simply considered, it is a menstruous cloth and dung." And their 36th error is,—"All the activity of a believer is to act to sin; so we can do nothing but sin, and we are to do nothing, nay, not obliged to pray, but when the Spirit moveth us, and that is the work of the Spirit: we are in it mere patients. So in Error 4th, he saith,—'If Christ will let me sin, let him look to it; upon his honour be it.'" Indeed, it standeth upon the honour of him who hath promised to keep us spotless until the day of Christ, and Christ is so an engaged Advocate to intercede for the saints when they sin, that the redeemed of the Lord fall not away, but be presented spotless before the Lord, in the day of Christ. But what is all this to annul? 1. All action of grace, and to soothe men up in a lazy dead faith. 2. To take away all commandments of duties so frequent in the word of grace, which teacheth us to "deny all ungodliness, and to live soberly, righteously, and godly, in this present world." (Tit., ii, 12.) 3. To make an opposition between Christ and his grace, the fountain and the stream, (John, i, 16; Tit., i, 14; 1 John, iii, 8).

Object. If the actions of grace be all turned upon this axletree of God's gracious will, what can I do, when I am indisposed to do good? *Ans.* If this be a rational question, then is no man condemned, because he believeth not in the only-begotten Son of God, contrary to John, iii, 18, 36; for reprobates are finally indisposed to believe. 2. Indisposition is our sin that we should be humbled for; and ink-water cannot wash a black cloth, sin excuseth not sin.

SERMON XV.

"*Then came she and worshipped him, saying, Lord, help me.*"—
VERSE 25.

CHRIST had denied her to be his, but she will not deny but Christ is her's: see how a believer is to carry himself towards Christ deserting, frowning. Christ, 1. Answered her not one word. 2. He gave an answer—but to the disciples, not to the woman. Oh dreadful! Christ refuseth to give her one word that may go between her, and hell and despair. 3. The answer that he giveth is sadder and heavier than no answer; it is as much as, Woman, I have nothing to do with thee; I quit my part of thee. Yet, 1. She is patient. 2. She believeth. 3. She waiteth on a better answer. 4. She continueth in praying. 5. Her love is not abated; she cometh and adoreth. 6. Acknowledgeth her own misery; "Lord, help me," and putteth Christ as God in his own room to be adored. 7. She taketh Christ aright up, and seeth the temptation to be a temptation. 8. She runneth to Christ; she came nearer to him, and runneth not from him; she clingeth to Christ, though Christ had cast her off.

1. Patient submission to God under desertion, is sweet. What though I saw no reason why I cry and shout, and God answereth not? 1. His comforts and his answers are his own free graces; he may do with his own what he thinks good, and grace is no debt. "Hear, O Lord, for thy own sake." (Dan., ix, 19.) 2. Infinite sovereignty may lay silence upon all hearts: good Hezekiah, "What shall I say? He hath spoken unto me, and himself hath done it." (Isa., xxxviii, 15.) It is an act of Heaven; I bear it with silence.

2. She believeth. There is a high and noble commandment laid upon the sad spirit: "He that walketh in darkness, and seeth no light, let him trust in the name of the Lord, and stay upon his God." (Isa., l, 10.) 2. Fill the field with faith, double or frequent acts of faith: "My God, my God, why hast thou forsaken me?" (Psal. xxii, 1). Two faiths are a double breastwork against the forts of hell. (Eph., vi, 16, 1 Thes., v, 8.) 3. In the greatest extremity believe, even as David in the borders of hell: "Yea, though I walk through

the valley of the shadow of death, I will fear no evil." (Psal. xxiii, 4.) It is a *litote;* I will believe good. It is a cold and a dark shadow to walk at death's right side, "Though he slay me, yet will I trust in him." (Job, xiii, 15.) See Stephen dying and believing both at once: Christ's very dead corpse and his grave in a sort believing: "My flesh also shall rest in hope." (Psal. xvi, 9.) How sweet to take faith's back band, subscribed by God's own hand, into the cold grave with thee, as Christ did; "Thou wilt not leave my soul in the grave." (Ver. 10.) 4. Faith saith, sense is a liar: fancy, sense, the flesh will say, "His archers compassed me round about, he cleaveth my reins asunder, and doth not spare, and poureth out my gall on the ground:" (Job, xvi, 13:) but faith saith, "I have a friend in heaven; also, now, my witness is in heaven." (Ver. 19.) Sense maketh a lie of God; "He hath also kindled his wrath against me, and taketh me for his enemy." (Job, xix, 11.) No, Job, thou art the friend of God: see how his faith cometh above the water, "I know that my friend by blood, or my Redeemer liveth." (Ver. 25.)

3. She waits in hope, and took not the first nor second answer: hope is long breathed, and at midnight prophesieth good of God: "Though I fall, I shall rise again:" (Mic., vii, 9). "Then I said, I am cast out of thy sight, yet I will look toward thy holy temple." (Jonah, ii, 4.) There is a seed of heaven in hope. When God did hide his face from Job, (Job, xiii, 24;) yet, "He also shall be my salvation:" (Ver. 16). There is a negative, and over-clouded hope in the soul at the saddest time; the believer dares not say, Christ will never come again: if he say it, it is in hot blood, and in haste, and he will take his word again. (Isa., viii, 17.)

4. She continueth in praying: she cried, "Lord, Son of David, have mercy upon me;" she has no answer: she crieth again, till the disciples are troubled with her shouts: she getteth a worse answer than no answer, yet she cometh and prayeth. We know the holy wilfulness of Jacob, "I will not let thee go till thou bless me." (Gen., xxxii, 26.) Rain calmeth the stormy wind: to vent out words in a sad time, is the way of God's children: "Thy wrath lieth hard upon me: My eye mourneth by reason of mine affliction." (Psal. lxxxviii, 7, 9.) And what then? "Lord, I have called daily upon thee, I have stretched out my hands to thee." (Psal. xxii, 2.) Christ in the borders of hell, prayed, and prayed again, and died praying.

5. She hath still love to Christ, and is not put from the duty of adoring. "Whom having not seen yet ye love." (1 Pet., i, 8.) The deserted soul seeth little: there must be love to Christ, where there is, 1. Faith in the dark; faith is with child of love. 2. Where the believer is willing that his pain and his hell may be matter of praising God: "Who is so great a god as our God?" (Psal. lxxvii, 13). The church was then deserted, as the psalm cleareth.

6. She putteth Christ in his chair of state, and adoreth him: the deserted soul saith, Be I what I will, He is Jehovah the Lord. Confession is good in saddest desertion, "I have sinned; what shall I do to thee, O preserver of man?" (Job, vii, 20). The seed of Jacob is in a hard case before God, (Lam., i, 17,) and under wrath, (verses 12–14). Yet, "The Lord is righteous, for I have sinned:" (ver. 16:) this maketh the soul charitable of God, how sad soever the dispensation be.

7. She seeth it is a trial, as is clear by her instant pursuing after Christ, after many repulses. It is great mercy, that God cometh not behind backs, and striketh not in the dark. "And I said, this is my infirmity:" (Psal. lxxvii, 10:) he gathereth his scattered thoughts, and taketh himself in the temptation. It is mercy, 1. To see the temptation in the face. Some lie under a dumb and a deaf temptation that wanteth all the five senses; Cain is murdered in the dark at midnight, with the temptation, and he knoweth not what it meaneth. 2. God's immediate hand is more to be looked at, than any other temptation. 3. Hence the conscience is timorous, and traverseth its ways under the trial. When a night traveller dare not trust the ground he walketh on, he is in a sad condition; he is under two evils, and hath neither comfort nor confidence. "He that walketh in darkness, and hath no light," (but some glimmering of star-light, or half moon under the earth, and knoweth not the ground he walketh on,) "let him trust in the name of the Lord." (Isa., l, 10.)

8. She runneth not away from Christ under desertion; but 1. She cometh to him. It is a question what deserted souls shall do in that case. See, 2, that you run not from Christ. It was a desertion that Saul was under, and a sad one we read of; but he maketh confession of his condition to the devil; a sad word; "I am sore distressed:" (1 Sam., xxviii, 15,) there is a heavy and lamentable reason given why; "the Philistines make war against me:" Why, that is not much; they make war always against the people of God: Nay, but here is the marrow and the soul of all vengeance, "God is departed from me." Why, foolish man, what availeth it thee to tell the devil, God is departed from thee? Judas was under a total de-

sertion; he went not to Christ, but to the murderers of Christ, to open his wound. "I have sinned:" fool! say that to the Saviour of sinners. The Church deserted, betaketh herself to Christ, and searcheth him out: "Saw ye Him whom my soul loveth?" (Cant., i, 5). It is a bad token, when men, conceiving themselves to be in calamity, make lies and policy their refuge.

Object. But it is a greater sin to go to Christ, being in a state of sin: What have I to do, to go to him whom I have offended so highly? *Ans.* To run from Christ under desertion, is two deaths. 1. Desertion is one, and if real, the saddest hell out of hell. 2. To flee from Christ and life, is another death; now to come to him, though he should kill thee for thy presumption, is but one death, and a little one in comparison of the other; and one little death is rather to be chosen, than two great deaths. 2. Consider how living a death it is, to be killed doing a duty, and aiming to flee into Christ: better die by Christ's own hand (if so it must be) as by another; and better be buried and lie dead at his feet, as to run away from him in a heavy desertion: if the believer must die, it is better his grave to be made under the throne, and under the feet of Jesus Christ, as to die in a state of strangeness and alienation from Christ, not daring to come nigh him. All the deserted ones that we read of, did flee in to himself. (Psal. xxxiv, xxxix, lxxxviii; Job, xiii, 15; Isa., xxxviii.) It is good to claim him as thy God, though he should deny thee; and creep unto him though he should throw thee out of his sight: better kiss the sword that killeth thee, and be slain with his own hand, as cast away thy confidence.

"*But she came and worshipped.*" An heavier

temptation cannot befall a soul tender of Christ's love, than to cry to God and not be answered; and to cry, and receive a flat and downright renouncing of the poor supplicant. Yet this doth not thrust her from a duty; she cometh, and worshippeth, and prayeth. It is a blessed mark, when a temptation thrusteth not off a soul from a duty. And 1. When the danger and sad trial is seen, it is good to go on. Christ knew before, he should suffer; and when they would apprehend him, yet he went to the garden to spend a piece of the night in prayer. It was told Paul by Agabus, if he went to Jerusalem, the Jews should bind him, and deliver him to the Gentiles: it was his duty to go, thither he professeth he will go: "What, mean ye to weep, and break my heart? I am ready not only to be bound, but to die for the name of Jesus." (Acts, xxi, 13.) Dying could not thrust him from a duty. Esther ran the hazard of death to go in to the king: yet conscience of a duty calling, she goeth on in faith; "If I perish, I perish." 2. In the act of suffering. Christ on the cross prayeth and converteth the thief; Paul, with an iron chain upon his body, preacheth Christ before Agrippa and his enemies, and preaching Christ was the crime: Paul and Silas, with bloody shoulders, must sing psalms in the stocks. 3. Indefinitely. After the trial, and when the temptation is on, yet the saints go on: "All this is come on us," (Psalm xliv, 17,) there is the temptation: the duty, "Yet we have not forgotten thee, neither dealt falsely in thy covenant." "Princes did speak against me," there is a temptation: yet here is a duty: "But thy servant did meditate on thy statutes." (Psalm cxix, 23.) "My soul fainteth for thy salvation, but I hope in thy word." (Ver. 81.) "The wicked have laid a snare for me, yet I erred not from thy precepts." (Ver. 110.) "Many are my persecutors and mine enemies, yet do I not decline from thy testimonies." (Ver. 157.) "They fought against me without a cause:" (Psal. cix, 3.) "For my love they were my adversaries, but I gave myself to prayer." (Ver. 4.)

1. It is a sign of a sweet humbled servant, who can take a buffet, and yet go about his master's service; and when a soul can pass through fire and water to be at a duty; for then, the conscience of the duty hath more prevailing power to act obedience, than the salt and bitterness of the temptation hath force to subdue and vanquish the spirit: it is likely grace hath the day, and better of corruption. 2. It argueth a soul well watched, and kept from the incursion of a house-sin, and a home-bred corruption; for the temptation setteth on the nearest corruption, as fire kindleth the nearest powder and dry timber, and so goeth along. "They prevented me in the day of my calamity;" (Psal. xviii, 18). "I was upright before him, and I kept myself from mine iniquity." (Ver. 23.) The devil hath a friend within us: now there be degrees of friends, some nearer of blood than other some; the man's own predominant is the dearer friend to Satan, than any other sin; if pride be the predominant, it is so Satan's first-born, he agents his business by pride. 3. So it may argue that the soul steeled and fortified with grace, taketh occasion from the sinfulness of the temptation, and the edge of it, to be more zealous and active in duties. David scoffed at by Michal, said, "I will be more vile yet." So, "All that see me laugh me to scorn, they shoot out the lip, they shake the head," (Psal. xxii, 7). "He trusted in the Lord," (Ver. 8). See here a heavy temp-

tation; but his faith diggeth deeper, to the first experience of God's goodness; "But thou art he that took me out of the womb," (Ver. 9). As the church mocked with this, "Sing us one of the songs of Zion," (Psal. cxxxvii,) raiseth an higher esteem of Zion, because Zion's songs are scoffed at: Let them mock Zion as they list, "But if I forget Zion," (Ver. 5.) then I pray God, "my tongue may cleave to the roof of my mouth." (Ver. 6.) So the thief, hearing Christ blasphemed and railed on by his fellow, doth take more boldness to extol him as a king; "Lord, remember me when thou comest to thy kingdom:" Grace appeareth the more gracious and active, that it hath an adversary; contraries in nature, as fire and water, put forth their greatest strength when they actually conflict together.

USE 1. Antinomians turn grace into a temptation, and then cast off all duties; as, "Christ has pardoned all sin; his righteousness imputed, is mine: What do you speak to me of law-duties?" The way that crieth down duties and sanctification, is not the way of grace; grace is an innocent thing, and will not take men off from duties; grace destroyeth not obedience: Christ hath made faith a friend to the law; the death of Christ destroyeth not grace's activity in duties. It is true, grace trusted in, becomes ourself, not grace; and self cannot storm heaven, and take Christ by violence: grace, though near of kindred to Christ, as it is received in us, is but a creature, and so may be made an idol, when we trust in it, and seek not Christ first, and before created grace: But believing and doing are blood-friends. (John, xi, 26).

USE 2. This would be heeded, that in difficulties

and straits, we keep from wicked ways; and being tempted, that we strive to come near the fore-runner's way. It was peculiar to Christ, to be angry, and not to sin; to be like us, "in all points tempted like as we are, yet without sin," (Heb., iv, 15,) with this difference, Christ was tempted, but cannot sin; the saints are tempted, but dare not sin. The law of God, honeyed with the love of Christ, hath a majesty and power to keep from sin. So Christ, made under the law for us, (Isa., liii, 7,) "was oppressed, he was afflicted," (oppression will make a sinful man mad,) but it could not work upon Christ: "He was oppressed, yet he opened not his mouth: he is brought as a lamb to the slaughter." So all Christ's followers did: they are tempted, but grace putteth a power of tenderness on them. Joseph tempted, saith, "How can I do this great wickedness, and sin against God?" (Gen., xxxix, 9). David is reproached by Shimei, but he dares not avenge himself. Job, heavily as any man tempted, yet "In all this, Job sinned not, nor charged God foolishly?" (Job, i, 22). I deny not, but the temptation doth sometimes obtain half a consent: Nabal tempted David, so that he resolved to be avenged. 2. It will leave a black and a crook behind it in some, for their whole life. Peter shall be all his life known to be one that once forsware his Lord. But this is fearful, when men both create temptations, by defending a bad cause, (as holy men may have an unholy cause) and then, can find no way to carry it out, but by crooked policy and calumnies. We are now pursued by malignants with an unjust war. To embrace peace upon any dishonourable terms to Christ, is to desert a duty for fear of a temptation: on the other side, to refuse an offer of peace, because many innocent persons have been killed, is also a yielding to a temptation; for by war, we kill many more innocent ones, and it is against the Lord's counsel, "Seek peace," (Psalm xxxiv, 14), that is, as much as, we are not to be patients only, but agents, even when we are wronged, in seeking peace. But what if peace flee from me? I confess that this is a temptation; then saith the Lord 'follow after it;' (the word *Darash* is *diokein.* Heb., xii, 14); the Syro-Chaldee is, 'run after peace,' compel peace and force it, as men follow an enemy: 'Let us pursue after things of peace,' (Rom., xiv, 19, *diokomen*).

USE 3. See the sweet use of faith under a sad temptation; faith trafficketh with Christ and Heaven in the dark, upon plain trust and credit, without seeing any surety or pawn; "Blessed are they that have not seen, and yet have believed, (John, xx, 29). And the reason is, because faith is sinewed and boned with spiritual courage; so as to keep a barred city against hell, yea, and to stand under impossibilities; and here is a weak woman, though not as a woman, yet as a believer, standing out against him, who is "The mighty God, the Father of ages, the prince of peace," (Isa., ix, 6). Faith only standeth out, and overcometh the sword, the world, and all afflictions, (1 John, v, 4). This is our victory, whereby one man overcometh the great and vast world.

SERMON XVI.

"*But he answered, and said, It is not meet to take the children's bread, and to cast it to the dogs. And she said, Truth, Lord, yet the dogs eat of the crumbs that fall from the master's table. And Jesus answered, and said unto her, O woman, great is thy faith, be it unto thee even as thou wilt: and her daughter was made whole from that very hour.*"—MATTHEW, XV, 26–28.

"*And when she came to her house, she found the devil gone out, and her daughter laid upon the bed.*"—MARK, vii, 30.

THE dispute between Christ and the woman goeth on: Christ bringeth a strong reason, (ver. 26,) why he should not heal her daughter; because she, and all her nation, not being in covenant with God, as are the Jews, the church of God, are but dogs, and profane, and unworthy of Christ, which is the bread ordained for the children.

When Christ humbleth, he may put us in remembrance of our nation, and national sins: "Look to the rock whence ye were hewn, and to the hole of the pit whence ye were digged," (Isa., li, 1). "I alone called Abraham, he was an idolater," (Hos., ix, 10). I found Israel like grapes in the wilderness; they should have been wild grapes rotting in the wilderness, had I not put them in my basket. "Son of man, cause Jerusalem to know her abomination," (Ezek., xvi, 2). How? Make them know the stock they came of, 'And say, Thus saith the Lord unto Jerusalem, thy birth and thy nativity is of the land of Canaan; thy father was an Amorite, and thy mother an Hittite,' (verse 3). When the Jew was to offer the first fruits to the Lord; "And thou shalt speak and say before the Lord thy God, A Syrian ready to perish was my father, and went down to Egypt to sojourn there," (Deut., xxvi, 5). Thus, the forgetting what we are by nature, addeth to our guiltiness: "And in all thine abominations, and thy whoredoms, thou hast not remembered the days of thy youth, when thou wast naked and bare, and wast polluted in thy blood," (Ezek., xvi, 22). So the Ephesians must be told how unfit they were by nature for Christ, being the very workhouse and shop of the devil, in which he wrought, (Eph., ii, 1–3). National sins have influence in their guilt and contagion on believers: 1. When they mourn not for them: God's displeasure should be our sorrow. 2. When they stand not in the gap to turn away wrath, (Ezek., xxii, 30). There were godly men that departed from ill, (Isa., lix); but God's quarrel was, that there was no intercessor, (verse 15). In fasting, believers, though pardoned, may have on them a burden of the sins of three nations, and be involved in that same wrath with them. National repentance is required of every one, no less than personal repentance. Who sorrows for the blood of malignants and rebels?—for their oaths, mocking, scoffing, massing? The sins of the land, idolatry, superstitious days, vain ceremonies, etc., have influence on a believer's conscience in his approach to God. But we are here to consider, that Christ doth two great and contrary works at once: 1. He humbleth the believing woman, in reproaching her as a profane dog, unworthy of the children's bread, that the will may be more broken for believing; And 2. He trieth and tempteth her, to see if she can, by reproaches, be taken off from Christ. A broken will is a broken heart, for will is the iron sinew in the heart: account merit and conceit of any good in thyself, but the uncleanness of a dog; and break will, that that proud thing may fall in two pieces at Christ's feet: and 3, believe, stick by thy point, that though a dog, yet thou art one of Christ's dogs, and then all is well. The best way to break the will, is, 1. To offer hell, and the coals of everlasting burning to it; yea, and when the soul is humbled, to humble it more. Christ knew, that this woman was lying in the dust; but he will have her below the dust, when he trieth her with such a humbling temptation. Many think, the troubled conscience should not be further humbled. They say, 'There is nothing for such a soul, but the honey and sweetness of consolations in the gospel.' Nay, but often that which troubleth them, is subtle and invisible pride; he will not believe for want of self-worthiness:—Oh! I dare not rest on Christ, nor apply the promises, because of my sinful unworthiness.' Now, if this be humility, it is the proudest humility in the world; for the soul thus troubled, saith, 'I am not good enough, nor rich enough for Christ and his fine gold.' And the truth is, he is not a good enough Papist, to give a ransom of self-worth, for that great ransom of blood which cannot be bought. But though thou shouldst buy Christ, the Father will not sell him. Christ is disposed to a sinner as a free gift, not as a wage or a hire. There is a difference between down-casting and saving humiliation. Down-casting may exceed measure, in the too much apprehension of the law-curses, and may be conjoined with much pride and self-love: but right and saving humiliation conjoined with faith, cannot overpass bounds; it ariseth often from the sense of grace rather than from the law; God giveth grace to the humble, and he giveth humility to the gracious, under the sense of rich grace, (1 Tim., i, 15, Eph., iii, 8, Tit., iii, 3–5, 2 Tim., i, 9). Nothing humbleth us more than an opinion of the power and excellency of grace. Grace known and apprehended in its worth, layeth down proud nature on the earth. Christ's grace, was Christ's account book to Paul; "But by the grace of God I am that I am," (1 Cor., xv, 9, 10). A borrowed garment, though of silk, will make a wise man humble: many sins pardoned, made much love to Christ, and much humility in the woman, (Luke, vii, 44,) and made her lay head and hair, yea, and heart also, under the soles of Christ's feet. No doubt, she thought basely of herself and her hair, remembering that grace put these feet to a sad and tiresome journey, to come into the world to seek the lost, and to be pierced with nails for her. There is courtesy in free grace, being the marrow and flower of unhired love, to kill high thoughts of a self-destroying sinner.

Observe, also, that not to dare to come to Christ, and believe and pray, because of unworthiness, such as is in dogs that are without the new city, (Rev., xxii, 15,) is but a very temptation. And Christ, under the notion of tempting and trying, offereth that to the woman, that she was too daring and bold, being a dog, to presume to ask for the children's bread. Hence have we to consider, how far the conscience of sin ought to stand in our way toward Christ. Hence these considerations; 1. Conscience of sin is to humble any; that is, to make out for Christ. "Saul, Saul, why persecutest thou me?" spoken by Christ brought Paul down off his high horse, and laid his soul in the dust. "Now we know, that what things soever the law saith, it saith to them who are under the law, that every mouth may be stopped, and all the world may become guilty before God." (Rom., iii, 19.) It is a speech taken from a malefactor, arraigned and panelled upon his head. When the judge objecteth, 'What say you? This and this treason is witnessed against you.' Alas! the poor man standeth speechless and dumb; his mouth is stopped, "That thou mayest remember thy old shame, and be confounded, and never open thy mouth any more, because of thy shame." (Ezek., xvi, 63.) Christ, then, hath the sinner's neck under his axe. What justice and law may do, that Christ may do. The captive taken in war, may be killed by the laws of war, if he refuse to submit. 2. No sin is unpardonable treason, but the sin against the Holy Ghost, and final impenitence. The gospel is a treaty of peace between parties in war; none are excepted but these two. 3. But what then, if a soul come to this,—'I have either sinned against the Holy Ghost, or certainly am on the borders of it, because Christ knocked long: and a year ago, or a long time from this, I remember of his farewell rap, when Christ knocking, took his last good night, with this word, 'He that is filthy, let him be filthy still,' and said, he would never come again. I grant an ill conscience can speak prophecy; (Exod., x, 28, 29). So Pharaoh did prophesy, and Cain also, (Gen., iv, 13, 14). But 2. I can yield, that there be some farewell knockings of Christ, after which, Christ is never seen or heard at the door of some men's hearts. Paul speaketh so to the Jews, "But seeing you put the gospel from you, and judge yourselves unworthy of everlasting life, lo, we turn to the Gentiles." (Acts, xiii, 46.) The like is Christ's language to them: "Then said Jesus to them, I go my way, and ye shall seek me, and shall die in your sins; whither I go, ye cannot come." (John, viii, 21.) I doubt if any can sin the sin against the Holy Ghost, and the sinner only, and no other complain of it; that sin breaketh out in prodigious acts of wickedness, as blood and persecution. Though it were true, that you were upon the borders of hell, yet the gospel, though it except you from actual mercy, yet excepts you not from the duty of believing and coming to Christ; and though such think and imagine, that they believe Christ is able to save and redeem them, only they doubt of his will, yet the truth is, the doubt of unbelief is more of the power of mercy and infinite grace in Christ than of his will; and my reason is, "that whosoever believeth, hath set to his seal that God is true;" (John, iii, 33;) and "He that believeth not God, hath made him a liar, because he believeth not the record that God gave of his Son." (1 John, v, 10.) Now, it is not God's testimony, nor any gospel truth, that such as sin against the Holy Ghost shall be pardoned; yea, the contrary is said, (Matt., xii, 31, 32). Yet these that sin against the Holy Ghost are condemned for unbelief, as all other unbelievers are. (John, iii, 18, 36.) Then such as fall in this sin, though they say infinite mercy can pardon them (but infinite mercy will not pardon them), should not belie God, by unbelieving these truths, for they are gospel truths: then must the unbelief of those that sin against the Holy Ghost, put a lie upon some gospel truth, and this can be only on the power of infinite mercy; and so they must say, Christ cannot save, though he would, for there is a power of Christ in mercy, no less than a will. If Francis Spira[1] go for

[1] A distinguished Venetian lawyer of the 16th century, who embraced the Reformation but afterwards recanted, to save his life. A short time

a despairing reprobate (which I dare not aver), yet, when he said, he believed Christ was able to save him, but he doubted of his will, he must not be so understood, as if it were so indeed. Unbelievers know not all the mysterious turnings of lying and self-deceiving unbelief. Unbelief may lie to men of itself, when it dare not belie the worth of that soul-redeeming ransom of Christ's blood. If he that sinneth against the Holy Ghost, could believe the power of infinite mercy, he should also believe the will and inclination of infinite mercy, for the power of mercy is the very power of a merciful will. I shall not then be afraid that that soul is lost, which hath high and capacious apprehensions of the worth, value, dignity, and power of that dear ransom, and of infinite mercy. It is faith to believe this gospel truth, which is, "That Christ is able to save to the utmost all that come to him." (Heb., vii, 25.) If I believe soundly what free grace can do, I believe soundly what free grace will do. It is true, Christ can save many, whom he never will save; but the faith of the power of mercy, and of his will to save, is of a far other consideration. It must then be the prevailing of a temptation, not to dare to come to Christ, because I am a dog, and unworthy, 1. Because sin is no porter put to watch the door of Christ's house of free grace: mercy keepeth the keys. Sin may object my evil deserving, but it cannot object Christ's rich deserving. 2. That which maketh me unworthy, and graceless, and unfit to be saved, may make Christ worthy, and gracious to save; my sin may be Christ's rich grace. Though sin maketh me unworthy of

after this, he was seized with such anguish on account of his apostacy, that he sickened and died in despair, A. D. 1548. The narrative of his death, which produced a deep sensation in Protestant countries, was in common circulation in Scotland till within these few years.

Christ, yet it maketh me a fit passive object for the physician Christ to work on, and maketh not Christ unworthy to save. If I feel sin, it then saith, Thou art the very person by name that Christ seeketh. Therefore is the sense of sin required as a condition in all that come to Christ, whether it be before conversion, or after conversion, when acts of faith are renewed.

Object.—'But we find by experience, that true poverty of spirit, and sense of sinful wretchedness, doth kill and destroy any sight of guilt and wickedness in myself: if I rightly see Christ, I shall not also see any unworthiness in myself.'

Answ.—This experience is not warranted by the word of truth. These may well consist together. 1. That felt and apprehended wretchedness of a sinner, may stand with a sight of Christ's riches of grace, is as evident, as the felt pain of the sting of the fiery scorpion, may stand with looking up to the brasen serpent, and being saved; yea, when the poor man said, "Lord, I believe, help my unbelief," (Mark, ix, 24,) he both was sensible of faith and unbelief. 2. Yea, the converted may well see grace and holiness in himself, (else, how shall he be thankful to Christ the giver?) and also see Christ, and believe in his righteousness. For holy walking cometh under a threefold consideration: 1. As a duty. 2. As a mean ordained of God that we should walk in, (Eph., ii, 10). 3. As a promise, or a thing promised in the new covenant. And in this threefold consideration, we may know how far we may build our peace upon any duties, as upon evidences of our state of grace. 1. As holy walking as a duty coming from us, is no ground of true peace, believers often seek in themselves, what they should seek in Christ; this is natural merit.

Often we argue from the measure of obedience, to deny grace altogether; this is a false way, especially, it is a false way of logic, to argue negatively, from want of such and such a measure of obedience, to deny you are in Christ: how we may argue affirmatively, we shall hear hereafter. 2. The duty is Christ's mean, not enjoined in a strict law way, but in a gospel way, as the commandment is oiled with a gospel spirit of love. Law and love are not contrary, as Antinomians do imagine; Christ has united, not only persons, but also graces and virtues. This way, the duty is a mean, and a way, not to the right of salvation, but to the actual possession of it; and as it is, or standeth stated before us in the letter of the gospel, in a moral commanding, or a doctrinal, or directing way, without the efficacy of grace, it can be nothing but a doctrinal mean, no more than the law way is; for all gospel precepts without grace, are as little available to us as the law. But, in the third notion, holy walking, as performed by that efficacious grace promised in the covenant of grace, is an argument on which we may build our peace, not as a cause, or a merit deserving peace, but as a grace threaded upon the free promise of God. So the saints have builded upon their sincere walking, as on a fruit of the covenant of grace promised to us, (Jer., xxxi, 33; xxxii, 38); for so duties speak the mercies promised in the covenant, 'And I will give them one heart, and one way, that they may fear me for ever.' (Ver. 39.) See Ezek., xxxvi, 27; Isa., liv, 13. Upon this ground Hezekiah, pleadeth with God, when he heard the sentence of death: 'Remember now, O Lord, I beseech thee, how I have walked before thee in truth, and with a perfect heart, and have done that which is good in thy sight;' (Isa., xxxviii,

3;) and David putteth his faith upon this, as a gracious fruit of grace promised in the covenant of grace. So David pleadeth, and in faith, "Preserve my soul: (Ps. lxxxvi, 2:) here is a prayer in faith—and upon what ground? "for I am holy." Now, this would seem pharisaical, and merit-like, if holiness did not relate to the free promise of the covenant of grace, in which God hath promised, and tied himself by covenant, to make his own children holy; and also, is resolved upon a proposition of the covenant of grace. God hath both promised to cause his covenanted ones walk before him in truth, as did Hezekiah; as we have it in Ezek., xxxvi, 27, and he has promised to save and deliver the upright in heart, as is clear in Psalm l, 23; xxxiv, 15; 1 Pet., iii, 12; Psalm cxlv, 18, 19.

So all the peace we can collect for our comfort, from holy walking, is resolved on a promise of free grace; and the duty as performed by the grace of the covenant, may, and doth lead us to the promise, and so, no ways from Christ, but to Christ. Holy walking is a faithful witness, and a true witness may lead any accused man to law-right. Holiness may lead me to the promise, and that is good law-right. If we cannot gather any assurance of our spiritual estate, from holy duties in us, such as are universal obedience, sincerity in keeping close to Christ, and love to the saints, because they may deceive us, and may be in hypocrites, as Doctor Crispe saith, then may faith also deceive us; for there be as many kinds of false faiths, as there be of counterfeit loves to the saints; and there is somewhat of Christ peculiar to the regenerate in their love, obedience, and sincerity, which they may discern to be a saving character, and badge of Christ, no less than in faith. 2. But here is the mystery: neither faith, nor anything inherent in us, can yield us certainty that we are in Christ, or any peace with God, in regard that all grace, all evidences of our good estate are without us in Christ; inherent holiness and duties are but fancies. When we then refuse the comforts of God, and peace from holy walking, as it is threaded and linked to the promise, we refuse Christ; especially under desertion, we bid Christ look away from us; and there is a wilfulness of unbelieving sorrow, so that Rachel will not be comforted. But when we refuse Christ's comforts, we refuse himself. She who refuseth to accept of a bracelet, or a gold ring, from him who suiteth her in marriage, she refuseth both his love and himself, in that she refuseth his love token.

Observe also, that Christ bringeth himself in, as a great householder in the gospel. In his house there be divers children, servants, dogs, and the house is broad, and open to all that come: there is bread in our Father's house for all. What bread? A great marriage supper: Here is a king's son married, Matt., xxii, Luke, xiv,) and many excellent dainties, and all dainties is Christ, the marrow of the gospel, that bread of life; "I am that bread of life," (John, vi, 48). He was the wheat that dieth and rotteth in the earth, and then taketh life, and bringeth forth fruit, (John, xii, 24). He is the wheat that suffered the winter frosts and storms, rain and winds, and went through the millstones of God's wrath, and was "bruised for our iniquities," (Isa., liii, 5;) "For it pleased the Lord to bruise him," (verse 10): Dakeo, is *contundere*, to grind as in a mortar, or mill; and he went through the oven and fiery furnace of the anger of God, before he could be bread for the king's table, and the children. 2. Every bread, is not the bread of children: Christ is not a loaf, nor a feast for the man that wanteth his wedding-garment: such a friend was never invited to the banquet, (Matt., xxii, 11, 12): and of those that loath Christ, and love their lusts better than him, Christ saith, "None of these men that were bidden, shall taste of my supper," (Luke, xiv, 24).

1. The children are parts of the house, and are more than children, heirs, even joint heirs with the eldest heir, Christ, (Rom., viii, 17), because Christ and the younger heirs divide heaven (to speak so) between them. And 1. The Spirit that raised Christ from the dead, dwelleth in them, (Rom., viii, 11). 2. They have one God, and one Father; Christ and we are Father's children; "Go to my brethren, and say to them, I ascend unto my Father and your Father, and to my God and your God," (John, xx, 17). 3. We must be together in one place; all the children must be in one house together, (John, xvii, 24). "And if I go, (it is not an *if* of doubting,) and prepare a place for you, I will come again, and receive you unto myself, that where I am, there ye may be also," (John, xiv, 3). "And where I am, there shall also my servant be," (John, xii, 26). 4. One resurrection, "Because I live, ye shall live also," (John, xiv, 19). Every believer is raised in Christ, but in order; "Every man in his own order, Christ first, as the first fruits," (1 Cor., xv, 23). 5. One heaven, and one kingdom, and one throne, (Luke, xxii, 29, Rev., iii, 21).

2. There be great odds between the spirit or mind of an heir or a son, and a servant. The heir will do much for the birth-right; take his life from him, ere you take his heritage from him. Esau's face dried, he wept no more, when his father blessed

him with the dew of heaven, and the fatness of the earth. A servant will not contend to be an heir.

3. " The servant abideth not in the house for ever, but the son abideth ever." (John, viii, 35.) The son's reward is all hope, as some courtiers attend princes upon hopes; servants have hand-payment, and present wages. Let every professor try his spirit and nature: if the spirit bend toward the inheritance, and heavenward, it is right: see who looketh to the last year of nonage and minority, and hath not an eye and heart on time. There is a latent hope in all troubles, in sons, as in a king's heir in a far country where he is not known, not honoured as one of a prince's blood, but neglected, injured—yea, in want and necessity; yet when he casteth his eye upon his over-sea hope, it cometh home to his heart with ease, "One day I shall be a king, in honour and wealth." 2. Try the free and ingenuous spirit of a son toward the father: there is not a nature, or an instinct in the servant, nor such an inward principle toward the lord of the house, as in a son: blood and nature is strong and prevalent; blood-bonds, nature-relations are mighty.

" *But Jesus said unto her, Let the children first be filled,*" (Mark, vii, 27). Christ denied not, but the woman and the Gentiles have a right to the bread of Christ's house, only, grace must keep an order; let the Jews first have the loaf broken to them, and then, let the Gentiles have the by-board, or the second table of Christ. Hence, observe Christ's wise attemperating of the temptation in these particulars: 1. That temptations are measured by grains and scruples to the saints. There is a seed of comfort and hope in Christ's glooming and frownings: he would say, When the children are filled with bread first, then, you that are dogs, shall also have your portion of the children's bread. There is a kiss, and bowels of compassion, under the lap of that covering and cloak of wrath, with which he is covered; for "in wrath, he remembers mercy," and moderateth anger; "Fury is not in me," (Isa., xxvii, 4). 2. Gospel trials and temptations are for a merciful end, that Paul may not be puffed up, or as he saith, "Lest I should be like a meteor lifted up in the air above measure,"[1] (2 Cor., xii, 7). "But we had the sentence of death in ourselves, (as condemned malefactors,) that we should not trust in ourselves," (2 Cor., i, 9). 3. God will not have them above our strength, but the burden and the back are proportioned, (1 Cor., x, 13). It is good that we know Christ breweth or mixeth our cup; he can sugar the salt and bitter wine with mercy. There is no desertion of the saints that we read of, but there is as much of Christ in it, as giveth it some taste and smell of heaven. Heaven is stamped upon the hell of the saints, life is written on their death: their grave and dead corpse are hot, and do breathe out life and glory; their ashes and dust smell of immortality and resurrection to life. Even when Christ is gone from the church, he leaveth a pawn or a pledge behind him, as love-sickness for the want of him, (Cant., iii, v). When Christ is nothing but an empty grave, and he himself is away, yet weeping for the want of him, without care of angels or apostles, when the beloved himself is gone, is somewhat of Christ; yea, he sendeth before him a messenger, to tell that the King himself is coming, as in a great summer drought, little drops go before the great shower, to make good report that the earth shall be refreshed.

[1] Ina me hyperairomai.—*Rutherf.*

1. Longings for him, 2. Waiting after him, 3. Christ in you seeking after Christ, are messengers of heaven sent before, to dress and adorn the lodging for the prince, who is on his journey coming to thee.

SERMON XVII.

"*And she said Truth, Lord, yet the dogs eat of the crumbs that fall from the master's table.*"—VERSE 27.

OBSERVE, 1. The woman's witty answer. By retortion in great quickness, by concession of the conclusion, and granting she was a dog, she borroweth the argument, and taketh it from Christ's mouth to prove her question. She argueth from the temptation: Let me be a dog, so I be a dog under Christ's feet at his table. Wisdom's scholars are not fools: Grace is a witty and understanding spirit, ripe and sharp; so it is said of Christ, (Isa., xi, 3). Grace has a sagacity to smell things excellently; so Prov., i, 4; the wisdom of God in the Proverbs, giveth subtlety to the simple; to such as may easily be milked, and flattered, and persuaded. In young ones, reason sleepeth, affection ruleth all: and grace furnisheth the soul with quick, sharp, deep thoughts, to know a devil and an angel, heaven and hell, and that "stolen waters are not sweet," (Heb., v, 14). Their spiritual senses are as wrestlers experienced, or as learned scholars in universities, acquainted with the knowledge of good and ill. 2. Faith is thus pregnant, as to draw saving conclusions from hard principles, and to extract the spirit of the promises. Christ came to save sinners; then, saith Paul, to save me, for "I am the chief of these sinners." (1 Tim., i, 15.) And though a temptation's language be the language of hell and unbelief, as thus, "Thou art a sinner, a lost and condemned one, and therefore hast nothing to do with Christ:" Faith argueth the language of heaven and the gospel from this, "I am a sinner, and a lost one; but one of Christ's sinners, and one of Christ's lost ones, and for that very same cause I belong to Christ."

3. Faith doth here contradict the temptation, and modestly refute Christ. If Christ say, 'Thou art a transgressor, from the womb;' *Answ.* 'I confess, Lord, but Christ died for transgressors.' 2. If he say, 'Thou art under a curse;' *Answ.* 'With a distinction; it is too true, Lord: so I am by nature, but Christ was made a curse for me.' 3. If he say, 'Thou hast holden me at the door;' 'I confess, Lord, it is so.' But if Christ say, 'I came not for thee, thou art a dog; to such belongeth not Christ, the bread of children:' You may then answer, 'O Lord, with all reverence to thy holy Majesty, it is not so; I am thine, thou didst come for me, the bread belongeth to me.' When a sinner dare not dispute his actions with Christ, yet he may dispute his estate: the state of sonship is not sin; and therefore, we must adhere to this, as Christ did when he was tempted; 'If thou be the Son of God.' He refused to yield that. If then Christ himself should say, 'Thou art a reprobate,' expound it as a temptation; far more, if Satan, if conscience, if the world say it, you are not to acknowledge these to be heralds sent to proclaim God's secrets. Job would not believe his friends in this. Then to be tempted

to deny your sonship and claim in Christ, may be your temptation, not your sin; injections of coals to try, may come immediately from God, as well as from Satan. It is good (say Antinomians) to lay the saints under a covenant of works, because it doth this good, to make us make sure our evidences, that Christ is ours. Yea, some desire a wakened conscience, that the terrors of God may chase them to Christ. But, 1. That is a murmuring against God's dispensation: let Christ tutor me as he thinketh good, he hath seven eyes, I have but one, and that too, dim. 2. We are not to make sad whom God hath not made sad, (Ezek., xiii, 22,) nor to make a lie of grace; Nor, 3. To usurp the devil's office, to accuse a brother, far less yourself.

"*Truth, Lord, the dogs.*"—Behold where humility sitteth. 1. Christ cannot put humility lower, it sitteth in the dust: "I am not worthy to be called thy son." (Luke, xv, 19.) O great Paul! What is less than nothing, and less than the least of all? "Unto me who am less than the least of all saints is this grace given." (Eph., iii, 8.) "I was a persecutor, a blasphemer, (1 Tim., i, 13). "I am the least of the Apostles." (1 Cor., xv, 9.) Humility is no daring grace; it dare scarce seek to be a door-keeper in heaven; it setteth itself in hell. 2. Though humility be well born, and of kin to sweet Jesus, who is lowly and meek, yet Christ, and Christ only, is humility's freehold. The humble soul knoweth no landlord but Christ, and is only grace's humble tenant: there is none to him but the Lord Jesus, with his rich ransom of blood, (1 Tim., i, 16, 17). So there is much humility in heaven. If it were possible that tears could be in heaven, the humble saints that are there, should not see Christ reach out a crown to set on their head, but they should weep, and hold away their head; yea, the glorified are ashamed to bear a crown of glory on their head, when they look Christ in the face, and so, cannot but cast down their crowns before the throne. (Rev., iv, 10.) 3. All the saints truly humbled cry up Christ, and down themselves; and in their own books are as far from Christ as any: "I am not worthy that thou shouldst come under my roof; but speak the word only, and my servant shall be healed." (Matt., viii, 8, 9.) We may gather from Job's pleading, (chap. xiv,) that humble saints think not themselves only below grace and mercy, but also below the glory of justice and wrath. "Man fleeth as a shadow, and continueth not. And dost thou open thine eyes upon such a one, and bring me into judgment with thee? Who can bring a clean thing out of an unclean? Not one." He would say, I am not only frail by condition of nature, being a shadow of clay (verses 1, 2,) but also by birth, sinful and unclean, by reason of sin original: I am therefore a party unworthy of the anger of God, as a beggar is not worthy of the wrath of the emperor, or a worm of the indignation of an angel. 4. Any man is nearer God, than the humble soul in his own eyes. "Our fathers trusted in thee," (Psalm xxii, 4). "I am a worm and no man," (ver. 6). Because humility is a soul smoothed, and lying level with itself, no higher than God hath set it, "I do not exercise myself in great matters, or in things too high for me." (Psalm cxxxi, 1.) The proud soul hath feathers broader than his nest. 5. The humble soul is a door-neighbour to grace. Christ is near a cast-down mourner in Sion, "to give him beauty for ashes, the garment of praise for the spirit of heaviness," (Isa., lxi, 3). Christ hath a napkin for the wet face of a humbled sinner. Christ, the chirurgeon of souls, hath a wheel to set in joint the broken heart, (Isa., lxi, 1). There is a Saviour's hand in heaven, to wheel in an ill-boned soul on earth, (Psalm li, 8). Oh, what consolation! Christ doth both seek and save the self-lost soul, (Luke, xix, 10). The lamb, one of the lowliest and meekest creatures, hath a bed beside the heart, and in the bosom of Christ: "He shall carry the lambs in his bosom," (Isa., xl, 11); yea, "He shall deliver the needy when he crieth; the poor also, and him that hath no helper," (Psalm lxxii, 12). The Lord giveth more grace, he resisteth the proud and giveth grace to the humble. Grace upon grace is for the humble, (James, iv, 6). 6. The humble cannot complain of God's dispensation. Humble David,—"But if the Lord say, I have no delight in thee, behold, here am I, let him do to me as seemeth good to him." (1 Sam., xv, 26.) That I am not fettered with the Prince of Darkness, is the debt of grace on me: then, that you are any thing less than timber and firewood for Tophet, put it up in Christ's account, and strike sail to Christ, and stoop to him. 7. Yet is the hope of the humble, green at the root; it shall not be as a broken tree, (Psalm ix, 18), 1. Because "God shall save the humble," (Job, xxii, 29); 2. "And hear his desire," (Psalm x, 17); 3. "Revive his spirit," (Isa., lvii, 15); 4. "Beautify him with salvation," (Psalm cxlix, 4); 5. "Honour him," (Prov., xv, 33); 6. "Satisfy him," (Psalm xxii, 26); 7. "Guide him in judgment," (Psalm xxv, 9); 8. "Increase his joy," (Isa., xxix, 19); 9. "Bless him," (Matt., v, 5,) and give him a sure inheritance. None can extol grace as the humble soul, "Not I, but the grace of God in me," (1 Cor., xv, 10). "I have written that ye be not puffed up for one against another; for who maketh thee to differ from another? and what hast thou that thou didst not receive?" (1 Cor.. iv, 6, 7.) Then, because thou art little in thine own eyes, put not thyself out of grace's writing, for God putteth thee in. (1 Cor., i, 27–29.) Grace is mercy given for nothing, and the promise is made to the humble. In the judgment of sense, every one is to esteem another better than himself, (Phil., ii, 3). Peter is to have a deeper sense of his own sinful condition, than of the sinful condition of Judas the traitor. Though Peter, being graced of God, owes more charity to himself than to Judas, when Judas is a known traitor, yet should not humility decline to that extreme, as to weaken faith, and to say, Because I am unworthy of pardon, therefore it is presumption to believe pardon of sins.

Use 1.—Beware of pride; the elephant's neck and knees, that cannot bow, God must break. "God knoweth the proud afar off," (Psalm cxxxviii, 6). The word (Gavoah) is the high man, the Scripture word, (James, iv, 6,) is *hyperephanos;* the proud man is an appearance, not a real thing, and an appearance more than enough. The phrase importeth two: 1. It is borrowed from men, who see things near hand, before they see things afar off; and so, more of their eyes is fixed on that which is near hand, and so, it is more delighted in. We see things afar off with less delight to the sense,[1] and with contempt. The humble man lieth near God's eye; the proud man is farther from his eye, and seen in the by, and with contempt by God. 2. A man seeth his enemy afar off, and loveth not to

[1] Lorinus, Quasi in transitu videre.

come near to him. God hath an old quarrel against pride, as one of the oldest enemies born in heaven, in the breast of the fallen angels, and thrown out of heaven, and it seeketh to be up at its own element, and country where it was born, as proud men are climbing and aspiring creatures; but God, afar off, resisteth the proud, and denieth grace, or any thing of heaven, to the proud Pharisee. When God first seeth a proud man, he saith, "Behold my enemy." The lowly man is Christ's friend.

USE 2.—Though the woman be a dog in her own eyes, and so a sinner, see, O sinner, rich mercy, that Christ should admit of dogs to his kingdom. Oh, grace! that Christ should black his fair hands (to speak so) in washing foul and defiled dogs. How unworthy sinners, and so foul sinners, that they should be under Christ's table, and eat his bread within the King's house! What a motion of free mercy, that Christ should lay his fair, spotless, and chaste love, upon so black, defiled, and whorish souls! Oh, what a favour, that Christ maketh the leopard and Ethiopian white for heaven! These two go together, "Who has loved us, and washed us." (Rev., i, 5.) Humble sinners have high thoughts of free grace: stand not afar off, come near, be washed, for free grace is not proud, when grace refuseth not dogs. Salvation must be a flower planted without hands, that groweth only out of the heart of Christ. Take humble thoughts of yourselves, and noble and high thoughts of excellent Jesus to heaven with you. A curse upon the creature's proud merits! If you make price with Christ, and compound with everlasting grace, you shame the glory of the ransom-payer. It is no shame to die in Christ's debt; all the angels, the cedars of heaven, are below

Christ; angels and saints shall be Christ's debtors, for eternity of ages; and, so long as God is God, sinners shall be in grace's account-book.

The truly humble, is the most thankful soul that is; unthankfulness is one of the sins of the age we live in. It floweth from, 1. Contemning and despising God's instruments: The valour of Jephthah is no mercy to Israel, because the elders hate and despise a bastard, (Judges, xi, 1, 2, 6). The curing of Naaman's leprosy is not looked on as a mercy: why? washing in Jordan must do it, and there be better rivers in his own land, in Damascus. Not only God, but all his instruments that he worketh by, must be eye-sweet to us, and carry God and omnipotency on their foreheads, else the mercy is no mercy to us. 2. Mercies cease to be mercies, when they are smoked and blackened with our apprehensions. David, (2 Sam., xviii, xix,) receiveth a great victory, and is established on his throne, which had been reeling and staggering of late; but there is one sad circumstance in that victory; his dear son Absalom was killed, and the mercy no mercy in David's apprehension: "Would God I had died for Absalom!" So a little cross can wash away the sense of a great mercy: the want of a draught of cold water, strangles the thankful memory of God's wonders done for his people's deliverance out of Egypt, and his dividing the Red sea. What a price would the godly in England have put on the removal of that which indeed was but a mass book, and the burdensome ceremonies, within these few years? But because this mercy is not moulded and shapen, according to the opinion of many, with such and such reformation and church-government, I am afraid there is fretting in too many, instead of the return of praise;

and hating of these, for whom they did sometimes pray. God grant, that the sufferings of the land, and this unnatural bloodshed, may be near an end! Except the land be further humbled, I fear the end of evils is not yet come. This is a directing of the Spirit of the Lord, to teach God how to shape and flower his mercies toward us. Is it not fitting there be water in our wine, and a thorn in our rose? Shall God draw the lineaments and proportion of his favours after the measure of my foot? Shall the Almighty be instructed to regulate his ways of supernatural providence according to the frame of our apprehensions? Oh, he is a wise Lord, and wonderful in counsel! Every mercy cannot be overlaid with sapphires and precious stones, nor must all our deliverances drop sweet smelling myrrh. God knoweth when and how to level and smooth all his favours, and remove all their knots, in a sweet proportion, to the main and principal end, the salvation of his own. There is a crook in our best desires, and a rule cannot admit of a crook, even in relation to the creature, far less, to him who doth all things after the counsel of his own will.

"*Truly, Lord, the dogs.*" See and consider this woman whose faith was great, as Christ saith, and so she was justified. She confesseth and esteemeth herself a dog, and so, an unworthy and profane person.

Doct. A justified believer is to confess his sins, and to have a sense and sorrow for them, though they be pardoned. The word is clear for both confession and sorrow for sin; though Antinomians make it a work of the flesh in the justified person, either to confess sin, or to sorrow for it, or to crave pardon for it. For confession, there is commandment, practice, promise. "Speak unto the children of Israel, when a man or a woman shall commit any sin that men commit to do a trespass against the Lord, and that person be guilty, then they shall confess their sin that they have done," (Numbers, v, 6). This is not a duty of the unconverted only, but tying all the children of Israel, men and women: "Confess your faults one to another," (James, v, 16). Now, it is not confession to men only, as if they were sins only before men, which the justified person committeth, and not sins in the court of heaven before God, as libertines teach; therefore it is added, "Confess—and pray one for another, that ye may be healed, for the effectual fervent prayer of a righteous man availeth much." Then, justified persons are to pray for pardon of sins confessed. I take it to be a precept, that as many as say, 'Our Father,' to God in prayer, should also say, 'Forgive us our sins, as we forgive them that sin against us.' And so, pardon of sins, by a justified person, and a son of God, is to be asked when we pray for daily bread, and the coming of Christ's kingdom: "Take with you words, and turn to the Lord; say unto him, Take away all iniquity," (Hos., xiv, 2). This must be a confession, that a people turned to the Lord are in their iniquities.

This is set down as a commendable practice: "Ezra confessed and weeped," (Ezra, x, 1). "And the seed of Israel separated themselves from all strangers, and stood and confessed their sins, and the iniquity of their fathers," (Neh., ix, 1, 2). "I prayed unto the Lord and made my confession," (Dan., ix, 4). So David: "I have sinned against the Lord," (2 Sam., xii, 13). "The church confesseth, "Thou art wroth, for we have sinned: But we are all as an unclean thing," (Isa., lxiv, 5, 6). "For our transgressions are multiplied before thee, and our sins testify against us," (Isa., lix, 12). "I have sinned against thee, O preserver of man," (Job, vii, 20). "My sins are more in number than the hairs of my head," (Psalm xl, 12). "Our iniquities testify against us,—our backslidings are many," (Jer., xiv, 7). It is a vain shift to say, The church prayeth and confesseth in name of the wicked party, not in name of the justified ones; for as many as were afflicted confessed their sins for the which the hand of God was upon them. Now God's hand was upon all: Daniel and Jeremiah were carried away captive; yea the whole seed of Jacob, (Isa., xlii, 24, 25, Isa., lxiv, 5–7). And Jeremiah, in name of the whole captive church, saith, "The Lord is righteous, for I have sinned," (Lament., i, 16). There is a promise made to these that confess: "Whoso confesseth and forsaketh their sins, shall have mercy," (Prov., xxviii, 13). "When I kept silence," (and confessed not) "my bones waxed old," "I said, I will confess my transgression unto the Lord, and thou forgavest the iniquity of my sin." (Psalm xxxii, 3, 5). And this is not an Old Testament spirit only; for the same promise is, "If we confess our sins, he is faithful and just to forgive," (1 John, i, 8, 9). "If they shall confess their iniquity, then will I remember my covenant with Jacob," (Lev., xxvi, 40, 42). Not to confess, is holden forth as a guiltiness: "Yet thou saidst, Because I am innocent, surely his anger shall turn from me; behold I will plead with thee, because thou sayest I have not sinned," (Jer., ii, 35). It is a token of impenitency: "No man repented him of his wickedness, saying, what have I done?" (Jerem., viii, 6).

Ephraim, God's dear child, is brought in, as

commended of God, and the Lord telleth over again Ephraim's prayers and sorrowing for sin: "I have surely heard Ephraim bemoaning himself," (Jerem., xxxi, 18). We have a precept for it in the New Testament; "Be afflicted, and mourn, and weep; let your laughter be turned to mourning, and your joy to heaviness. Humble yourselves in the sight of the Lord and he shall lift you up." (James, iv, 9, 10). Now, there is better reason to mourn for sin, because they did lust, war, and were contentious, than because there were afflictions on them. Nature will cause any to cry when punishment is on them; but not nature but grace, not the flesh but the Spirit causeth men sorrow for sin as sin: "If then their uncircumcised hearts be humbled, and they then accept of the punishment of their iniquity, then I will remember my covenant with Jacob," (Lev., xxvi, 41, 42). 2. To mourn for sin, is a grace promised under the New Testament: "And I will pour upon the house of David, and upon the inhabitants of Jerusalem, the Spirit of grace and supplication, and they shall look upon me whom they have pierced, and they shall mourn, as one mourneth for his only-begotten son," (Zech., xii, 10). 3. Those for whom the consolations of Christ are ordained, are the mourners in Zion; but the consolations of Christ are not for legal mourners, and such as are weary and laden for sin, and yet never come to Christ nor believe: there is no promise made to such mourners as Cain and Judas were. Can we say, that God promiseth grace and mercy to any acts of the flesh, or of unbelief? 4. It is a mark of a conscience in a right frame, to be affected with a sense of the least sin, as David was one in whose conscience there remained the character of a stripe, when he but cut the lap of Saul's robe, (1 Sam., xxiv). 5. And when wicked men sin, their conscience is past feeling, (Ephes., iv, 19): and seared as with an hot iron, (1 Tim., iv, 2).

It is not an argument of faith, apprehending sin pardoned, not to mourn for sin, and confess it; for if this be a good argument, that if we, being justified, cannot, but out of unbelief, sorrow for a sin, that before God is no sin; as it is (Jerem., l, 20,) fully removed and taken away, (John, i, 29, Micah, vii, 19,) cast in the depths of the sea, (as libertines argue); for then (say they) we were both to believe that that sin remaineth, and maketh the justified person liable to eternal wrath, and so, to sorrow for it, as sin before God; and also to believe that it is taken away, and maketh the person not liable to eternal wrath; which are contradictory. If this, I say, were a good argument, then were we not to eschew evil, and to be averse to the acting of sin, before it be committed; for by the doctrine of Antinomians, all sins, even before they be committed, yea, from eternity, say some, are as fully taken away and pardoned, as after they be committed, and as when we do now believe and repent: For if we were to have a will averse to the acting of sin, before it be committed, it must be upon this ground, that it is sin before God, and not taken away by Christ's death, else we should not abstain from sin as sin. But this is a false ground to Antinomians, and inconsistent with the object of faith, which is, to believe this truth, that all sins, past, present, and to come, are equally removed, pardoned, yea, and in Christ taken away, as if they never had been. And so, sorrow for sin committed, being an act of the sanctified will displeased with sin, if it be unlawful, the will of the justified person is not to be displeased with it ere it be committed; but by the contrary, if he is not to be displeased with sin committed, but rather to will its commission; not to sorrow for it, because he believeth it is pardoned, and in God's court it is no sin to him, being in Christ. By the same ground, ere it be committed, in God's court it is no sin; and so, neither can he be displeased with it ere it be committed, but may also will it, and believe it is pardoned, and he ought to have no act of remorse, nor reluctance of conscience, which is God's solicitor, before the committing of it. For how is it not equally an act of the flesh and unbelief, to fear sin to be committed, as not pardoned in Christ, as to fear sin already committed, as not pardoned? If it be a lie, and an act of unbelief, for any justified person to say,—'Lord, I have sinned; O God, thou knowest my foolishness, and my sins are not hid from thee,' as justified David saith, (Psal. lxix, 5,) in regard all his sins are pardoned, and the man in faith, contrary to the sense of his weak flesh, is to believe that they are all taken away,—upon the same pretended ground of faith, he is to say, 'Lord, I shall never sin: though I am to commit adultery, and to murder innocent Uriah to-morrow, yet thou, O God, neither to-morrow, nor at any time, dost see my foolishness and sins,—because the sins to come are equally removed and taken away in the free justification of grace, as the sins already past. Mr. Eaton saith,—'To hold, that when God hath justified both us and our works, God yet seeth us in the imperfection of our sanctification, is another evident mark of an hypocrite, that was never yet truly humbled for the imperfection of his sanctification. But these imperfections of our sanctification are left in us to our sense and feeling, that they may be healed in our justification.' And he bringeth divers reasons to prove, 'That we are not both righteous in the sight of God, and yet sinners in ourselves.' Let me answer, that Antinomians in this, join hands with the Council of Trent, who curse us Protestants, because we say, 'The guilt of original sin is taken away in baptism, but that sin, and that which is essentially sin, dwelleth in us, while we are here, as the sad complaints of justified saints do testify,' as Chemnitius observeth. Yea, Andradius saith, as Antinomians do, that we put blasphemy upon Christ's merits and grace, as if he could not in a moment wash us perfectly from all sin. And what arguments Papists in this point use, the same doth Eaton and Antinomians use also. Yea, but justified Job saith, (chap. ix, 30, 31,) "If I wash myself with snow-water, and make my hands never so clean, yet shalt thou plunge me in the ditch, and mine own clothes shall abhor me." "Behold I am vile, what shall I answer thee? (chap. xl, 4). Thus Job, after he was by God's pen declared an upright man, saith of his own ways, in his sufferings. And David, a justified man, saith, "Enter not into judgment with thy servant, for in thy sight shall no flesh be justified," (Psalm cxliii, 2): yet Job and David were no hypocrites.

SERMON XVIII.

NAY, give me leave to say, that Antinomians make justification and free grace, their commonplace of divinity, as if they only had seen the visions of the Almighty, and no other. But they are utterly ignorant thereof; for they confound and mix what the Word distinguisheth, because justification is only a removal of sin by a law-way, so that in law it cannot actually condemn: There is no condemnation to them that are in Christ Jesus,[1] (Rom., viii, 1). So that in law, all obligation to external punishment, called *reatus personæ*, the guiltiness of the sinner, is removed, and he shall never be condemned for sin, because Christ did bear that guilt for him. Hence we say, in this regard it is blasphemy to say, that tears of sinners do wash away sin; that sorrow for sin and fasting pacifieth, or removeth God's wrath. For my part, I never used such popish and unsavoury speeches: Papists do, and we must distinguish between the lax rhetoric, and the strict divinity of Fathers. But 2. Justification is not an abolition of sin in its real essence and physical indwelling. Justified Paul sigheth and crieth, "I am carnal, sold under sin. I know that in me, that is, in my flesh, dwelleth no good. O wretched man that I am, who shall deliver me from the body of this death?" (Rom., vii, 14, 18, 24). Now, if the sense of the corrupt flesh make these complaints in Job, David, Paul, and if sinful flesh opposite to faith, apprehending the just contrary in Christ who justifieth the sinner, dwell not in us,—then 1. David, Job, and Paul, did lie in these confessions; for to speak contrary to the language of justifying faith, must be a lie. 2. They were not really carnal, and sold under sin, but only according to the sinful doubting and apprehension of the flesh. Paul's crying out of the body of sin, was an

[1] *Ouden katakrima;* he saith not *ouden katakriton,* nothing that deserveth condemnation, *nihil condemnabile.—Rutherford.*

irrational, fleshly, and hypocritical complaint. 3. We are not to grow in the grace of sanctification, and abstinence from yielding to the motions of the flesh, because, if there be no sinful imperfections in our sanctification, we are not to grow in grace really, but only in the false and hypocritical apprehension of the flesh. 4. If God see nothing of sin in the saints after their justification, then there can be no sin in them after justification; and so, the justified cannot sin, except they may sin, and yet God cannot see them sin, contrary to Psalms lxix, 5, cxxxix, 1–3. Yet John saith, even of himself, and of those who have an Advocate in heaven, (1 John, ii, 1,) "That if we say we have no sin, we deceive ourselves, and the truth is not in us," (1 John, i, 8). Now, he cannot speak of men as considered in the state of nature and unjustified: because, to answer a doubt of weak consciences, who said, 'Oh! if we have sin, then are we eternally lost and condemned,' he answereth, 1. The justified are to confess, (verse 9,) and God is faithful to forgive. 2. He answereth, "If we sin, we have an Advocate with the Father," (1 John, ii, 1). 5. It must inevitably follow, that Christ commanding these who have a Father in heaven, to pray, 'Forgive us our sins,' commandeth them daily to pray out of a fleshly doubting, not from the spirit of faith. I had rather say with Scripture, that all the justified saints must take down their top-sail, and go to heaven halting, and that they carry their bolts and fetters of indwelling sin through the field of free grace, even to the gates of glory, Christ daily washing, and renewing pardons, and we daily defiling, to the end that grace may be grace.

6 Yea, the Scripture is most clear, that the fairest

face that is now shining in glory, was once even in the kingdom of grace, and in the state of justification, blacked with sin, and sin-burnt, by reason of sin dwelling in them; "For there is no man that sinneth not." (1 Kings, viii, 46.) This is a black put on the faces of all men dwelling on the earth, amongst which you must reckon justified and pardoned souls, "For there is not a just man upon earth, that doeth good and sinneth not." (Eccl., vii, 20.) Then there is a thorn in our fairest rose; David's sun shines not so bright, but there is a cloud going over it; in every justified man's good he doth, in every sacrifice that he offereth, there is some dung. 'The sun hath looked on him.' Augustine had the same controversy, but on another ground, with Julian, who also of old, conceited that justified souls were free of inherent sin, as libertines now teach; but Augustine saith always, 'That sin dwelleth in the regenerate, but it is not imputed, and concupiscence after baptism is removed;[1] not that it is not, but that in the court of justice it is not reckoned on our score.' By which it is more than evident, that justification is not such an abolition of sin, in its root and essence, as shall be in the state of glory, when root and branch shall be abolished; and not only shall justification free us, as it doth in this life, from all law-guilt, and obligation to wrath, which is but the Second Act of sin, the effect, not the essence of sin, but also, sanctification being perfected, all indwelling of sin shall be removed. Sin in the justified hath but house-room, and stayeth within the walls as a captive, an underling, a servant,—it hath not the keys of the house to command all, nor the sceptre to rule: all the keys are upon Christ's shoulder:

[1] Non ut non sit, sed ut non imputetur.

far less, hath it a law power to condemn. Therefore saith Augustine excellently,[1] "*God healeth the sinner from his guiltiness* (it is a law-word, and a law-cure) *presently, but from his infirmity by degrees, by little and little.*"[2] The holiest in this life, is but the dawning of the morning; we are half-night half-day: "Who can say I have made my heart pure, I am clean from sin?" (Prov., xx, 9.) Who can say, I have a clean heart, and not lie? Libertines can say it in a higher manner than Papists, who acknowledge that venials, little sins, and motes, are in us always in this life.

But it may be, this is the Old Testament spirit that speaketh, as they say; but the apostle, (Rom., iii,) applieth the Psalm xiv, that stoppeth all mouths of the world, as so many guilty malefactors at the high bar of heaven: and he proveth, that no flesh, not David, nor the holiest on earth, can be justified by works, either done by the strength of nature, or by the help of grace.—Now, if there be no indwelling sin in the justified person, we answer not Papists and Pelagians, who say, 'That we are justified by works done by the help and aid of grace after regeneration, but not by the works that we perform by the strength of nature;' for if there be no indwelling sin in the regenerated, all their good works must be perfect and sinless, and can draw no contagion from an impure heart; because if there be no indwelling sin, and no imperfect sanctifi-

[1] Cont. Julian, Lib. 6, c. 5. "Sanat vitiatum a reatu statim, ab infirmitate paulatim."

[2] And Gregory, Moral, Lib. 29, c. 2. "Quid in hac vita omnes qui veritatem sequimur, nisi aurora sumus? Aurora enim noctem præteriisse nunciat, nec tamen diei claritatem illa satis ostendit; sed dum illam pellit, et hanc suscipit, lucem tenebris permixtam tenet, sic nos quædam jam quæ lucis sunt agimus, et tamen in quibusdam adhuc tenebrarum reliquiis non caremus."

cation in us (as Mr. Eaton saith it is hypocrisy so to think or say), how can an impure heart defile these works that are done by the aid of grace? For that which is not, hath no operations at all: if there be no contagious fountain, and no indwelling sin, but root and branch be removed in justification, then such a fountain cannot defile the actions; "In many things we offend all" (James, iii, 2); (ptaiomen apantes,) a metaphor from travellers walking on stony or slippery ground. "O wretched man that I am, who shall deliver me from the body of this death?" (Rom., vii, 24.) If this was but the flesh and unbelief that made this complaint, then the combat between the flesh and the spirit shall come from the flesh. Now the conflict of two contraries, such as are the flesh and the spirit, is not from the one more than the other, but equally from both: the conflict between fire and water, is neither from the fire only, nor from the water only, but from both yoking together. Yea, certain it is, that the flesh cannot, and doth not complain of its own motions against the spirit; sin cannot complain of sin; it is the renewed part that complaineth of the stirrings and motions of the unrenewed part: Satan is not divided against Satan, nor sin against sin. It is true, the sins of the justified are said to be sought and not found, (Jer., l, 20,) and our transgressions are said "to be blotted out, and blotted out as a thick cloud, and to be remembered no more," (Isa., xliii, 25; xliv, 22; Ps. li, 1,) "and to be subdued and cast into the depths of the sea," (Mic., vii, 19,) "and we washed," (Rev., i, 5;) "and made whiter than the snow." (Ps. li, 2.) And Christ's church is so "undefiled," so "fair as the moon, clear as the sun," (Cant., v, 2; vi, 10,) that Christ himself giveth a testimony of her,

"Thou art all fair, my love, there is no spot in thee;" (Cant., iv, 7;) all which are true in a law sense, and in legal and moral freedom from sin, in regard that the sins of the justified and washed in Christ's blood, shall no more be charged upon them to their condemnation, than if they had never committed any sins at all; and as if their sins, were no sins to witness against them in judgment, they being clothed with Christ's white and spotless righteousness; for they are, in their actual guilt, as touching the law-sting and power, as no sins, no debts, but obliterated in the book of God's account, and as a blotted out cloud, which is no cloud; in which regard they must be white and fair whom Christ washeth.

I profess, it is sweet to be dipped in the new "fountain opened to the house of David, and the inhabitants of Jerusalem for sin and for uncleanness," and under the sweet and fair hand of the Mediator, that he might wash us: I know he should not be ashamed of his labour, but should make fair and white work. But, in regard of the inherent root, essence, and formal being of sin, the saints are not freed and delivered from sin; but these same sins, though broken in their dominion to command as tyrants, and removed and taken away,[1] in their law-demerit and guilt; yet do remain and dwell in the saints while they are here in this life. And these two removals of sin differ much: the former is a law-removal of sin, not the removal of the essence and being of sin; the other removal, is a physical removal in root and branch, and therefore, done by degrees, according to the measure of begun sanctification, and shall never be perfect in this life, till that habit of sanctification, which is contrary to

[1] Quoad actualem reatum Æternæ mortis.—*Ruth.*

sin, physically considered, shall be introduced, and the person perfected in glory: Whereas the former removal is so perfect, as the person is made spotless, and whiter than snow; which two removals of sin may be thus illustrated: There is a man defiled with leprosy in his body,—this is a physical contagion; the same man is condemned to die for a high point of treason against the state and prince—this is a law-contagion. The physician cureth him of his leprosy by a physical expulsion of the disease, but by degrees, and by little and little, and maketh, at length, his skin, as the skin of a young child. The prince and state send to him a free pardon of his treason, and he is at once perfectly acquitted from his guilt; but the prince's pardon doth not physically and really expel out of his person the shame, the inherent blot and infamy of his foul and treacherous disloyalty that he committed against prince and state, so as this pardon should transubstantiate and change him by a physical transmutation, into a person as innocent and blameless, as any the most loyal subject of the kingdom: the pardon putteth only upon him a law-change, and a moral immunity and freedom from a shameful death. And Christ's pardon in like manner doth remove a law-obligation to eternal death, so as there is no condemnation to the man; but it removeth not the inherent and physical blot, nor the real obliquity between his foul sin, and the spiritual law of God; nor doth it make him perfectly sinless and holy, as if he had never sinned, as Antinomians dream. So, the justification of the saints, is like the free acquitting of a broken man that hath borrowed thousands, and is unable to pay: the cancelling of his bill freeth him in law, from paying the sums, but doth in no case make him a man that never borrowed money; nor doth it free him from that inherent blot of injustice, in regard of which he is a broken man, who hath wasted his neighbour's goods. But perfected sanctification expelleth sin in its essence, being root and branch in its dominion, lordly power indwelling, so that it is no more: and this is like the expelling of night-darkness out of the whole body of the air, by the presence of the sun diffusing its beams and light from east to west, and north and south. I grant, the habit of sanctification perfected in glory, doth not make it a false proposition, that such a pardoned and washed saint never sinned, for what is done, can never be undone; that were a speaking contradiction: but it putteth the man in that state, that he is as free of the indwelling of the body of sin, and perfectly holy, as the body of the air at noon-day is free of darkness, and qualified with inherent light. Now, Antinomians cannot endure (especially Mr. Eaton, their chief leader,) that we say, that sanctification is imperfect in this life, or that the indwelling of sin can consist with free justification, and remission of sins in Christ's blood. But let us turn our eyes a little toward the wisdom of God's free dispensation, to scan the reasons why our Lord will have justified saints to go halting to heaven.

1. He can, at our first conversion, make us glorified and perfected saints; but it is his wisdom to take a time and succession to perfect his saints: he took about thirty and three years on earth for the work of our redemption, and would for three days lodge in the grave, as it were a neighbour to "our father, corruption, and the worm, our brother and sister," (Job, xvii, 14,) "though he saw no corruption," (Psalm xvi, 10). He hath been dressing up the high palace of glory, his

Father's house, these sixteen hundred years. If he be pleased to take months and years to the work of the applying of the purchased redemption, whereas, he might and could have done it in one instant, as he created light out of darkness with one word, we are to be silent: his wisdom in so doing, is sufficient for us. The second heaven, and the new light in the redeemed soul, is done by continued acts of omnipotency; the first heaven was sooner made. Shall it seem hard to us, that our midnight, and our full noon day-light of grace, are not existent in one instant together? We are to wait on in patience; and not to fret, that we cannot at our first conversion, pray out of us the indwelling body of sin, and sigh out the weight and sin that doth so hardly beset us, (Heb., xii, 1). God is wise who will have our day to break and dawn by degrees, and our shadows to flee away, and our sun to rise to noon-day light through length of time. If a creature, yea, the most excellent of created angels, should but sit at the helm of this great world, to rule and govern all things but for forty-eight hours, the sun should not rise in due time, the walls and covering of the great building of the world should fall, the globe of the world, and of the whole earth "should reel to and fro, and stagger like a drunken man," all should go to confusion; and so, if we had a world of grace of our own carving, and had it in our wise choice to go, from the first moment of our new birth, to heaven, without sin, we should lose ourselves by the way, and take on new debt, that should require the new and fresh crucifying of the Lord of glory: we should be no better tutors, governors, and lords to ourselves, than Adam, and the angels that fell. The weight of a saint's heaven and hell upon his own clay-shoulders, is a heaven put to a great hazard, or rather to a remediless loss: I shall easily grant that it is sure that my heaven be upon Christ's shoulders.

2. Grace worketh suitably to the nature of the patients. The vessel would be prepared with the frequent sense of grace, before Christ pour in it the habit of glory. It is fit we see and feel the shaping and sewing of every piece of the wedding-garment, and the framing, moulding, and fitting of the crown of glory, for the head of the citizen of heaven; yea, the repeated sense and frequent experiences of grace in the ups and downs in the way, the falls and risings again of the traveller, the revolutions and changes of the spiritual condition, the new moon, the darkened moon, the full moon in the Spirit's ebbing and flowing, raiseth in the heart of saints, in their way to the country, a rank smell of that fairest rose and lily of Sharon, Jesus Christ, the delight of men and angels;—that as travellers at night talk of their foul way, and of the praises of their guide; and battle being ended, soldiers number their wounds, extol the valour, skill, and courage of their leader and captain;—so, the glorified soldiers may take loads of experiences of free-grace to heaven with them, and there speak of their way, and their country, and of the praises of Him who hath "redeemed them out of all nations, tongues, and languages." The half-drowned man shaketh his head, and drieth his garments before the sun on the shore, with joy and comfort. The impressions of the kisses of the face of Him that sitteth on the throne, are the deeper, that the frequent experiences of grace have been many. Much dirty and dangerous way, and the lively and hearty welcome of glory, suit well together.

3. As there is much, yea, an exceeding weight of

glory in heaven, so it is convenient, that the way to heaven be strewed and covered with roses of renewed acts of free grace, and Christ's repeated expressions of new pardon, one expression coming after another;—that, since the saints pray daily, 'forgive us our sins,' it is in the wisdom of God fitting, that as glory in heaven is one continued act of happiness for all eternity, so the grace that maketh the old and sinful man a new creature, should be one continued act of grace. And, as many streams and rivers are one water, and one spring in the fountain; and many lines, one in the centre; and thousands of generations of men, are but one man in the first father, Adam;—so, multiplied acts of grace in the saints, from the first moment of their conversion, to the period and first hour of their glorification, are but one fountain-grace in God, revealed in the mediator, Christ: and there can be no reason, why our first conversion should be free grace, and the perseverance of the saints in grace, and all their steps in the way should not also be grace. Grace is not only singly in the saints, but grace and peace must be multiplied on them.

4. The standing and prorogated intercession and advocation of Jesus Christ, every day upon occasion of new committed sins, (1 John, ii, 1, 2,) and the golden altar that hath been hot these 1600 years, (Rev., viii, 3, 4,) with the fresh prayers of the saints, must have a daily use, so long as Christ is in the office of the great, true, and exalted High Priest, now passed into the Holy of Holies; and better it is that Christ act grace again and again in heaven, as we sin again and again on earth, than that the act of our High Priest's intercession had been all but one act on the cross. And the way to heaven was made long, and

falls there must be in the way, to the end that I might lodge many nights and months by the way, with my guide Christ, and that my expences and charges in the way might be free grace.

5. Faith hath its work in our gradual mortification. We believe that Christ shall perfect what he hath begun; so it was needful, that winter, and months of spring and summer, go before our harvest, and reaping of the fruits of the tree of life.

6. Christ works in the lower kingdom, as making the higher kingdom the copy and sampler of his working. Now, it is most suitable for flowers and roses, that must be transplanted, to grow up in the high garden beside the tree of life, and to blossom out glory for all eternity, that they grow for a time in the land of grace, that they may take kindly with the soil. So, the lower and higher gardens of glory and grace differ not in nature; what groweth in the one, can well grow in the other: they cannot suit with the happiness of that land, except they have experienced the holiness of continued grace in this land. And Christ maketh storms of sin to blow upon his young heirs for their winter, God keeping life at the root, that they may be fitter for an eternally green flourishing summer of glory. And when Christ consecrated himself through many afflictions, that he might be an heir suitable for glory, he being brought through fire and water, hot and cold, and many changes, to heaven, and so came to eternal happiness through many years' continued holiness, it was not fit that Christ, who was to make heirs like his rule and sampler, should bring them to glory with a leap and a step, from a justified condition, to a glorified estate, without an intervening progress in sanctification and holiness. Christ un-

derstandeth well the fundamental laws of the higher city, the new Jerusalem. The frame of the government of that kingdom is, that none be received as free citizens of glory, but such as have served apprentices, minors, little children, under tutors to grace and the way of holiness. He is of too short standing, who cometh hot and smoking out from his lusts, a justified sinner, to step immediately into glory; and so, here is a stranger welcomed to heaven from hell,—a child of Satan, playing at the devil's fireside yesterday, or the last hour; now this day, this same very hour, he must be enrolled amongst those who walk with the Lamb, in white. Some soldiers, I grant, are advanced to be high commanders, *per saltum*, by a leap, but it is for some piece of rare service to the prince and state; and it is like the repenting thief, who, in few hours' space, had been in three several kingdoms; in the state of nature, the kingdom of darkness, and the kingdom of grace, and that day with Christ in paradise. But this is, I conceive, rare: and give me leave to say, princes at their coronation do some extraordinary acts of grace, by privilege of the new crown, that they may handsel the new throne with acts of mercy. Christ was now in an act of pure unmixed grace, actually and formally redeeming the lost world on the cross, and was now this day crowned by his mother the Church, and installed King-Redeemer of saints, and therefore would handsel paradise with a sinner, by a privilege of matchless grace: there is but one example of it in all the Scripture.

7. The way to heaven is sweeter, that it should be here *nulla dies sine linea*, that every day and hour that we sin (as every hour we contract new debt), Christ's free grace might have its daily flux, the "fountain

opened to the house of David," daily running, renewed forgiveness going along with "this day, our daily bread:" hence these noble acts of grace. 1. Every sin, the least omission by law, is hell, (Deut., xxvii, 26, Gal., iii, 10). Two sins must be two hells, seven sins, seven hells: then multiplied sins, to the number of the hairs of David's head, (Psalm xl, 12,) and not sins only, but innumerable iniquities, must cause the account of Christ's free grace to swell and arise to a deliverance from two, from seven, from innumerable hells. Oh, grace, every day! every hour! So then, the rebel brought nine times a-day, twenty times a-day, for the space of forty years, by his prince's grace, from under the axe, how fair and sweet are the multiplied pardons and reprivals of grace, to speak so! Here are multitudes of multiplied redemptions, here is plenteous redemption: I defile every hour, Christ washeth; I fall, grace raiseth me; I come this day, this morning, under the reverence of justice, grace pardoneth me; and so along, till grace puts me into heaven. "The Lamb's book of life" containeth not only the names of those who are ordained for that blessed end of eternal life, but also, the means leading to the end. Then here are written all the sins, all the pardons of free grace, since the first Adam sinned. Oh, but the book of life must be a huge volume! Oh, how large, and broad, and long, must the accounts of the grace of Christ be! 2. We are not saved completely, because justified; but we are expectants of the divinity of immediate vision, and "groan within ourselves, waiting for the adoption, the redemption of our body, and are saved by hope." (Rom., viii, 23, 24.) In regard of title, we are saved completely; but in another sense, we are but lords and kings in title only;

we are far from the lands, rents, crown, and our Father's house, and so, are not saved, till our feet stand within the streets of the New Jerusalem. 3. In this consideration, we sigh in our fetters and bolts, and sin remaineth in us, for our exercise and humiliation, that we may have an habitual engagement to Jesus Christ and his grace. That soul loveth much to whom much is forgiven; and, especially, when in sense and frequent experiences, much and multiplied backslidings are forgiven.

Object. 1.—'But justification is one indivisible act of grace, pardoning all sins, past, present, and to come; and is not a successive and continued act, in progress always, such as is sanctification; for we are but once justified.' I answer by these following assertions:

1.—There is a double notion of justification, as Dr. Abbot teacheth us. There is a universal, and properly so called justification; there is a partial, and improperly so called justification: or, give me leave to say, there is a justification of the person, of the state; or a justification repeated, or rather a reiterated remission; I doubt, if it be called a justification. The former justification doth include, 1. The act of atonement made by Christ on the cross, for all the sins of all the elect of God, past, present, and to come. This act is not tied to believing, nor are we properly justified, in regard of this act. But, 2. There is a justification formal, of which Paul speaketh, (Rom., iii, 4, Gal., iii, iv, and v,) which goeth along in order of cause, time, and a required condition of apprehending Christ's righteousness. And this justification of the person, while he believeth, is but once done, and that, when the believer doth first lay hold on Christ, and righteousness imputed in his blood. There is, 3. A remission, and taking away of sin. Now, according to these, we are to consider of doing away sin in a threefold notion; for, though justification essentially include remission and pardon of sin, yet every remission doth not include justification, properly so called.

Asser. 2.—This threefold taking away of sins, I clear from the Scripture. 1. Christ taketh away our sins on the cross, causatively, and by way of merit, while as he suffereth for our sins on the cross. So, "Behold the Lamb of God that taketh away the sins of the world," (John, i, 29). "He was made sin for us," (1 Cor., v, 21). "Christ blotted out the hand-writing of ordinances that was against us, which was contrary to us, and took it out of the way, nailing it to the cross," (Colos., ii, 14). "Who, his own self, bare our sins on the tree," (1 Pet., ii, 24). "He made his soul an offering for sin," (Isa., liii, 10). This atonement of blood was typified in Aaron, who was to lay both his hands on the head of the live goat, and to confess the sins of the people, and did translate them off from the people; "so as the goat was to bear upon him all their iniquities, into a land not inhabited," (Levit., xvi, 20–22). Now, this was the paying of a ransom for us, and a legal translation of the eternal punishment of our sins; but it is not justification, nor ever called justification. There is a sort of imputation of sin to Christ here, and a sum paid for me; but, with leave, no formal imputation, no forensical, and no personal law-reckoning to me, who am not yet born, far less, cited before a tribunal, and absolved from sin. When Christ had completely paid this sum, Christ was justified legally, as a public person, and all his seed fundamentally, meritoriously, causatively, but not in their persons.

There is a second removal of sin, and that is, when the believer is justified by faith. Paul, "Even as David," (saith he,) "also describeth the blessedness of the man, unto whom God imputeth righteousness without works," saying "Blessed are they whose iniquities are forgiven, and whose sins are covered. Blessed is the man to whom the Lord imputeth no sin," (Rom., iv, 6–8). This is the blessedness of a man born, living, believing. Now, we say improperly, the heirs of a king not born are blessed.[1] So, if Christ's removal of sins on the cross were justification, all Christ's seed, and we believers of the Gentiles, who were not then born when Christ died, should be blessed and justified before we be born. Now, in this, which is formally the justification of the believing sinner, the believer's person is accepted, reconciled, justified, and really translated by a law-change from one state to another. I mean not, that there is a physical infusion of a new habit of sanctification, and an expulsion of an old habit, as Papists teach, confounding regeneration, or sanctification, with justification. But there is a real change of the state of the person: "And such were some of you; but ye are washed, but ye are sanctified, but ye are justified," (1 Cor., vi, 11); then they were sometime not justified. 2. There is here a real removal of all sins, and a pardon and relaxation from the eternal punishment of all sins; as well of sins to come, and not yet committed, as of sins past, present, and already committed; so as sins not yet committed, shall no more involve the believer in the punishment of eternal wrath, than sins past or present. Yet, 3. The sins not committed, though virtually pardoned (with correction and submission) are not for-

[1] Non entis nulla sunt accidentia.—*Rutherf.*

mally pardoned. That which is not sin at all, but only in a naked potency, it must be pardoned only in that notion that it is a sin, and not first formally remitted, and then afterward committed: yet is it paid for, and the person freed from all actual condemnation for it—but withal, conditionally and virtually, so he believe in Christ, and renew his repentance; which graces God shall infallibly give him, because the calling and gifts of God are without repentance. And of this third removal of sin, is that petition which Christ hath taught justified persons to ask of God, "Forgive us our sins, as we forgive them that sin against us." And Nathan saith to David, "The Lord also hath put away thy sin, thou shalt not die," (2 Sam., xii, 13). David, before he contracted this horrible guilt of murder and adultery, was "a man according to God's own heart," and so his person was justified: this way, God daily taketh away sin: "For therein is the righteousness of God revealed from faith to faith, as it is written, The just shall live by faith," (Rom., i, 17). Now, the life of faith justifying, is not one single act of faith, such as is at our first personal, relative, and universal absolution; but the believer liveth by renewed and often repeated acts of faith, such as is, "To walk from faith to faith." The least faith[1] doth justify; but the gospel requireth a growth in faith. In this sense, remission is a continued, and one prorogated act of free grace, from our first moment of believing, to the day of putting the crown on our head.

If any object that I am contrary to myself, in that I sometimes did write, that justification is a plenary pardon, in one indivisible act of all sins, past, present,

[1] Even the *minimum quod sic.—Rutherf.*

and to come, and therefore sin cannot be oftener than once pardoned—If I should answer, that the knowledge we have, especially in so supernatural a mystery, is but the twilight, or the day-star's glimmering of sinful men, it might suffice; but I judge, that I speak nothing contrary to that.

Asser. 3. For two formal justifications of a believer, I utterly deny, which is that which Arminians press not a little; yea, and the justification of the person, and his acceptance in God's favour, is but one act: I never fall from that acceptance, once being in court and grace. I illustrate it thus: There is a catholic pardon in a statute of Parliament, for grace to all traitors, and that for treasons past, and also to come, upon condition, that after new treasons committed, they address themselves to the public register of the state, and cause insert their names in the blank of that act of grace printed, and in the keeping of some officer of state: now, though any one be pardoned at his first lapse, fully, if he fail again and again, and yet perform the condition prescribed in law, we cannot say he hath obtained twenty, a hundred, yea, as many several pardons of grace, as he hath failed against king and state—it is but one public act of grace made use of several times. So, here, in the gospel, there is a written act of the grace of God in Jesus Christ,—remission to all under the treason of sin against the royal crown and glory of the Most High, the supreme Lawgiver, and that to the acceptation of the person of the traitor in full favour, when he shall have in his conscience the transumpt or transcript of it at first; and also for grace and pardon of all after-slips, and sins against the glory of the Redeemer (so he sin not against the only flower of the prerogative royal, the operation of the Holy Ghost in a special manner) upon condition, he walk from faith to faith, and renew his address to Christ, the great Lord of the rolls, who keepeth the book of life;—now, I cannot see here many pardons of grace, but only, the double extract or copy of the first act of free grace.

Object. 2. But the sins pardoned to the justified person, after the first justification of his person, were never pardoned before, and they are now pardoned; therefore, there must be two justifications.

Ans. They were virtually pardoned, and so, as he shall never come to condemnation for any sins past, or to come, but the man now standeth justified in the court; whereas before his first believing, God looked at him, as a judge doth at a guilty person, whose person he absolveth from all punishment, because his surety hath given a ransom for him, and he holdeth forth that ransom to the judge: but the man in all his after faults is so far forth a sinner, as that which he hath done, though he be a justified David, displeaseth the Lord, (2 Sam., xi, 27); and in so far is he pardoned. But God now looketh on him, as a father on an offending son; and this son doth not hold forth a new ransom to God, but only renew the former: nor doth it infer a new acceptance of his person that he had not before, 3. Nor place in God any new love of free complacency and good will; but only a further manifestation thereof, and a greater measure of the love of benevolence. 4. It is the same act of free grace, that God putteth forth in pardoning his son now fallen in sin, and in accepting of his person at first. 2. It is the same ransom of Christ's atonement of his dear blood, that his faith layeth hold on now, as before. 3. The pardon of this sin committed by a justified son, is not the freeing of him from the eternal punishment of this sin, as if he had been under eternal wrath for it before;—for at his first believing, when his person was accepted, he was fully and freely pardoned, and freed from all the obligation to eternal wrath, that all or any of his sins past, present, or to come, might subject him unto;—but it is the renewing of the certainty of the sufficiency of Christ's ransom, as applied to take away that sin in particular, and that by a renewed act of faith. Now, the renewed apprehension of the grace of God in the same ransom of blood for righteousness in Christ, as applied to this new guiltiness, maketh not a new forensical and law-act, but doth only apply the Lord's first act of grace to this particular sin; nor do I mean, that faith, for remission of sins committed, after a soul is in the state of justification, is nothing else but a mere reflex act, by which we apprehend and know the first acceptance of a sinner to righteousness; for it is a direct act, apprehending the former grace of a sufficient ransom, as applied to this new contracted guiltiness; for the sinner is condemned for unbelief, (John, iii, 18, 36,) and because he believeth not, he is liable to the wrath of God. Now he is not condemned, because he doth not to his own sense know, feel, and apply the remission of sins, and satisfaction purchased in Christ's blood for him: because then, he should be condemned, because he doth not believe a lie; for there was never any such remission purchased for him: he is condemned, not for want of sense and actual knowledge of any such pardon, but for want of confiding on Christ, as on him who hath made a sufficient atonement for all that believe; and so, justifying faith is some other thing, than the sense of purchased pardon of sins.

Object. 3. Then may I, with the like boldness, believe the remission of these sins that I am to commit, and so, sin boldly, because I am persuaded, they cannot prevail to condemn me eternally, as I may with boldness believe the remission of sins already committed.

Answ. There is a boldness of faith; and, 2, a sinful boldness. In regard of boldness of faith, I am to believe the sufficiency of that invaluable ransom, that it cannot be more or less, nor intended or remitted, but doth lie under the eye of Justice, and equally accepted of God, as able to remove the eternal guilt of all sins, past, present, as also of those to come. But it were sinful boldness to commit sin, because Christ hath paid for it: it is a motive to the contrary, not to live to ourselves, but to him who died for us, because Christ bare our sins on his own body on the tree, (1 Pet., iii, 24; 1 Pet., i, 18; Gal., i, 4; Rom., vi, 1–4; 1 Pet., iv, 1, 2.) For though I be persuaded there is no fear of eternal wrath in sins to be committed, for my faith believeth freedom from that, in regard of all sins; there be other stronger motives to eschew sin, than fear of hell; even fear of violating infinite love and mercy: there is a more prevailing and efficacious power in apprehended love, to keep from sin (it being saving grace,) than in fear of hell, which of itself is no grace. 2. Fear of punishment of sin as sin, is to keep from sin, though it be not fear of eternal punishment: the eternity of punishment is no ways essential to punishment. Libertines closely remove this motive, who will have no sin, as sin in God's court, punished in the believer. It is not punished in order to satisfaction of justice, but it followeth not that it is not punishable as sin.

Object. It is mercenary, and peculiar to hirelings, to abstain from sin for fear of stripes, or to serve God for hope of reward.

Answ. To abstain from sin, for fear of punishment, as the only and greatest evil (whereas the evil of sin is far greater, and so more to be feared) is mercenary: Indeed, we teach that no man should, upon that fear, abstain from sin. 2. To serve God for hope of heaven, as a created good to ourselves, separated in the intention from God himself and holiness, is peculiar to hirelings, but not to serve God simply for heaven. Moses did it, (Heb., xi, 25, 26.) It is Christ's argument in stirring up his disciples to suffer for righteousness; "For great is your reward in heaven." (Matt., v, 12.) And it is no less mercenary which libertines teach, that to serve God for actual hire in hand already purchased, to wit, for deliverance from hell, and a purchased redemption, than what we teach, that we may serve God for hope of good to come, if the intention in both be not steeled with grace, and free of selfishness.

SERMON XIX.

OBJECT. But the gospel, from the law of love, not the law itself, forbiddeth the believer to sin; neither teach we, (say they,) that the gospel maketh sin to be no sin, but it only maketh it to be no more my sin, but Christ's, and counted on his score, who was wounded for my iniquities, and was my surety; and therefore, his payment is my payment, so as we have no more conscience of sins.

Answ. It is true, the gospel speaketh no contradictions, and maketh not sin to be no sin, or David's adultery not to be a violation of the Seventh Commandment: indeed, it maketh Peter's denial of Christ, not to be Peter's sin in a legal and forensic way; but that Peter, believing in Christ, who justifieth the ungodly, shall not be condemned for that, nor for any other sin—that, and all his other sins with that, are counted upon Christ's score. But the denial of Christ, in another relation, is the sin of Peter only, to wit, according to the physical inherency of it, in that it proceeded from Peter's lust, and body of sin dwelling in him, and not any way from Christ Jesus, and in that it is against Christ's express commandment, who charged Peter to confess his Lord and Master.

But Antinomians, and by name Dr. Crispe, teach us, that not only the guilt of sin, but sin itself, really, and inherently, was laid upon Christ, in regard Christ was not, by way of supposition only, or imagination, counted the sinner, but made sin. And 2. In regard, not only the guilt of sin, but sin itself, was laid upon Christ; for, saith Dr. Crispe, 'The guilt of sin, and sin itself, are all one.' When Joseph's brethren were accused for spies, they say, "We are guilty concerning our brother, in that we saw the anguish of his soul, when he besought us, and we would not hear." (Gen., xlii, 21). Reuben expoundeth the meaning, "Did not I say to you, Sin not against the lad? But you would not hearken unto me; and, therefore, behold, we are guilty." (verse 22.) What is that? We did sin against the child. To be guilty, therefore, and to commit a sin, is all one; they are but two words expressing the same thing. 2. Suppose a malefactor be asked, Guilty, or not guilty? He answers, Not guilty: What doth he mean? He means, he hath not done the fact that was laid to his charge. When the jury is asked, Guilty, or not guilty? the jury saith, Guilty. What do they mean? Do they mean any thing in respect of punishment? No: The jury hath nothing to do with that, but only in matter of fact; that is, whether the fact be done, or not done?—It had been extreme injustice to punish Christ, if sin had not been on him, and if he had been at his arraignment, completely and absolutely innocent; even as if a judge should hang a man, though there were nothing found against him. Man is a broken debtor, and Christ a surety: God is content to take Christ's single bond, and looketh for no other paymaster but Christ: Sin was really translated upon Christ, else it was false, that the Lord laid on him the iniquities of us all; yea, by this transaction of sin, Christ doth now become, or did become, when our sins were laid on him, as really and truly the person that had all these sins, as those men who did commit them, really and truly, had them themselves. So Christ was made sin itself; we are made righteousness in him:—this is no imagination. But as we are actual and real sinners in Adam, so here is a real act: God doth really pass over sin upon Christ, still keeping this fast, that Christ acted no sin; so that, in respect of the act, not one sin of the believer is Christ's: But in respect of transaction, in respect of passing of accounts from one head to another, in respect of that, there is reality of making of Christ to be sin. If a judge will think such a man to be a malefactor, and by reason of his thoughts that he is a malefactor, he will actually hang this man, is there any justice in such an act? If God will but suppose Christ to have sin upon him, and knows that he hath it not, but others have the sins upon them, and upon this supposition will execute Christ, what will you call this? "He shall bear the sins of many;" (Isa., liii). Doth a man bear a thing on him in a way of supposition? Or, where there is bearing, is there not real weight? The Lamb of God taketh away the sins of the world, (John, i, 29). Can it sink into a reasonable person, that a thing should be taken away, and yet be left behind? It is a flat contradiction. If a man be to receive money at such a place, and he doth take this money away with him, is the money left in the place where it was, when he hath taken it away? Although I have searched the Scripture as narrowly as possibly I may, yet this I find, that throughout the whole Scripture, there is not one scripture that speaketh of imputing our sins to Christ; but still the Holy Ghost speaketh of sin not imputed to us, and of righteousness imputed to us."

Let me answer, That in all this, you shall find grace turned into wantonness. In all this man's sermons, there is not one word to stir up to the duties of sanctification and holiness; but there is much in these words, and several other passages of his two little volumes of sermons, to depress, and cry down holiness and walking with God. I shall therefore say a little on this, and deliver truth shortly in these positions:

POSITION 1. No believer's sin is so counted upon Christ's score, as that it leaveth off to be the believer's sin, according to its physical and real indwelling. It is true, it is Christ's sin by law-imputation, and legal obligation to satisfactory punishment, and only laid upon Christ in that notion. Yet it is so the believer's sin, as he is to mourn for this very thing, that Christ was pierced and crucified to remove the guilt, and the obligation to satisfactory punishment: "And they shall look upon me whom they have pierced, and they shall mourn for him, as one mourneth for his only son." (Zech., xii, 10.) Yea, it is so the believer's sin, even when he believeth that his original corruption is pardoned; yet it dwelleth in him, having the complete essence and being of sin; so as if he should say, he had no sin, and nothing in him contrary to the holy law of God, he should deceive himself, and the truth should not be in him, (1 John, i, 8). Yea, let him be a Paul, not under the law, but being dead to the law, (Rom., vii, 6,) as touching all actual obligation to eternal death; yet in regard of the real essence of sin, and proper contrariety that sin hath to God's righteous law, he crieth out, "For we know that the law is spiritual, but I am carnal, and sold under sin," (ver. 14,) "Now it is no more I," (ver. 17,) (sanctified and pardoned I,) who am in Christ, "dead to the law," (Rom., viii, 1;) freed from condemnation that "do sin, but sin that dwelleth in me." (Rom., vii, 6.) If there were no sinful I (to speak so) and no corrupt self in Paul, which breaketh out into sin, and this indwelling sin were as really in its essence, and its being, removed, and taken close out of Paul, as money taken really out of a place, is no more left in that place than if it had never been there; surely, then, justified saints were as clean as these, who are up before the throne, clothed in white. And when Paul saith, "It is no more I that do sin, but sin that dwelleth in me," he should speak contradictions, and say, It is no more I that do sin, but it is I that do sin: there should be in justified Paul, no law in his members warring against the law of his mind, as he saith, (Rom., vii, 23); no body of death leading him captive to the law of sin, (verse 24); no flesh lusting against the spirit, hindering the regenerated to do the good that they would. As Paul speaketh, (Gal., v, 17,) there should be no members on earth to be crucified; as it is in Col., iii, 5; no old man to be put off, no corruption, no deceitful lusts in us to be abated; as we are charged, Eph., iv, 22, 23; no fleshly lusts in us, which war against the soul, as 1 Pet., ii, 11; no weight, no sin that doth so easily beset us, to be laid aside by the regenerated and justified, who are to run their race with patience: contrary to the Spirit of God, speaking the contrary, (Heb., xii, 1, 2). Yea, there shall be no original sin remaining in the justified person, which can be named sin; nothing in them lusting against the spirit, nothing to be mortified, crucified, resisted; nothing to be work for the grace of God; nothing to be a field and plat of ground to be laboured on by the spirit by faith; nothing to be the seed and rise of humiliation: the sinner may go to heaven, and be nothing in Christ's debt, to help him against indwelling sin, for that guest is so taken away, as money that was in a place, and is every penny really removed to another place: Yea, it is a flat contradiction (say Antinomians) "to be a pardoned soul, and yet to have sin dwelling in the soul."

Posit. 2. The guilt of sin, and sin itself, are not one and the same thing, but far different things. That I may prove the point, let the terms be considered. There be two things in sin very considerable: 1. The blot, defilement, and blackness of sin; which, I conceive, is nothing but the absence and privation of that moral rectitude, the want of that whiteness, innocency, and righteousness, which the holy and clean law of the Lord requireth to be in the actions, inclinations, and powers of the soul of a reasonable creature. 2. There is the guilt of sin; that is, somewhat which issueth from this blot and blackness of sin, according to which, the person is liable and obnoxious to eternal punishment. This is the debt of sin, the law obligation to satisfaction passive for sin: just as there be two things in debt, so these two are in sin. For when a man borroweth money, and profusely and lavishly spendeth it, this is injustice against his brother, in matter of his goods, and a breach of the Eighth Commandment. Again, this breach in relation to policy, to the magistrate and the law of the land, putteth this broken man under another relation, that he is formally a debtor; and so, it is just, that he either pay the money, or suffer for this act of injustice, and satisfy the law of the Fifth Commandment, which is, that he satisfy the law and the magistrate, the public father, tutor of a wronged and oppressed brother. Now, here be two things in debt: 1. An unjust thing; a hurting of our brother in his goods: this is a blot, and a thing privately contrary to justice. 2. A just thing, a guilt, a just debt, according to which it is most just, that the broken man either pay or suffer. Now, these two, as all contraries do, they make a number, as just and unjust must be two things, and two contrary things. I know there be cavils and subtleties of schoolmen, touching the blot,[1] and the guilt[2] of sin; but this is the naked truth which I have declared. Some say, 'the blot of sin, is that uncleanness of sin which is washed away by the blood of the Lord Jesus;

[1] Or macula peccati. [2] Reatus.

and this is nothing but the very guilt of sin, which is wholly removed in justification.' But I easily answer, The blot of sin hath divers relations, and these contrary one to another: As, 1, there is the blot of sin in relation to the holy law, as it is a privation of the rectitude and holiness that the spiritual law requireth; and it is formally sin, and not the guilt of sin; in which consideration, as nothing removeth blindness but seeing eyes, or deafness but hearing ears, so nothing formally removeth sin, but only the perfect habit of accomplished sanctification; and so, the blot of sin, is not that which is formally removed in justification, but only in perfected sanctification.

2. The blot of sin in relation to God, as offended and injured, putteth on the habit of guilt, and so, it is washed away in the "fountain opened to the house of David," and formally removed in justification; but now, it is not formally considered as sin, but according to that which is accidental in sin; viz., obligation to punishment, which may be, and is removed from sin, the true essence and nature of sin being saved whole and entire. Hence sin hath divers considerations: 1. As sin is contrary to the righteousness and holiness of the law, it is formally sin, and this essential form and life of sin remaineth in us while we live, sin being in the act of dying, or a passion rather to be crucified, and in the way to its grave and perfect destruction, which shall be when glory shall grow up out of the stalk of grace, and sanctification shall be perfected; for grace is the bud, glory the fruit; grace the spring and summer,—glory the harvest. As sin is a blackness contrary to the innocency that the law requireth, and as it blotteth and defileth the soul, it is a spot, a filthy and deformed thing, abasing the crea-

ture, making the creature black, crooked, defiled like the skin of the Ethiopian, or spotted like the leopard, (Jer., xiii, 23.) 3. As sin is a blot that maketh the creature impure, unclean, and contrary and hateful to God; so it is a blot and unclean thing to God, and that two ways:—1. As it is contrary to God's holy law, it is formally sin, as is before said. 2. As it offendeth and injureth God in his honour and glory of supreme authority, to command what is just and holy, it is an offence and a provocation, (Isa., iii, 8; Psalm lxxviii, 17,) a displeasing of God, (1 Cor., x, 5; 2 Sam., xi, 27,) a grieving of him and his Spirit, (Eph., iv, 30; Gen., vi, 6; Psalm xcv, 10,) a tempting of God, (Psalm lxxviii, 18; xcv, 9; Acts, xv, 10,) a wearying of the Lord, and making him to serve, (Isa., xliii, 24; vii, 15,) a loading of the Lord, (Isa., i, 24,) a pressing of the Lord, as a cart is pressed under a heavy load of sheaves, (Amos, ii, 13,) and so is punished with everlasting punishment. Hence there is a two-fold guilt, one fundamental, potential, the guilt of sin as sin; this is all one with sin, being the very essence, soul, and formal being of sin; and this guilt of sin you cannot remove from sin, so as sin shall remain sin; take this away, and you take away sin itself. But this is removed in sanctification as perfected, not in justification. As all the arguments of Dr. Crispe go along in their strength, to prove that the guilt of sin, the fundamental guilt of sin, and sin itself, are all one, so we shall yield all to him, but with no gain to his bad cause. For Joseph's brethren say, Truly we sinned, or were guilty against our brother. (Gen., xlii, 22.) This is nothing, but we trespassed against our brother; this is not spoken so much of guilt, as of sin itself. And the malefactor saying he is not guilty, meaneth of fundamental guilt, or the guilt of sin, and that he hath not committed the crime charged upon him.

But there is another guilt in sin, called the guilt or obligation to punishment, the actual guilt, or actual obligation of the person who hath sinned,[1] to punishment; and this guilt is a thing far different from sin itself, and is separable from sin, and may be, and is removed from sin, without the destruction of the essence of sin, and is fully removed in justification. Now that this guilt is different from sin, I prove, 1. Because that which our blessed Surety took upon him for our cause, without taking to him any thing which is essential in sin, such as is to be a sinner like us, to do violence, to be justly accused of sin, that is different from sin; but Christ took on him the guilt of our sin, that is, the actual obligation to be punished for sin, while as he bare our sins in his own body on the tree, (1 Pet., ii, 24,) "And was wounded for our transgressions, and bruised for our iniquities, and did bear on him the chastisement of our peace," (Isa., liii, 5,) "and died for our offences," (Rom., iv, 25; v, 6). And this punishment Christ could not have borne, except by law he had obliged himself, as our Surety, to pay our debts, (Heb., x, 4–8, and vii, 22.) Now that in all his life and sufferings he did no violence, committed no sin, nor touched any contagion of sin in his own person, is evident; because he was holy, harmless, undefiled, and separated from sinners, (Heb., vii, 26; iv, 15; Isaiah, liii, 9). The proposition is sure; for if Christ was so made sin, and punished for sin, and liable to suffer for sin, and yet had not any sinful or blameworthy guilt on him; then that guilt of the person by which any is liable to punishment for sin, is some

[1] Reatus pœnæ, reatus personæ, reatus actualis.—*Rutherford.*

other thing than sin, and the blame-worthy guilt that is in sin; forasmuch as they are really separated, the one being in Christ, and the other not being in him, nay, nor could it be in him.

2. The cause cannot be one and the same with the effect, nor the subject and foundation one with the adjunct, and that which resulteth from the foundation. But sin is the cause, foundation, and subject, from which guilt, or actual obligation to punishment issueth, because therefore is the sinner under guilt-personal, and actual obligation to punishment, because he hath sinned, and is under the guilt of transgression. As he is therefore in law and justice a guilty debtor to suffer evil of punishment, because against law and justice he is a bad deserving sinner, in doing against, and so by a sin-guilt, hath transgressed a law;—for all evil of punishment is a daughter which lay in the womb of the evil of sin; and the guilt of the latter ill of punishment must flow from the former; to wit, from the ill of sin;—so, to be guilty, or obliged to eternal punishment, is a fruit and result, or consequent of the fundamental and intrinsical guilt of sin.

3. An unjust and sinful deviation from the holy will of God revealed in his law, and hateful to, and punishable by God, cannot be one and the same thing with that which is just, and agreeable to the just and holy will of God: but sin itself, in its formal being, is a deviation from the holy will of God revealed in his law, sin being defined by John, "A transgression of the law," and is hateful to, and punishable by the Lord. But the guilt of sin, of which we now speak, is nothing but the demerit, and actual obligation to eternal punishment, and is no unjust thing, no transgression of God's will revealed in his law: yea, the

demerit of sin is a most just thing, and the actual obligation to punishment is most just and holy, and agreeable to God's just will: and obligation to punishment can neither be punishable nor hateful to God; yea, it is just with God, that the sinner be under law-obligation, to eat the fruits of the tree of his own planting, to have his teeth set on edge with the sour grapes which he ate himself.

4. He that borroweth money, and profusely and lavishly spendeth it, is in that a transgressor against the Eighth Commandment; he committeth an act of injustice against his brother. Now this act of injustice cannot formally or intrinsically be the sin or sinful guilt of the innocent surety. No law of God or man can make actions evil and sinful, that are physically, inherently, intrinsically, really, the unjust actions of the doer, the formal sin, or intrinsical and fundamental sinful guilt of another man, who, in that action, is innocent, and is not a member, a hand, or a foot of the man that committed that fault, which I speak for. The sons of Adam, who intrinsically sinned in Adam, and, by God's supreme will, were made a part of Adam, yet the surety is formally made a debtor, and by law obliged to pay the debt; and it is an act of justice that he pay the debt: his promise to the creditor maketh him a debtor; but his promise to the creditor putteth no act of injustice in lavishly spending his neighbour's goods on him, for in that, he is innocent, and cannot be charged morally, as a faulty and a broken bankrupt; the fruit and effect of the broken man's injustice, doth only lie upon him, in regard of his promise. There be three brethren born of the same parents, Adam, John, Thomas. Suppose we then, that the law of the city or kingdom is so,

that one brother may die for his brother. John murdereth Thomas traitorously, under trust; by law then John ought to die. The elder brother, Adam, out of love, interposeth himself to the judge, to die for his younger brother, John: in this case, Adam by law ought to die, and he is in law reputed and counted the murderer; but truly, not morally, not intrinsically, for he can be reproached formally with no act of treacherous dealing, as if under trust he had stabbed his brother, for he did no such act. If shame by accident accompany his public laying down of his life, it is morally no reproach, no intrinsical blot to him; yea, that Adam dieth for John the murderer, it is through his own free consent, an act of extreme love; in relation to the judge, it is a most just act, and in law only, in imputation and legal account, he is the murderer. But, poor soul! he never thought, nor acted any treachery or cruelty against his brother.

Posit. 3. Hence this position: Christ was made sin, or imputed the sinner, and died for us sinners. The second Adam, "the First-begotten among many brethren," suffered for his younger brethren, and so, by free consenting to be our Surety, and to die for us, (Psalm xl, 6–8; Heb., x, 5–7; John, x, 17, 18; xiv, 31; Matt., xxvi, 46; Mark, xiv, 42; John, xviii, 7, 8,) he was made by law-account sin for us, as the sinner, (John, xv, 13; 2 Cor., v, 21,) to die for us, (Rom., iv, 25,) and the Lord laid upon him the iniquities of us all, (Isa., liii, 6; 1 Pet., ii, 24, 25). But I judge it blasphemy to say, 'By this transaction of sin upon Christ, Christ doth now become, or did become, when our sins were laid on him, as really and truly the person that did all these sins, as these men who did commit them, really and truly had these sins on them themselves.' For the elect believers in Christ were intrinsically, formally, inherently adulterers, murderers, "disobedient, serving divers lusts;" (Titus, iii, 3); "Dead in sins and trespasses; by nature the children of wrath," (Ephes., ii, 1); and in their own persons acted all these acts of wickedness, so as sin doth formally denominate them sinners; as whiteness in snow, in milk, in the wall, denominateth all these white. But Christ never is, never was, intrinsically, formally, inherently the adulterer, a disobedient person; nor is sin personally in Christ, to denominate him as really and intrinsically a sinner, as David, Isaiah, Peter, Paul, for whom he died; for "He did never violence; neither was there any deceit in his mouth," (Isa., liii, 9). There was no fundamental guilt, nor any bad deserving in him. How then was he a sinner, or made sin for us? I answer, By mere imputation, and law-account, and no other way.

But the libertine saith, 'It were the greatest injustice in the world, to punish Christ, if sin had not been on him really. If he had been at his arraignment completely, and absolutely innocent, and if only in imagination, and by a lying supposition, which wanteth all reality in the thing, God should put Christ to death for these sins that he knoweth Christ to be free of, this were as if a judge should hang a malefactor, whom in conscience he knew to be free from all sin, and could find nothing against him.'

But I answer, law-imputation is a most real thing, and no imagination, nor any lying supposition; as a man that is surety for his broken brother, who hath wasted the creditor's goods, is truly surety and really the debtor, and his obligation to pay for his broken friend is real, and most just, on two grounds: 1. That he gave faith and promise, and writ and seal, that, his friend failing, he should pay. 2. The creditor accepted him as a real law-debtor and paymaster in that case, and yet the surety in his person did neither borrow the money, nor lavishly waste it, and he hath in his person neither conscience nor guilt of injustice toward his brother. And, in regard of personal contagion of sinful guilt, Christ was completely and absolutely innocent in his arraignment, as one that neither acted sin, nor could he be the formal subject of sin, in whom the blot of it was intrinsically, or really inherent. But, in regard that Christ was willing to strike hands with God, and to plight his faith and soul in pawn, and did willingly sign with his hand an act of cautionry as our Surety, (Psalm xl, 6–8; Heb., x, 3–10), and the Lord accepted him as Surety, and "laid our sins on him," (Isa., lvi, 6; 2 Cor., v, 21; John, iii, 19; Rom., v,) he "was made sin;" that is, he was made a debtor and a law-paymaster, so constituted by his own and his Father's will. So that God did no act of injustice in punishing Christ, nor was he in law absolutely innocent, but nocent and guilty; that is to say, in regard of his law-place, or law-condition, he was by imputation liable and obnoxious to actual satisfaction and punishment for our sins; yet he was[1] a sinner, a debtor by imputation, a debtor by law, by place, by office, and served himself heir to our sins, and the miseries following sin. Now, he was not in imagination, and in a false and a lying supposition, made sin: imputation is not a lie, but as truly and really a real law-deed, as Judah offered himself surety for Benjamin, and was in law, and really, a bondman to Joseph,

[1] Debitor factus, non intrinsice; debitor legaliter, non personaliter; debitor ratione conditionis et officii, non ratione personæ.—*Rutherford.*

and might have been so dealt with as a real slave, if he had plighted himself instead of Benjamin. And the surety, by the words of his own mouth, and by his covenant and promise, is really and truly ensnared, as a true and real debtor in law; as a roe is really in the hand of the hunter, and a bird in the fowler's net, being once caught and in hands, (Prov., vi, 1–5.) He is no debtor by imagination; he is not supposed to be what he is not indeed by the law of God, and nature, and all laws.[1] A man's promise fetcheth him within the law-compass of a real debtor. So Christ was under bail, and a law-act of surety by his own act, his own word of promise and covenant: 'Thou hast given me a body, I have taken the debts and sins of my poor brethren on me; crave me, Lord, as only pay-master.' "Lo, here am I, to do thy will," (Ps. xl, 6–8; Heb., x, 4–8; John, x, 18).

Now, there are but these two in sin,—1. The act committed against the law of God: 2. The debt and obligation to punishment is clear; and though Dr. Crispe denies that sin was imputed to Christ, at least, he cannot see or read it in all the Scripture, yet he granteth the thing itself. But I prove both the one and the other.

And, 1. That Christ committed and did no act nor deed against law, for which he should be intrinsically and inherently the sinner, is clear: because that "holy thing Jesus," being God-man, could not sin, nor did he ever any violence or deceit. (Isa., liii, 9, Heb., iv, 15, viii, 26.) 2. The inherent viciousness, and sinful blot of sin, which followeth upon the physical act of sin, being once done and committed by David, Peter, and all the elect of God, cannot come out by a

[1] Promissum cadit in reale debitum.—*Rutherford.*

real transmigration, and true and physical derivation, or removal from one agent and subject to another, to inhere in and denominate another subject: the same whiteness in number that was in milk, cannot remove out of it, and reside and dwell in another subject.[1] No law in the world, no covenant, no transaction imaginable can effectuate this, that the real wickedness once committed by David, should really and truly remove out of him, and go in, and reside in, and denominate the man Christ a wicked person. It is an everlasting contradiction, that the treacherous murdering of innocent Uriah should remove out of him into the Son of David, Jesus Christ, and denominate him the murderer of Uriah, so as the same murder can be said to be committed by David only, and not by David only, but by the man Christ. It must then be a lie, a dream, and palpable untruth, to make Jesus Christ intrinsically the sinner and murderer.

Judge, then, if this doctrine be of God, which Dr. Crispe, right down, hath asserted to the world in print, Sermon iii, volume ii, p. 84, "God made Christ a transgressor. No transgressor in the world was such a transgressor as Christ was." P. 88, "You will never have quietness of spirit in respect of sin, till you have received this principle, that it is iniquity itself that the Lord hath laid on Christ. Now, when I say with the prophet, It is iniquity itself that the Lord hath laid on Christ, I mean, as the prophet doth, it is the fault or the transgression itself; and to speak more fully, that erring and straying like sheep—that very erring, and straying, and transgressing, is passed off from thee, and is laid upon Christ. To speak it more plainly, Hast thou been an idolater? Hast thou been a blasphemer?

[1] It is a principle of nature, Idem numero accidens, non migrat e subjecto in subjectum.—*Rutherford.*

Hast thou been a despiser of God's word, and a trampler upon him? Hast thou been a profaner of his name and ordinances? Hast thou been a murderer, an adulterer, a thief, a liar, a drunkard? Reckon up what thou canst against thyself; if thou hast part in the Lord Christ, all these transgressions of thine, become actually the transgressions of Christ, and so cease to be thine, and thou ceasest to be a transgressor from that time they were laid upon Christ, to the last hour of thy life. Mark it well. Christ himself is not so completely righteous, but we are as righteous as he was; nor we so completely sinful, but Christ became, being made sin, as completely sinful as we. Nay, more, the righteousness that Christ hath with the Father, we are the same righteousness, for we are made the righteousness of God: that very sinfulness that we were, Christ is made that very sinfulness before God."

Ans. 1. No scripture calleth Christ the thief, the murderer, the adulterer, the idolater; God avert from pious hearts such blasphemies! He may by a figure be called Sin, and be said to "be made sin for us," but that is by mere imputation; as if you would say, 'The surety is the broken and riotous waster.' All that have common sense, know this to be a figurative and improper speech; that is, he is in law liable to pay the debts of the broken waster; and the law-guilt and law-obligation that was in the broken man, is transferred on him by his own promise. But no man in his right wits can say, that the broken man is as intrinsically just, as sober a manager of his goods, as free from all intrinsical fault, and sin of injustice, and breach of the Eighth Commandment, as the innocent surety. No sober wit can say, that the injustice and injury done by the broken man to his brother, and against the Eighth Commandment, "Thou shalt not steal," is nothing formally, but the very just and real debt that the surety hath taken upon him; and that the surety is as guilty of the same very fault and sin of wastery that is inherent in the broken bankrupt, as the bankrupt himself. And it is as great blasphemy to say, Christ is as guilty, and as inherently faulty, and no less a transgressor of the Sixth and Seventh Commandment, by killing Uriah, and deflowering Bathsheba, than ever David was; and that David was as free from the inherent fundamental guilt of these sins from eternity (for libertines will needs have our sins from eternity to lie on Christ, and our persons before all time justified) as Christ himself is. 1. God made Christ sin; God made not David to murder Uriah. Then Christ must be one way a sinner, David another way; the one by imputation, the other by real inherency. 2. David was intrinsically a transgressor of a law, Christ not so. 3. David was washed and pardoned in the blood of Christ, Christ not so. Then David's righteousness is but borrowed, and Christ's righteousness his own.

2. There is an essential righteousness that Christ hath with the Father, and it is communicable neither to men nor angels, no more than God can communicate with the creature any other of his essential attributes, such as are infinite justice, infinite mercy, infinite grace, holiness, goodness, omnipotence, eternity, immensity. It is only the cautionary, the surety-righteousness of Christ-God, that is made ours; and that we are as completely righteous as Christ, is divinity not borrowed from the fountain of the holy Scripture, but the man's own dream: for the broken debtor is never so righteous as the surety, except in

this sense, he is *æque*, but not *æqualiter*—he is righteous as the surety who has paid the sum for him, in regard that the creditor can no more in law charge him with the sum, than he can in law charge the surety who hath completely paid it: So are we in Christ freed from the guilt of eternal wrath, in that the Lord can no more in law charge sin to actual condemnation in the believer, than he can put Christ to death again, or give a new ransom for us.

But this is but formally a righteousness, in regard of freedom from the punishment of sin. But, as I have said, the surety is more righteous, simply, 1. In regard the surety never broke faith to the creditor; the broken debtor hath broken to him. 2. The surety never injured the creditor by injustice done against the Eighth Commandment, but the broken man hath failed in this. But I would be resolved what truth can be in those: "Who can say, I have made my heart clean?" (Prov., xx, 9.) "Who can bring a clean thing out of an unclean? No, not one," (Job, xiv, 5). "There is not a just man upon earth, that doeth good, and sinneth not," (Eccl., vii, 20). "If we say we have no sin, we deceive ourselves, and the truth is not in us," (1 John, i, 8).

If we be completely as righteous as Christ, and if, as Crispe divines, all the idolatry, thefts, murders of the redeemed, become actually the transgressions of Christ, and so cease to be the transgressions of the sinners, from that time they were laid upon Christ, to the hour of their death, can he determine the time, when persecuting Saul's blasphemies, and bloody outrages to the saints, were laid upon Christ? I conceive he will say, from eternity they were laid upon Christ, and before he believed: certainly this was an untruth then, "Saul made havoc of the church," even when he did make havoc of the church, and ere he believed; for if Saul persecuting, and all the elect unconverted, yet disobedient, and boiling in their lusts, be as righteous as Christ all their life, it is most false that ever they were dead in sin, or sometimes disobedient. If it be said, The elect considered in themselves and in nature are sinners, but considered as men in Christ, they are as righteous as Christ, it helpeth not: for we must not dream of and fancy considerations, that have no reality and truth in them; for all now born since our Lord died, I am persuaded, by the doctrine of Antinomians, were never, nor can they be real and true objects of this consideration; for, from that time that their sins were laid upon Christ, to the last hour of their life, they are as righteous as Christ, and so washed and justified. Now, their sins were laid upon Christ, as some libertines say, from eternity; as others, from that day that he died on the cross.

Sins taken away by Christ's blood, saith Dr. Crispe, are no sins of the saints: 'Christ did take them away, and bear their weight, even in the fault and sin itself, and not the guilt only, and not by supposition or mere imputation only, and that from eternity.' But when Antinomians confess that Christ acted no sin, so that in respect of the act (the sinful act against the law of God must be here understood), not one sin of the believer's is Christ's, but only in respect of passing accounts from one head to another. This is all the truth we here plead for; because the act (or somewhat answerable to that) done against the spiritual law of God is sin itself, and essentially sin: if this was never upon Christ, then sin itself was never upon Christ. Now, there is no other thing remaining in sin but the debt, guilt, or obligation of sin that can be laid on Christ; and the truth is, the Scripture expoundeth the laying our sins upon Christ, to be nothing but God punishing Christ for our sins, as Isa., liii, 4. The cause and formal reason, why Christ did bear our griefs and carry our sorrows, is, "Because the Lord laid on him the iniquity of us all," (ver. 6,) and is so expounded in 1 Pet., ii. Whereas it is said, that "Christ suffered for us," (ver. 21,) and an objection is removed, (ver. 22,) Why should he suffer? did he sin? The apostle answereth, by concession of the antecedent, and by denying the consequence: "He did no sin (personally), neither was guile found in his mouth." But it followeth not, that he should not suffer legally, and for others, the punishment due to them; so his sufferings are expounded, (verse 24,) "Who his own self bare our sins in his own body on the tree." Now, how did Christ bear our sins? On the tree; that is, by suffering. And Paul evidently distinguisheth, (Gal., iii,) between two sorts of persons that are cursed; the sinners that abide not in all that is written in the law to do them, (ver. 10,) these are intrinsically, and in their person cursed, as being sinners in their person, and so, the intrinsical objects of divine hatred, and a curse and abominable to God.

Yea, but Christ was also cursed—but how? Not intrinsically. God is never said to hate his Son Christ, nor to abhor him, as he doth sin, which personally resideth in the man who acteth sin in his own person; therefore the Lord's forsaking of Christ his Son, is not an intrinsical detesting, or a moral abhorring of Christ, but an extrinsical, a penal, or a judicial suspending of the beams and rays (as Cyril saith), or the overclouding of his favour, in the comfortable shining on the soul of his own Son. And it is not said that Christ was cursed, but only, "He was made a curse for us," (ver. 13); that is, the fruits and effects of God's curse, the punishment due to sinners, even that satisfactory and penal curse and punishment which infinite justice requireth, was laid upon Christ, while, as he died upon the cross, and suffered the effects of God's wrath upon his soul for our sins. Then he must be the sinner only by imputation, except Antinomians show to us, how a person is made sin, or accounted the sinner, and yet, is neither a sinner, by inherent and personal acting of sin, nor yet by law-imputation. And truly it is bad divinity for Dr. Crispe to say, 'As we are actual and real sinners, in Adam, so here, God passeth really sin over upon Christ. For we sinned intrinsically in Adam, as parts, as members, as being in his loins, and we are thence "by nature the children of wrath," (Ephes., ii); but it is blasphemy to say, that our blessed Saviour sinned intrinsically in us, as part or member of the redeemed, or that he is a son of God's wrath, for sin intrinsically inherent in him, as it is in us.

Further, Christ's bearing of our iniquities is an obvious Hebraism, and all one with the bearing, not of the intrinsical and fundamental guilt of sin, but of the extrinsical guilt, or debt and punishment of sin. So Exod., xxviii, 38, "A mitre shall be on Aaron's forehead, that Aaron may bear the iniquity of the holy things;" Heb. *(Venasa)* signifieth to carry, or the seventy turn it, *exairei*, Aaron shall take away or bear the punishment of the violation of the holy things. Moses saith to Aaron's sons, "God hath given you the sin-offering, to bear the iniquity of the congregation." (Lev., x, 17.) Aaron and his sons did bear the sins of the people, as types of Christ, not by an intrinsical guilt put on them, but by mere imputation: "And the goat shall bear upon him all the iniquities of the children of Israel unto a land not inhabited," (Lev., xvi, 22). The priest prayed that the sins, that is, the punishment of the sins of the people, might be laid on the goat. "Aaron and his sons are to bear the iniquity of the sanctuary," (Numb., xviii, 1); that is, the punishment of their iniquity, in that they were punished, if any of the sanctuary polluted the holy things of God: "The witness who seeth and heareth a swearing, and doth not utter it, he shall bear his iniquity," (Lev., v, 1); that is, saith Vatablus, and all the interpreters, "the punishment of his iniquity." Yet say ye, "Why? doth not the son bear the iniquity of the father?" (Ezek., xviii, 19.) "The soul that sinneth shall die, the son shall not bear the iniquity of the father," (ver. 20). "Because thou hast forgotten me,—bear thou also thy lewdness and thy whoredom," (Ezek., xxiii, 35). In the same very sense, Christ "was once offered to bear the sins of many," (Heb., ix, 28): "He did bear our sins on his body on the tree," (1 Pet., ii, 24): "He did bear the sins of many," (Isa., liii, 12); he did bear heavy punishment, death, and the wrath of God, for the sins of many: "The Lord laid the iniquity of us all on him," (ver. 6). And "He was oppressed, he was afflicted, yet opened he not his mouth," (ver. 7). He was exacted, or payment of violence sought of him. Christ was put to a fine, condemned to pay an amercement or forfeit, or Christ was pursued as paymaster and surety for us: the Father pursued Christ's bond, that he should now, at the appointed day, tell down the sum, the great ransom-money of his life for sinners, who were broken men. Justice gave in a broad and large claim against Jesus Christ, in which were written all the sins of the elect; and Christ opened not his mouth, but was dumb as a lamb led to the shambles, and his silence was as much as, 'Lord, I grant, I yield to all the accounts in this sad claim.' You will not confess your guiltiness, O sinners in Christ, nor take with riots, murders, oaths, and all your sins; but the surety Christ was craved, and all your accounts demanded of him, and he confessed debt, and granted all, —"He was numbered," (ver. 12,)—he was reputed, and written up in the count amongst thieves: This was mere imputation, he was not a wicked man indeed. And consider how, he is called "despised and rejected of men," (ver. 3). Christ in himself, and intrinsically, was the glory, the flower, the prince of men, even at his lowest; he must then be abased below all men, in regard of imputation, and that penal degrading of Christ.[1] He was in himself the mighty God, the Prince of Peace, more than above men and angels; the chief of the kindred of men, the fairest among the sons of men, even at his lowest: but in regard of his low condition, he was made the off-scouring, or the dross or refuse of all men, as if not a christianed creature.

When our divines say, Christ took our place, and we have his condition; Christ was made us, and made the sinner; it is true only in a legal sense: as we say, the advocate is the client, or the guilty man, because

[1] So as it is said of him (*Chadal ishim*), which is, as Vatablus expoundeth it, so contemptible a man, that men would not admit him in company of men. *Sanctius* saith, "He was not numbered amongst men; he was so despised, that he was the lowest among the lowest of men, or the *minimum quod sic* of men, as it is, Psal. xxii, 6, 'A worm, no man,' nobody, not in the class or rank of men."—*Rutherford*.

the advocate beareth his name and person; and what the accused man could in law say before the judge, in his own defence, that the advocate saith for him. The advocate saith, 'I cannot in law die for this crime, for such reasons.' So the surety in law, or in a legal substitution, is the broken man. The surety saith, 'The debt is mine, all the wants, all the poverty, all the debts and burdens of my broken friend be on me;' —and the rich surety having paid all, can say, 'I have paid all; I am in law free.' My friend and surety hath done all, and paid all for me; and that is as good, in the court of justice, as if I had paid in my own person all. For the truth is, there be not two debts, and two bonds, and two sums, nor two debtors; the broken man and the surety are in law but one person, one party addebted—which of them pay, it is all one to law and justice: it is all one sum they owe. The believer in Christ is put in Christ's law-place, and Christ by law is put in his place. Christ, made surety, saith, 'I am the sinner, O Justice, all my broken friends' wants, all their debts be upon me; my life for their life, my soul for my brethren's souls, my glory, my heaven, for my kinsmen's glory and heaven.' The law's bloody bond, was the curse of God upon the sinner, upon the debtor: Christ changed bonds and obligations with us, and putteth out our name, and putteth in his own name in the bloody bond; and where the law readeth, 'the curse of God upon the debtor,' Christ is assignee to this bond, and the gospel readeth it, 'the curse of God upon the rich surety.' (Gal., iii, 13.) Hear then the boldness of faith: "Now, then, there is no condemnation to those that are in Jesus Christ." What challenges Satan or conscience can make against the beli ›ver (for justice being put to silence by Christ, maketh none) hear an answer: 'I was condemned, I was judged, I was crucified for sin, when my surety, Christ, was condemned, judged, and crucified for my sins; and what would you have more of a man than his life? It was a man's life and soul, my life, that my surety offered up to God for sin, and I have paid all, because my surety hath paid all.' And the truth is, it is not two debts, one that the believer owes to God's justice, and another that Christ paid; but the debt that Christ paid is our very debt, and sins, which he did bear on his own body on the tree, (1 Pet., ii, 24). But though it be true in a legal sense, that the surety is the broken man, yet it is true only in regard of the law punishment, or ill of punishment that is laid upon him: for I take Doctor Crispe's words from his own pen. "Suppose (saith he) a malefactor be asked, Guilty or not guilty? he answereth, Not guilty,—what doth he mean? He meaneth, he hath not done the fact that was laid to his charge." Then, not to do the fact of sin, to Dr. Crispe, is not to be guilty. Now, I assume, that Jesus Christ did never any sinful fact, as he also confesseth: then Christ was punished for sin, and yet was never guilty of sin. This must be the greatest injustice in the world to punish a man for sin, altogether free of the guilt of sin. Except Antinomians distinguish, with us, between sinful guilt and penal guilt, they shall never expede themselves.

Now, though it be true, that in law, the debtor and the surety be both one legal person, yet intrinsically they are not one. The broken debtor, as such, may be an unjust man, and the surety a faithful and just man; so that the surety, as a satisfying surety, removeth only the punishment due to the debtor for his injustice; but he removeth not formally injustice, except he be such a surety as Christ, who can both pay the debt, and so remove the ill of punishment; and also, infuse holiness, and sanctify, and remove the evil of sin. Hence, in justification formally, Christ only taketh away the punishment of everlasting fire, and eternal condemnation due to sin. But he removeth not sin itself: sin itself is removed in sanctification, and by degrees. Justification taketh the sting out of the serpent, but doth not formally kill the serpent; the serpent is killed by another act of grace, by infused and perfected sanctification. Justification is a forensical and a legal act, and removeth the power of the law, which involveth the sinner in a curse. Now, the strength, or the legal sting of sin, is the law, (1 Cor., xv, 56;) so we may judge how false this divinity is, which Dr. Crispe asserteth, "You will never (saith he) have quietness of spirit, in respect of sin, till you have received this principle, that it is not the guilt of iniquity only, but iniquity itself, that the Lord laid on Christ;" for it is true, quietness and peace of faith with God floweth from justification, (Rom., v, 1;) and the assurance that Christ hath pardoned sin, and hath removed the penal guilt, the punishment of eternal condemnation from sin; but that the conscience should be quiet, that is, that it should not have also a care to believe that Christ will sanctify thoroughly, and perfect his good work in us, is most false. For though a soul be justified and freed from the guilt of eternal punishment, and so, the spirit is no more to be afraid and disquieted for eternal wrath and hell, which should never have been feared as the greatest evil, in regard that sin, as sin, is more to be feared than hell as hell; —yet there be two other acts of disquietness of spirit, laudable and commendable, even in the saints after they are justified, and the guilt of eternal punishment removed. As, 1. The believer is to have a holy anxiety and care of spirit (I do not call it a troubled conscience) to improve his faith, in believing that Christ will perfect what he hath begun. 2. He is to be grieved that sin dwelleth in him, and to groan and cry as a captive in fetters, out of the sense of his wretched estate, as Paul doth, (Rom., vii, 23, 24).

Antinomians will have the justified to be so quiet in spirit, as if Christ had removed sin in root and branch, buds and stump; whereas, only the eternal punishment, and fear of eternal condemnation, is removed in justification. But there is a worse thing remaining in sin after this, and more to be feared, and a more real and rational ground of disquietness of spirit; and that is the fundamental, intrinsical, and sinful guilt of sin, which Christ never took on him, and is not removed in justification, but only in the gradual and successive perfection of sanctification. And so, being justified, I am to be secure, and to enjoy a sound peace and quietness of spirit, in freedom from eternal wrath. But yet am I to be disquieted, grieved, yea, to sorrow that such a guest as sin lodgeth in me and with me; even as an ingenuous and honest-hearted debtor is to rejoice and be glad in the goodness and grace of his gracious surety, who hath paid his debt, and never to fear that the law or justice can go against him, to arrest and imprison him for that debt, which is now completely paid by his surety. But if the surety gave his back-bond to pay him service of love, and service of sorrow and remorse, for his injustice and sinful lavishing of his neighbour's goods, which did necessitate his loving surety to hurt himself, and be at a great loss for him; he owes to his surety the debt of love, and disquietness of spirit, in so far as the blot of his wastery, and the shame of his riotous youth, lieth on him all his days. Antinomians conceive, that there ought to be no disquietness of spirit, no remorse, no trouble of mind, but that which hath its rise and spring from sins apprehended as not pardoned, and from the fear of eternal punishment to be inflicted for these sins: and it is true, that such a troubled and perplexed soul, which is once in the state of justification, is but the issue and brood of unbelief, and ariseth from the flesh prevailing over the spirit in such sorrow: Yea, or if confession of sin arise from this spring of servile and slavish fear, it is not a work of faith, except that a conditional fear of eternal wrath, if a David fallen in adultery and treacherous murder, or a Peter overtaken with a denying of his Saviour before men, shall not renew his repentance: and faith in Christ is required in all the justified, for the perfecting of their salvation, and final perseverance. But there is another remorse and sorrow, according to God, required in all the justified, and it is this; that though they are not to fear condemnation with a legal fear, so as to distrust God, and be afraid of eternal wrath, yet he who is ransomed by Christ, though he can never recompense the free grace, nor pay a satisfactory ransom for so great and rich a love, he is under a back-bond, or a re-obligation of love, service, and obedience to him that ransomed him. And this law of love and thankfulness is not, as libertines and others conceive, a positive and simply supernatural gospel-obligation; for the law of both nature and nations requires, that the captive be thankful to the ransom payer.

I grant that the particular commandments are positive and supernatural; so the justified is obliged by this back-bond and gospel re-obligation to confess sin dwelling in him, to groan, and sigh, and sorrow under it—to be troubled and grieved in spirit, for sin as sin dwelling in his members, and rebelling against the law of his mind, and keeping him in bondage; to walk humbly and softly all his days, by reason of the running issue of sin, and to strive by all means to walk worthy of Christ. And this in the general, is the law of nature, from which Christ hath in no sort exempted us, (Matt., vii, 12; 1 Cor., xi, 14; Eph., v, 28, 29). Now, as a man having fallen from a high place upon a rock, and hath broken bones of thighs and legs; though he be cured, and can walk abroad, yet all his days he halteth in his walking: or like one that is cured of an extreme fever-tertian, at such and such seasons some fit of the disease recurreth, yet is he not to doubt of the fidelity and love of the chirurgeon and physician, who hath really cured him, in so far as he is in capacity in this life to be cured;—and, therefore, as he is to walk warily, and with circumspection all his days, caring for his crazed body, so is he to be thankful to those who recovered him; and may be sad and heavy now and then, that by his own folly and temerity he hurt his body. For even sins pardoned, as concerning their eternal guilt, by our sovereign physician Christ, in justification, lay a law on us to serve our physician, Christ, in these positive commandments of obedience, love, sorrow, softness of spirit, with a care to sin no more, though we must needs halt and slip all our days; yet not so to sorrow, as to call in doubt the reality of pardoning grace.

SERMON XX.

YEA, the law from the highest bended love, even from love with all the whole soul, and all its strength, (Matt., xxii,) forbiddeth all sin, no less than the gospel of love, which gospel doth spiritualise the law to the believer, but not abolish it. The gospel addeth a new argument of gospel love: because Christ hath died for me, therefore I will keep that same law of God I was under before; only, now, I fear not actual condemnation, which is accidental to the law, for Christ and the confirmed angels keep the law, as a rule of life, yet without any fear of actual condemnation. Nor doth the gospel more make David's adultery not to be against the Seventh Commandment to David, than it maketh the Israelites' spoiling of the Egyptians of their ear-rings and jewels, to be no breach of the Eighth Commandment. The grace of Christ doth privilege the believer from condemnation, which condemnation is a mere accident, which doth go and come without hurting the essence of the law, and its commanding and eternal moral-directing power. The law saith, Do and live; there is no exception of this —it is the will of God eternal, as God is eternal, and obligeth us in heaven, and for ever, (Rev., xxii, 5). But this, 'if you do not, you shall die,' hath a large exception; Christ my Son shall die for you; and this, 'if you keep not the law, you are condemned,' to the believer is abolished. And when we are (Rom., vii,) said to be freed from our first husband, as the woman is freed by law from her dead husband, and may, without sin, marry another, and we not under the law; the word (law) is taken only for the law, as given to the sinner. Now, the law should have been law, though sin had never been, and is law to the elect angels, who never sinned; and that is only the law, under the notion of that sad office of eternal condemnation. The law could never have been law, except it had promised eternal life to those who do the law. But it both is, and should have been law to believers in Jesus Christ, to the elect angels, and yet it doth not, it cannot actually condemn them.

But that the gospel maketh adultery to be no sin to believers, is a blasphemous assertion. Then commit adultery, murder, whore, steal; O believer! these are not sins to thee,—but Christ's sins, not thine. Oh, turn not the grace of God into wantonness! The believer hath no conscience of sins; that is, he in conscience is not to fear everlasting condemnation;—that is most true, because Christ hath delivered him from that wrath to come, (Rom., viii, 1; John, v, 24). Faith of eternal life by Jesus Christ, cannot consist with fear of eternal condemnation; for then, with a legal and an evangelic faith, one person should be obliged to believe things contradictory, and yet, both faiths oblige us to give credence and assent. But that the believer hath no conscience of sin, that is, that he is to believe there is nothing in him that is sin, is to believe a lie, (1 John, i, 8, 9). That he is to confess no sin, and to be grieved in conscience for no sin, and to sorrow for no sin; that he is to be wearied and laden with no sin,—that he is to groan under the burden of no sin, as failing against the love of him that gave a ransom for him,—this is a blasphemous easiness of conscience, yea, of a conscience past feeling. Beloved in the Lord, the gospel forbiddeth sorrow, fear, and agony of conscience, in a believer apprehending eternal wrath; such a one once truly believing in Christ as the Saviour of sinners, and his Saviour, and now believing the contrary, must believe that his Lord is really changed, that he hath forgotten to be merciful, that he hath falsified and altered his covenant, oath, and promise; this were to make God a liar. But the gospel forbiddeth not, but commandeth, that the justified person sorrow for sin; yea, it commandeth carefulness to forbear clearing of the offender, as being in Christ, and desiring to flee to Christ; indignation against himself, in not forgiving himself, fear of offending love and law in Christ, vehement desire to have peace confirmed, zeal for God, revenge to afflict the soul. (2 Cor., vii, 10, 11.) And in this sense it is blasphemy to say, that the gospel taketh away all conscience of sin. Believers humbled for sin, are to be taken off all law-thoughts and fear of eternal condemnation, and all thoughts that sorrow is a penance, and satisfactory to offended justice, as we are ready to conceit of our evangelic rejoicing, and holiest works. But they are to sorrow for offended love, for the body of sin breaking out in scandals. I may then have peace with God, in the assurance of remission and removal of eternal wrath, and yet not peace with my own conscience, 1. Because I may be persuaded, that God in Christ hath forgiven me; yet am I not to forgive myself. 2. I am to believe, that in Christ I am delivered from eternal wrath, and justified in Christ; and yet, to sorrow that I have sinned against Christ's love. 3. I may have peace, sense of peace, and pardon in Christ; and yet a necessary unquietness, sorrow, and tears, that I should have been so unthankful to so lovely a Redeemer. So Christ doth commend the woman's tears, as a sign of love, and of the sense of many sins pardoned, "Thou gavest me no water for my feet;" but "she hath washed my feet with tears." (Luke, vii, 44.) Yet many sins were forgiven her, (verse 47).

Hence, I may, First, believe the remission of that sin for which I am to sorrow, and for the remission of which I am to pray, and which I am to confess. Nathan said to David, "Thy sin is pardoned:" yet the Spirit of God, after that, both confessed, sorrowed, prayed for pardon in David. 2. We may comfort those that mourn for sin, from assurance of pardon, and yet exhort them to be humbled and afflicted in spirit, and to confess, sorrow, and pray for pardon: So Antinomians, rejoicing evermore after justification, without sorrow, remorse, down-casting for sin at all, is but fleshly wantonness. I may have, and ought to have, a disquieted spirit, and no peace with myself, and yet peace with God, even as the sea after a storm, and when the winds are gone, and the air is calmed, hath yet a raging and a great motion, by reason of wind enclosed in the bowels of the sea; and after the cool of a mighty fever, yet are the humours in the body stirred and distempered.

1. But we are hence led to find out resolution for divers cases of consciences after justification. 1. Many dare not question their state of justification, and so are freed from the storms of apprehended wrath, arising from the guilt of sin. Yet there is another storm within the bowels of the sea, arising from the indwelling of the body of guilt. The storm before justification is less free, less ingenuous, more servile, as looking to that eternal wrath hanging over the soul for unpardoned sin: this is more free, and is a peaceable, a

gracious, and heavenly storm raised, not for sin unpardoned, and the eternal punishment thereof, but for sin as sin, as indwelling; not for the penal guilt and the sting of hell, in sin, but for the sinful guilt and the wounding of Christ. 2. It is impossible this latter storm can be in the soul, till the sentence of justification be pronounced; as none can have the moved bowels of a son for the offence of a father, till he be a son.

2. Another case is, that many have an absolute, loose, and lax peace and calmness, great confidence of deliverance from eternal wrath, and so, of a supposed pardon, whose peace is convinced to be but a base outside, and mere painting and gilding, because there is in them no storm for sin as sin, and for the over-motions of boiling lusts; no tenderness to walk spiritually. A faith that eateth out the bottom and bowels of conscience, of declining sin, and walking with God, is the justification of the Antinomians, of the old Gnostics, of the natural men: all our professors are cured, none, or few, are healed.

3. Full assurance that Christ hath delivered Paul from condemnation, yea, so full and real, as produceth thanksgiving and triumphing in Christ, (Rom., vii, 25, viii, 1, 2,) may and doth consist with complaints and outcries of a wretched condition for the indwelling of the body of sin, (Rom., vii, 14–16, 23, 24). Then the justified, that are whole, not sick, not pained, are yet in their sins, and not justified, whatever Antinomians say on the contrary.

4. The flesh in the justified cannot complain of indwelling sin; but the flesh, mixed with some life of Christ, may raise a false alarm of sins not pardoned, which are really pardoned. Some false grief may,

and often hath, its rise from a false and imaginary ground; as a sanctified soul may praise God, through occasion of a lying report of the victory of the church, when there is no such matter. A sanctified child may spiritually mourn for the supposed death of his father, or that he hath offended his father according to the flesh, when his father is neither dead, nor offended at all. So, gracious affections, as gracious, may work spiritually upon supposed and false grounds, when there is no cause,—as, that the soul hath grieved his heavenly Father, and that he is displeased, when it is not so.

5. Sin indwelling is a greater evil, than the feared evil of ten hells; and, therefore, there is more cause of sorrow for sin, confession, unquietness of spirit after justification, than before; because sin, the only true object of fear and disquietude of spirit, is both a guest dwelling in the soul, and is more really and distinctly apprehended as a spiritual evil, after the light of faith hath shown us the sinfulness of sin, than ever it was discovered to be before.

6. I doubt, if justified souls are to be refuted in their complaints and fears, for the indwelling of sin, providing they fear not eternal wrath: which fear is contrary to faith; and so they fear not, and sorrow not, for that God hath changed the court, and the wind of his love turned in the contrary air, and he hath forgotten to be merciful.

7. Faith chargeth us to believe that grace shall, at length, finally subdue sin. And, as boatmen labour with oars, to promote their course in sailing, even when wind, sails, and tide are doing somewhat to promote the course; so doth faith, which purifieth the heart, set the soul on work "to perfect holiness in the fear of

God," and believeth also, that God shall work both to will and to do.

It is not then good physic for many exercised in conscience, especially after their first conversion, to apply only the honey and sweetness of consolations of the gospel, as if there were not any need of humiliation, and sorrow for sin. Yet it is to be cleared, that, 1. Sorrow for sin, is no satisfaction for sin; for the pride of merit is crafty, and can creep in at a small hole. We think there is no repentance where there be no tears; and God of purpose withholdeth tears, as knowing, when water goes out, wind cometh in. 2. They are tenderly to be bound up and comforted, in whom sin riseth up with a witness. Oh, what pity and humble on-looking should be here! For a hell of pain in the body is nothing; wheels, racks, whips, hot-irons, breaking of bones is nothing; but half a hell in the spirit, is a whole hell. The upper hell, the grave, to Hezekiah, is like to swallow him up, when dipped in the lower hell, and covered with the apprehension of wrath. O sweet Jesus! what a mercy that thou swallowed up all hells to believers, and calmed the sea of hell.

Use 1. If in justification, sins be blotted out, cast in the depths of the sea, and removed, as if they never had been, the state of justification must be a condition of sound blessedness, the most desirable life in the world, even as David also described the blessedness of the man unto whom God imputeth righteousness without works. "Blessed are they whose iniquities are forgiven, and whose sins are covered." (Rom., iv, 6, 7.) For, consider, 1. What an act of grace it is in a prince, to take a condemned malefactor from under the axe, the rack, the wheel, and so many hours' torture, before he end his miserable life. Or, 2. Suppose he were condemned to be tortured leisurely, and his life continued and prorogated, that bones, sinews, lungs, joints, might be pained for twenty or thirty years, so much of his flesh cut off every day, such a bone broken, and by art the bone cured again, and the flesh restored, that he might, for thirty years' space, every day be dying, and yet never die. Or, 3. Imagine a man could be kept alive in torment in this case, from sleep, ease, food, clothing, five hundred years, or a thousand years, and boiling all the time in a cauldron full of melted lead; and say the soul could dwell in a body under the rack, the wheel, the lashes and scourges of scorpions, and whips of iron, the man bleeding, crying, in the act of dying for pain, gnawing his tongue for ten hundred years: Now, suppose a mighty prince, by an act of free grace, could and would deliver this man from all this pain and torture, and give him a life in perfect health, in ten hundred paradises of joy, pleasure, worldly happiness, and a day all the thousand years without a night, a summer all this time, without cloud, storm, winter; all the honour, acclamations, love, and service of a world of men and angels,—clothe this man with all the most complete delights, perfections, and virtues of mind and body—set him ten thousand degrees of elevation, to the top of all imaginable happiness, above Solomon in his highest royalty, or Adam in his first innocency, or angels in their most transcendent glory and happiness: —Yea, 4. In our conception, we may extend the former misery and pain, and all this happiness, to the length of ten thousand years;—this should be thought incomparably the highest act of grace and love that any creature could extend to his fellow-creature. And yet, all this were but a shadow of grace, in comparison of the love and rich grace of God in Christ, in the justification of a sinner.

Consider we are freed from the guilt of sin in justification. Now, this is the eternal debt of sin, that remaineth after sin, that none can wash away but Christ, and that this remaineth after sin is acted. 2. That it remaineth for eternity. 3. That it is a misery we are only in justification delivered from, is clear in Scripture, 1. Because sin is a debt: After the borrowed money is spent and gone, somewhat in law and justice remaineth, and this is debt or obligation to make payment to the creditor. So the Scripture speaketh, "For though thou wash thee with nitre, and take thee much soap, yet thy iniquity is marked before me." (Jer., ii, 22.) *Borith* is an herb that fullers use for washing and purging; yet is sin such a leopard-spot, that no art, no industry of the creature can remove it: "the sin of Judah is written with a pen of iron, and the point of a diamond; it is graven upon the table of their heart, and the horns of your altars." (Jer., xvii, 1.) There is writ remaining after sin is acted. 2. Writ written with a pen of iron and diamond, to endure for eternity. 3. Not written only, but engraved, and indented upon the conscience. When David rent the robe of Saul, his heart smote him, so that it left a hole, or the mark of the stripe behind it; (1 Sam., xxiv, 5;) as when a burning iron is put on the face of an evil-doer, it leaveth behind it a brand, or a stigma. This is terrible, that this brand is eternal; as the prophet prayeth, "Let the iniquities of his fathers be remembered with the Lord; and let not the sin of his mother be blotted out; let them be before the Lord continually." (Psal.

cix, 14, 15.) O dreadful! The sins of wicked men shall stand up in heaven before the justice of God, so long as God shall live, and that is for ever and ever. So the Lord sweareth by the excellency of Jacob, that is, by himself, "Surely, I will never forget any of their works." (Amos, viii, 7.) All that ever came before me, all that came not in by me, the door and the way, they are thieves and robbers. (John, x, 8.) The false prophets, many of them, were dead, yet being dead (saith Christ) this day they are, in regard of guilt, thieves and robbers. To this day, above sixteen hundred years, the Jews are guilty murderers, though their fathers, who slew the Lord of glory, be dead. This day, Cain is a murderer, Judas a traitor, and shall be, so long as God shall live and be God. Now, without shedding of Christ's blood, there is no remission of sins, (Heb., ix, 22). To be delivered from eternal debt, and entitled to an eternal kingdom, is a life most desirable, and maketh the sinner to stand in the books of Christ, as the eternally engaged debtor of grace. Young heirs, know your blessedness aright. Sinners under eternal debt; you laugh, sport, rejoice; and you are firebrands of wrath. You go singing, and shaking and tinkling your bolts and fetters of black and unmixed vengeance. Alas! how can you sleep? How can you laugh and sing?

"*Eat the crumbs.*" The dogs desire but the least, and (to speak so) the refuse of Christ. The meanest and worst things of Christ (to speak so) are incomparably to be desired above all things. 1. Any thing of Christ is desirable; but to lay hold on the skirt of a Jew, (Zech., x, 23,) because Christ that is with him is good—yea, the dust of Zion is a thing that the servants of God take pleasure in, (Psal. cii, 14). The dust and stones of Zion are not like the earth; and the mules[1] of the holy grave, as papists fondly dream, and are but earth, but because the Lord Christ dwelleth there, therefore are they desirable. The people carried their old harps to Babylon with them, and Joseph's bones must be carried out of Egypt to Canaan. Why? Canaan was Christ's land, his dwelling. Why? but we are to love the ground which Christ's feet treadeth on. This I say, not that I judge it holy earth—that is Popish superstition—but that such is Christ's excellency, that any thing that hath the poorest relation to him, is desirable for him. 2. A poor woman, sought no more of him, but to wash the feet of Christ, and kiss them. (Luke, vii.) Another woman, "If I may but touch the border of his garment, I shall be whole." (Matt., ix, 21.) Mary Magdalene sought but to have her arms filled with his dead body. She saith, weeping, to the gardener, as she supposed, "Sir, if thou hast borne him hence, tell me where thou hast laid him, and I will take him away." (John, xx, 15.) To Joseph of Arimathea, his bloody winding sheet, and his dead, and holed, and torn body in his arms, are sweet. Christ's clay is silver, and his brass gold. 3. Christ's sharpest rebukes are sweet oil; the wounds and the holes that the sweet Mediator maketh in the soul, when he smiteth with the rod of his mouth, are with child of comforts; he rebuked not the serpent, as not minding salvation to Satan, but rebuked Eve, intending the promised seed for her. Oh, what sweetness of love is that expression, "For since I spake against Ephraim, I do earnestly remember him; I will surely have mercy on him, saith the Lord." (Jer., xxxi, 20.) Then rebuking of Ephraim, which is called speaking against him, is dipped in mercy. "My people

[1] Clods of a grave.

are bent to backsliding;" this is a rebuke sharp enough Yet He chides himself friends with the people, "How shall I give thee up, O Ephraim; mine heart is turned within me." (Hosea, xi, 7, 8.) Here is kissing, and love wrapped about rebukes. So Jer., iii, 1. "Thou hast played the harlot with many lovers:" but see mercy: "Yet return to me, saith the Lord." 4. His black and sour cross is sweet, and honeyed with comfort; his dead body a bundle of myrrh, (Cant., i, 13,) the smell of which is strong and fragrant, and sweateth out precious gum, rejoicing in tribulations. Count it joy, all joy, when you fall into divers temptations, (James, i, 2). The eagles smell heaven in the cross, and Christ in it; yea, the refuse, and the worst of Christ's cross, the shame and the reproaches of Christ, are sweeter and more choice to Moses, than the treasures, riches, yea, than the kingdom of Egypt, and the glory of it, (Heb., xi, 26, 27,)—yea, the shame and blushing on Christ's fair face, which he suffered under the cross, is fairer than rubies and gold, and hath the colour of the heaven of heavens. (Heb., xii, 2.) Nebuchadnezzar hath more pain and torment in persecuting, than the three children had in being persecuted. (Dan., iv, 19.) There is pain and fury in active persecution: "He was full of fury, and the form of his visage changed;" but there is joy unspeakable, and glorious, in passive persecution. Christ's sanctified cross droppeth honey; Christ's gloomings, and sad desertions, though to the believer they be death and hell, yet have much of heaven in them. So, Psalm xxx, 7, "Thou turnedst away thy face, and I was troubled;" (*Niuhal*) I was troubled like a withered flower, that loseth sap and vigour; (so, Exod., xv, 15, "The dukes of Edom (*Niuhaln*) were amazed;") yet at that time David prayed, cried, and was heard. (ver. 8–10.)

The sweetest communion that Christ seeketh of us on earth is prayer, (Cant., ii, 14, and Cant., v). Desertion is death itself, and a death to the soul: "I opened to my beloved, and my beloved had withdrawn himself, and was gone." And what was the Church's case? "My soul went forth from me." The Arabic, "My soul departed, I died;" so is death described by the like phrase, (Gen., xxxv, 18,) Rachel's soul was in departing, for she died: And when men are stricken with sudden fear, the heart is said to go out: So, (Gen., xlii, 28,) the soul of Joseph's brethren departed, that is, they were extremely amazed, when they found their money in their sacks. The like was the case of the Church when Christ departed, she died for sorrow, the soul departed from the soul, because her Lord and beloved was gone. Yet even that death, that soul-hell in the want of Christ was a heaven, it was a sweet and a comfortable season; then hath she a communion with him in a most heavenly manner, 1. Asking at the watchman for him. 2. In binding sad charges on the daughters of Jerusalem, to commend her to God by prayer. 3. Then was she sick of love for him. 4. Then fell she out in that large love-rapture, in a most heavenly praise of him in all his virtues, "My well-beloved is white and ruddy, and the chief amongst ten thousand." Here, then, the hell that Christ throweth the saints in, in their desertions, is their heaven.

The meanest and lowest relation with Christ is honour. John Baptist placeth an honour in unloosing the latchets of his shoes, and thinketh, to bear his shoes is more honour than he deserveth, (John, i, 27). David, a great prophet, appointed to be a king: Oh, if I might be so near the Lord, as to be a door-keeper in his house, (Psal. lxxxiv, 10). He putteth a happiness on the sparrow and the swallow, that may build their nests beside the Lord's altar. Then the fragments and crumbs that his dogs eat, must be the dainties of heaven, and Christ's water the wine of heaven. Now, if any, the lowest thing of Christ, the morsel of his dogs, be desirable, how sweet must himself be? If the parings of his bread be sweet, what must the great loaf, Christ himself, be? Christ himself is so taking a lover, he hath a face that would ravish love out of devils, so they had grace to see his beauty; he could lead captive all hearts in hell with the loveliness of his countenance, which is white and ruddy, and pleasant as Lebanon, if they had eyes to behold him. Oh, he himself is an unknown lover; he hath neither brim nor bottom; his gospel is the unsearchable riches of Christ. His gospel is but a creature; how unsearchable must he himself be? The wise man, putteth a riddle upon all the wisest on the earth, Solomon and all: What is his name? We know neither name nor thing; (Prov., xxx, 4). "Who shall preach his generation?" (Isa., liii, 8.) Oh, what a mercy, that he will give sinners leave to love him! Or honour us so much, that we may lay our black and spotted love, on so lovely and fair a Saviour! That such an infinite and desirable love as Christ's love, should come (to borrow that expression,) within the sides of thy love and heart, is a wonder. Alas, it is a narrow circle, and not capacious to contain him and his love, that passeth knowledge, (Eph., iii, 19); it overpasseth and transcendeth far the narrow comprehension of created knowledge, either of men or angels.

To seek grace is desirable: but suppose any person were a mass, and nothing but composed of pure grace, and yet want Christ himself, he should be but a broken lamed creature. Put a soul in heaven, and let him be hated of Christ (if that were possible), heaven should be hell. Imagine devils were standing with their black chains of darkness, even up in the heaven of heavens, and the plague of being hated of Christ on their soul, and that they could see Him that sitteth on the throne, and somewhat of the rays and beams of that fulness of God that is in Christ; yet should devils still be devils, they wanting Christ, the heaven of angels and glorified men. What a flower! what a rose of love and light must Christ be, who filleth with smell, light, beauty, the four sides, east and west, south and north, of the heaven of heavens, and his glory! Suppose in the hour of our last farewell to time, all creatures void of reason, heavens, stars, light, air, earth, sea, dry land, birds, fishes, beasts, were in a capacity to love us, and they, with men and angels, should let out upon us the fulness, yea the sea of all their love (as it is a sweet thing to be lovely and desirable to many), yet this were nothing to him who is all desires or all loves, (Cant., v, 16).[1] He is a mass of love, and love itself; lovely in the womb, the Ancient of Days became young for me; lovely in the cross, even when despised and numbered with thieves; lovely in the grave, lovely at the right hand of God, lovely in his second appearance in glory: yea, all desirable, his countenance white and ruddy; his head a golden head; (Cant., vi, 10, 11;) his headship and government desirable; his locks bushy and black; his counsels deep, various, unsearchable; his eyes as doves, chaste, pure, and can behold no iniquity; his cheeks,

[1] So Vatablus rendereth it, *Christus est totus desideria.—Rutherford.*

or two sides of his face, as a bed of spices and sweet smelling flowers; his face manly, comely as Lebanon; his lips like lilies, dropping sweet smelling myrrh; his gospel smelleth of heaven: his hands pure, his works holy, fair, as gold rings set with beryl: his belly, or breast and bowels, as bright ivory overlaid with sapphires—that is, his breast and belly, that containeth his bowels, his heart and affections, are as ivory, bright and glorious; and as ivory overlaid, covered, and adorned with sapphires, that are precious stones of a sea-blue and heavenly colour, because his bowels and inward affections are full of love, tenderness of mercy, and the compassion of his heart most heavenly: his legs are pillars of marble, set upon sockets of fine gold; his ways and government like marble pillars, upright, white, pure, and set on gold, solid, firm, stable, that Christ cannot slip or fall; his sceptre, a sceptre of righteousness, and his kingdom eternal, and cannot be shaken: his countenance as the mountain Lebanon, his person eminent, goodly, high, great, tall, fruitful as cedars: his mouth most sweet, his words and testimonies as honey, or the honey-comb. Yea, all creatures are weak, and Christ strong; all base, he precious; all empty, he full; all black, he fair; all foolish and vain, he wise, and the only counsellor, deep in his counsels and ways. The special evangelic sin that we are guilty of is unbelief, (John, xvi, 9,) and this floweth from a low estimation we have of Christ; and therefore these considerations are to be weighed in our estimation of Christ.

1. The wisdom or folly of any man is most seen in the estimative faculty, for it denominateth a man wise. Many are great judges, and learned, as the magicians of Chaldea, and philosophers, who know wonders

hidden things, and causes of things, and yet are not wise, but fools. (Rom., i, 21,) and vain in their imaginations, because there is a great defect in their estimative faculty in the choice of a God, (ver. 22, 23) The practical mind is blinded, and they choose darkness for light, evil for good, a creature for their God. "By faith Moses, when he was come to age, refused to be called the son of Pharaoh's daughter; and chose rather to suffer affliction with the people of God, than to enjoy the pleasures of sin for a season." (Heb., xi, 25.) And how is his faith made faith? And how is it evident, that he was not a raw, ignorant, and foolish child, when he made the choice; but a man ripe, come to years, and so, as wise as he was old? It is proved, because his estimative faculty was right, "Esteeming the reproach of Christ greater riches, than the treasures of Egypt." He is a wise man who maketh a wise choice, and for this cause, Esau is called a profane man; (Heb., xii, 26;) he had not wisdom to put a difference between the excellency of the birthright, and a morsel of meat. A profane wicked man hath not wisdom to esteem God and Christ above the creature, but confoundeth the one with the other.

2. Our esteem of Christ is to be pure, chaste, spiritual, and so to work purely; that is, the formal reason why we esteem of Christ, must be, because he is Christ, and not because summer goeth with Christ; nay, not because he comforteth, but because he is God, the Redeemer and Mediator. It is a chaste love, and a chaste esteem, if the wife choose to love her husband, because he is her husband, as the sense esteemeth white to be white, under the notion of such a colour. The operation of every faculty is most pure, and kindly, when it is carried toward its object, according to its formal

reason, without any mixture of other respects; extraneous and by-reasons are more whorish, less connatural, not so chaste: there is some wax in our honey, and this we should take heed unto; the elective power is a tender piece of the soul.

3. Estimation produceth love, even the love of Christ; and love is a great favourite, and is much at court, and dwelleth constantly with the king. To be much with Christ, especially in secret, late and early, and to give much time to converse with Christ, speaketh much love; and the love of Christ is of the same largeness and quantity with grace, for grace and love keep proportion one with another.

4. He who duly esteemeth Christ, is a noble bidder, and so a noble and liberal buyer. He out-biddeth Esau; what is pottage to Christ? he over-biddeth Judas; what is silver to Christ? Yea, *all things*, is the greatest count can be cast up; for it includeth all prices, all sums; it taketh in heaven, as it is a created thing. Then, all things, the vast and huge globe and circle of the capacious world, and all excellencies within its bosom or belly; nations, all nations; angels, all angels; gold, all gold; jewels, all jewels; honour and delights, all honour, all delights, and every *all* beside, lieth before Christ, as feathers, dung, shadows, nothing. To wash a sinner, is the eminency of love, and the highest esteem of him: but, oh, what a mercy, that Christ should defile his precious, sinless, royal, and princely blood, by dipping in such a loathsome, foul, and deformed creature as a sinner is, (Rev., i, 5).

"*Dogs eat the crumbs.*" Here be degrees of persons and things in our Father's house, children and dogs; yet dogs which the lord of the house owneth. Here is a high table and bread; and a by-board, or an after-table, and crumbs for dogs. Here be persons of honour, kings' sons clothed in scarlet, and sitting with the king at dinner, when his spikenard sendeth forth a smell; and here be some under the table, at the feet of Christ, waiting to receive the little drops of the great honey-comb of rich grace that falleth from him. Follow Christ, and grace shall fall from him; his steps drop fatness, especially in his palace. There be in our Lord's house little children, babes; there be in it also experienced ancient fathers (for grace hath grey hairs for wisdom, not for weakness); there be strong men also. (1 John, ii, 12–14). Christ was once a little stone, but he grew a great mountain that filled the whole earth, yea, and the heaven too: Christ is a growing hild. In Christ's lower firmament, there be stars of the first and second magnitude; and in his house, vessels of great and of small quantity, cups and flagons, (Isa., xxii, 24,) yet all are fastened upon the golden nail, Jesus Christ. 2. All are in the way, the plants all growing; but one is a grain of mustard seed, and a rose not broken out to the flower, and another is a great tree. It is morning, and but the glimmering of the rays of the day-star in one; and it is high sun, perfect day, near the noon-day with another. Strong father Abraham, mighty in believing, was once a babe on the breasts, that could neither creep, nor stand, nor walk. The love of Christ in its first rise, is a drop of dew that came out of the womb of the morning; the mother, in one night, brought forth an host, and innumerable millions of such babes, and covered the face of the earth with them. But this drop of dew groweth to a sea that swelleth up above hell and the grave, (Cant., viii, 6, 7); it is more than all the floods and seas of the earth, and floateth up to the heaven of heavens, and up, and in, it must be upon Christ. Ye see not Christ, yet ye love him, (1 Pet., i, 8). It overfloweth Christ, and taketh him, and ravisheth his heart. It is a strong chain that bindeth Christ, when the grave, sin, death, devils, could not bind him, (Cant., iv, 9; Acts, ii, 24). 3. Christ's way of administration is a growing way; his kingdom is not a standing, nor a sitting, nor a sleeping kingdom, but it is walking and posting: "Thy kingdom come:" An increasing kingdom, a growing peace, "Of the increase of his government and peace there shall be no end," (Isaiah, ix, 7). In regard of duration, even in heaven, there shall be a growing of his kingdom. There is not yesterday, and to-morrow, and the next year, in heaven; yet there is a negative increase; glory and peace shall ascend in continuance, and never come to an height, the sun never decline; the long day of Christ's glory and peace shall never end. Christ is saying even now, 'Father, I must have all my children up with me, that where I am, there they may be also.' And therefore the Head draws up to him now a finger, then a toe; now an arm, then a leg; he hath been these sixteen hundred years since his ascension, drawing up by death, whole churches, the saints at Corinth, at Rome, at Philippi. The seven candlesticks, and the seven stars of Asia, are long ago up above Orion and the seven stars; and are now shining up before the throne. This consecrated Captain of our salvation will not sleep, till his Father's house be filled; till all the numerous offspring, and the generations of the first-born, be up under one roof with their Father. Heaven is a growing family, the Lord of the house hath been gathering his flocks into the fair fields of the land of praises, ever since the first Abel died; and down all along, the believers were gathered to their fathers.

USE 1. Is, that we despise not the day of small things. God's beginning of great works is small. What could be said of a poor woman's throwing of a stool at the man who did first read the new service book in Edinburgh? It was not looked at as any eminent passage of divine providence; yet it grew, till it came up to armies of men, the shaking of three kingdoms, the sound of the trumpet, the voice of the alarm, the lifting up of the Lord's standard, destruction upon destruction, garments rolled in blood;—and goeth on in strength, that the vengeance of the Lord, and the vengeance of his temple, may pursue the land of graven images, and awake the kings of the earth to rise in battle against the great whore of Babylon, that the Jews may return to their Messiah, and Israel and Judah ask the way to Zion, with their faces thitherward, weeping as they go; that the forces of the Gentiles, and the kingdoms of the world, may become the kingdoms of God and of his Son Jesus Christ. And this act of a despised woman, was one of the first steps of Omnipotency; God then began to open the mouth of the vial of his wrath, to let out a little drop of vengeance upon the seat of the Beast; and ever since, the right arm of the Lord awaking, hath been in action, and in a growing battle against all that worshipped the Beast, and received his mark on their right hand, and their forehead. And who knoweth but Christ is in the act of conquering, to create a new thing on the earth, and subdue the people to himself? Omnipotency can derive a sea, a world of noble and glorious works, from as small a fountain as a straw, a ram-horn, yea, jaw-bone of a dead ass. God can put forth omnipotency in all its flowers and golden branches of overpowering and incomparable excellencies, upon mere nothing: the wind is an empty unsolid thing, the sea a fluid and soft and ebbing creature; yet the wind is God's chariot, he rideth on it; and the sea his walk, his paths are in the great waters.

USE 2. A crumb that falleth from Christ's table, hath in it the nature of bread. Some weak ones complain, Oh, I have not the heart of God, like David, nor the strong faith of Abraham, to offer my son to death for Christ; nor the burning fire of the zeal of Moses, to wish my name may be razed out of the book of life, that the Lord may be glorified; nor the high esteem of Christ, to judge all but loss and dung for Jesus Christ, as Paul did. But what if Christ set the whole loaf before the children? Is it not well, if thou lie but under Christ's feet, to have the crumbs of mercy that slip through the fingers of Christ? The lowest room in heaven, even behind the door, is heaven. 1. There is the lowest measure, or grain of saving grace, and it is saving grace; a drop of dew is water, no less than the great globe and sphere of the whole element of water, is water; a glimmering of morn-dawning light is light, and of the same nature with the noon-light that is in the great body of the sun: the motion of a child newly formed in the belly, is an act of life, no less than the walking and breathing of a man of thirty years of age, in his flower and highest vigour of life; the first stirrings of the new birth, are the workings and operations of the Holy Ghost; and the love of God, even now shed abroad in our hearts by the Holy Ghost, shall remain the same in nature with us in heaven, (1 Cor., xiii, 8–10). 2. Christ doth own the bruised reed, and the smoking flax, so far forth, as not to crush the one, nor to quench the other; and can with tender cautiousness of compassion, stoop, and with his arm go between the lamb on the margin and brink of hell, as to save it from falling down headlong over the brow of the mountain. He "healeth the broken in heart," (Psal. cxlvii, 3,) and as a surgeon (so Vatablus expoundeth it) "bindeth up their wounds," and putteth the broken bones in their native place again. And whereas young ones are easily affrighted, yea, and distracted with fear, when sudden cries and hideous war-shouts surprise them, Christ affrighteth not weak consciences with shouts, to put poor tender souls out of their wits with the shouts of armies, of the terrors of hell in the conscience; yea, the meek Lord Jesus "shall not cry nor lift up (a shout) nor cause his voice be heard in the street," (Isaiah, xlii, 2). Oh, what bowels! what stirrings, and boilings, and wrestlings of a pained heart touched with sorrow, are in Christ Jesus! When he saw the people scattered as sheep having no shepherd, he was bowelled in heart, his bowels were moved with compassion for them, (Matt., ix, 36). Oh, how sweet! that thy sinful weakness should be sorrow and pain to the bowels and heart of Jesus Christ, so as infirmity is your sin, and Christ's pity and compassion. Can the father see the child sweat, wrestle under an over-load till his back be near broken, and he cry, "I am gone," and his bowels not be moved to pity, and his hands not stretched out to help? Were not the bowels and heart of that mother made of a piece of the nether mill-stone; had she not sucked the milk and breast of a tiger, and seemed rather to be the whelp of a lion, than a woman, who should see her young child drowned, and wrestling with the water, and crying for her help, and yet she should not stir, nor be moved in heart, nor run to help? This is but a shadow of the compassion that is in that heart dwelling in a body personally united to the blessed Godhead in Jesus Christ.

We should have tender hearts toward weak ones; considering, 1. That Christ cannot disinherit a son for weakness. 2. Love is not broken with a straw, or a little infirmity. 3. All the vessels of Christ's house are not of one size. 4. Some men's infirmities are as transparent crystal, easily seen through; others have infirmities under their garments. 5. We shall see many in heaven, whom we judged to be cast-aways, while they lived with us on earth. 6. Many go to heaven with you, and you hear not the sound of their feet in their journey.

SERMON XXI.

"*Then Jesus answered, and said unto her, O woman, great is thy faith,*" etc.

THIS is the last passage of the text, containing a commendation of the woman, given to her by Christ in her face. 2. An answer according to her desire. 3. The effect of her praying with instancy and pressing importunity of faith. The devil is cast out of her daughter.

Christ acknowledgeth here, that instancy of praying in faith, will overcome God, and Satan, and all the saddest temptations that can befall the child of God. Hence, observe what acts of efficacious power instant and earnest prayer putteth forth upon God, and how the clay-creature doth work upon, and prevail with the great Potter and former of all things.

1. Prayer is a messenger, and a swift and winged post despatched up to court. David sent away this post early in the morning, with morning wings: "My voice shalt thou hear in the morning." (Psal. v, 3.) The post is himself, for the word is, I will address my person, as in battle array. "Set thyself in order before me, (and) stand up," saith Elihu to Job; or, I will address my words, (Job, xxxiii, 5). "Now he hath not directed his words against me." (Job, xxxii, 14.) The seventy render it *purastesomai soi;* and David sent himself to heaven, not only as a post, but as the word (*Atsappeh*) soundeth, 'I will look up, or, espy;' as one that keepeth watch and ward, waiting for an answer from God, as the word is, (Hab., ii, 1, and Psal. xviii, 6.) "In my distress I called upon the Lord,—and my cry came before him, even into his ears."

2. Prayer putteth a challenge upon God, for his covenant's sake and his promise; that is greater boldness, than to speak to God and wait on; "Our adversaries have trodden down thy sanctuary: We are thine, thou never barest rule over them, they were not called by thy name," (Isa., lxiii, 18, 19). "Behold, O Lord, and consider, to whom thou hast done this." (Lam., ii, 20.) O Lord, why hast thou made us to err from thy ways, and hardened our heart from thy fear? Return for thy servants' sake, the tribes of thine inheritance." (Isa., lxiii, 17.) Hence is there a

holy chiding with God: "O my God, I cry in the daytime, and thou hearest not, and in the night season, and am not silent." (Psal. xxii, 2.) "How long wilt thou forget me, O Lord, for ever? How long wilt thou hide thy face from me?" (Psal. xiii, 1.)

3. It putteth God to great straits and suffering, even to the moving of his soul, (Jer., xxxi). When God heareth Ephraim bemoaning himself in prayer, it putteth God to a sort of pinch and condolency: "Is Ephraim my dear son? Is he my pleasant child? For since I spake against him, I do earnestly remember him still; therefore my bowels are troubled for him." (ver. 20.) Is Isaac, an earthly father, moved, and his heart rent and torn with the weeping and tears of Esau, his son, so as he must confer some blessing upon him; far more must the bowels of our Father, infinite in mercy, be turned within him, at the weeping and tears of a praying and crying Church.

4. When God seemeth to sleep, in regard that his work, and the wheels of his providence are at a stand, prayer awakeneth God, and putteth him on action: "Arise, O Lord, in thine anger, lift up thyself because of the rage of mine enemies; awake for the judgment thou hast commanded," (Psal. vii, 6). "Awake, why sleepest thou, O Lord! Arise, cast us not off for ever." (Psal. xliv, 23.) Both the words (*Gnurah* and *Hakitsa*) signify to awake out of sleep: so prayer putteth God on noble acts of omnipotency, as to bow the heavens and come down, (Isa., lxiv, 1,) to shake and put on work all creatures in heaven and earth, for the saving of one poor man, (Psal. xviii); as when the sick child crieth for pain, all the sons and servants, yea, the father of the house, and mother, are set on work, and put to business for his health. Hence when David

prayed, "The earth shook, the foundations of the hills were moved, for the Lord was wroth; smoke and fiery coals went out of his mouth; he bowed the heavens and came down, he rode upon a cherub, and did fly upon the wings of the wind." (Psal. xviii, 6, 7.) So it did put the Lord to divide the Red sea; to break the prison doors and iron chains, to deliver Peter, Paul, and Silas.

5. It acteth so upon God, that it putteth the crown upon Christ's head, and heighteneth the footstool of his throne; so much doth that prayer, "thy kingdom come," hold forth; and that last prayer of the church, which the Spirit and the Bride uttereth, "Even so, come, Lord Jesus," (Rev., xxii,) is a hastening of that glorious marriage-day, when the Bride, the Lamb's wife shall be married on Jesus Christ; and a ripening of the glory of God, and of Christ the King and Head mystical of his body the Church. The glory of infinite justice, and saving grace in the redemption of men, is like a fair rose, but inclosed within its green leaves in this life. But when Christ shall appear, this rose shall be opened and cast out in breadth, its fair and beautiful leaves to be seen and smelled openly by men and angels. In very deed, this prayer, "Even so, come, Lord Jesus," is summons for the last judgment, for the full manifestation of the highest glory of Christ, in the final and consummate illustration of free grace and mercy, in the complete redemption of all the prisoners of hope, only for the declaration of the supreme Judge's glory; who shall then do execution on Satan, his angels, Antichrist, and all slaves of hell: so that though prayer made not the world, yet it may unmake it, and set up a new heaven and a new earth.

6. Prayer is a binding of God, that he cannot de-

part; and layeth chains on his hands, and buildeth a wall or an hedge of thorns in his way, that he cannot destroy his people: "And there is none that calleth upon thy name, and stirreth up himself to take hold of thee;" (Isa., lxiv, 7;) there is none to lay hands on thee; "And I sought for a man amongst them that should make up the hedge, and stand in the gap, (or in the rupture made by war,) before me for the land, that I should not destroy it, but I found none." (Ezek., xxii, 30.) If a Moses or a Samuel should intercede by prayer, that the Lord would spare the land, his prayer should be a hedge or a wall to stand in the way of justice, to hinder the Lord to destroy his people.

7. Prayer is a heavenly violence to God expressed in divers powerful expressions; as, 1. The faithful watchmen pray and cry to God so hard, that they give the Lord no rest, no silence, till he establish Jerusalem. (Isa., lxii, 6, 7.) 2. Praying is a sort of striving with the Lord: "I beseech you,—strive with me, in prayers to God for me." (Rom., xv, 30). 3. Jacob by prayer wrestled with the Lord; and the Lord, as if he had been straitened, saith, "Send me away, dismiss me. And Jacob said, I will not dismiss thee, till thou bless me:" (Gen., xxxii). Which is well expounded by Hosea, chap. xii, 4. Jacob had a princely power over the Angel, and prevailed, he wept, and made supplication to him. He was either a princedom in prayer over God, which is the true reason of the name Israel; or, as others think, he stood right up, and his prayer did not bow, nor was broken, when a temptation lay on him as heavy as a mill-stone: even when the Lord said he would depart from him, yet he prevailed under that weight. So, (Exod., xxxii, 10,) when Moses was praying for the people, the Lord

said to Moses, "Let me alone that I may destroy them." The Chaldee translates it, 'Leave off thy prayer before me.' All which tendeth to this, that prayer is a prince, and a mighty, wrestling, prevailing king, that hath strong bones, and strong arms, to be victorious with God. We know the parable of the widow, (Luke, xviii,) who by importunity obtained of the unjust judge, that he should avenge her of her adversary. The scope of which parable is, that prayers without fainting, putteth such a labour and a trouble upon God, that he must hear and answer the desires of his children. So doth the Lord resemble himself to a master of a family gone to bed with his children, who yet being wearied by the knocking of his neighbour, cannot choose but rise in the night, and lend him bread, to strangers come to his house.

8. Some also say, that prayer commandeth God, as Isa., xlv, 11: "Ask of me things to come concerning my sons, and concerning the work of my hand command ye me." Which place, though it may well bear another interpretation, yet is this not beside the scope of the text; for sure it is, that God hath laid a sort of law on himself, in regard of his binding promise, to hear the prayers of his children; and that he cometh down from the throne of his sovereignty, to submit himself to his own promise of hearing prayers, (Psalm xxxiv, 15; lxv, 2; cxlv, 18, 19; Matt., vii, 7, 8; John, xiv, 13, 14).

Use 1. If prayer prevail over God and Christ, even to the overcoming of the Devil, then much more will a praying people prevail over hell and malignants. It were wisdom then for malignants, to yield and strike sail to those, who can by prayer set Omnipotency on work, and engage the Strength of Israel against them. Amalek had Omnipotency against them, and a harder party than spears, and bows, and armed men, in that praying Moses was against them. The third Psalm was a strong piece against Absalom and Ahithophel, and all that conspired against David. Christ's prayers for the perfecting of his own body, and gathering in his first-born, include in them a curse upon all those that hinder the gathering in of his flock. woe to the enemies, then, against whom our Intercessor prayeth curses; the prayers of Christ against his enemies shall blast them and their counsels, and all their war-undertakings.

USE 2. Some are discouraged; they can neither fight for Christ, nor do any thing to promote this cause, as wanting strength of body and means. Nay, but if thou canst pray, thou dost set the whole wheels of Omnipotency on work, for the building of the Lord's house; in which regard, the prayer of a sick and poor man shall do more in war for the cause of God, than twenty thousand men. It was not Ahasuerus, nor the grace that Esther found in the eyes of the king, that saved the whole church of the Jews from destruction, but the prayers of Esther and her maids. It is true, an angel brought Peter out of prison, (Acts, xii,) but what stirred that wheel in heaven? Here's the cause, "Prayer was made without ceasing to God for Peter, by the church:" (Verse 5). Prayer, prayer can put a reeling and tottering on king and court, pope, prelate, and Babylon: we are to pray the king of the bottomless pit, the man of sin, the graven images of apostate Rome, out of the world. Prayer can yoke all the swords in Europe against the Whore. Every one who hath the spirit of adoption, though poor and rejected of men, by prayer hath powerful influence on all the nations of the earth, on all Europe, on the ends of the earth, on the hearts of the Jews, on Turks and Indians. Prayer can reach as far as Omnipotency, accompanied by the wise decree of our Lord; and the poorest girl or maid that can pray, doth lend a strong lift to heighten the footstool of Christ's royal throne. Children and poor maids, by prayer, may put the crown on Christ's head, and hold up his throne, and may store and increase heaven by praying, "Thy kingdom come," and enlarge hell, and fill the pits with the dead bodies of Christ's enemies; and may, by prayer, bind kings in fetters, chain up and confine devils, subdue kingdoms.

"*Great is thy faith.*" For the clearing of these words, we are to consider three points; 1. What faith is. 2. What a great faith is. 3. Why he saith 'thy faith,' appropriating it to the woman. Now, of faith I shall speak, 1. A word of preparations for faith; 2. Of the grounds and necessary motives to faith; 3. Of the ingredients of faith; 4. Of the sinner's warrants to believe; 5. Of divers sorts of false and ill rooted faiths.

1. There be some preparations which go before faith: 1. Faith is a seed of heaven; it is not sown by the "good husbandman" in unploughed and in fallow ground; Christ soweth not amongst thorns. We are "builded on the faith;" stones are hewn, rubbish removed, before one stone be laid. 2. Every act of grace in God is an act of Omnipotency, and so requireth not time or succession: God might have set up the frame of the world in all its fulness, with less than one thought, or act of his will put forth by Omnipotency. Yet did our Lord subject the acts of creating the first world to the rule of time, and to a circle of

evening and morning, nights and days; so doth the Lord set up a new world of faith, in a soul void of faith, by degrees. There is a time, when there is neither perfect night nor perfect day, but the twilight of the morning; and God, notwithstanding, created the morning, no less than the noon-day sun. There is a half summer, and a half spring, in the close of the spring, which God made. The embryo, or birth, not yet animated, is neither seed only, nor a man-child only; so is a convert in his first framing, neither perfectly untamed corruption, because there is a crack and a thraw in the iron-sinew of the neck; nor is he a thorough child of light; but as we say, in the dead-throe, "in the place of breaking forth of children," as Hosea speaketh. A child with his head come forth of the womb, and no more, and so half born only; so is the convert, while he is in the making, not taken off Christ's wheels; half in the borders of hell, and looking afar off at the suburbs of heaven, not far from the kingdom of heaven.

But, 2. This bridge over the water, between the kingdom of darkness and the state of saving grace, hath no necessary connection with that kingdom of the Son of God's love, but such as it hath from the sole and mere decree of the free election of grace; and therefore, many reprobates may enter the bridge, and never go along to the other bank of the river. God breaketh the bridge, this being the very division and parting of these two unsearchable ways of election and reprobation, yet so as the sin in cutting the bridge, is the guilt of the reprobate man;—as many births die in the breaking forth out of the womb, divers roses in the bud are blasted, and never see harvest, through the fault of the seed, not of the sun.

3. It is true, the new creation and life of God is virtually *seminaliter* in these preparations, as the seed is a tree in hope, the blossom an apple, the foundation a palace in its beginning: so half a desire in the non-converted, is love-sickness for Christ in the seed; legal humiliation is in hope, evangelical repentance, and mortification. But, as the seed and the growing tree differ not gradually only, but in nature and specifically; as a thing without life, is not of that same nature and essence, with a creature that hath a vegetative life and growth; so the preparatory good affections of desire, hunger, sorrow, humiliation, going before conversion, differ specifically from those renewed affections which follow after; the former being acts of grace, but not of saving grace, which goeth along with the decree of the election of grace, and of like latitude with it; the latter being the native and con-natural fruits of the Spirit, of which the apostle speaketh, (Gal., v, 22, 23). In which regard, no man is morally, and in regard of a divine promise, such as this,—"Do this, and this, and God shall bestow on you, the grace of conversion,"—fitter, and in a nearer disposition to conversion than another: 1. Because we read not of any such promise in the gospel; 2. Because amongst things void of life, all are equally void of life, and here there are no degrees of more or less life, no intention, no remission or slacking of the degrees of life. For even as an ape or a horse are as equally no men, as stones and dead earth are no men; though an ape or a horse have life common to them with men, which stones and earth have not, yet they are equally as destitute of reason and an intellectual life, which is the only life of a man as a man, as stones and earth are; so Saul, only humbled by the terrors

of the law, and sick of half-raw desires of Christ, is no less yet a creature void of the life of God, than when he was in the highest pitch of obstinacy, spitting out blood and murders on the face of that Lord Jesus whom he persecuted. And in this regard, conversion is no less pure grace, every way free to Saul humbled, and so, having only half a thirst and desire of Christ, than if he were yet in the fever of his highest blasphemy, thirsting after the blood of the saints.

4. Yet are the saints thus prepared and humbled, but not converted materially, physically, or as it were, passively nearer Christ; and in relation to God's eternal election of grace, who maketh this a step relative to his eternal love, they are under the reach of Christ's love, and at the elbow of the right arm of the Father, who draweth souls to the Son, (John, vi, 44). And in the gospel-bounds and fields, or lists of free grace, as the height and rage of a fever is near a cool and a return to health, and yet most contrary to health; and the utmost flowing of the sea, when it is at the remotest score of the coast, is a disposition to an ebbing, though most contrary to a low ebb; so are the humbled souls who have some lame and maimed estimative power of light, to put half a price on Christ, and find apprehended sin, the mouth, throat, and out-entry of hell, in that case most contrary to Christ. A fish within that circle of the water that the net casteth, is no less living in its own element of water, than if it were in the bosom of the ocean, some hundred miles distant from fisher or net; yet is it in a near disposition to be catched.

For grounds of faith to lead us on to believing, consider, 1. two words, (Col., i, 27,) spoken of the object of faith. 1. It is named "The riches of the glory of this mystery among the Gentiles; 2, which is," saith Paul, "Christ in you, the hope of glory." Now, faith leadeth us to a mystery that none knoweth, but such as are the intimate friends of Christ, and are put upon all Christ's secret cabinet councils. 2. Glory is so taking a lover, that it will deprive a natural man of his sleep; but the glory of a kingdom revealed in the gospel, is the flower, marrow, and spirits of all glory imaginable. 3. What is riches of glory? "That I should preach, the gold mine of the riches of the glory of Christ,"[1] (Eph., iii, 8,) so deep, that none can find them out, and so large, that when they are found out, men and angels shall not find their bottom. Oh, what foldings, and turnings, and inextricable windings of glory, are lapped up in Christ! Yea, treasures, all treasures are in him, (Col., ii, 3,) so it is called, (2 Cor., iv, 17,) *baros doxes*, a weight of glory. But, 2. A weight eternal, a weight aged, and full of ages of glory. 3. An exceeding great weight, and not that only; but, 4. a far more exceeding and eternal weight of glory.[2] Do but weigh how weighty precious Jesus Christ is, how heavy and how massy and ponderous the crown is, and what millions of diamonds, rubies, sapphires, and precious stones do shine, and cast out rays and beams of pure and unmixed glory out of his crown! What smiles and kisses breathing out glory on thy now sinful face, shall come out of Christ. Now the light of faith, even as a lantern, or a day-star in a cloudy dawning, leadeth thee up to this.

2. "Christ in you the hope of glory." How in them? By faith, (Eph., iii, 17). Christ, the hope of glory, is Christ the glory hoped for, by a figure; that

[1] Anexichniaston plouton tou Christou.—*Rutherford.*

[2] No orator in the Greek tongue hath any so superlative expression, *kath hyperbolen eis hyperbolen aionion baros doxes.—Rutherford.*

is, faith putteth Christ and heaven in you by hope. So, in the believer, there is Christ the Lamb, the throne, the glorified angels, and sinless and blessed musicians that stand in a circle about the throne, praising Him that liveth for ever. All these are in the believer by faith; and in him is heaven, the tree of life, the higher paradise, the river of water of life; unto all these faith entitleth the soul, and they be all nothing to Christ, the hope of glory. Even the only-begotten son and heir of a king, is called the hope of his house, the only hope of his house; but, in regard the heirs of mortal kings are mortal, the house is weak, and standeth but upon one foot, when he hath but one mortal heir. Now, it is the infinite perfection of God, that he can have but one son who is infinite, and the same eternal and immortal God with the Father, and that he cannot die. So Christ standeth the only hope of the house of heaven, a king by hope, the king of hope; and all hope of the captives and sons of hope, and all the glory of his Father's house hangeth upon him: Christ hath all the heirs upon his shoulder, and faith investeth the believer to all this power and glory.

Faith must be so much the more precious, as that it layeth hold, for its possession, on God, and on the garland, marrow (if any comparison here can stand) and flower of all God's attributes, the righteousness of Christ. 2. The free grace of God, the most taking, heart-ravishing attribute in God, and most suitable to our sinful condition. 3. The high and deep love of God, and love which dwelleth in and with the noble and excellent blood that satisfieth infinite justice. There is no such glory, by any act of obedience tendered to God, by Adam in his innocent condition, or by angels which never sinned.

3. There is as great a necessity of faith as of life; for the justified man must "live by faith." There is no grace so catholic: it being of necessity interwoven in all our actions, as they fall under moral consideration; not only in supernatural actions, but also in all our natural and civil actions, in so far as they must be spiritualised, in relation to God's honour, (1 Cor., x, 31). So as Joshua, Baruch, Samson, David, did fight battles, kill men, subdue kingdoms by faith, (Heb., xi, 32, 33,) so must the soldier now fight by that same faith, and so are the saints to eat, drink, sleep, journey, buy, sell by faith. We are not to put on faith as a cloak, or an upper garment, when we go to the streets, fields, or church, and then lay it aside in the house, at table, or in bed; yea, the renewed man is not to eat and sleep, because the light of reason and the law of nature teacheth him so to do, or the convenience of a calling; for then, all those actions shall be resolved in the same principles, and formal reason of moral performance of them, in the believer, as in the carnal man, in whom a natural spirit is steersman; and then we do but, in these actions, "walk in the light of our own fire, and the sparks that we ourselves have kindled," and shall not see to go to bed, "but lie down in sorrow," (Isa., l, 11). But we are to set faith as the plummet and line to regulate these actions, to do them, 1. Because He who hath bought us with a price, commandeth us by the light of nature. 2. And the light of faith is to moderate us in eating, drinking, sleeping, according to Christian sobriety, in the measure of the action. 3. Faith teacheth us not to eat, that we may eat; or for a natural or civil end. Grace heighteneth the natural intention to a supernatural end, and to do all these for God and his service, (1

Cor., x, 31). And "whatsoever we do" (though but civil service, as servants to earthly masters in a civil calling, in trading, in arts), "we are to do all as to the Lord, not unto men," (Col., iii, 23).

Then Christ, acting and moving by the light of faith, is the formal reason and principle in which lastly and formally (*ultimatè*) all our actions are resolved. 2. Look of how much worth and price thy soul is; of as great necessity is faith, except thou wouldst look for the gospel vengeance, the day, or the ages of eternal vengeance at Christ's appearance, (2 Thess., i, 8; Isa., lxi, 2; John, iii, 18–36; viii, 24).

"But if it be so, that faith is required in all that I do, the business of salvation (may some say) is hard and difficult work. Where shall I have faith for every stirring of my foot?" I answer, as all our actions, except where imagination is principle of the act, must be deliberate, and so the actions of a rational man, so must they be moral. Now, there is no morality in a man who is a citizen of the church, but the morality of faith; for it is a duty laid upon every one within the visible church, that all his actions moral be watered and lustered with faith. And the truth is, the work of our salvation being compared to sailing, (Heb., vi, 19,) and to fighting, (2 Tim., iv, 7; 2 Tim., ii, 3, 4,) it is very like a ship, which requireth many hands, and much attentive carefulness in the owner and sailors. Now the mast is hurt, then somewhat wanting in the deck; now the helm is faulty, then the cords are to be repaired; or the anchor is broken, or she taketh in underwater, or the sail is torn, or the motion slow. There is charge to the owner, and much work to all hands. And how many things are required to a huge body of an army? So many thousand men must be liable to so many thousand wants. Some are sick, some wounded, some a-dying, some hungry, some naked, some fall off the army, and are catched by the enemy; some be faint, some too bold and precipitate; yea, armour, houses, bread, drink, fire, tents, physicians, workmen, mattocks, spades, bridges, ladders, horses, engines of war, art and skill, medicine, counsel, courage, intelligence, and a thousand things of this kind are requisite; and seldom is an army, but there be some one inconvenience or other in this needy and cumbersome huge body. And when is the business of salvation not at a stand one way or other? Is there not either one piece or other, the shield of faith, or the anchor of hope, or the breast-plate of righteousness, or some the like, broken or faulty? Is not our Guide, who hath seven eyes, ten times a-day cumbered with us? Must not Christ solder our broken weapons, sew our torn sails, repair one breach or other in us? In a thousand the like, faith is to improve the free grace, the omnipotence, the unchangeable love of Christ, to promote his own work, and to "work in us to will, and to do, according to his good pleasure," (Phil., ii, 13).

Now, for the ingredients of faith: 1. There be in us, (2 Cor., x, 5,) *Logismoi*, great forts raised against the light of faith; these natural discourses in the mind, that are great works and heights, strongholds builded against Christ. The prime faculty, reason, the discoursive power (*dianoia*,) that thinketh she hath wit enough against Christ, and to keep the man out of all danger of eternal salvation, overtoppeth and outgroweth all gospel truths: Christ must overpower carnal, fat, rank and heady soldiers, called thoughts, every thought, and so kill some that will not be taken, and lead captive other thoughts to the obedience of faith. Reason is a predominant bone in itself. The carnal mind neither will, nor can keep rank as an obedient soldier under the law of God, (Rom., viii, 7). It is much for fine, silken, and golden reason, to say to Christ, Lord, there is more of a beast in me than of a man, I have not the understanding of a man. (Prov., xxx, 2.) The learned, the schoolmen seldom believe, except grey-haired wit turn a child, and go to school again, to learn from Christ the new art of believing; for there was never an act of unbelief in any, but it grew out of this proud and rank stalk of a lofty wit. Therefore, Christ breaks out a new window in the soul, and brings in a new sun that flesh and blood never saw, nor heard of before, (Matt., xvi, 17). 2. Faith hath low and creeping affections to the creature: but when the affections are big with child of the creature, as, 1. They are strained and swelled in their acts, faith is no faith, but a delusion. The rich man speaketh with all his heart, and with good-will of his full barns; and it is clear, he had neither faith nor hope towards eternity, (Luke, xii, 19, 20). For every word being (as we say) of the length of a cubit, a foot and a half, he casteth forth words of pulling down, building greater houses, and scraping in all; his goods are[1] "my goods, all my births and bowels, and all my good things;" for he had no other good things, and there is no apostrophe in the words: he speaketh them with a full sound, and we speak with good will these things that we tell to our soul. Faith hath but half words and half affections touching the world; half acts, or broken acts in the affections, closing with the creature, smell of a faith with child of eternity. To

[1] Ta gennemata mou, kai ta agatha mou.—*Rutherford.*

make the excellency of the creature a matter of mere opinion; to reckon the world's witchcrafts of lust, gain, glory, but uncertain and topic arguments to conclude a Godhead, and a golden heaven in the creature, is the height of the wisdom of faith. So Paul, "I am crucified with Christ." (Gal., ii, 20.) O then (may some say), Paul, you are a dead man. He saith, No. "Nevertheless, I live," but I live the life of faith, "For Christ liveth in me." All his motions toward the creature were half dead, like the vital motions of a crucified man half out of the world, and his acts of faith were lively and vital, and high-tuned, like the highest note in the music-song. Faith cannot break, and violently rend asunder the two sides of the affections, with too violent and intense acts of love, joy, fear, desire, sorrow, as these are terminated upon the creature. It is true, faith clippeth nothing from the utmost and most superlative pitch of the love of God, of desire, fear, sorrow, joy, as they act upon God; but addeth wind to the sails in that flux of the soul's way toward God. But faith moderateth and lesseneth all these in relation to the creature; so the faith, which hath its direct aspect toward eternity, and looketh on the shortness of sliding away time, and the transient wheeling away of the poor figure of this world, (1 Cor., vii, 29–31,) turneth all these acts into but half a face on the creature, and into leisurely and leaden motions, or half to non-acts, as if made up of heavenly contradictions: "Having wives, having not wives; weeping, not weeping; rejoicing, not rejoicing; buying, not possessing; using the world, not using the world." (ver. 29–31.) When the saints throng through the press and crowd of the creatures (for the world is a bushy and rank wood), thorns take hold of their garments, and retard them in their way. Faith looseth their garments, and riddeth them of such thorny friends as are too kind to them in their journey. Who diggeth for iron and tin in the earth with mattocks of gold? What wise man would make a web of cloth of gold, a net to catch fish? Expences should overgrow gains. There is much of the metal of heaven in the soul. Faith would forbid us to wear out the threads of this immortal spirit; such as are love, joy, fear, sorrow, upon pieces of corruptible clay. Alas, is it faith's light that setteth men a-work to make the soul a golden needle, and the precious powers and perfections thereof, threads of silver, to sew together pieces of sackcloth and old rotten rags? What better, I pray you, is the finest of the web in the whole system of creation? Certainly, the heavens must be a thread of better wool than the clay earth; yet, if you should break your immortal spirit, and bend all the acts to the highest extent of your affections, to conquer thousands of acres of ground in the heavens, and entitle your soul to that inheritance, as to your only patrimony without Christ, faith's day-light should discover to you, that this finest part of that web of creation, with which you desire to clothe your precious soul, is but base wool, and rotten thread, and though beautiful and well dyed to the eye, yet, "The heavens, even all of them, shall wax old like a garment." (Psal. cii, 26.) And the wisdom of faith knoweth a shop, where there is a more excellent suit of clothes for the soul, and a more precious piece of the heaven to dwell in; even a house which is from heaven, with which you shall be clothed, when life shall eat up death and mortality. (2 Cor., v, 1, 2.)

2. The creatures are below the affections of the

believer, and his affections conquer them, as having the vantage of the mount above all the creatures. So Paul maketh an elegant contrariety, (Phil., iii, 19, 20,) between those whose heart, senses, mind, find neither smell, taste, nor wisdom, but in earthly things, and those who by faith look to heaven, and dwell there. And the temporary's heart is below the world, and the creatures are up in the mount above him. So (Matt., xiii, 7–22,) the thorns or cares of riches have the forestart of the earth, and sap above faith, or the good seed: for the seed was cast in the earth, when the thorns had been there before, and had the vantage of the season and the soil both. The first love is often strongest. The martyrs (Heb., xi, 35,) had poor and weak thoughts of this life, and would not accept and welcome life and deliverance from death; but had strong acts of faith and love toward a better resurrection. It is a soul's strong faith, that bringeth him to wonder at nothing; never to love much, nor fear much, nor sorrow much, nor joy much, nor weep much, nor laugh much, nor hope much, nor despair much, when the creature is the object of all these acts. There is nothing great, not the world's all things, to him who is possessed with that righteousness which is of God by faith," (Phil., iii, 8, 9). Men that talk with good will and all their heart, of their learning, books, of their own acts, good works, wisdom, court, honour, valour in war, flocks, lands, gold, monies, children, friends, travels, are to examine if faith be not a chaste thing, and that acts of whoredom with the creature, and of believing in Christ, are scarce consistent. Let your affections move toward the creature without great sound of feet.

3. There must be self-forsaking in believing. 1. An affirming, and an Ay to grace, is a negation and

denial to itself: "I laboured more abundantly than they all; yet not I, but the grace of God, which was with me." (1 Cor., xv, 10.) To deny that you are Christ's, or that you have any grace (if Christ have any thing of his in you), is not self-denial, but grace-denial, and God-denial; deny the work of the Spirit, and deny himself. It is a saying of humility, "I am black;" and of faith, "but comely as the tents of Kedar, as the curtains of Solomon;" (Cant., i, 5;) and, "I slept, but my heart waked." (Cant., v, 1.) It is faith to hold fast your state of adoption: "Lord, I am thine." 2. When our self maketh a suit to self, and putteth in a bill to the flesh, "O pity thyself; Rejoice, O young man, in thy youth," it is self-renouncing to deny this request to the flesh. And faith only can give an answer to self declining the cross: "He that denieth me before men, him will I deny before my Father and his holy angels," saith Christ. And another answer faith giveth, (Rom., viii, 12). I am not debtor to thee, O flesh; I owe thee nothing. And it is faith's word of answer, "But know thou, that for all these things, God will bring thee unto judgment." (Eccles., xi, 9.) 3. Faith putteth the soul into that condition, that self may be plucked from self without great violence, as an apple full of the tree and of harvest sap is with a small motion plucked off the stalk. "I am ready," I have myself in readiness,[1] "not only to be bound, but also to die at Jerusalem, for the name of the Lord Jesus." (Acts, xxi, 13.) Certainly, faith saw here more in Jesus of excellency and sweetness, than there could be of bitterness in bonds and death, to self.

4. There is a denial of the creature, and a bill of

[1] Ego etoimos echo.—*Rutherford.*

defiance sent to all the lovers of the world, when Ephraim is brought to this act of believing; "For in thee the fatherless findeth mercy." (Hos., xiv, 3.) Then it is said, "Ashur shall not save us; we will not ride upon horses." That creature that we trust on, we ride upon it, as Israel did upon the horses of Assyria and Egypt. But, in this regard, faith dismounteth the believer, and abaseth him to walk on foot. All the creatures are ships to the believer without a bottom; they are empty and weak. David forbiddeth us to ride on a prince, (Psalm cxlvi, 3, 4,) for that horse shall faint, and fall to clay. God alloweth Scotland to help England, but will not have the souls of his children in England to ride upon an army of another nation, and to trust in them for salvation. To make fire, is not so proper to fire,—to give light, not so kindly to the sun,—as salvation is God's only due; and, therefore, let England in this, walk on foot, and trust in the Lord.

5. The fifth ingredient also in faith is, that it is bottomed upon the sense and pain of a lost condition. Poverty is the nearest capacity of believing. This is Faith's method,—Be condemned, and be saved,—be hanged, and be pardoned; be sick, and be healed; (Matt., ix, 13; James, iv, 7, 8; Matt., xi, 28; Luke, xix, 10). Faith is a flower of Christ's only planting, yet it groweth out of no soil, but out of the margin and bank of the lake of fire and brimstone, in regard there be none so fit for Christ and heaven, as those who are self-sick, and self-condemned to hell. This is a foundation to Christ, that because the man is broken and has not bread, therefore he must be sold, and Christ must buy him, and take him home to his fireside, and clothe him, and feed him. The chased

man, pursued upon death and life, who hath not a way for life, but one nick of a rock; if he miss that, he is a dead man, had he a hundred lives. So is the believer pursued for blood; there is but one city of refuge in heaven, or out of heaven; this is only—only Jesus Christ, the great rock. And it is true, it is in a manner forced faith, and forced love cast upon Christ, upon a great venture; yet we may make necessity here the greatest virtue, or the highest grace, and that is,—to come to Christ. Satan doth but ride upon the weakness of many, proving that they are not worthy of Christ; which is the way of a sophist, to prove an evident truth that cannot be denied. But there is no greater vantage can be had against sin and Satan than this; Because I am unworthy of Christ, and out of measure sinful, and I find it is so, (Satan and conscience teaching me that truth, to bring me on a false conclusion,) therefore ought I, therefore must I come to Christ, unworthy as I am. For free grace is moved from within itself from God's good will, only without any motion or action from sin, to put itself forth upon the sinner, to the end, that sin, being exceeding sinful, grace may be abundantly grace. And no thanks to Satan, for suggesting a true principle—Thou art unworthy of Christ—to suggest a false conclusion, Therefore thou art not to come to Christ; for the contrary arguing is gospel-logic. Satan's reasoning should be good, if there were no way but the law to give life. But because there is a Saviour, a gospel, and a new and living way to heaven, the contrary arguing is the sinner's life and happiness.

6. The sixth ingredient in faith is, that the sinner can lay hold on the promise, 1. Not simply, but with relation to the precept; for presumptuous souls plunge

in their foul souls in fair and precious promises; and this is the faith of Antinomians: for the promise is not holden forth to sinners as sinners, but as to such sinners; for we make faith to be an act of a sinner humbled, wearied, laden, poor, self-condemned. Now, these be not all sinners, but only some kind of sinners. Antinomians make faith an act of a lofty Pharisee, of a vile person, applying with an immediate touch, his hot, boiling, and smoking lusts to Christ's wounds, blood, merits, without any conscience of a precedent commandment, that the person thus believing should be humbled, wearied, laden, grieved for sin. I confess this is hasty hot work, and maketh faith a stride, or one single step; but it is a wanton, fleshly, and a presumptuous immediate work, to lay hold on the promises of mercy and be saved. This is the absolute and loose faith that Papists and Arminians slander our doctrine withal, because we reject all foregoing merits, good works, congruous dispositions, preparations moving God to convert this man, because he hath such preparations, and to reject and to leave another man to his own hardness of heart, because he hath no such payment in hand, by which he may redeem and buy conversion, and the grace of effectual calling: especially, they building all upon a Babel of their own brick and clay, that free will in all acts of obedience before or after conversion, is absolutely indifferent; to do, or not do; to obey, or not obey; to choose heaven and life, hell or death, as it pleaseth, as being free and loosed from all predetermination, and foregoing motion, acting or bowing of the will, coming either from God's natural, or his efficacious or supernatural Providence. And so the Papist and Arminian on the one extremity, enthroneth Nature, and extolleth proud merit, and abaseth Christ and free grace. The Familist, libertine, and Antinomian, on a contrary extremity and opposition, turn man into a block, and make him a mere patient in the way to heaven; and, under pretence of exalting Christ and free grace, set up the flesh, liberty, licence, looseness on the throne, and make the way to heaven on the other extremity, as broad, as to comply with all presumptuous, proud, fleshly men, walking after their lusts, and yet, as they dream, believing in Christ.

2. The soul seeth Christ in all his beauty, excellency, treasures of free grace, lapped up with the curtain of many precious promises. Now, the natural man, knowing the literal meaning and sense of the promises, seeth in them but words of gold, and things afar off; and in truth, taketh heaven to be a beautiful and golden fancy, and the gospel promises, a shower of precious rubies, sapphires, diamonds, fallen out of the clouds only in a night dream; and therefore jeers and scoffs at the day of judgment, and at heaven and hell, (2 Pet., iii, 1–3). For, can every capacity smell and taste the unsearchable riches of Christ, the fulness of God in the womb of the promises, by meditating on them, and sending them, in their sweetness and heavenly excellency, down to the affections to embrace them? No, it cannot be, that words, and sounds, and syllables, can so work upon a natural spirit. If you show not to a buyer precious and rare commodities, and bring them not before the sun, he shall never be taken so with things hidden in your coffers, as to be in love with them, and to sell all he hath and buy them. Preachers cannot, nay, it is not in their power to make the natural spirit see the beauty of Christ. Paul preacheth it, but the gospel is hidden from the

blinded man, (2 Cor., iv, 3). If I cannot communicate light, far less can I infuse love in the soul of a lost man. 3. Literal knowledge of Christ, is not in the power of natural men; but laying down this ground, that a Pharisee lend eyes and ears to Christ and his miracles, the light of the gospel worketh as a natural agent; for, make open windows in a house, whether the indweller will, or he will not, the sun shall dart in day-light upon the house. "Then cried Jesus, in the temple, as he taught, saying, ye both know me, and ye know whence I am." (John, viii, 28.) And there is a covering upon the spiritual senses and faculties of the soul of natural men, that though eyes, and ears, and mind, and soul be opened, yet it is as impossible for the natural spirit, or the preacher, to remove that covering, as to remove a mountain, it being as heavy as a mountain. And therefore, there be three bad signs in a natural spirit:—1. His light, which is but literal, is a burden to him; it but vexeth him to know Christ; and if a beam of light fall in on the apple of the eye of a natural conscience, it is as a thorn between the bone and the flesh; the man shall not sleep, and yet he is not sick. I doubt if either Ahithophel or Judas, wakened with their light, could sleep. 2. Though a promise should dispute and argue Christ in at the door of the natural man's soul, as the gospel, by way of arguing, may do much, (John, vii, 28; xii, 37; Heb., xi, 1), the word of the gospel being a rational convincing syllogism, as Christ saith, "But now they have both seen and hated both me and my Father; (John, xv, 24); yet men may see the principles and the conclusion, and hate and practically suspend the assent from the conclusion.

3. Conversion is feared as a great danger by natural

men, lest the promises put them on the pain, and the main mill of godliness. For men do flee nothing but that which they apprehend as evil, dangerous, and so the true object of fear. Now, when Felix and Agrippa were both upon the wheels, I cannot say that conversion formally was begun; yet materially it was. The one trembled, and so was afraid, and fled, and did put Paul away till another time; then he saw the danger of grace: (Acts, xxiv, 25, 26:) the other saith, he was half a Christian, (but it was the poorest half,) and "he arose and went aside," (Acts, xxvi, 28, 30, 31). The natural spirit may be convinced by the promises, and have the pap in his mouth, but dare not milk out the sap and sweetness of the promises: "Their eyes they have closed, lest at any time they should see with their eyes, and hear with their ears, and should understand with their heart, and should be converted, and I should heal them." (Matt., xiii, 15.) So is it, Isa., vi, 10, in which words, conversion is feared as an evil, as is clear. So one wretch said, he was once in danger to be catched, when a Puritan preacher, as he said, 'was preaching with divine power, and evidence of the Spirit of God.'

4. The true believer's soul hath influence on the promises to act upon them, to draw comfort out of them: "Unless thy law had been my delight, I should have perished in mine affliction." (Psalm cxix, 92.) "My soul fainteth for thy salvation: but I hope in thy word." (Verse 81.) And there is a reciprocation of actions here; the word acteth upon the soul again: "This is my comfort in my affliction, for thy word hath quickened me." (Psalm cxix, 50.) A dead faith is like a dead hand; a living hand may lay hold on a dead hand: but there is no reciprocation of actions

here, the dead hand cannot lay hold on the living hand. So the living wife may kiss and embrace the dead husband, but there can come no reciprocal act of life from the dead husband to her, nor can he kiss and embrace her. The promise may act upon the natural spirit, to move and affect him; but he can put forth no vital act upon the promise to embrace it, or lay hold upon the promise. But the promise acteth upon the believer to quicken him, and he again putteth forth an act of life to embrace the promise, and putteth forth on it some act of vital heat to adhere and cleave to, and with warmness of heart to love it. And here the case is, as when the living hand layeth hold on the living hand; they warm one another mutually, according to that which Paul saith, "But I follow after, if that I may apprehend that for which also I am apprehended of Christ Jesus." (Phil., iii, 12.) Here be two living things, Christ, and believing Paul, acting mutually one upon another; there is a heart and a life upon each side.

5. Faith under fainting, and great straits, can so improve the promise, as to put an holy and modest challenge upon God. So afflicted David saith, "Remember the word unto thy servant, upon which thou hast caused me to hope; (Psalm cxix, 49;) and the Church, "Do not abhor us, for thy name's sake; do not disgrace the throne of thy glory; remember, break not thy covenant with us." (Jer., xiv, 21.) And the Lord commanded that this challenge be put on him, "Put me in remembrance, let us plead together:" (Isa., xliii, 26). Then he giveth faith leave to plead on the contrary with God.

Natural spirits faint, and cannot so far own the promise, as to plead with God by their right and just claim to the promise. Now, the fourth point concerning faith is, What grounds and warrants the sinner hath to believe?

4. It is an ordinary challenge made by Satan, conscience, and the Arminian. Since Christ died not for all and every one of mankind; and all are not chosen to life eternal, but only those on whom the Lord is pleased, according to the free decree of election to confer the grace of believing; what warrant can the unworthy sinner have to believe, and to own the merits of Christ; for he knoweth nothing of the election or reprobation that are hidden in God's eternal mind? For answer,

1. It is no presumption in me to believe in Christ before I know whether I be chosen to salvation or not; for nothing can hinder me in this case to believe, save only presumption, as the adversaries say. But it is not presumption; because presumption is, when the soul is lifted up, and towered like an high building, as the word is, (Hab., ii, 4). And therefore, the lifted up man, *(Gnophel)*, is he that hideth himself in a high castle, as every unbelieving presumptuous soul hath his own castle: the unbeliever hath either one Ophel, or high tower, or other; either the king, friends, riches, or his own wisdom, for his God on which he resteth, beside the God that the Scripture recommendeth to us, as our only rock and soul-confidence. All men on earth live, and do all moral actions, even when they go on in a wicked life, as slaves of hell, to work all uncleanness with greediness, upon some ground of faith, though a most false and counterfeit faith, that they shall prosper by evil doing, and that sin shall make them happy. So, " The wicked man praiseth the wicked man; (Psalm x, 3); then he

must believe that wickedness maketh men praiseworthy; and this belief is but presumptuous confiding, and resting on a tower of his own building. Now, to believe in Christ, though the decree of election be not revealed to me, is no presumption; for I am not obliged, before I believe, to know that I am elected to glory; it being one of God's secrets not revealed in the word, but made manifest to me, after I believe, and am sealed unto the day of redemption. And, therefore, in a humble resting on Christ, though the soul know not his election, which is not revealed in the word, in that condition there can be no pride nor presumption; for he is self-wise and presumptuous, who intrudeth "into those things that he hath not seen," (Colos., ii, 18,) knoweth not that which God hath revealed, and so which he ought to know. Now the believer ought not to know that he is elected to glory, he being yet an unbeliever; so his knowledge cannot deviate from a rule which doth not oblige to conformity therewith, as with a rule. The portrait of Cæsar doth not err from the sampler, because it is not like a bull or a horse, because neither a bull nor a horse is the due sampler.

2. To warrant an unworthy humble sinner to believe, there is no need of a positive warrant, or of a voice to say, Thou art elected to glory, therefore believe. The word is near thee in thy mouth; yea, there is a commandment laid upon the humbled sinner: Come, O weary and laden sinner, to Christ, and be eased. Now, when the wind bloweth sweetly and fair upon an humbled sinner who is elected to glory, there goeth the spirit of the gospel along with this commandment: and the word of commandment, and the spirit united in one, acteth and worketh so upon

the soul, that the humbled sinner cannot be deluded and led on a rock of presumption; for this spirit joineth and closeth with his spirit, and he, as one of Christ's sheep, knoweth this to be the voice of Christ. I grant, when the same command of faith cometh to the ears of a reprobate, he may, upon a false ground, believe, or rather presume; he neither being rightly humbled and fitted for Christ; nor can the reprobate know and discern the wind of the Spirit, breathing with the command, and acting upon his spirit, because that wind neither can, nor doth breathe upon any reprobate. And there is no need of any positive warrant, to ascertain a child of God to believe, beside the commandment of faith, enlivened and quickened with the Spirit going along with it; for that command, so quickened, doth put such a real stamp of an evident testimony that he hath claim to Christ, on whom the Spirit and the command doth so act, that he seeketh no more any other evidence to prove his claim to Christ, than the lamb needeth any evidence to prove, that of ten hundred sheep, this only that offereth to it her paps and milk, must be its dam or mother, and none of the rest of the flock.

But how do I know, that it is the Spirit that goeth along with the commandment of believing? It may be a delusion. *Ans.* Beside that a deluding spirit, for the most part, doth not go every way along with the word, if this spirit keep God's order, to work upon the humbled and self-despairing sinner, who is willing to receive Christ upon his own condition, it is not like to a deluding spirit; for if the word of commandment to believe, and the spirit agree in one, it cannot be a delusion; fancy leadeth no man to faith. 2. When objects of life work upon life, they cannot deceive especially all the senses, hearing, seeing, tasting, feeling, smelling. The excellency and sweetness of Christ going along with the word, cannot be delusion: a man may imagine that he seeth and heareth, and yet his senses may be deceived; but that all the senses, especially all the spiritual senses, and that a man imagineth that he liveth a natural life, and is dead, is rare.

3. Faith can stand upon one foot, even on a general word; hence, this is a gospel word in the Prophets, which requireth faith, Turn to the Lord for he is merciful, (Jer., iii, 12; Joel, ii, 13; John, iv, 2). And because a general promise received with heart-adherence and confidence giveth glory to God; and if it be holden forth to a humbled soul, who is now within the lists and bounds of grace, and, for any thing that the person thus laden with sin knoweth on the contrary, (for the secrets of election and reprobation belong to the Lord) Christ mindeth and intendeth to him salvation, therefore he is to believe.

4. This would be considered, that unbelief breaketh with Christ first, before Christ break with the unbeliever; and the elect of God findeth no more, nor any higher favour in the kind of external means to open the Lamb's book of life, which is sealed and closed with God's own hand, than the commandment of believing. Now, when our Lord maketh offer of the kingdom of sons, to slaves, and casteth his jewel of Christ offered in the gospel, in the lap and bosom of a bastard, whatever be the Lord's secret decree and purpose in so doing, the bastard is to take God at his word, and to catch the opportunity of God's love in so far; and if he do it not, the gospel offer to the reprobate being a treaty of peace, then the treaty breaketh off first upon his side; for Christ cometh within a

mile of mercy, to meet the sinner, and the sinner cometh not the fourth part of a mile, yea, not half a step of love and thankful obedience, to meet Christ; and so, Christ killeth the unbeliever with the sweetness of the preventing courtesy of offered mercy.

5. But if the sinner be wearied and laden, and seeth, though through a cloud only, Christ only must help and save; if not, he is utterly and eternally lost. What is there upon Christ's part to hinder thee to believe, O guilty wretch? Oh, (saith he,) I fear Christ only offereth himself to me, but he mindeth no salvation to me? *Answ.* Is not this to raise an evil report and slander on the holy One of Israel? For Christ's offer is really an offer, and in so far, it is real love, though it cannot infer the love of election to glory, yet the total denial of this offer openeth up the black seal of reprobation to heathens without the church. And therefore it is love to thee, if thou be humbled for sin; 2. And have half an eye to the unsearchable riches of gospel mercy; 3. And be self-condemned; 4. And have half a desire of Christ: thou mayest expound love by love, and lay hold on the promise, and be saved. An error of humble love to Christ, is no error.

That which is next, is a word of the essential principle of true faith, and that is a proportionable measure of grace, required in faith. (Phil., i, 29.) Men naturally imagine, that faith is a work of nature; hence that speech of a multitude of atheists, "I believe all my days, I believe night and day;" but they never believe at all, who think and say, they believe always. The Jews asserted, that they believed Moses always, and so oppose themselves to the man altogether born in sin, (John, ix, 28, 29, compared with verse 34). 1. But Christ told them, they neither believed the Messiah nor Moses, (John, v, 35–37.) Nature worketh always alike, and without intermission or freedom. The floods always move, the fountain always casts out streams, the fire always burneth, the lamb always fleeth from the wolf; but the wind of the Spirit doth not always enact the soul to believe. They are not in an ill case, who wrestle with unbelief, and find the heart and take it, in the ways of doubting and terrors, as feeling that believing is a motion up the mount, and somewhat violent. Facile and con-natural acts cannot be supernatural acts of faith. It is no bad sign, to complain of a low ebb sea, and of neither moon-light nor star-light. 2. It is impossible they can submit to give the glory of believing to God, in whose heart there is a rotten principle destructive of faith, and that is, an ambitious humour of seeking glory from men, (John, v, 44). Little faith there is in kings' courts; faith dwelleth not in a high spirit. 3. Such as take religion by the hand upon false and bastard motives, as the summer of the gospel, and fame, ease, gain, honour, cannot believe. A thorny faith is no faith, (Matt., xiii, 22). A carnal man's faith must be true to its own principles, and must lie level with externals; so as court, ease, the world, and its sweet adjuncts, are a measuring line to a rotten-rooted faith neither longer nor broader than time, it goeth not one span length within the lists of eternity. 4. Fancy cannot be faith. Such as have not gospel knowledge of Christ, cannot believe; but must do as the traveller, who unawares setteth his foot on a serpent in the way, and suddenly starteth backward six steps for one, (John, vi, 66). So do they that fancy all the gospel to be a carnal or a moral discourse. 5. Those cannot have faith, in whose heart the gospel lieth above ground, devils and sin having made the heart hard like the summer streets, with daily treading and walking on them. (Matt., xiii, 19.) A stony faith, or a faith that groweth out of a stone, cannot be a saving faith. There is a heart that is a daily walk, in which the devil (as it were) aireth himself. 6. If Christ have given the last knock at the door, and all in-passages be closed up, and heart inspirations gone, there can be no more any sort of faith there, (Eph., iv, 19; 2 Tim., iv, 2). The heart is like a dried-up arm in some; all the oil in the bones is spent. 7. Loose walking with greediness, argues, that hell hath taken fire on the outworks of the soul. Hell in the hands and tongue, as in the out-wheels, must argue hell and unbelief in the heart and the in-wheels. 1. Loose believers go to heaven by miracles; I dare go to hell for a man, if such a one go to heaven, who liveth profanely, and saith, he hath a good heart within. 2. The going in ways of blood, extortion, covetousness, idolatry, belieth the decree of election to glory. Grace leadeth no man to the east, with his face and motion close to the west. 3. This way of working by contraries is not God's way: God can work by contraries; but he will not have us to work by contraries. There is some heaven of holiness in the court-gate to the heaven of happiness. 8. Faith overlooketh time, (Heb., xi, 10). Abraham looked for another city. Faith in Moses was great with child of heaven; (ver. 25,) he had an eye to the recompence of reward. Eternity of glory is the birth of faith. Oh! we look not to the declining of our sun; it is high afternoon of our piece of day; eleven hours are gone, and the twelfth hour is on the wheels, and I see not my own grey-hairs. It is upon the margin and borders of night, and I know not where to lodge. We are like the man swimming through broad waters, and he knoweth not what is before him; he swimmeth through deeper and deeper parts of the river, and at length, a cramp and a stitch cometh on arms and legs, and he sinketh to the bottom, and drowns. We swim through days, weeks, months, years, winters, and are daily deeper in time; till at length death bereave us of strength of legs and arms, and we sink over head and ears in eternity. Oh! who, like the sleepy man, is loosing his clothes, and putting off the garments of darkness, and would gladly sleep with Christ? Men are close-buttoned, and like day-men, when it is dark night. It is fearful to lie down with our day-clothes, (Job, xx, 11). Sin is a sad winding-sheet. Oh! what believer saith, I would have a suit of clothes for the high court and throne, to be an assay, to see how a suit of glory would become me?—This much for faith.

SERMON XXII.

NOW, a word of a strong and great faith, and withal, of a weak and fainting faith. For the most, I go not from the text, to find out the ingredients of a great faith.

1. A strong praying and a crying faith, is a great faith. So must Christ's faith have been, who prayed with strong cries and tears. Strong faith maketh sore sides in praying, as this woman prayed with good will: there is an efficacious desire to be rid of a sinful temptation, as Paul prayed thrice to

be freed of the prick in the flesh. Their faith is weak, who dare not pray against some idol sins; or, 2, If they pray, it is but gently, with a wish not to be heard.

2. The woman's crying,—her instant pleading in faith, yea, 1, above the disciples' care for her; yea, above Christ's seeming glooms, who denied her to be his, who reproached her as a dog, argueth great grace, great humility, with strong adherence; and so, great faith.

2. For faith saileth sometimes with a strong tide and a fair wind; according as the moon hath an aspect on the sun, so is it full or not full. When the wheels are set right to the sun, the clock moveth and goeth right. The fairer and more clear sight that faith hath of Christ, the stronger are the acts of faith. It cannot be denied, that faith hath a good and an ill day: because grace is various, it is no strong proof that it is not grace.

3. To put faith in all its parts in light, in staying on Christ, in affiance, in adherence, in self-diffidence, in submissive assenting forth in all its acts, and to lift the soul all off the earth, requireth Christ's high spring-tide: it is not easy to put all the powers that do act in faith afloat, especially because a strong faith is a great vessel; and therefore, more of Christ's tide is required for weighing anchor and launching forth. The wings of a sparrow should not raise an eagle off the earth; the limbs of a pismire could not suit with a horse or an elephant: there is need of a strong winged soul to believe, especially against hope.

4. To believe Christ, when midnight speaketh blackness of wrath, requireth eyes and light of miracles; yea, it is a greater work than the very miracles of

Christ, (John, xiv, 12). But especially when Christ is absent, it is with the soul, as with a clock, in which the wheels are broken, the passes or weights are fallen down.

Object. 1. But I aim and endeavour to believe, but can do nothing, and, without His grace, my violence to heaven is without fruit. *Ans.* It is true the Semi-pelagians' halving of the work of believing, and the glory of it, between co-operating grace and will, as if nature could divide the spoil with the grace of Christ, is damnable pride; but it is God's way to halve the work between Christ within, in regard of the habit of grace, and Christ without, in regard of the assisting grace of God: "While he was yet a great way off, his father saw him, and ran, and fell on his neck, and kissed him." (Luke, xv, 20.) Christ rewardeth not nature's aims with grace, nor doth he make gifts the work, and grace the hire, or nature's labour the race, and grace the garland. But he rewardeth grace with grace, and that of mere grace, (John, xv, 3). He hath in his decree and promise marshalled such and such acts of grace to stand beside others, and that by covenant: and therefore believe, that you may believe; pray, that you may pray.

Object. 2. But who can act saving grace, without the blowing of saving grace? I can no more do it, than I can command the west wind to blow when I list *Ans.* I grant all, nor do I speak this to insinuate, that free-will sitteth at the helm, or that grace sleepeth, and will waketh; the contrary is an evident truth. Yet give me leave to say, there is odds between blowing of the wind, and making ready the sails. Though seamen cannot make wind, nor is it their fault to want wind, yet can they prepare the sails, and hoist them up to welcome the wind. We cannot create the breathings of the Spirit; yet are we to miss these breathings? and this is, a fitting of the sails, and we are to join with the Spirit's breathings. Christ bindeth up the winds in his garment, so as, if one look of faith, or half a spiritual groan, should ransom me from hell, I have it not in stock; therefore hath God ordered such a dispensation, that in all stirrings of grace, the first spring, the fountain-rise of calling Jesus, Lord, shall be up in heaven at the right hand of the Father; and the far end of any gracious thought, is as far above me, as the heart of Christ, who is in the heaven of heavens, is above the earth, though ye think nothing of it. And better Christ be my steward, and that the gospel be at the end of all acts of grace, as that Christ be free-will's debtor.—More reason that Christ be creditor, than debtor to his redeemed ones. 2. I know the child of God may be so far forth lazy, as that it is his fault that the wind bloweth not, if we speak of a moral cause. 3. It is his part to join with the working of assisting grace: "Whereunto I also labour, striving according to his working, which worketh in me mightily." (Col., i, 29.) The Lord hath, by free promise, laid holy bands on himself, to give predeterminating grace to his own children to persevere to the end, and to prevent apostacy and heinous sins, inconsistent with saving faith; (1 Cor., i, 8, Jude, 24, Jerem., xxxii, 39–41, Is., liv, 10, lix, 21, 22, Luke, xxii, 32, 1 John, ii, 1, 2,) yet so as he hath reserved a liberty to himself, to co-operate with them in particular acts, as it shall be their sin, not his withdrawing of grace that maketh them guilty, to the end we know we are in grace's debt, in all good and supernatural acts. So (2 Chron., xxxii, 31,) Hezekiah was tried of God in the business of the king of Babylon's ambassadors, that the king might see, that he could not walk to heaven on clay legs, or by his own strength. And the reason is clear: God cannot make a promise of contributing this bowing and predeterminating grace, but in a way suitable to free grace; for God cannot change grace unto natural debt, it remaining grace, for so it should be grace, and no grace, which is a contradiction. 2. The Lord hath reserved liberty to himself in this promise, that in this or that particular act (the omission whereof may consist with perseverance in grace), he may contribute his influence of grace, or not contribute it. So David hath not actual grace at his will and nod, to eschew adultery and murder as he pleaseth; nor Peter to decline an evil hour, when he shall be tempted to forswear his Saviour Christ; nor hath Heman in his hand, (Psalm lxxxviii,) nor the deserted church power, (Psalm lxxvii,) to pray, and believe, and rejoice in the salvation of God, at the disposition of free-will: but the key is up in the hands of the kingly Intercessor, at the right hand of the Father, that must open the heart. It is far to fetch, as far as the heaven of heavens, to make wind and sailing to Christ-ward; therefore, 3. Seasons of acts of grace to believe, to walk in any warmness of love to Christ and his members, are fruits of royal liberty and free grace. Who hath the key of the house of wine, to stay the soul with the flagons and apples of love? Certainly, it is the king himself, that taketh the spouse into his banqueting house, (Cant., ii, 4). And yet, so as the omission of all supernatural duties, yea, our laziness in the manner of doing, our failings and sins, are imputed to ourselves, and not to the not blowing of the wind of the Holy Spirit, nor to the want of the efficacious motion of the Spirit, as Libertines teach, with Arminians; for we so sin through the want of the motions of efficacious grace, as through the want of a physical, not of a moral cause; and so, as we are most willing to want that influence, and so are guilty before the Lord.

God hath reasons strong and convincing why he worketh thus; 1. It suiteth not Grace to work by engagement; the spirit of the living creatures is within every wheel of Christ, that it must move from an inward principle: the motion of saving grace, is Christ's heart wheeled about by itself, and by no foreign cause without itself: love worketh as love without boon or bribe from men or angels. Grace is both wages and work, the race and the gold to itself. 2. God delights to have men and angels his debtors. Grace holdeth an open and a free inn, with all the dainties that Christ can make, to all comers and goers, for nothing but thanks, and heartily welcome. Grace maketh no gain of my work. The sweating of angels, and of the thousand thousands that sing up the glory of Christ before the high throne, is no income to Christ's rent. Grace would not be grace, if it could traffic, or buy, or sell with a creature. Angels and men stand in the books of free grace for millions of borrowed sums. Christ's blood and deep love may be praised, but never recompensed. Christ's love hath filled this world, and the new paradise with debtors; and angels can neither read, nor sum, nor cast up the accounts of free grace. 3. That we cannot be masters of one good act, without His preventing grace, evidenceth what nature is, and maketh grace both my staff and my convoy in at heaven's gates; nature and free-will must stoop and do homage to Christ. There is a glory active, and a glory passive, as there is also grace active and passive; free-will is active under grace, and passive also; and therefore, grace and mercy is to the saints and upon the saints: nature emptieth its lamp upon the golden pipe, the rich grace of the Mediator, and free-will moveth and runneth, but not but as moved, driven, and breathed upon by free grace. But as concerning glory, it hath a more eminent and noble relation: glory shall be on the saints as a garment, as a crown, for they shall be glorified. But no glory to the saints, but only to the Lamb, to the flower of the glory of glory, Jesus, the celebrated, eminent, most high and adored Prince of the kings of the earth. And, therefore, there is room and place left for sin and shame to free-will in the business of predeterminating grace, that nature can but sigh and sin, and grace sing, and be spotless and innocent. Christ so draweth, as we sin in not being drawn; Christ so taketh and allureth, that it is our guilt that we are not taken and overcome with the smell of the King's ointments. So is sin the field out of which springeth the rose, the flower of free and unhired grace. Sin must go with us as near to heaven, as to the threshold of the gates, that the sinner may halt and crook, when he moveth his foot on the threshold-stone of glory; that so, pardoning grace may enter the new city with us. 4. The Lord will have us take to heaven with us, a book of the psalms and praises of grace, that in that land we may extol and advance free grace, and may hold the book in our hand all the way, and sigh, and weep, and sing, and adore the Saviour of free grace, and may take grace's bill in our hand into heaven with us. Oh, how sweet to be grace's drowned and over-burdened debtor! It is good here to borrow much, and profess inability, for eternity, to pay, that heaven may be a house full of broken men, who have borrowed millions from Christ, but can never repay more, than to read and sing the praises of grace's free bill, and say, Glory, glory, to the Lamb that sitteth upon the throne for evermore: praising for ever in heaven, must be in lieu of paying debt. 1. God is not behind, nor wanting to the gracious soul, for there is a promise of grace here. 2. There is an intercession at hand, and that more mighty now, than at Christ's first ascension, and shall be more mighty when all Israel shall be converted. There is a stirring required in a gracious spirit, but with sense of nature's weakness, so as he is "to arise, and be doing, and the Lord shall be with him;" and he is so to blow upon the coals, as if he could his alone do, though not without the faith of dependence upon an immediate acting from heaven.

Obj. 3. Adam, yet sinless, was to believe weakness and sin in himself, before he sinned. *Ans.* Not so, but he was to have that which, by analogy, answereth to sense of sin, that is, a sinless consciousness and solicitude, that if God should withdraw his stirring and predeterminating influence of corroborating him to will and to do (you may call it grace), he should fall; and that legs in paradise, without actual assistance, could not bear the bulk and weight of Adam's connatural and constant walking with God, that Adam might know, before he was a debtor to justice, that he had need of mercy, or the free goodness of a surety, such as Jesus Christ, to prevent debt, no less than to pay debt; even as angels are debtors to Christ their head, for redemption from all possible sins, no less than we are (though the degrees of altitude of grace varieth much), the obliged underlings of such a bountiful landlord, for redemption from actual misery.

3. That is a great faith, that is not broken with a temptation, but 1. Taketh strength from a temptation; as some run more swiftly after a fall, that they may recompense their loss of time; and that is great faith, that argueth from a temptation, as this woman doth. 2. That is Job's great faith, (chap. ii, 3). "That he still holdeth fast his integrity;" the word (*Hazak*) is, to hold with strength and power: he keepeth fast, and with violence, his innocency, and faith maketh him stronger than he was. The word is used, (Psalm cxlvii, 13), for making stronger the bars of ports. And it is Job's praise, (chap. i, 22,) "In all this Job sinned not, nor charged God with folly." 3. It is a strong faith in this woman, that, in a manner, conquers Omnipotency by believing. Yea, Satan, winds, fire from heaven, wife, Sabeans, yea, apprehended wrath, cannot prevail with Job to subdue his faith: in all he standeth by this, "Though the Lord should slay me, I will trust in him." (Job, xv, 13.) It is great faith to be at holding and drawing with God; and yet believe and pray, (Hosea, xii, 3; Gen., xxxii, 26,) and not let the Lord alone, nor give him any rest, (Isa., lxii, 6, 7,) till he answer. As suppose thy prayers were never heard, and the acts of believing were but darts thrown at heaven and the throne without any effect; yet because prayer and believing are acts of honouring God, though they never benefit thee, it argueth strong grace, and so great faith, that it can be said, there be ten years, twenty years of reiterated acts of faith, and prayers of such a man lying up before the throne, yea, in Christ the High Priest's bosom. Let God make of my faith what he will, yet am I to believe: continued

believing is Christ's due, though it should never be to me gain of comfort or success. That is, a weak man who is thrown down on his back with a blast of wind, or made to stagger with the cast of a straw, or a feather;—the temporary faith is in this seen to be soft, that it is broken with persecution; "When the sun riseth anon, he is offended, and withereth quickly." (Matt., xiii, 21.) Some spirit of soft clay for a scratch with a pin on his credit, casteth away all his confidence, despaireth, and hangeth himself as Ahithophel. Such a temptation would not once draw blood of a strong believer. Straws, and feathers, and flax do quickly take fire, and are made ashes in a moment; but not so gold: there is bones and metal in strong faith; so the martyr's faith, that could not be broken with torments, is proved to be a great faith: Their bodies were racked out as a drum,[1] and beaten to death after racking, and they would not accept a deliverance. (Heb., xi, 35.) Why? Faith looked to a better resurrection. He who sweateth, panteth up the brow of the mount after Christ, and carrieth death on his back, must have this strong faith, that Christ is worthy of tortures. A strong faith can bear hell on its shoulders, the grave and the sorrows of death, and not crack, nor be broken, (Psal. xviii, 4–6; cxvi, 3, 4).

4. That faith is argued to be strong, that hath no light of comfort, but walketh in darkness upon the margin and borders of a hundred deaths, and yet stays upon the Lord, (Isa., l, 11). So this woman had no comfort, nor ground of sense of comfort from Christ, except rough answers and reproaches; yet she believeth, and so, must be strong in the faith, (Psal. iii, 6). David's faith standeth straight without a crook, when

[1] Etympanisthesan.—*Rutherford.*

ten thousand deaths are round about him; (and Psal. xxiii, 4,) he feareth no ill, when he walks in the cold and dark valley of the shadow of black death. Heman, (Psal. lxxxviii, 7,) "Thy wrath lieth hard on me, thou hast afflicted me with all thy waves:" then, in his sense, God could do no more to drown him; not waves. but all waves, all God's waves were on him, and above him; yet (verse 9,) "Lord, I have called daily upon thee." Then he believed daily. Hezekiah's comforts are at a hard pinch, (Isa., xxxix, 14,) "Mine eyes fail with looking upward, O Lord, I am oppressed;" yet praying, argueth, believing, "Lord, undertake for me." We must think Christ's sense of comforts was ebb and low when he wept, cried, (Heb., v, 7,) and was forsaken of God; yet then his faith is doubled, as the cable of an anchor is doubled, when the storm is more than ordinary,—"My God, my God." David chideth his cast-down soul when there is no glimpse of comfort, with strong faith, "Hope thou in God, for I shall yet praise him." (Psal. xlii, 11.) In swimming well, the less natural helps to hold up the chin and head, the greater wave, if the swimmer be carried strongly through, as it were in despite of the stream, there is the more art. Art may counterbalance strength, and sometimes wisdom is better than strength. The less comfort, if yet you believe at midnight, when the spirit is overwhelmed, the more is the art of believing. When an inward principle is weak, we help it with externals. That the child must be allured with rewards, as with apples, a penny, or the like, it is because his sight and desire of the beauty and excellency of learning and arts, is but weak or nothing at all. Sense and comforts are external subsidies and helps to faith, and those that cannot believe but upon feelings, and sense of the sweetness of comforts, are hence argued to have weak and broken inclinations and principles of faith. The more freeness and ingenuity of spirit that is in believing, the more strength of faith; for that is most con-natural, that hath least need of hire. You need not give hire, reward, or bribes to the mother's affection, to work upon her, and cause her to love her child: love can hardly be hired; nature is stronger than rewards or any externals. Comforts are but the hire of serving of God, and the results of believing in a sad condition.

There be some cautions here that are considerable. 1. God leadeth some strong ones to heaven, whose affections are soft as David's were, (Psalms xxxv, 13; cxix, 25, 28; cxxxvi, 53; vi, 6). And yet faith is strong, (Psal. xxii, 1). God possibly immediately working upon the assenting, or believing faculty, leaving the affections to their own native disposition. 2. God useth some privileged dispensations, so as a strong believer shall doubt upon no good ground, (Psal. cxvi, 11), God so disposing, that grace may appear to be grace, and the man but flesh. 3. Softness of affection, and light of comfort, may by accident concur with strong acts of believing; for, with these, in many, there is little light, much faith, and they should, without those apples given to children, strongly believe; and God, to confirm his own, of mere indulgence sweeteneth affections.

But if God give comforts, ordinarily it is a sort of indulgence of grace, or the grace of grace. It is true, rejoicing falleth under a gospel commandment, (Phil., iv, 4,) yet so, as God hath not tied the sweet of the comfort of believing to believing, that you may know its strength of faith, that is, the principle of strong faith, as intense and strong habits make strong acts. God keepeth some in a sad condition all their life, who are experienced believers, and they never feel the comfort of faith till the splendour of glory glance on their eyes; as one experienced believer, kept under sadness and fear for eighteen years, at length came to this, 'I enjoy and rejoice, with joy unspeakable and glorious;' but he lived not long after. Another living in sadness all his life, died with comforts admirable. And 3. Let this be put as a case of conscience, why divers believing, and joying much in God's salvation all their life, yet die in great conflicts, and, to beholders, with little expression of comfort and feeling; as divers of the saints die. Certainly, God, 1. walketh in liberty here. 2. He would not have us to limit the breathings of the Holy Ghost to jump with our hour of dying. 3. We may make an idol of a begun heaven, as if it were more excellent than Christ. To conclude, little evidence, much adherence, speaketh a strong faith.

SERMON XXIII.

5. THE woman had no apparent evidences of believing; yet did she hang by one single thread of the word of the mercies of the Son of David. The more that the word of promise hath influence in believing, and the less of convincing reason and appearances, the greater faith. Abraham had a promise of a son in whom the nations of the world should be blessed. (Rom., iv.) But, 1. There was no appearance of this in nature; Abraham and Sarah, at this

time, were, between them, two hundred years old, lacking ten, and so, no natural hope of a child. 2. He had but one promise for his faith; we have twenty, an hundred; yet, "He, against hope, believed in hope." (Rom., iv, 18.) It is an elegant figure, having the form of a contradiction,—there was no hope, yet he had hope. "Not being weak in the faith:" (Verse 19.) Then, "he was strong in the faith," and gave glory to God, as it is, verse 20. 3. He staggered not through unbelief. Then it is an argument of a weak faith, to dispute according to the principles of natural logic with God: to go on upon God's naked word, without reasoning, is a strong faith, especially when the course of Providence saith the contrary. The word of promise is the mother and seed of faith, (1 Pet., i, 23): the more of the seed, the more of the birth. Wine that is separated from the mother, doth sooner corrupt; that is strongest faith, that hath most of its seed and mother, that is, of the word of promise in it. Abraham had nothing on earth to sustain his faith in killing his son, but only a naked commandment of God; all other things were contrary to the fact: yet is faith strongest when it standeth on its own basis and legs, and that is, the word of Omnipotency—the word of promise. Other pillars of faith are rotten and sandy foundations; inspirations beside and without the word, are the natural faith's unwritten traditions. Every thing is strongest on its own pillars that God and nature hath appointed for it. The earth hangeth by God and nature's statute in the midst of the air. If the earth were up in the orb or sphere of the moon, it should not be so sure as it is now; and if the sea, fountains, and floods were up in the clouds, they would not be so free from perishing, as they now are. Faith is seated most firmly on a word of Him who is able to perform what he hath said. Wicked men are seeking good in blood, in wars, in the destruction of the church, of the reformation and covenant of God; yet their actions are not seated on a word of promise, but on a threatening that destruction shall come on them as a whirlwind. Therefore is not the wicked man's bread sure, when the child of God hath bread, sleep, peace, immunity from the sword, (in so far as the sword is a curse), and that by the covenant of promise. This woman had one gospel word, mercy from the Messiah, David's son.

6. That is a strong faith, which can forego much for Christ, and the hope of heaven. Moses was strong in the faith in this, who refused the treasures of Egypt, the honour of a princedom, and to be called "The son of Pharaoh's daughter." (Heb., xi, 26.) For he had an eye, an eagle's look, and eye to heaven, to the recompence of reward. Abraham foregoeth country and inheritances for God; "By faith he sojourned in the land of promise, as in a strange country, dwelling in tabernacles." (Heb., xi, 9.) 1. He sojourned. 2. He played the pilgrim. 3. He dwelt not in castles and cities, though the land was his by promise, and his grandson, Jacob, disposed of it in his testament, (Gen., xlix, 10,) "For he looked for a city which hath foundations," (to the strong faith, all cities are bottomless except heaven,) "whose maker and builder is God." Now, this woman's faith is great in this;—she looked for a temporary deliverance from Satan's power to her daughter, under the notion of one of the sure mercies of David, and that by faith, which inheriteth all the promises. Not to see beyond time and death, not see the gold at the race's

end, fainteth the traveller: a sight of the fair city, is as a draught of wine to the fainting traveller; it addeth legs and strength to him. Heaven is down-ground when faith seeth it; it is, when sight faileth us, toilsome, and up the mount. When Stephen in a near distance heard the music of heaven, his countenance did shine; he did leap to be at it: "I see heaven open, and Jesus standing on the right hand of God."

7. It is great faith to pray, and persevere, and watch unto praying, as this woman did, when Christ seemeth to forbid to pray; as he both reproached this woman in her praying, as if it had been but the crying of a dog, and said, he was not sent for her. When the promise and Christ seem to look away from you, and to refuse you, yea, to forbid you to believe; then to believe is great faith: actions in nature going on in strength, when contrary actions do countermand them, must be carried with prevailing strength. It is strength of nature that the palm tree groweth under great weights; it is prevalency of nature, that mighty rivers, when they swell over banks, do break over all oppositions. Satan hath a commission to burn and slay; a strong faith quencheth all his fiery darts, (Eph., vi, 16). "Let me alone," saith the Lord to Jacob, (Gen., xxxii, 25, 26); pray no more. Jacob's strong faith doth meet with this commandment thus, "I will not let thee alone, I must pray on till thou bless me." Strong faith beateth down misapprehensions of promises, or of Christ, and layeth hold on Christ under his mask of wrath, and covered with a cloud. (Lam., iii, 9.)

8. Great boldness in the faith, argueth great faith. There be three things in faith, in this notion: 1. An agony and a wrestling of faith, (Col., i, 29,) which is

a heavenly violence in believing: 2. To be carried with a great measure of persuasion and conviction, with full and hoisted up sails in believing, (Col., ii, 2). There is a rich assurance of faith. Not that only, but in the abstract, there is the riches of assurance. There is all riches of assurance; all riches of the full assurance of faith. So strong prevailing light, produceth a strong faith: alas! it is but twilight of evidence that we have. 3. To be bold, and to put on a heavenly stoutness and daring, in venturing with familiarity unto the throne of grace, is a strong faith, (Heb., x, 22; iv, 16). We are to come with liberty, and holy boldness to the throne, as children to their father: so the church, with heavenly familiarity, and the daring of grace and faith, prayeth, "Let him kiss me with the kisses of his mouth." (Cant., i, 2.) John's leaning on Christ's bosom, is not familiarity of love only, but of faith also: "In whom we have boldness and access, with confidence, by faith," (Eph., iii, 12). Faith dare go unto the throne; and to the Holy of Holies: (Heb., x, 19). Faith blusheth not.

9. That which leadeth a man, with Paul and Silas, to sing psalms in the stocks, in prison, and in scourges, that is a strong faith. Job is hence known to be strong in the faith, because, being made a most miserable man in regard of heavy afflictions, he could bless God. A strong faith prophesieth glad tidings out of the fire, out at the window of the prison, and rejoiceth in bonds, (Mic., vii, 8, 9; Isa., lii, 1, 2; liv, 1–4). "To glory in tribulation," is an argument of one justified by faith, (Rom., v, 1–3); and the greater glorification of Christ's chains and cross, is a stronger reason to conclude a strong faith.

10. To wait in patience for God all the day long, is

an argument of great faith: "He that believeth shall not make haste; (Isa., xxviii, 16); he shall not be confounded with shame, (so the Seventy translate it, and Paul after them, Rom., ix, 33); as those that flee from the enemy out of hastiness, procured by base fear, which is a shame. It proveth believing, and a valorous keeping the field without flying, and so, continued waiting on God, to be of kin to believing; and the longer the thread of hope be, though it were seventy years long, (as Hab., ii, 1, 2,) or though it were as long as a cable going between the earth and the heaven, "up within the veil," (Heb., vi, 19,) the stronger the faith must be. Unbelief not being chained to Christ, leapeth overboard at first, as the wicked king said in the haste of unbelief, "What should I wait any longer on the Lord?" (2 Kings, vi, 33.) Faith is a grace for winter, to give God leisure to bring summer in his own season. The reasons of our weakness be two: 1. We see Israel and their dough on their shoulders wearied and tired, lately come out of the brick furnace, wandering without one foot of heritage, forty years in the wilderness, and four hundred years in Egypt; (Acts, vii, 6;) this looketh like poverty: to believe the other mystery in the other side or page of providence, the glory of dividing the Red sea, and of giving seven mighty nations to his people, and their buildings, lands, vineyards, gardens; is a strong faith. 2. The furnace is a thing void of reason and art, and so knoweth little that by it the goldsmith maketh an excellent and comely vessel of gold. It is great faith to believe, that God, by crooked instruments, and fire and sword, shall refine a church and erect a glorious building, and these malignant instruments are as ignorant of the art of divine providence, as coals and fuel arc of the art and intention of the goldsmith, (Mic., iv, 12; Isa., x, 5–7). The axe and saw know nothing of art, nor the sword any thing of justice. Prelates papists, malignants in the three kingdoms, understand nothing of God's deep counsel upon themselves, in that God, by a fire of their kindling, is burning themselves, and taking away the tin and brass, and reprobate metal, and refining the Spouse of Christ; they serve a great service, but know not the master of the work.

11. An humble faith, such as was in this woman, is a great faith. The more sins that are pardoned, as it inferreth the more love to Christ, (Luke, vii, 47,) so the unworthier a soul is in itself to believe pardon in Christ, argueth the greater faith. It must be a greater faith, to believe the pardon of ten thousand talents, than to believe the forgiveness of five hundred pence. Christ esteemeth it the greatest faith in Israel, that the centurion abaseth himself, as one unworthy to come under one roof with him; and that he exalteth Christ in his omnipotency, to believe that he can command all diseases at his nod, (Matt., viii, 8–10).

12. A strong desire of a communion with Christ, is an argument of a strong faith. "Surely, I come quickly;" (Rev., xxii, 20). Faith answereth with a hearty desire, "Amen, even so, come, Lord Jesus," and, 2 Pet., iii, 12.[1] Faith desireth an union with Christ, and a marriage union. The reason is, strong faith cometh from strong love; and strong coals of desiring to be dissolved, and to be with Christ, (Phil.,

[1] These two are conjoined; the one is a word of faith *(prosdokontas)*, "Looking for;" the other, a word of earnest desire, *spoudontas*,—'hasting after,' (Stephanus, *votis accelerantes*,) "the coming of the day of the Lord."—*Rutherford.*

i, 23,) burneth in at heaven's door; love-sickness for glory goeth as high, as the lowest step of the throne that the Lamb Christ sitteth on; and it is faith and love together, that desireth Christ to mend his pace, and saith, "Make haste, my beloved, and be as a roe or young hart upon the mountains of spices." (Cant., viii, 14). The fervour of love challengeth time, and the slow-moving wheels of years and months, and reckoneth an hour for a day, and a day for a year, "Oh, when wilt thou come to me?" (Psalm ci, 2). So, hope deferred is a child-birth pain, and a sickness of the soul, (Prov., xiii, 12). Faith with love cannot endure a marrow; faith putteth Christ to posting, and "leaping over mountains, and skipping over hills," (Cant., ii, 8;) and addeth wings to him, to flee more quickly. Yet is there a caution here most considerable: Faith both walketh leisurely, and with leaden feet, and moveth swiftly with eagle's wings. Faith, in regard of love, and desire of union with God, is swift, and hath strong motions for a union; yea, a love-sickness to be at the top of the mount, to be satiated with a feast of Christ's enjoyed face; but, in regard of a wise assurance, that God's time is fittest, it maketh no haste. So, to wait on, and to haste, may stand together, (2 Pet., iii, 10).

13. Faith effectual by, or with child of love and good works, is a strong faith: "Remembering your work of faith;" (1 Thess., i, 3;) faith effectual. (Philem., 6.) There be bones in a strong faith; yea, sap and life. How many thousands of apples be there virtually in a tree that beareth fruit for thirty or forty years together? So, it is said of Stephen, that he was "full of faith and power," (Acts, vi, 8;) and Barnabas, "full of the Holy Ghost, and of faith."

(Acts, xi, 24.) What is then a small faith, or a weak faith, is easily known. 1. A faith void of all doubting, is not a weak faith, nor yet the strong faith. Antinomians err many ways in this point: 1. 'After the revelation of the Spirit, neither devil nor sin can make the soul to doubt,' say they. Yea, but the spirit of revelation was in Jeremiah, who doubted when he complained to God of God; (Jer., xv, 18). Wilt thou be to me altogether as a liar, and as waters that fail? (Jer., xx, 7–9, 14–16.) Job doubted, when he said, "Wherefore hidest thou thy face, and holdest me for thine enemy?" (Job, xiii, 14.) And Asaph, (Psalm lxxiii, 13), Heman, (Psalm lxxxviii, 13–15), and the Church, (Psalm lxxvii). Yet all these were "sealed by the Spirit unto the day of redemption." 2. This is like the foul error of the Arminians, who, with the Socinians, hold, that as there be three degrees of believers, 1. Some babes; 2. Some aged; so there is a third sort of truly perfect ones, who do not sin from the root of concupiscence, 'the combat between the flesh and the spirit now ceasing, only they sin through inadvertency or some error, or overclouding of their light,' as Adam and the angels sinned, there being no inward principle of corruption in them. Hence some libertines say, those that are in Christ can no more sin, and not walk with God, than the sun can leave off to give light, or fire to cast heat, or a fountain to send out streams, in regard that the Spirit actuateth them to walk with God by such a necessary impulsion that destroyeth all freedom of will; and if they sin, they are not to be blamed, because the Spirit moveth them not to abstinence from sin, and to holy walking. But Paul, "a chosen vessel," and a strong believer, complaineth of the indwelling of sin, of his carnality, and the flesh lusting against the spirit, and of his captivity under sin, (Rom., vii, 14–17,) which must argue his imperfect faith, liable to the distemper of sinful doubtings. It is also a great error to say, That to call in question, whether God be my Father after, or upon the commission of some heinous sins, as murder, incest, etc., doth prove a man to be in the covenant of works.

Now there be sundry sorts of doubtings opposed to faith. In the renewed, there is, 1. A natural doubting; and, as all popery is natural and carnal, so this strangeness of affection by which men are unkind to Christ, and never persuaded of God's favour in Jesus Christ, argueth the party to be under the law, and not in Christ. This doubting may, and doth in carnal men consist with presumption, and a moral false persuasion, that natural men have all of them, till their conscience be wakened, that they shall be saved. 'Why? I am not a murderer, a sorcerer, etc. Why? Or, how can God throw me into hell?' So it is made up of real lies and contradictions; yet they have no divine certainty of salvation. For, ask a natural man, Have you a full assurance of salvation, as you say, that you always believe and doubt not? He shall be there at a stand, and answer, Who can have a full assurance? But I hope well, I believe well, night and day. And so doubt Papists also, and they have a lie in their right hand; 'it cannot stand with God's mercy or justice, since I am not this, and this, to throw me into hell.' So is unbelief a lie: "And of whom hast thou been afraid and feared, that thou hast lied and hast not remembered me?" (Isa., lvii, 11.) 2. There is an occasional doubting that riseth by starts upon wicked men, out of an evil conscience of sin, but it vanisheth as a cloud; as in Pharaoh's confession, "I and my people have sinned." This argueth a law-spirit, rising and falling asleep again. 3. There is a final doubting of despair, like the doom passed on the condemned malefactor; as in Cain, (Gen., iv, 13, 14;) in Saul, (1 Sam., xxviii, 15, 16). All these conclude men under the law, and the curse of it. But there is, 4. A doubting in the believers, which, though a sin, yet (if I might have leave to borrow the expression) is a godly sin; not because it is not a sin indeed, and so, opposite to grace and godliness, but a gracious sin, in regard of the person and adjuncts, it being a neighbour to saving grace; and no reprobate can be capable of this sin, no more than Pagans, or flagitious and extremely wicked men can be capable of the sin against the Holy Ghost. So beggars are remotest from high and personal treason, because they have never that honour to come near the king's person. So David's bones, not Saul's bones, were broken, humbled bones. (Psalm li, 10.) For a humbled heart is called *(Nidcheh)* broken, and bruised with a fear of God's wrath for sin; and the converted soul's moisture is turned to the drought of summer; and his bones waxen old with roaring all the day, God withholding the joy of his salvation. (Psalm xxxii, 3, 4.) This doubting befalleth never any reprobate under the law or covenant of works; and so, though it be an ill thing, yet it is a good sign, as out-breaking of boils in the body are in themselves diseases, infirmities, distempers, and contrary to perfect health; yet they are often good signs and arguments of strength of life, and much vital heat and healthiness of constitution. That affections of the child of God, under incest, murder, or other heinous sins be stirred, that sorrow be wakened and rise, when our Father is offended, and when our Lord frowneth and standeth behind the wall, and goeth away, is lawful; yea, it speaketh tenderness of love, softness of heart. But that they be so far wakened, as to doubt, and fear that the Lord be changed, that he hath forgotten to be merciful, that is sinful doubting; but doth noways conclude, that the person is under the covenant of works, but the contrary rather, that grace sitteth and bordereth with this doubting; and so, that the person is under grace, not under the law. Even where faith is strong, it is not ever in the same temper. Health most vigorous will vary in its degrees, and decrease at times of distemper, and yet be strong, and have much of life in it. Take the strong and experienced Christian's life in its whole continued frame, and for the most part, he hath the better of all temptations; but, take him in a certain stage, or nick of providence, when he is not himself, and he is below his ordinary strength, even in that wherein he excelleth. If a gracious temper of meekness like Christ, was not the predominant element of grace in Moses, yet it was in a great measure in him, he bearing the name with Him, who best knoweth names, and things, of the meekest man in the earth. Yet in that which was his flower, he proved weaker than himself, and spake unadvisedly with his lips. Our highest graces may meet with an ill hour. Job, by the testimony of the Holy Ghost, is patient; "ye have heard of the patience of Job." And, (chap. iii,) we have heard of the cursing passion of Job, also. Believing is like sailing, which is not always equal; often strength of wind will blow the ship twenty miles backward. 2. The smallest measure of faith, is sincere adherence to Christ. Not that negative adherence simply, by which some may say, I dare not for a world quit my part in Christ, or give up with him. Natural spirits may have a natural tenderness, by which they dare not quit Christ, and give up with him; yet there is no saving faith in natural spirits: but there is in the believer some positive adherence under, or with the negative, by which there is a power of love and kindness, making the soul to cleave to Christ. There may be great weakness with this, and great failings, and yet faith unfeigned. We have need of much charity to those that are weak in faith. A reed, a broken reed may grow; and Christ will not break it. A buried believer is a believer. If Christ have a near relation of blood to a piece of blue clay, and the dead corpse of a believer, seeing in his flesh there is the seed and hope of a resurrection, as the seed and hope of harvest is, in rotting and dying grains of wheat sown in the cold earth, as is clear, (Psalm xvi, 9; 1 Cor., xv, 42–44), much more the relation of mercy remaineth in Christ, toward the wrestling, deserted, and self-dead believer.

Now, this smallest measure of faith may consist, 1. With much ignorance of God, as it was with the believing disciples, who continued with Christ in his temptations, confessed him, believed and adhered to him, when many went back, and departed from him, (Luke, xxii, 28, 29; Matt., xvi, 16, 17; John, vi, 66–69;) and yet were ignorant of great points of faith, as of his death, (Matt., xvi, 21, 22,) and of his resurrection, (John, xx, 9). 2. So there be great faintings and doubtings, when a storm ariseth, and the soul is sinking, (Matt., viii, 25–27; Matt., xiv). 3. Yet a little faith is faith. As touching a fainting faith, it is not always a weak faith that fainteth;

strong and healthy bodies may have fevers and deliquiums. For the causes of fainting are, 1. The want of the influence of mercy, and of stirring or exciting grace, causeth fainting. "As we are mercied we faint not;" we degenerate not. (2 Cor., iv, 1.)[1] It is in the bosom of Christ, and lieth about the bowels of our merciful High Priest, that keepeth from fainting. If our Intercessor pray not, we faint: "I have prayed that thy faith may not be eclipsed."[2] (Luke, xxii, 32.) The moon is in a certain death, and soon in an eclipse; so is faith under fainting. 2. Fear of wrath may cause distraction, and hanging of mind, and uncertainty, where there is strong faith; (Psalm lxxxviii, 14, 15, compared with ver. 8, 9). As apprehensions report of God, so are we affected in believing; yet may it be collected from Matt., x, 19, "In that hour it shall be given you," that Christ holdeth the head of a fainting believer. 3. The dependence of faith will faint, when Christ withdraweth love, though he inflict no anger. The ingenuity of grace gathereth fear from a cloud, though there be no storm. 4. A soul dead in himself, and that cannot put out faith in acts, for want of light and comfort, is a weak faith. A tree in winter is a living tree. There may be life, where there is little stirring or motion. 5. That faith that seemed smallest to the man himself, is sometimes in itself greatest. 1. In sad desertions there is most of faith, and least of sense of faith, (Psalm xxii, 1). 2. A suffering faith, may be small to the sufferer. Many of the martyrs, in their own sense, were in a dead and unbelieving condition. Yet Christ is more commended for a suffering faith than any, in that he did run, endure the cross, for the glory that was before him. (Heb., xii,

[1] Ouk ekkakoumen.—*Rutherf.* [2] Me ekleipe.—*Rutherf.*

1–3.) He saw heaven; and his faith went through hell to be at heaven. There is a high commendation put on the suffering faith of those who were tried with bonds, imprisonment, sawn asunder, mocked, slain with the sword, of whom the world was not worthy. (Heb., xi, 37, 38.) This is not put upon the active and doing faith, which is put upon the passive faith; nor is so much said of these, who, by faith, pulled down the walls of Jericho; of Gideon, Baruch, Samson, and such as by faith subdued kingdoms. The reason is, suffering is a loss of being and well-being. Those who, by doing, give away their evil-being for Christ, and crucify their lusts for him, are dear to him; but such as die for Christ, they give away both being and well-being. Moses and Paul, who, in a manner, were content to go to hell, with believing that God's glory in saving the people of God, was to be preferred to their eternal being and well-being, behoved to have great faith. 3. The faith that is weak, in regard of intention of degrees, may be a great faith, in regard of extension. The children of God, whose life is the walk of faith, (2 Cor., v, 7,) may have but a small measure of faith: Yet it is a constant and well breathed faith, good at the long race, that carrieth a soul through; in, 1. His natural capacity to believe God will feed him: And, 2. In his civil relations, as a father, son, servant, magistrate. 3. In his spiritual condition, in the duties of the first table; in all which capacities we are to walk by faith, yea, to eat, drink, sleep; to laugh, to weep, as concerning the ordering of all these heavenward by faith. All the saints that go by heaven believing and ordering all these conditions by faith, have not always a faith as great as Abraham, as Moses. Weak legs carry some through the earth many thousand miles. A sorry and small vessel, in comparison of others, may sail about the globe of the whole earth. The wings of a sparrow or a dove, can carry these little birds through as much sea and land, as the wings of an eagle doth carry the eagle.

But ere I go from this point, I crave leave to add somewhat, 1. Of the least and smallest measure of faith: 2. Of the condition of the child of God under it.

Touching the former, I only say, there is a degree of fire, and a coal so small, that less cannot be, the thing remaining fire, having the nature, essence, and properties of fire. And when any is in a deliquium or swoon, the man hath life, but it is kept in narrow bounds; there is breathing only; some vital heat; some internal motion in the heart, and vital, and animal spirits, but no more to prove life almost, than the man is a dead corpse. Yet somewhat there is to distinguish him from dead clay, for friends will not bury a swooning man wilfully and knowingly. So at the lowest condition of the weakest faith that the believer is in, some fire and coal of love and faith there is, and some smoking, though little fire, and possibly we cannot give it a name. Yet if the just live by faith, there must be some measure of faith; some smoking of love to Christ; some discerning of an ill condition. No man on earth, in a sleep, hath a reflex act to know that he sleepeth; no dead corpse knoweth itself to be dead. Never sleeping man could say, nay, not Adam in his first sleep, when God formed the woman out of a rib of his side, 'Now, I am sleeping.' No man naturally dead, can say, 'Now am I dead, and I lie among the worms and corruption.' Death maketh no report of death. But the believer can say, at his lowest condition, "I sleep, but my heart waketh;" (Cant., v, 1,) and he who saith, "Lord, quicken me," (Psalm cxix,) must say, "Lord, I am dead:" yet to say, "Lord, quicken me," and to feel and know deadness, are acts of the life of grace. A saint in this condition, may love Christ through half a dream, and half-sleeping half-waking retain honourable thoughts of Christ, (Job, xiii, 15; and xix, 25–27). Some have said, in hell they should love Christ. This truth is in it, that in such a pain and sad condition of suffering as the damned are in, (sin, despair, or God's hating of them excepted,) saints can believe and love Christ. (Psalm xxii, 1,) at least, desire to have leave to love Christ; for the evil of sin may, the evil of punishment cannot quench the love of Christ, which is stronger than death—than hell, (Cant., viii, 6, 7). The soul, at the lowest condition, is like the man who hath engaged his lands for so great a sum, as may be a just price to buy the land; and so, in effect, he hath sold the land, but with a reversion; he keepeth the reversion, and so by law, within such a time, he may redeem his mortgaged inheritance. The weakest of believers, at his lowest ebb, keepeth the reversion of Christ. He may, by some grievous sin, be under such a terrible desertion, as to put the inheritance of heaven to a too great hazard of being lost, and in appearance, and in his own sense, and in the sense of many, all is gone; yet then, to say nothing of the invisible chain of God's unchangeable decree of election, which the strongest arms of devils and hell cannot break, there is fire under the embers,—sap and life in the root of the oak tree. God saith of the bud of this vine tree, though the man neither see nor hear it, "Destroy it not, for there is a blessing in it."

As touching the Second, the question may be, What

remaineth for him in this condition, to know his condition, or what can he do? I answer, 1. When Christ hath left his bed, and is gone, he is to keep warm the seat that Christ was in. I do not say that the Church was at the lowest ebb, yet a desertion there was, and a sad one. (Cant., v, 6.) But in this condition she openeth her heart to Christ: "I rose up to open to my Beloved." 2. There be some "Droppings of myrrh from her hands," some sense of Christ. (ver. 5.) 3. "I called him, but he answered me not;" there remaineth a faculty of praying. 4. A love-sickness. Hence it is evident, in the lowest and ebbest condition of a fainting faith, there is something answerable to this; and this is, to love the smell of Christ that he hath left behind him, when he himself is gone; it is to desire to behold, with love and longing, the print of his feet, the chair of love that he sat in.

Hence, though you feel no work of sanctification, his seat is kept by some spiritual meditations, as to consider, what kind of love it is that Christ hath bestowed on sinners, for that he loved his own before he died for them, his love being the cause why he died for them; and still, after the purchased redemption, he loveth them, and intercedeth for them up at the right hand of God. And this is as much as to say, Christ hath loved you, and repenteth not of his love; love made him die for you, and if it were to do again, he would die over again for you, (Rom., viii, 33, 34; 1 Tim., iii, 16). And suppose we that there were need that Christ should die twice, or four times, or an hundred, or millions of times, and that he had ten thousand millions of lives, and that our sins should have required that he should first die for one believer, and then die again the second time for another, and then the third time for another;—and so that he must, for every several elect person, have died a several death; love, love should have put him upon all these deaths willingly. And, therefore, if the believer had ten loves, as many loves in one as there be elected men and angels, all had been too little for Christ; and when the believer hath been serving and praising up in the highest temple, as many millions of ages of years, (or a track of eternity answerable to that duration of ages,) as the number of the sand on all the coasts in earth, of all the stars in heaven, of all the flowers, herbs, plants, leaves of trees, that have been, or shall be from the creation of God, to the taking down of the workmanship of heaven and earth; yet shall he be as much in Christ's debt for this infinite love, when that time is ended, as when he first opened his mouth in the first breathing out of praises in the state of glory. 2. He may turn over in his mind all the promises; and the literal revolution of them in the mind, though it be but a deed or act of the understanding and memory, may cast fire on the affections, in which there resideth a habit of grace: though there be no fire in the bellows, yet blowing with the bellows may waken up, and kindle fire in the hearth where there is little. The habit of grace is often as sparks of fire on the hearth, under the ashes, and may be kindled up, and made a fire. 3. When faith is weakest, and the soul under a winter and a dead eclipse, it is fit to keep the heart in a passive frame of receiving of him again; as to sorrow for sin, and to put to the door unrepented sins; as when the king goeth abroad, to sweep the chamber for his return. Missing of Christ, longing for his return, inquisition for him, "Watchmen, saw ye him?" love-sickness for him, putteth the soul in a sweet passive capacity to receive him again, (Cant., iii, 1–5). 4. When the Church is in bed sleeping, yet she is charged to open, (Cant., v, 2). To weep at the noise of Christ's knock, when you cannot rise, is somewhat; a prisoner may stir his legs, and cause the iron fetters tinkle, though he cannot get out; there is some strength when we are bidden, "Lift up the hands that hang down, and the feeble knees." (Heb., xii, 12.) Motion will make fire. 5. Especially Christ sleepeth least, when his child is in a high fever; love watcheth then most at the bed-side.

SERMON XXIV.

"THY *faith.*" Faith is so Christ's, as the fountain and the cause, that it is ours, as agents moved and acted by Christ. Hence it is a foul error to say, 'That there is no inherent righteousness in the saints, and no graces in the souls of believers, but in Christ only.' There is water, even "the Spirit poured on the dry ground," (Isa., xliv, 3); God's Spirit put within us," (Ezek., xxxvi, 26, 27); "the Spirit of grace and of supplication poured on the house of David," (Zech., xii, 10); "a well within the saints, springing up to life everlasting," (John, iv, 14). The Father and the Son, through the operation of grace, take up house in them, (John, xiv, 23). Such a new stock and plant of heaven set in them, as they have the "anointing dwelling in them," (1 John, ii, 27). "The seed of God abiding in them," (1 John, iii, 9). "Unfeigned faith dwelling in Timothy," (2 Tim., i, 5). Grace in them, as fire under ashes, (2 Tim., i, 6). And a new divine nature, (2 Pet., i, 4). An inward man," (2 Cor., iv, 16). "Christ in you the hope of glory." (Col., i, 27.) Nor are the faculties of the soul, and the workings thereof in our conversion destroyed, as some say, as if the Holy Ghost should come instead of these; for Christ taketh down old work, and maketh a new building for himself, but the stones are ours, the soul remaining in its powers and operations; the understanding and will remain, but opened, (Luke, xxiv, 45; John, xxi, 18; Eph., i, 17, 18; Eph., iv, 23, 24). Christ removeth the rubbish and the frowardness, and overgildeth our stones; it is our matter, and his workmanship. Hence we are agents. Grace teacheth no man to be lazy; for, because all the moral actions of the renewed are commanded of God, if we by grace were no agents in these, but mere patients, and Christ and the Holy Ghost the only immediate agents,—in the omitting of believing, praying, praising, hearing; in not doing all our natural and civil actions for God, and in a spiritual way; yea, and in our forbearing to murder, whore, blaspheme, etc., (for, by the grace of Christ the saints abstain from sin), we should not sin; —all these wicked acts were to be imputed to the grace of Christ, and the Holy Ghost, which is blasphemy, and a flat turning of the grace of God into wantonness. Now we are, by grace, to be agents, to purge ourselves, (1 John, iii, 3,) to run with enlarged hearts in God's way, (Psalm cxix, 32,) to stir up, and blow upon grace under ashes, (2 Tim., i, 6;) "To walk in Christ as we have received him," (Col., ii, 6;) "To keep ourselves in the love of God," (Jude, 21).

Use.—We are to be careful of the stock, not to hurt

or waste the stock of grace. He who is spending his stock, before it be long shall have nothing. Cast not water upon your own coal, to quench the Spirit, or to grieve it. See what grows out of your stock; what income and crop of the fruits of the Spirit shall return to Christ. The Lord demandeth of every child of God, what, and where is the stock, and where is the rent of heaven? It is the virtue of the merchant to increase the stock; and, in all losses to strive to keep it whole. There is a wasting of the habit of grace, which is a dangerous thing, (Eph., iv, 30). There is a sadding of the Spirit, and a rubbing off of some letters or characters of the broad seal of the Spirit, which is forbidden; even as break some spokes or axletree of the wheels of a great work, and the mill or horologe is at a stand, and can work nothing. Beware, that no wards of the conscience be broken, for fear that the key of David that openeth the heart, fit them not, or suit not with the lock. David brake a ward, and a sprent of the new heart, by his adultery and bloodshed, and therefore, no artificer but one only in heaven, could put the lock in frame again, (Psalm li, 10). The new creation is like a curious horologe, made of crystal glass; it must be warily and tenderly handled: the frame of the workmanship of "the Holy Ghost dwelling in us," (2 Tim., i, 14,) must be kept from the least craze or thraw in all the wheels and turnings thereof; yea, the least mote must not rest on it.

Quest.—What must be done to keep in good temper the new creation? *Ans.* 1. Beware to go to bed and sleep with a bone broken or disjointed in the inner man. It is good to be disquieted in spirit, as if there were an aching in the bones, after some great sin not repented nor bewailed. When Peter, by denying his Lord, had rotted a bone, or a joint of the new man in himself, he rested not well that night; "He went out, and wept bitterly," (Matt., xxvi, 57). Jeremiah made a rash and passionate vow, to speak no more in the name of the Lord; but he could not sleep with that coal of fire in his bones, (Jer., xx, 9). 2. Put the keeping of the new creature off your hand;—make it a pawn committed to Christ's keeping, (2 Tim., i, 12,)—let him answer for it,—be not you under the burden of it yourself. The habit of grace, and the man put under lock and key to Christ, is in sure keeping; consider what cometh of him, (Jude, 24). This is a broken world, there be many loose-handed devils going abroad through the earth; there be robbers lying await in the way to heaven, to take the crown from us, (Rev., iii, 11). The believer, who hath a stock of grace, must be at holding and drawing with men and devils. "Commit the keeping of your souls to the faithful Creator;" but be not you idle, do it in "well-doing," (1 Pet., iv, 19). 3. Deal kindly with Christ, when you have him; break not with Christ, if you would keep the habit of grace safe; do nothing against your state. Grieving of the Holy Ghost, is unworthy of the condition of a redeemed one; your place cannot consist with walking after the flesh. The camp you are in cannot well bear compliance with the flesh; "You have put on the Lord Jesus," (Rom., xiii, 14). You cannot lay in for, nor victual such a castle as the flesh; for some exercise a providence, and lay in provision for the flesh. 4. To be doing good, keepeth the habit of grace in exercise, and in life also; for grace is of the nature of life, and life is preserved by motion, and the frequent operations of life; yea, with this difference, the natural life may be worn out, and consumed away, with too frequent and violent labour and toil. This life is increased by assiduous walking with God; for "Every branch that beareth fruit in Christ, my Father (saith he) purgeth it, that it may bring forth more fruit." (John, xv, 2.)

"*Be it unto thee as thou wilt.*"—Christ cannot long dissemble (to speak so), and keep up his love; he tried this woman hardly, now he praiseth her in her face,—"Great is thy faith,"—and granteth her desire to the full. If there was such a brotherly and natural compassion in Joseph, (Gen., xliii, 30,) Joseph's bowels yearned, they were hot, and, "Joseph could not refrain himself,"[1] (Gen., xlv, 1); his love was like a hot furnace and it was like to make a captive of him, and to overcome him: now, the man Christ, hath the same heart and bowels of a man; and I conceive, as Christ was a man void of sin, so the acts of natural virtues, as to pity the afflicted, were stronger in him than in us. Sin blunteth natural faculties, especially such as incline to acts laudable and good—such as are love, compassion to the miserable; and sin boweth, or rather breaketh natural acts that are indifferent in their nature, and farther removed from morality, and maketh them intense above nature, sin being a violent thing. So, in natural men, there is little power in carnal reason over acts of generation, hunger, thirst, sleep, and such as have their rise from the sensitive soul. Christ having strength of sinless reason natural, far above Adam, was strong in the acts of the former kind, and moderate in the other; especially, being a High Priest that matcheth us in natural passions, (Heb., iv, 15). Even,

[1] Vatablus noteth, that the Hebrew word is, 'He could not do violence to himself.'—*Rutherford.*

in a sympathy, and having these same passions that we have, he wept over Jerusalem, (Luke, xix). When they were crying Hosanna to Him, and occasion of joy furnished to him, yet he wept over the city, and spake words of compassion, but broken and imprisoned with sighing and sorrow, "Oh, if thou knew, even thou," (Ver. 41, 42). Now, what compassion must be in him, when his compassion had such an edge? Joseph is nothing to him, he having taken a man's heart to go along with the saints to heaven, sighing, weeping, mourning, "tempted in all these, as we are, but without sin," (Heb., iv, 15). Now, though there be no passions, as there are no infirmities in God, yet the flower, the blossom, the excellency of all these are infinitely in God: he striketh, and trieth, and yet pitieth: Israel cry to the Lord in their bondage, he giveth them a hard answer, "Go to the gods," (saith he,) "that ye have chosen, and let them deliver you." They still are in bondage, and weep upon him; "The Lord's soul was grieved," (Judg., x, 16), (Hebrew, "Cut short for the miseries of Israel"). So Jer., xxxi: Two evils befall Ephraim, one is, God's correcting hand; another is, bemoaning and sorrow for sin; both are trials. But how doth God express himself toward Ephraim? "Is Ephraim my dear son? Is he a son of consolation?" (Verse 20.) So the Hebrew, "Is he my dainty child? For since I spake against him I do earnestly remember him still, therefore my bowels are troubled for him." Observe the in-come of God's consolations, after sad and heavy trials: "O, thou afflicted, tossed with tempest, and not comforted, behold, I will lay thy stones with fair colours, and thy foundations with sapphires." (Isa., liv, 11.) "Comfort ye, comfort ye my people, saith our God. Speak to the heart of Jerusalem, and cry to her that her warfare is accomplished." (Isaiah, xl, 1, 2.) There is a violence of heavenly passion in Christ's love; it will come out at length: tempted ones, wait on, you shall see Christ as Christ, in the end of the day: Christ is well worthy a day's weeping, and a day's waiting on. Compassion strangled and inclosed in Christ, must break out; it easeth Christ's mind, that his bowels of mercy find a vent. Pity kept within God's bowels (to speak so) paineth him, it must come out: "Mine heart is turned within me, my repentings are kindled together." (Hos., xi, 8.) Oh, how rude and inhuman hath sin made our nature! His love who died for us, brake heaven, and rent the two sides of the firmament, as it were, asunder: our Lord descended, and was made a man in all things like us, except sin. But, oh, the first, nay, the doubled summons of Christ's love is not obeyed. Love crieth, we are deaf; Christ's love hunteth no other prey but our heart, and he cannot have it. After Christ hath tempted a soul, he must put it in his heart; it is an ease and comfort to Christ, to ease and comfort the tempted. He is now trying Britain, and giving his bride a cup of blood and tears to drink; but who knows what bowels, what turnings of heart, what motions of compassion are in the man, Christ, now in heaven! Those who shall live to see the Lord take his bride in his arms, and embrace her after these many temptations that now your eyes see, shall subscribe to the truth of this; and those who find Christ's love-embracements, after desertions, know this. Should we suppose that there were in Christ but this one attribute of tender compassion toward his own tempted ones, it should make him altogether lovely to us. For the motion of tender mercy in

Christ, upon the supposition of free love that he died for his own, is natural, he having taken a man's heart to heaven with him, and borrowed nature from us: as our compassionate High Priest, he cannot but pity; mercy acteth as a natural agent in him. Now, suppose we that the mother were eternal, and her child eternal, but eternally weak; compassion should eternally flow from the mother to the child. Suppose a fair rose to grow eternally, and the summer sun to shine near it eternally, and life and sap to keep it vigorous eternally; it should cast out a sweet smell, and offer its beauty to the eyes and senses eternally. In Jesus Christ, the heart and tender bowels of the sweetest, mildest, and most compassionate nature of man that God can possibly form, have met with eternal and infinite mercy in God-Christ; and to say nothing, that mercy in Christ-man hath been putting forth the sweet-smelling acts of love, without tiring, summer and winter, night and day, these sixteen hundred years; and that, even now, while you read this, he is casting out acts of love and mercy—an eternal High Priest could do no other thing for ever, but compassionate his own redeemed flesh. Mercy chooseth a lover freely, Jacob, not Esau; this man, not that man; the fool, not the wise man; the beggar, not the prince; the servant, not the master; but, having once made choice, it worketh necessarily and eternally. Christ's love hath no vacation, no cessation; but when he tempteth, smiteth, afflicteth, trieth, love and tender mercy work in the dark. Joseph's bowels were upon action, and busy, when his brethren saw no such thing, even when he was accusing them as spies, and dealing roughly with them. When the sword of the Lord, drunken, swelled, and fatted with blood, is now raging in the three kingdoms, mercy is in our High Priest, and his bowels are rolled within him, though we cannot see Christ's inner side. It is likely, the place, (Heb., iv, 15,) is but an allusive exposition of the rolled and moved "bowels of God," (Jer., xxxi, 20). Christ is, as it were, in heaven burning, and flaming in a passion of compassion toward his weak ones. He is not only touched, but pained "with our infirmities," so the word doth bear. We shall not do well, to make the tempted condition that either the church or a soul is in, the rule of God's love: God's fiery dispensation in Zion, or in a soul, in the burning bush, speaketh not always wrath. Make not false commentaries on Christ's tempting dispensation. Hell is accidental to the love of Christ, and cannot change it. Suppose Christ's tender mercy were in the midst of the flames of hell, yet there mercy should be mercy, and work as mercy, and not belie itself.

Never a rod of God upon any elect child of God (save upon Christ only) did speak satisfactory vengeance for sin. *Quest.*—Why? Is not Christ now red in his apparel, and his garments dyed and dipped in blood; and hath he not put on vengeance as a garment, in the three kingdoms? *Answ.*—Yes, and for the provocations of England, their unrepented idolatry, superstition, vanity, pride, security, unthankfulness to God, who hath broken the rod of the oppressor, and delivered them from pressures of conscience under Episcopacy, a mass service, and burdensome ceremonies; and for the sins of the king, queen, court, prelates and prophets; the persecuting and killing the witnesses of Christ in Queen Mary's days, and in the late prelates' time; and the present injustice, careless and remiss minding religion; and their labouring to spoil the kingdom of Christ of that power that Christ hath given to his people of church discipline, and translating it to their parliament to make church discipline parliament discipline, confounding so the two kingdoms; their tolerating blasphemous sects, some denying the godhead of Christ, some his kingly office to sanctify and govern his people, some his priestly, some his prophetical office; and many other sins of prophets and people, not repented of; and most of these sins, and many others, and especially the breach of the covenant in Scotland;—these two kingdoms are to fear heavy judgments, and that their calamity is not yet at an end; but rather, "one woe is passed, but another cometh," except these lands be humbled, and lie in the dust before the Lord. Yet, in all this, the dispensation of God, though bloody, is but the Lord saying, as of old, so now to Britain, "And I will turn my hand upon thee, and purely purge away thy dross, and take away all thy tin. And I will restore thy judges as at the first, and thy counsellors as at the beginning; afterward thou shalt be called the city of righteousness, the faithful city. Zion shall be redeemed with judgment, and her converts with righteousness." (Isa., i, 25–27.)

2. A rough dispensation of Christ, cannot abide long rough to the saints, he must answer, and ease the pain of the woman's broken spirit. It is a night's pain to Christ, to cause the tears run down the cheeks of his church all the night,—he cannot but bring a day-light of joy, before the sun's ordinary time to rise, (Psalm xxx, 5.) Christ smiteth, and weepeth for compassion, both at once. Tender mercy in Christ moveth as much, if not more, within than without. The mother's bowels are as much on work within,

when the child is but upon her breasts, and he is not capable to know a mother as a mother; and love as love, as ever. When the deserted is but new and hot come out of the second womb, and a babe born over again, yet, in a spiritual fever, he is as much as ever in the bowels of Christ, though he be not in that case capable of the sense and actual apprehension of Christ, as Christ, and of the sense of Christ's love, as his love: "Since the time that I sufficiently talked with him in correcting him, or since the time of my sufficiency of speaking against him, in remembering him, I do remember him." (Jerem., xxxi, 20.) I spake much in mine anger against him, and half against my will; I did chide him, and scourge him; but my moved bowels, the stirrings of a compassionating heart, did contradict (in a manner) my rough correcting: my heart came out of me, with every rough word and stroke. The sun and nature work long, and many years under earth, in the generation of gold and silver, ere we see gold and silver. God, and his servant Nature, did us a pleasure and a great favour in that kind, in secret, down in the bowels of the earth, to make unseen and concealed provision for our purses: this secret love to us acted down in the dark, is no love to us, till we find it, and see it; yet is nature in a mystery under a veil, sweating under earth to bring forth for us metals, trees, herbs, flowers, corn for our service, but we see no harvest at that time. Christ's bowels are sweating, and as much labouring in child-birth, pain of compassion, and love, and tender mercy towards us, when we are in an ague, and a fit of desertion, as at any time; but we are loved of Christ and pitied, and we know no such thing. All Christ's answers and words to this woman, till now, were but interpretations and proclamations of wrath, and rejecting of her, as not one of the lost sheep of the house of Israel; a dog under the table, not a child of the house. Love came never above ground till now; yet did Christ's affection and love yearn upon her all the time.

Out of all this we collect, Christ may love persons, and yet his dispensation may be so rough, as that to their sense, there is no ground of being assured that Christ loveth them, till he shall be pleased to manifest it. Hence we may gather these propositions, to be considered for the times:

PROPOS. 1. God's free and unhired love, is the cause of our redemption, vocation, sanctification, and eternal salvation: he loved us in our blood, and while we were polluted in our blood. (Ezek., xvi, 6, 8.) When we were the lost world, (John, iii, 16,) ungodly, (Rom., v, 6,) enemies, (ver. 10,) he quickened us, called us, when dead in sins, (Eph., ii, 1,) without works, (2 Tim., i, 9). The bill of grace is Christ's welcome, and pay nothing.

PROPOS. 2. Our divines say, God loveth the persons of the elect, but hateth their sins. Mr. Denne is offended at this, and so are the Arminians for the same reason; "If God hate the works of iniquity, he cannot but hate the persons and workers of iniquity also." It is true, the Lord hateth so the persons of the elect for their sins, as he taketh vengeance of their sins on their surety, Christ; but this consisteth with the Lord's loving of their persons to eternal salvation. The truth is, God's affection *ad intra* of hatred and displeasure, never so passeth on the persons of the elect, as on the persons of the reprobate: he had thoughts of love and peace, in secret, from eternity, to his own elect; he did frame a heaven, a Saviour for them, before all time.

PROPOS. 3. Our divines do rightly teach, that there is a twofold love in God; a love of well-willing,[1] which he did bear to them before the world was, and it is called the love of election. Of this love, Paul speaketh. "I have loved Jacob, and hated Esau." (Rom., ix, 13.) This is fountain-love, the well-head of all our salvation. There is another love called a love of complacency,[2] a love of justification (so Mr. Denne termeth it,) which presupposeth faith, 'without which it is impossible to please God,' (Heb., xi, 6). Of this Christ speaketh, "He that loveth me shall be loved of my Father, and I will love him, and will manifest myself to him." (John, xiv, 21.) "If a man love me he will keep my words, and my Father will love him, and we will come unto him, and make our abode with him." (ver. 23.) So Christ, the wisdom of God, saith, "I love them that love me," (Prov., viii, 17). And so Christ speaketh of his love to his redeemed and sanctified spouse, "Thou hast ravished my heart, my sister, my spouse; thou hast ravished my heart with one of thine eyes, with one chain of thy neck." (Cant., iv, 9.) Holiness and the image of God is the object of this love, not the cause nor any hire. It is not so properly love as the other. God rather loveth persons, desiring well and good to them, than things. Mr. Denne is not content with this distinction; and why? 'The love of election and the love of justification,' saith he, 'are not divers loves or divers degrees of love, but divers manifestations of one and the same infinite love: as when a father hath conveyed an inheritance to his son; here is no new love from the father to the son, but

[1] Amor benevolentiæ. [2] Amor complacentiæ.

a new manifestation of that love wherewith the father loved the son before.' *Ans.* Men should not take on them to refute they know not what: not any protestant divines ever taught, that there is a new love in God, or any new degree of love in God, that was not in him before. Arminians, indeed, tell us of new love, new desires, and of ebbing and flowing; love and hatred succeeding one to another in God's mind:—these Vorstian blasphemies we disclaim. It is, indeed, one and the same simple and holy will of God, by which he loved Peter and John from eternity, and chose them to salvation, and by which he so loveth them in time, as of free grace he bestoweth on them faith, holiness, pardon in Christ, and followeth these with his love: and the former is called his love of good will to their person, ere they do good or ill;—the latter his love of complacency to their state, and the Lord's new workmanship in them; as with the same love the husband chooseth such a one for his wife, and loveth her, being now his married spouse.

Obj. 2. Men like those whom they love, and so doth God. *Ans.* We grant all; these terms of God's good loving, and good liking, are chosen of divines to express the thing. God loveth and liketh Jacob, not Esau, from eternity, ere he believe or do good; but he doth not so love and like Jacob from eternity, to bestow faith and the image of the second Adam on him, till in time he hear the word, and be humbled for sin. And the truth is, the love of complacency is not a new act of God's will, that ariseth in God in time, but the declaration of God's love of good will in this effect, that God is pleased to bestow faith and his beauty of holiness, which maketh the soul lovely to God; and it is rather the effect of eternal love, than love. And God hath a love of complacency toward the persons of the elect, and love of good will (though not of choosing good will toward them) for their holiness. (Cant., iv, 9.)

Obj. 3. It is absurd that God should love the elect with infinite love to choose them to salvation, as touching their persons, and withal to hate them with an infinite hatred, as workers of iniquity. *Ans.* It were absurd, I grant, if God's hatred to the elect as sinners, were any immanent affection in God opposite to his love, by which he should be averse to their persons. But God's hatred to the elect, because they are sinners, is nothing but his displeasure against sin, (not against the person,) so as he is to inflict satisfactory punishment on the surety, Christ, for their sin. A father may so love his prodigal son, as to retain a purpose to make him inheritor of a kingdom (if he had a crown for himself) and to pay his debts, and yet both hate and punish his profuse and lavish wasting of his goods.

Mr. Denne would teach us how love and hatred towards sinners doth consist. "The law (saith he) and the gospel speak divers things: the one being the manifestation of God's justice, tells us what we are by nature; the other, the manifestation of God's mercy, tells us what we are by God's mercy in Jesus Christ. The law curseth and condemneth the sinner; the gospel blesseth and justifieth the ungodly. *Ans.* What is this else but that which Mr. Denne and other Antinomians condemn in us? How can one and the same unchangeable God curse, condemn, and so hate sinners, as to punish them eternally, and yet bless, justify, and love to eternal salvation their persons, except they teach the same very thing which we do? For the law and the gospel are no more contrary one to another, than love to the persons of the elect, and hatred and revenging justice to their sins. Mr. Denne would further clear the point thus: "Whatever wrath the law speaketh, it is to the sinner under the law; although the elect are sinners in the judgment of the law, sense, reason, yea ofttimes conscience, yet, having their sins translated into the Son of God (in whom they are elected) they are righteous in Christ the Mediator. *Ans.* The law speaketh wrath, in regard of its reign and dominion to death, to the elect not yet converted, and to the reprobate, without exception of persons. But it cannot speak wrath to the believer, though he be one that daily sins, and is under the law; that is, under the rule of the law. Now, to be under the law, to Paul, is to be under the damnation of the law. (Rom., vi, vii.) In which regard, believers are not under the law, but under the sweet reign of pardoning grace; yet are they under the law as a tutor, a guide, a rule. And that the rule and reign of the law are different, is evident, 1. Because the ruling power of the law is an essential ingredient of the law, without the which, the law is not the law. The reign or damnation of the law agreeth to the law by accident, in so far as man is a sinner, which is a state accidental to the law. 2. The law is a rule, and hath a proper guidance and tutory over the confirmed angels, and should have had over man, if he had never sinned; but the law can have no reign to death over the confirmed angels, and man, in that case; as the jailor, hath no power over the man, who was never an evil doer. 1. We are sinners in the judgment of law, both sin dwelling in us; and 2. The guilt of the law lying on us to condemnation. But being once in Christ, and justified, we remain sinners, as touching the indwelling blot; but we are not sinners, as we are justified in Christ, as touching the law-obligation to eternal condemnation, from which we are fully freed. But the justified and redeemed of Christ, remain as formally and inherently sinners, as milk is formally white, a raven black. Justification removeth not the indwelling of sin; and so, in regard of sense, reason, and conscience, we are sinners to our dying day, but not condemned sinners. Mr. Denne objecteth—we pray daily, "Forgive us our sins;" then we are not righteous in Christ: he answereth, that Protestants say, we beg greater certainty and assurance of forgiveness. But not content with this answer, he addeth, "When we pray for forgiveness, we magnify His grace, who hath freely given us forgiveness: it were not folly to a condemned person, having received a pardon, and being assured of it, to fall down and say, Pardon me, my lord the king. *Ans.* What Protestant divines say in this, we acknowledge; but if we seek only a fuller certainty of forgiveness in this petition, and not also the application of the general pardon, as appropriated to the sins we daily fall in, I see no other thing we seek, but a greater measure of faith, to lay hold on remission. I should ask a warrant of Scripture to prove, that forgiveness of sin signifieth assurance of the pardon of sin. 2. That to seek forgiveness daily, is to glorify and magnify him from whom we once received forgiveness, is not to purpose, for that is a general in all petitions that we put up to God, no less than in this. 3. If a pardoned malefactor, having assurance he were pardoned, should fall down and beg pardon of the king, and not rather tender him thanks and blessings for a received pardon, I should believe he called in question the king's favour; but should he every day, when he eateth bread, beg pardon from the king, as we beg daily forgiveness, he might be charged with more than ordinary folly. Mr. Denne—God loves us in blood (saith he) and pollution, as well before conversion, as after conversion. And though faith procure not God's love and favour, yet it serveth us for other uses, that we may be sealed by believing, (Eph., i, 13,) and may thereby know the love of God. It is said, he that believeth not, is damned; not because his believing doth alter or change his estate before God, but because God hath promised, that he will not only give us remission, but also faith for our consolation; and so, faith becometh a note, and a mark of life everlasting, as final infidelity is of eternal condemnation. *Ans.* It is true, God loveth the elect before conversion equally as after conversion, in regard of that free love of election, that moved him to give his Son to death for them, (John, iii, 16,) and to call them effectually, (2 Tim., i, 9; Eph., ii, 1–4; Tit., iii, 3, 4).

Propos. 4. It is a palpable untruth, that the elect, by believing in Christ, and being translated from death to life in their conversion to God, are equally loved of God before conversion, as after conversion, if we speak of God's love of complacency; for though the inward affection and love of God, as it is an immanent and indwelling act in God, be eternal, and have not its rise in time, and be not like the love of man to man, which is like the sea ebbing and flowing; or the moon, which admitteth of a cloudy and dark visage, and of an enlightened and full condition; yet as the same love of God is terminated upon sinful men, or rather, that which is called the love of complacency, which is indeed the effect of God's love; it is not every way one and the same, after conversion and before; as it is the same fountain and spring that runneth in its streams toward the south, which, by art and industry of men, may be made to run toward the north: the change is in the streams, not in the fountain; yet we say the fountain now runneth not southward, as it did before, but northward. Also, give me leave to doubt, if these same very visible sun-beams, that did fall upon Adam and Eve, do this summer fall upon us; yet, I doubt not, but the same sun that did shine the first six hours of the creation, on the garden of Paradise, shineth upon all our gardens and orchards that now are. So God's love is one and the same toward the elect before time, and while they are wallowing in the state of sinful and depraved nature, and now, when they are changed in the spirits of their mind. But it may well be said that God loveth his Church, as washed, as fair, and spotless, (Cant., iv, 7,) and that he doth now say of her, "How fair is thy love, my sister, my spouse! how much better is thy love than wine, and the smell of thine ointments than all spices?" (Cant., iv, 10.) Whereas, the Lord said before of her, "Thy birth and thy nativity is of the land of Canaan; thy father was an Amorite, thy mother an Hittite; as for thy nativity, in the day that thou wast born, thy navel was not cut, neither wast thou washed in water to supple thee; thou wast not salted at all, nor swaddled at all; (Ezek., xvi, 3, 4). "And when I passed by thee, and saw thee polluted in thy blood, I said unto thee, when thou wast in thy blood, live." (ver. 6.) And all this the Lord might speak to the same Church yet unconverted; and at that time, the Lord could not utter that expression of love, to say to a bloody and polluted church, as he doth, "Thou art all fair, my love, there is not a spot in thee." (Cant., iv, 7.) Now, could it be said, that the Father and the Son love such a church, as such as loveth the Father, and keepeth the words of the Son; as it is, (John, xiv, 21, 23,) what the church was; not fair, not spotless, but filthy, polluted, not washed, not justified as yet? And though it be true, that faith procures not God's love and favour (it is a calumny, that ever a protestant divine taught any such thing); for the work of God's eternal love in election to glory, or his hatred in reprobation, is not the yesterday or to-day's-birth of our faith, or our unbelief; yet that believing, or our effectual conversion maketh no alteration or change in our state before God, is a gross untruth. Faith and conversion make indeed no change of any state in the Ancient of days, in the Strength of Israel, who cannot lie or repent; and putteth not God from the state of a reprobating or hating, or a not loving and choosing God; whereas, before he was such, who did love and choose us to salvation. The Lord is our witness, we asserted the contrary doctrine of free grace, against Arminians and Papists.

PROPOS. 5. Our believing and conversion to God, doth alter and change our state before God, 1. Because God esteemed an unbeliever that which he was, —even an unbeliever, a child of wrath, one that is disobedient, serving divers lusts; a soul unwashed, polluted in his blood before his conversion to God: but being once converted, and graced to believe, his state before God is altered and changed, even in the court of heaven; in the Lord's books he is another man, he goeth now for a fair and undefiled soul. The church that was in a polluted, filthy, and miserable condition, (Ezek., xvi, 3–8,) is now in Christ's heart as a seal, (Cant., viii, 6,) so fair, as her beauty ravisheth the heart of Christ. Now, Christ nameth things according to their nature. 2. The condition is so changed before God, that "It cometh to pass, that in the place where it was said to them, Ye are not my people, there it shall be said unto them, ye are the sons of the living God." (Hos., i, 10.) "Which in time past, were not a people, but are now the people of God; which had not obtained mercy, but now have obtained mercy." (1 Pet., ii, 10.) The words of Scripture, that import a real change, do prove the same; as Col., i, 12, "Who hath made us meet, (or sufficiently qualified us,) to be partakers of the inheritance of the saints in light." Christ is a qualified workman, and changeth hell, and the most untoward timber of hell, to heaven, and to a vessel of glory. It is a vain thing to dream, that Christ hath no other esteem and warmness of heart to us, when we are dead in sins and trespasses, and posting as in a horse-race after the devil, who rideth, and acteth, and breatheth in the children of disobedience; and when he hath raised and quickened us for his great love, and placed us in heaven with Christ, "And made us kings and priests unto God." (Eph., ii, 1–4.) Then the state of hell and death, should be the very state of grace and heaven, before God. "A new creature, (2 Cor., v, 7). "Light in the Lord," (Eph., v, 8). "Partakers of the divine nature," (2 Pet., i, 4). "Renewed in the spirit of the mind," (Eph., iv, 23). "Such as are begotten again, unto a lively hope, by the resurrection of Jesus Christ from the dead," (1 Pet., i, 3). "Born again, not of corruptible seed," (1 Pet., i, 23). "Kings and priests unto God," (Rev., i, 5). "A generation of kings and priests unto God," (1 Pet., ii, 9,) must be in their state some other thing than old creatures, than darkness, than unrenewed, uncircumcised old men, slaves of sin, persecutors, blasphemers, injurious persons. The Lord speaketh of a change great enough; "Since thou wast precious in my sight; thou hast been honourable, and I have loved thee." (Isa., xliii, 4.) Were the children of wrath from eternity honourable? No: were they more precious and honourable actually before God from eternity, than the rest of the nations? No; the contrary is evident, (Ezek., xvi, 3; Deut., vii, 7, 8; Psal. cxlvii, 19, 20; Deut., xxvi, 5). Certainly, if faith or conversion to God, (a special part of which is faith), doth not alter the state of believers before God, then are they believers, and actually converted before God, and so, justified from eternity. When were they then sinners? Never; their sins were just no sins from eternity, and blotted away as a cloud, as a thick cloud, as it is, Isa., xliv, 22,—and that from eternity, and from eternity sought and not found, because pardoned, (Jer., v, 20). "No more remembered," (Isa., xliii, 25). Now they were justified from eternity, and ere they believe in him that justifieth the ungodly, no other ways than in God's decree and eternal purpose.

But the truth is, this is the principal false and rotten pillar of all libertinism, which I evert thus, and they shall never be able to answer it: If faith be so far forth a manifestation of our justification before God, because justification was in the sight of God actually done from eternity, before all time, then are we never ungodly, and actually sinners before God: 'For it is impossible,' say Antinomians, 'that God can both hate us, as ungodly, and love us, as justified in Christ; and it is vain and nonsense,' say they, 'that God loved the persons from eternity, and hated the sins; or that he loved the elect with the love of election, or love of good-will, and did not also love them with the love of justification,'—this is their term, not mine—'or with the love of complacency, and his good liking to faith in them.' Then, say I, from eternity the justified were never ungodly, never sinners, never the heirs of wrath, never such as served divers lusts, and were disobedient, polluted in their own blood: which is downright contrary to the word of truth.

Observe the principle of Antinomians:—We are not justified by faith, say they. How then? Because 'we are justified from eternity, only we are said by Paul to be justified by faith, in that, by faith, we come to the knowledge and assurance of the state of election, and of justification, and God's act of not imputing sin to us, which acts were passed upon us from eternity, and before the children had done good or evil,' (Rom., ix, 13). And observe the words of Mr. Henry Denne to this purpose:—'I do believe,' saith he, 'sin to be of that hideous nature, and the justice of God so perfect, that he cannot but hate the person unto whom he imputeth, and upon whom he chargeth sin; if so be, the person charged cannot give full, perfect, and present satisfaction; and yet will I not say, that the Son of God, upon whom all our iniquities were charged, was at any time *filius odii*, a son of hatred, (for the Father was eternally well pleased with him): the reason is, that our sins were no sooner charged upon him, but that he had given full and perfect satisfaction, being the Lamb slain from the foundation of the world,' (Rev., xiii, 8).

Answ. 1. If God cannot but hate the person upon whom he chargeth sin, either God never charged our sins upon Christ contrarv to Scripture, (Isaiah, liii, 6;

1 Pet., ii, 23, 24; 2 Cor., v, 21,) or then he hated Christ; which no sound divine dare say. The payment and satisfaction which Christ made, cannot hinder Christ to hate sin; and so the person upon whom sin is (as Antinomians teach, while as they refuse this distinction), no more than the satisfaction that Christ made for sin, can hinder itself, or hinder Christ to die for sin; for if God should hate Christ, it should be satisfactory hatred, and penal.

2. I much wonder, if God, from eternity, charged sin upon his Son Christ, (for the place he citeth, Rev., xiii, 8, and the judgment of Antinomians so expounding it, evinceth this to be his meaning), how Christ from eternity could give full, perfect, and present satisfaction, to prevent the hatred of his Father, is not imaginable. Indeed, when Christ gave satisfaction, I believe that it was full and perfect: but that Christ from eternity gave present satisfaction, and that to make us actually justified from all eternity, is a point no head can conceive, except Herod, Pilate, Jews, and Gentiles, the traitor Judas, and all who were wicked actors in killing of Christ, be men uncreated, who had existence and being, and sinned from eternity. This lieth fairly for the eternal world of Aristotle. Then, surely, faith doth not bring us to the knowledge only of our state of justification, as past, and done from eternity, as if election to glory, and the love of God therein, and justification, and that love, as manifested by faith, were two co-eternal twins, both at once begotten from eternity. Sure I am, we are justified by faith; but sure I am, we are not elected and chosen to life eternal by faith. And if to be justified by faith be, as our masters (though ignorantly) teach, nothing but this, that we come to the knowledge of our justi-

fication by faith, as by a sign, even as the day-star maketh not the sun to rise, it being only a sign that the sun shall rise, and that justification is as old a child of free love, as election to life; then, say I, Paul might have taken the like pains to prove these propositions: "We are chosen to glory before the world was, by faith, and not by the good works of the law:" And this, "Men are reprobated from eternity by final unbelief." For sure it is, that we come to the knowledge of our election to glory, by believing; not to say, that Paul's large dispute with justiciaries, was not, whether we know and apprehend our own justification by the works of the law, or by faith in Christ.

3. If Antinomians say, that Christ was slain for our sins from eternity, not actually, but only in God's eternal purpose, and they must say, either he was the Lamb, actually crucified for us from eternity (which is a new eternal world,) and we are actually justified from eternity, and our sins imputed to Christ, and actually translated off us, and laid on him, and so our sins actually pardoned from eternity—or then they must say, Christ was the Lamb slain from eternity, not actually, not really, but only in the decree and gracious purpose of God: now, that is, I grant, sound divinity. Christ died not from eternity; but God only decreed and purposed, that in the fulness of time he should die. But then it must follow, that God did not actually charge sin on Christ from eternity, and that Christ did not actually from eternity justify the ungodly, but only in his eternal purpose he did justify the ungodly. Then the ungodly are justified in time;—and when is this time? I believe the word of God, that it is never, till the poor soul believes; even as the sinner is

condemned, and under wrath, but never till he misbelieves, and rejects the Son of God.

But 4. If the meaning (that Christ is the Lamb slain for our sins from eternity) be, that he is slain only in God's purpose, then we are no more justified and pardoned from eternity, and so before we believe, than the world was created from eternity. Now, in the Antinomian sense, as we are justified by faith, that is, we come to know that we were in God's mind actually justified, then it may be said, the world was created by faith; for through faith we understand that the world was created; (Heb., xi, 3;) and God laid our sins upon Christ by faith: and Christ died for us, and bare our sins, on his own body, on the tree, by faith. For, by faith, we come to know, that God made the world; but because the knowledge and apprehension of the creation, (may some say,) is not a point serving for peace of conscience and Christian consolation, which yet is false (every point of saving faith is apt to breed peace and consolation), yet certainly, we come to know and apprehend, that God laid our sins upon Christ, by faith, (Isa., liii, 6:) and that Christ died for us, and bare our sins on his own body on the tree, by faith, and by faith only, to our peace and consolation. And so, if justification by faith be nothing but the manifestation of God's love to us, in imputing our sins to Christ, and have no subordinate organical act in our justification, but we be justified before we believe, and that from eternity, upon the very same ground, God created the world by faith, Christ died for our sins by faith.

5. Yea, in this sense, the world must be created from eternity, and all things which fell out in time, fell out in eternity; because, as Christ was the Lamb slain

from eternity, in God's eternal purpose, so were all things, and the world created from eternity in God's purpose and decree. But things that only have being in the decree of God, are not simply, nor have they any being at all; and, therefore, our free justification from eternity had no being, but only was to be, and actually is, when God giveth us faith to lay hold on the remission of our sins.

Nor is it enough to say, that faith is only given for our joy and consolation, and not for the alteration and change of our state; that of unjustified, we may be justified: for this layeth down these false grounds, 1. The believer is so in every moment of time to rejoice, as he is never to sorrow for sin, nor to confess sin, because sins were pardoned from all eternity; but so, neither after a soul believes, nor before he believes, is he to confess sins, or mourn for them; because both after and before, yea, from eternity, sins are not at all, but removed in Christ. 2. It layeth down this ground, that we are justified no more by faith, than by the works done, by the saving grace of God after regeneration; and that Paul in the Epistle to the Romans and Galatians, does contend with justiciaries, how these who were from eternity justified, shall come to know and apprehend, for their own peace, joy, and consolation, that they were justified and elected to glory—whether men may know this by faith in Christ, or by the works of the law. But, 1. This is not the state of the question between Paul and the justiciaries. For (Rom., iii,) Paul concludeth strongly, we are really and indeed changed from a state of sin, unto a state of justification even before God; not because, by keeping the law, we know we are justified, but because all have sinned, and are come short of the glory of God, and so are inherently wicked, abominable, doers of ill, and condemned therefore before God, from David's testimony, (Psalms xiv, liii). This argument concludeth real and intrinsical condemnation, not the knowledge of condemnation, nor the knowledge that we are not justified by the works of the law. Paul proveth that we are justified as David and Abraham were. (Rom., iv.) Now they are not said to be justified by faith, because they come by faith to the knowledge of their justification. For Abraham's righteousness, and the blessedness of the justified man, opposed to the curse of the law, from which we are freed in justification, (Gal., iii, 10–13,) is the real fruit of justification, and of believing in him that justifieth the ungodly, (Rom., iv, 1–9). But this blessedness, and freedom from the curse of the law, is not any fruit, or effect, or consequent of our knowledge and apprehension of our justification in Christ, as if we were, before we believe, blessed and freed from the curse of the law; because even the elect, before they believe, are under the curse, and are not blessed: 1. Because they are, before they believe, the children of wrath, (Eph., ii, 2). *Ergo*, they are under the curse. 2. Because Paul and the elect, before they be under grace and belief, were under the law, and so, under wrath: (Rom., vi, 14–17:) "Wherefore, my brethren, ye also are become dead to the law, by the body of Christ, that ye should be married to another." (Rom., vii, 4.) "For when we were in the flesh, the motions of sins, which were by the law, did work in our members, to bring forth fruit unto death. But now, we are delivered from the law, that being dead wherein we were held; that we should serve in newness of spirit, and not in oldness of the letter." (ver. 5, 6.) Hence it is clear, there was a time when Paul, and the elect at Rome were servants of sin, (Rom., vi, 20, 21,) under the lusts and motions of sin, which work in their members to bring forth fruit, that is, sins to death eternal, (Rom., vii, 5;) *ergo*, they were then under the curse of the law, and so, far from blessedness, and the servants of sin, (Rom., vi, 20,) and persons in the flesh. But the case is changed; they are now not the servants of sin, but servants of righteousness, (Rom., vi, 22,) married to a new husband, Jesus Christ, (Rom., vii, 4). Whence came this change of two contrary states, yea, and before God contrary? (for before God, it cannot be one state, to be servants of sin, under the law, and servants of God, and under grace). Certainly, from faith on our part, or some other grace in us—at least, there must be something of grace by which the alteration from a cursed estate to a blessed estate is made. Then faith is not a naked manifestation of the blessedness of justification, to the which we were entitled before we believed; for before we believed, we were in a cursed estate. This also may be added, that if faith be but a declaration or manifestation that we are justified before we believe, Paul had no reason to deny that we are justified—that is, that we know to our comfort, by works of holiness, that we are justified; for works of sanctification are evident witnesses that we are in Christ, and are justified, (2 Cor., v, 17; 1 John, iii, 14; ii, 3; James, ii, 24, 25; 2 Peter, i, 10). 3. It layeth down this false ground, that grace is nothing in us, but a mere comfortable sense and apprehension of free love, and grace is conceived to be only and wholly in Christ; so that there is no inherent grace in the believer, by which he is distinguished from an unbeliever; sanctification and duties flowing from the habit of grace are nothing but dreams of legal men: Christ justifying the sinner is all and sum in the elect; strict and precise walking conduce nothing to salvation. 'To think that it can do any thing in order to salvation, is to worship,' saith Mr. Denne, 'an angry Deity; to satisfy justice with our works, fastings, tears, duties.' Therefore our

Propos. 6. is, That it is a vain distinction of Mr. Denne, who would have a reconciliation of God to man, and of man to God; 1. Because we read that man is reconciled to God, (Rom., v, 10; 2 Cor., v, 18–20; Col., i, 20, 21; Eph., ii, 16). Man is the enemy, whereas in Adam he was a friend, and in Christ, the second Adam, he is made a friend. But that God is reconciled to man, or changed toward his own elect from an enemy, and a God that hateth their persons, into a friend and lover of them, I never read: if at any time God be said to be comforted toward his people, or eased, these are borrowed speeches. 2. Love of election, yea, the love that putteth God on work to redeem, call, justify, sanctify the elect, is no love bought with hire, yea, the price of redemption which Christ gave for sinners, cannot buy eternal love. Blood, and the blood of God shed, cannot wadset ancient love; all the sins of devils, of men, cannot forfeit it: make sins, floods and seas, and ten thousand worlds of rivers, they cannot quench that eternal coal and flame in the breast of so free a lover as God;— in a word, the shed blood of Christ is an effect, not a cause of infinite love. 3. What, then, doth reconciliation place any new thing in God? No. Doth it turn him from a hater into a lover? No. Reconciliation active on the Lord's part, is a change of his outward dispensation, not of his inward affections. "Fury is not in me," he saith himself, (Isa., xxvii, 4). He cannot wax hot and fiery in the acts of his spotless and holy will. Reconciliation turneth not the heart, but the hand of the Lord upon the little ones, as he speaketh, so that he cannot deal with or punish his elect, as otherwise he would do. The Lord's justice may be satisfied, his love cannot be bribed or hired, and the effect of justice, the inflicting of infinite wrath, is diverted, as a river that runneth east, hath been made to run west, and an issue of blood in one member of the body, hath been diverted to run in another channel. Justice was to run through the elect of God in the due and legal punishment of the sinner, (which yet is extraneous to the just and eternal will of God;) but infinite wise mercy, caused that river to run in another vein, through the soul of Jesus Christ.

Propos. 7. Joy of the Holy Ghost is a fruit of the kingdom of grace, (Rom., xiv, 17). But not that joy spoken of, Rev., xxi, 4, and Isa., xxxv, 10, which excludeth all tears, death, sorrow, crying, all sighing, as Mr. Denne dreameth; so as joy can no more be separated from the subjects of that kingdom, than light from the sun, heat from the fire, or ebbing and flowing can be stopped in waters, as he saith. Far less is it true, that actual love and obedience do inseparably follow this condition, except we were made angels, when we are once justified. Nor is the kingdom of God spoken of, 1 Cor., vi, 9, 10, and the seeing of God, Heb., xii, 14, the kingdom, or state of grace, or the seeing of God in a vision of faith here in this life; but of the kingdom of glory and of the vision ot God in the other life, as Mr. Denne expoundeth it, that he may elude all necessity of holiness; but that which floweth from no obligation of any law or commandment of God, but which is in our power of love to perform or not perform, if we perform it not, it is no transgression of any law of God.

1. Mr. Denne himself granteth, page 84, 'God is not like some niggardly man, who will not bid us welcome to his house, unless we bring our cost with us.' Nor is holiness required of us without faith, and before we believe and enter citizens of the kingdom of grace; nay, by this interpretation, 1 Cor., vi, we must be justified and washed before we can inherit this kingdom, (verses 9–11). But we are not to be washed and justified, before we inherit the kingdom of grace, and before we believe; for so, we should be justified and washed before we be justified and washed. And the like I say of the kingdom of God, (John, iii, 3.) For it should follow that a man must be born again, ere he be born again, if he must be born again ere he enter a subject of the kingdom of grace. Nay, not any such condition can go before man's reconciliation to God.

PROPOS. 8. Christ can love dearly, and tempt roughly both at once. 1. His love consisteth not in a taking his Church into his bosom, and a continual, and never interrupted laying of her between his breasts; yea, tempting floweth from the love of God, nor is it any act of justice, yea to take vengeance on the inventions of his people (satisfying justice he cannot exercise toward his elect; yet, a punishing and correcting justice, he may, and doth, put forth on them), but it hath its rise from love. All the wheels of God's dispensation, sweet or sour, are rolled upon this axle-tree of free love: the bowels of Christ act, move, and breathe all dispensations to the saints, through no other pipe and channel, but free and tender compassion, so as mercy is an immediate actor, when the Lord is wasting his church with bloody wars. And, which is wonderful, Mercy is Christ's armour-bearer, and Mercy immediately killeth, even when Death climbeth in at the windows, and enters into the house of the believer, either in a pestilence known to come from no creature or second cause, or in the raging sword, when "the carcases of men fall as dung in the open field, and as the handful after the harvest men, and there be none to bury them," (Jer., ix, 21, 22). 2. Tempting mercy is wise mercy; it were not a tempting mercy, if we saw all the secrets of love, and the reasons why the Lord buildeth Zion with blood. Even the elect and beloved of God, though they be in Christ's court, they are not always upon his council, (John, xiii, 7). Many are within the walls of the palace, that are not in the king's parlour, and taken into his house of wine. The love of Christ hath its own mysteries and unknown secrets; as why one saint is led to heaven, and to men's eye "the candlestick of the Almighty shineth on his tabernacle, and he washeth his steps in oil," he is rich, holy, prosperous; and another no less dear to Christ, never laugheth till he be within the gates of heaven, but eateth the bread of sorrow all his days; his face never dryeth till he be in glory, is a secret of heaven. The love of Christ is often veiled and covered, and we know not what he meaneth: but he hasteth to show mercy.

Use. This should make us very charitable of Christ when he frowneth, and covereth himself with a cloud, and very inclinable to pardon (if I may so speak) rough and bloody dispensations in Christ. He loveth, and he bleedeth, scourgeth, and giveth his own child a cup of gall and wormwood. Could we in silence believe it is Christ with two garments on him at once—Christ clothed with love, wrapt in the unseen mystery of tenderness of compassion, and yet his upper garment is vengeance, and rolled in blood, we should kiss the edge of Christ's bloody sword. So we are to believe, for Christ at one time "travaileth in the greatness of his strength, and speaketh in righteousness, and is mighty to save," and at the same time his upper garment is blood. (Isaiah, lxiii, 1.) It is true, it is the blood of his enemies; but it is often the blood of the children of his own house and sanctuary, (Ezek., ix, 6; 1 Peter, iv, 17). And what more concerneth us, than to keep our first love to Christ, when he multiplieth our widows in the three kingdoms, as the sand of the sea, and bringeth against the mother of the young men a spoiler at noonday? (Jer., xv, 8.) This woman stayed on her watchtower, and now, the vision speaketh mercy to her. Say they were injuries that Christ inflicteth (which is a blasphemous impossibility) yet it is Christ, it is the Lord, let him do what seemeth good to him. The absolute liberty of the potter closeth the mouth of the clay vessel, if it could speak, (Rom., ix). That unbelief hath no reason to stomach and dispute against hell's fire coming from him, who hath absolute dominion over us. As devils and wicked men burn in hell with eternal fretting against God for their pain; so, if it were possible, that the elect and regenerate were thrown into hell, they are to have eternal charity and love to the holy and just Lord, and to believe his eternal love.

SERMON XXV.

"BE *it unto thee as thou wilt.*" *(Genethto soi;)* it is a word of Omnipotency, to create being. It is spoken of Satan, and to Satan, (Mark, ix, 25; Luke, iv, 35). 2. None can speak to leprosy, but Christ, "Be thou clean." (Matt., viii, 3; Luke, iv, 39.) 3. Christ can speak to stark death: "Jesus cried with a loud voice, Lazarus, come forth." (John, xi, 43, v, 28.) 4. He can speak to life, in the abstract, "Come from the four winds, O breath, breathe upon these slain, that they may live." (Ezek., xxxvii, 9.) 5. God can speak to mother-nothing, as if Nothing had ears and reason, and could hear; "He calleth things that are not, as though they were." (Rom., iv, 17.) He did but nod upon nothing, and out of nothing there compeared before him "the great host of heaven and earth, and all things in them," (Psalm xxxiii, 9). 6. There is a language of providence, by which every being, as being, hath a power obediential to hear what God saith, and do it: "The Lord spake to the fish, and it vomited out Jonah on the dry land." (Jonah, ii, 10.) "And he rose and rebuked the wind, and said unto the sea, Peace, be still; and the wind ceased, and there was a great calm." (Mark, iv, 39.) What wise man can boast the sea? What ears have the senseless and lifeless waters? Yet they hear Christ's language—they speak, 'Yonder standeth our Creator boasting us, and therefore we will obey,' (Isaiah, l, 2). Here himself speak: "Behold, at my rebuke, I dry up the sea," (Psalm cxiv). There is a question put upon the creatures, that they can well answer, "What aileth thee, O thou sea, that thou fleddest? thou, Jordan, that thou wast driven backward?" (Verse 5.) What ailed you, "Ye mountains, that ye skipped like rams, and ye little hills, like lambs?" (Verse 6.) Good reason, saith the Spirit: "Tremble, thou earth, at the presence of the Lord, at the presence of the God of Jacob." (Verse 7.)

This obediential power is not any quality created in the creature different from their being, for God may use any creature to infinite effects of omnipotency; and so there should be infinite created qualities in every finite creature. 2. This obediential power was in that mother-nothing, out of which God, by an omnipotent act of creation, extracted all the host of creatures that now are; and it is in that other mother-nothing, yet objected to omnipotency, according to which, God may create infinite more worlds than now are, so it please him. It is then nothing but a non-repugnancy to hear and obey God in these particulars: As, 1. Omnipotency of strong grace can speak to sin, which none can do, but God: "I said to thee, when thou wast in thy blood, live." (Ezek., xvi, 6.) This mandate of omnipotent grace is spoken to Jerusalem as hardened and cold, dead in sin, wherefore he saith, "Awake, thou that sleepest, and arise from the dead, and Christ shall give thee light." (Eph., v, 14.) This is a commandment of Omnipotency, given out of sinful rebellion. If Omnipotency say, 'See, ye blind; hear, ye deaf;'—grace is a king over sin, and Omnipotency a mighty conqueror: rebellion cannot stand before the grace of God: could we resign rebellious and dead hearts to God, he should change them, though we be most unable to master them. 2. Mere nothing is a servant to Omnipotency. He sendeth his mandate or statute of heaven to mere nothing; and darkness, as the serjeant and pursuivant of God, must send out light, by virtue of a creating mandate, (2 Cor., iv, 6). 3. Every creature is under the awe of Omnipotency, and dare not without (as it were) a written and signed ordinance and statute of the Almighty, exercise their natural operations. As the Lord sendeth an awful mandate to the sea, and God saith, Do not ebb and flow, and the sea is dried up at his rebuke; "The waters saw thee, O God, the waters saw thee, they were afraid." (Psalm lxxvii, 16.) So saith he, 'Winds, blow not; seas, rage not; fire, burn not; lions, devour not; sun, move not; clouds, rain not; devils, hurt not; waters, overwhelm not; sword, destroy not:' and they all obey. 4. There is a power obediential in creatures, to be instruments, that can be elevated above, and contrary to their nature, to miracles; as clay to be a plaister to blind eyes, to make them see, whereas clay can put out seeing eyes. By this, iron can swim, Peter walk in the sea; yea, devils and men crossing God's moral will, fulfill his eternal counsel, according to that, Ps. cxix, 91: "All are thy servants;" hell, devils, cavaliers, malignants, Papists, are God's servants. 5. By this power, whereas nature must have time and hours to work, yet nature followeth the swift pace of Omnipotency. The fever departeth from Peter's mother-in-law in an instant. 6. By this power, creatures creep into nothing, when God commandeth them so to do. God putteth his arm to the heaven, and shaketh it, and the hangings, pillars, walls, plenishing of the house of heaven and earth, are all dissolved: all the old tenants of the world, the heavens, which have sitten in God's house five thousand years, at the first warning of their Almighty Landlord, must remove and retire into nothing, if God so command them.

Use 1. It is comfort to the believer that all things are possible. Faith hath Omnipotency at its service: the sword and wars are gone, the enemies of the Lord broken, the temple built, Babylon plagued, at the nod of faith. Devils cannot stand, when Christ's mandate chargeth them to fall.

Use 2. It is but little that we can do; let us have hosts of men, we cannot have the victory. Let man be swift, yet the race is not to the swift; let him be strong, yet the battle is not to the strong; let him be wise and learned, neither is bread to the wise, nor yet riches to men of understanding, (Eccles., ix, 11). 1. The word of the Almighty is his deed also; "He spake, and it was done, he commanded, and it stood fast;" (Psalm xxxiii, 9;) for he himself spake, and it was. The Lord's word giveth being to things; by the contrary, men's deeds are nothing but words; so the lives, being, and actions of the kings of Israel and Judah, are called (*Dibre hajamim*), words of days. They are the acts and deeds of men living and dying, and compassed with days: for the deeds and acts of men are but words; they live, and speak a little on earth, and die; their acts are of as little worth, and reality, as the airing out, or breathing forth of words. The greatest prince maketh a sound for a time, as one that speaketh words, and then he is gone, and lieth silent in the grave. Solomon did many acts, but they are called words only, (1 Kings, xi, 41): "And the rest of the acts of Solomon, (Hebrew, 'The rest of the words of Solomon,') are written in the books of the Acts, (Hebrew, 'of the words') of Solomon." "And the rest of the words which Amon did, are written in the book of the words of the days of the kings of Judah." (2 Kings, xxi, 25.) We use not properly to do or act words, but to speak words; but the holy language maketh man, and all his noble acts, but words, and would express that he is a creature of no great action, and can say more than he can do. Strong and mighty man is but a creature of words; he is a speaking body of clay, and can do but little. We boast much, that this and that we shall do; God hath a lock and a chain of iron on all the creatures: armies are not to be feared, the Lord smites the horse and the rider, and maketh war to cease unto the end of the earth; he breaketh the bow, and cutteth the spear in sunder; he burneth the chariot in the fire, (Psalm xlvi, 9). Be not afraid of clay, (Isaiah, li, 12).

USE 3. If the Lord's word create the being of things, then are we to conceive of him, as of an independent sovereign: we forget this, and worship a dependent God. If I suffer the people to go to worship at Jerusalem (saith Jeroboam) I shall lose both life and kingdom; God had promised the contrary, to establish him and his kingdom, so he would 'do what is right in the sight of the Lord,' (1 Kings, xi, 37, 38). But he believed, that God, in the fulfilling of his promise, must depend upon the calves set up at Dan and Bethel. So the Jews will have God, in the preserving of their kingdom and place, to depend upon the sinful murdering of the Lord of glory; (John, xi, 48,) yea, we imagine, that God cannot carry on the work of reformation, except we comply with some sort of antichristian prelate. The king thinketh he cannot be a monarch, except he have a prerogative to play the tyrant; and his throne must fall, except the antichrist, and blood, and unlawful peace with the bloody Irish murderers, and destroying of the Lord's redeemed flock in both kingdoms, be the bloody pillars of his throne and royal power. So God cannot save us, if France, Denmark, Spain, and Ireland come against these kingdoms; we are so wasted, except we make a peace dishonourable to Jesus Christ, and his prerogative royal. All this is to place God in a state of dependency: we are too wickedly careful how God shall acquit himself in his office of governing the world. Ere you or I were born, the Lord governed the world and his church without a miscarry (the church's heaven cannot be marred in Christ's hand); and when we are rotten in the dust, he shall carry on all in righteousness and wisdom: but we take it ill, if we cannot have a Providence as fair and eye-sweet as white paper, though indeed there be not one spot in God's ways. So Martha, "Lord, if thou hadst been here, my brother had not died; (John, xi, 21,) but Christ-God, in preserving lives, dependeth not on his own bodily presence here or there. Another complaineth, 'God hath forgotten me, he is not my God.' Why? 'Because I walk in darkness, and have no light, nor any sense of his love: it is the black and dead hour of midnight with me.' So the church argueth, (Isa., xlix, 14, 15; Psalm lxxvii, 3–9). But his unchangeable love depends not on the ebbing and flowing of your transient, and up and down sense: in this, you worship a dependent God.

There is no rule without God to regulate him, or yet to straighten him in his walking. We are not to misplace God; for though the God of hosts hath purposed to stain *(Lechallel)*, to cast a blot on, and profane the pride of all glory, (Isa., xxiii, 9,) and suffer

Parliaments, Assemblies, armies, councils of war, statesmen, the godly, the princes, judges, pastors, men of wisdom, learning, eloquence, parts, to miscarry in this great service against Babylon, it is to cry down the creature's garland, and the rose of their eminency, that when all spots of sacrilege and idol-confidence in men are washed off the work, the Lord only may be exalted. It is our wisdom to suffer God to be wise for us. Yea, Antinomians will have Christ no independent Redeemer; but to them his grace shall not be perfect in pardoning, except all sin in root and branch be removed from the justified, and they made as sinless as Adam before his fall, and the elect angels. Yea, how many connections of Providence do we spin and twist out of our own head?—as, How happy had we been, if the king had remained with the parliament, to countenance it! Yea, but rather how unhappy; for our reformation had been as an untimely birth, if so it had been. How blessed should I have been, saith another, if I had been rich and learned! Yea, rather, you should have dishonoured God in that condition. The catholic and mother sin is, God must be dependent, we independent.

USE 4. All of us have need of a devil, one or other, to exercise and humble us: but we go wrong to work, when we think to make good our party against the devil by our own strength. This woman yoked Christ and the devil together, and would not yoke with him her alone, and the success is blessed. We go to dispute with temptations ourselves, by reason: you shall not dispute Satan to hell with all your logic; nor can policy and state-wit calm the Prince of the bottomless pit, who is let loose now in these three kingdoms to kill with the sword. The horseman, upon the red and bloody horse, and his footman, Death, are posting through the kingdoms. More wrestling by prayer, the putting of Satan in Christ's grips, by faith effectual, by love, and sincere humiliation, should create peace; for peace is a work of creation. There is but one only can create: I mean, God, by, or at the exercise of these graces, should create peace. We lie bleeding and dying under our lusts, because Christ was not entrusted with mortification. If we gave in a bill of complaint against our devils, as this woman did, Christ should loose Satan's works and help us.

"*Be it unto thee.*"—Faith obtaineth the most excellent favours, refined mercies; and these are immediate favours, acts of immediate Omnipotency. Christ sent an immediate post to the Devil, though in a remote place, (it is an act of immediate creation) and Satan must be gone. No creature here interveneth; it is Christ's *genetheto*, his omnipotent Be it so, that doth the turn. It is not faith, it is not a good angel expelling an evil one, nor one devil beating another, nor the disciples helping the woman, though they also did cast out devils. The more immediate mercies be, the more love-expressions of God in them; the first roses, the first trees, and plants that God's own immediate art produced, and in which nature could not share, are the most perfect creatures; the rest of the creatures, after the fall, come not near in goodness and beauty to God's first sampler; which are, as it were, the first assays of Omnipotency. The greatest mercies are most immediate; these be sweet favours that come, as it were, hot and new, immediately from God himself. See it in all the excellent things that God giveth us, especially in these four: 1. In Christ; 2. Grace; 3. Glory; 4. Comfort. Christ is God's highest love-gift. Now Christ, the Mediator, was given without any medium, or any intervening mediator. God, out of the mere bottom of free love, giveth Christ. The Lord Christ was not given by so much as request, or counsel of men or angels. Christ, "by himself purged our sins," (Heb., i, 3). He "gave himself a ransom for all," (1 Tim., ii, 6). "Who his own self bare our sins in his own body on the tree." (1 Pet., ii, 24.) He satisfied and paid in his own person. It was not a deputed work: God, the Lord of life, in proper person, redeemed us. Christ's love to us was not deputy-love—he loved us not by a vicar; Christ is given freely as a Redeemer, is more essentially a gift of free grace, to speak so, than the grace of faith, which is given to those who hear and are humbled for sin. And Christ given to die for sinners, is a more immediate and pure gift of grace, than remission of sins and eternal life, which are given to us upon condition of faith; whereas a Redeemer is given to die for us, without any condition, thought, desire, any sweating or endeavour in man or angel. 2. So is grace given out of grace: saving grace is made out of nothing, not out of the potency of the matter. The new heart is a creation; and, as it is grace, is framed without tools, agents, art, or service. Grace issueth immediately out of Christ's heart; he hath no hire, no payment for it; non-payment, no money, is grace's hire. 3. And heaven is given, not by art, not by merit, not for sweating; but how? "It is the Father's will;" (Luke, xii, 32;) and 4. "God shall wipe all tears from their eyes." (Rev., xxi, 21.) It is the sweeter, that no napkin, but his own immediate hand, shall wipe my sinful face.

In heaven, the vision of Him that sitteth upon the

throne is immediate; the mirror or looking-glass of Word and Sacraments being removed, there is but a vision of God "face to face;" (1 Cor., xiii, 12). "And I saw no temple therein." (Rev., xxi, 22.) If any should ask tidings and say, 'John, what sawest thou in that new city? Was there any temple, any priests, any prophets, any candlesticks there?' He should answer, 'Oh, you know not what you speak! I saw no temple there; I saw a more glorious sight than all the temples of the earth; I saw the Lamb, the King in the midst of them; I saw Christ, the fountain of heaven. And though ye should know Moses, David, Paul, in glory, you should be so taken with beholding the face of the Lamb for evermore in an immediate vision, that you find no leisure to look over your shoulder to Moses or any other; "for the Lord God Almighty and the Lamb are the temple of it." It must be sweeter, when the sweet immediate hand of Jesus Christ shall pluck the soul-delighting roses of the high garden, and hold them to your senses with an immediate touch, so as you shall see, behold, smell, and touch his hand with the rose, and when he shall put immediately in your mouth the apples of the tree of life, and the King himself shall make himself, as it were, your cup-bearer; for there shall be neither need of pastor, prophet, or of any Christian brother, but only Christ himself, to hold to your head "a cup of the water of life," "And he showed me a pure river of water of life, clear as crystal, proceeding out of the throne of God, and of the Lamb. (Rev., xxii, 1, 2.) "He showed me;" which He?—"the Lord God Almighty and the Lamb: "He that talked with me, who had a golden reed to measure the city;" "He who carried me away in the spirit to a great and high mountain, and showed me the great city, the holy Jerusalem, descending out of heaven from God." (Rev., xxi, and xxii.) No created angel could show to John "the Bride, the Lamb's wife." And what is that, 'He showed me?' He made me see. Is that but a naked cast of the eye, or a speculation? No, it is more; he himself who only reveals all the secrets of God, "and measures the temple with a golden reed," he only gave me a drink of the water of life immediately; for to see, in the holy language, is to enjoy, (Heb., xii, 14; Rev., xxii, 4; Jer., xvii, 6; Psal. xxxiv, 12; Job, xix, 26). And then, "he showed me," must be this in good sense, 'He, he the uncreated King himself made me, or caused me to enjoy.' Messengers carry love-letters; now, there is no need of love-letters between the Lord Jesus and "the Bride, the Lamb's wife," in this condition. Certain it is, a draught of such water at the well-head must be sweetest; then immediate comforts, in a heavy condition, must be sweetest also; as in heavy desertions, word, ministry, pastors, prayer, and ordinances, cannot raise up the spirit. What doth the Lord else speak in this? No less than that mediation of means is but mediation of means, and Christ is Christ. Means in a soul sickness, yea, apostles, angels, watchmen fail; but Christ himself, with his immediate action, faileth not, (Cant., iii, 1–4; John, xx, 8–17). Christ himself, immediately by himself, will do in a moment, that which all means, all ordinances, all sweatings, all endeavours cannot do.

I do not now cry down means, and extol immediate inspirations: the latter I deny not in some cases; but I only compare means and Christ. And is not this an experience of some who are brought to the margin and black borders of hell and despairing, all creature comforts having failed them, and they having received the sentence of the second death? Yet Christ cometh with an immediate glimpse, like a fire-flaught in the air, which letteth the lost and bewildered traveller, in an extremely dark night, see a lodging at hand, whereas otherwise he should have fallen in a pit, and lost himself: and in a moment, in the twinkling of an eye, the Lord having rebuked the winds and the stormy tempests in the soul, there is a calm and peace, (Psal. xxxi, 22; Jonah, ii, 4). Christ is speedy, and swift as a roe; his leap is but a stride over a whole mountain at once, over many "mountains and hills," (Cant., ii, 8,) especially, in his immediates, when he comforts by himself. He then maketh no use of a deputy sun to shine, or of borrowed light; the sun himself riseth with his own immediate salvation, and his own immediate wings; and we see it was Christ's immediate love, yea comfort, because immediate carrieth with it the heat and smell of Christ's own hand, it hath the immediate warmness of Christ's bosom-consolation; it was an act of tender mercy that came hot and smoking from the heart of Christ; the immediate coal of love smelling of the perfume of the hearth it came last from, and that was heaven, and the bowels of Christ. Waters carried from a precious fountain in a vessel many hundred miles, are not so sweet as at the well-head; because they are separated from the fountain, they lose much of their virtue. Sometimes it is so long since the rose was plucked, that the colour and smell which it had, while it grew on its own stalk, are quite gone. Look how inferior art (which is but medicine for sick nature) is to nature in its beauty and strength: as painted physic can neither purge nor cure, so far are all means and ordinances, being but the deputies of Christ, below Christ himself. What is Paul? What is Apollos? Put all the prophets, all the apostles, all the patriarchs, all the chiefest of saints in one flower, I confess they should cast forth an excellent smell, like the outer borders of the garden of the high paradise; but all their excellency should be mediate excellency, and but somewhat of Christ—but alas! as low, as very nothing to Christ, as the smallest drop of dew that sense can apprehend, to ten thousand worlds of seas, fountains, and floods. We defraud our spirits of much sweetness, because we go no further in our desires than to creature excellency; we rest on mediate comforts, because mediate: painted things do work but objectively: only a painted meadow casteth no smell, a painted tree bringeth forth no apples; the comforts and sweetness of the creatures have somewhat of daubing in them, in comparison of Jesus Christ; all reality, and truth of excellency, is in him.

And we know, God marreth the borrowed influence of means. Armies, parliaments, learning, and all miscarry; therefore, there was never a reformation, nor a great work wrought on earth, but Omnipotency put forth many immediate acts in it. The Lord would not be beholden to Moses; he "himself divided the Red sea." He would not engage himself to fountains and vine-trees, but "he gave them water out of the rock." He would not borrow from the earth, and sowing, reaping, and ploughing, bread for his people's food; he would "give them the bread of angels" from heaven immediately. He would have no engines at the taking of Jericho; the blowing of rams' horns was a sign, not a cause; God immediately cast down the walls. He would not have a sword drawn, nor a drop of blood shed, in the people's return from Babylon, but the Lord putteth an immediate impulsion upon the spirit of Cyrus, as if he had been in a dead sleep; and he being awaked by God only, sendeth the people away. And the temple must be builded again, but how? Neither by King nor Parliament, nor armies; for, "Not by might, nor by power, but by my Spirit, saith the Lord." (Zech., iv, 6.) When Babylon is to be destroyed (as the work is even now on the wheels in Britain), a mighty angel took up the great millstone, and threw it in the sea. (Rev., xviii, 21.) Though it be a vision by comparison, yet it holdeth forth an immediate work of God in the ruin of Babylon; and angels pour their vials "on the sea, on the sun, on the river Euphrates," to make for the destruction of Babylon. And, in delivering of Lot, angels did work. God himself spake to Noah for making an ark. Although angels be creatures, yet the Lord's action by them is more immediate, than when he worketh by natural causes. When the judges scourge and imprison the apostles, no man will speak for them; the immediate power of God doth it, the chains fall off legs and arms; immediate providence is a key also to open the prison doors, and they are saved. There is a bloody war at the taking of the ark, and thirty thousand footmen of Israel killed, (1 Sam., iv, 10, 11,) but there is not a sword drawn when it is rescued. The ark cometh home,—it is alone God's immediate providence that driveth and acteth upon two milch kine to bring it home again, (1 Sam., vi, 12–14). Who knoweth but when our strength of two kingdoms hath failed us, the Lord shall make kine to bring home his kingdom and reformation to our doors?

Were it possible that creatures could work salvation for us, and freedom from the sword, and sure peace in

England, Scotland, and Ireland, without God, or any subordination to him, let it be a deliverance from the creature only, it should be no deliverance, but a curse: that which maketh salvation to be salvation, is, that God hath a finger of power, and an influence of free grace in it. Oh, but this putteth the lustre, sweetness, and smell of heaven on it, that it is "the salvation of the Lord," (Exod., xiv, 13). In regard of irresistible efficacy and success, under-causes, though chained to the influence of God, are but idol-causes; they lie as ciphers, and do nothing, no more than a lame arm can master a sword: "The Lord worketh all our works for us;" and he is daily marring, and shall further mar our armies, parliaments, councils, undertakings, to the end that more of Christ may appear in these wars, than in other wars. Some immediate power must close and crown this glorious work in Britain; God must be alone, and appear alone, and only Jehovah must be visible "in the mount," to the end that bleeding England, long afflicted Scotland. and wasted Ireland, may, with one shout, cry, "Not unto us, O Lord, not unto us, but unto thy name be the glory." This discovereth the deceit of our confidence: for when the Lord and the creature work together for our good, Asa, though his heart was perfect, possibly seeth not whether he trust on the Lord or on the physician; and yet the Scripture saith, when he was diseased in his feet, there was a worse disease about his heart. For, because "he sought to the physicians," he is blamed; yet to seek to physicians is lawful: but the Spirit of God blameth his seeking to the physicians, and saith, (2 Chron., xvi, 12,) "He sought not the Lord in his sickness;" and the reason is given, "Because he was in the physicians." So the

Hebrew readeth it: he is said, "not to seek the Lord," not because he sought to the physicians, for that had not been a sin, but because he was wholly, the whole man, soul and all, in, 'or on the physicians;' his care, pains, and heart, was all on the physicians. So also the Greek expresses great care and diligence by the like phrase, (1 Tim., iv, 15,) "Give thyself to these things."[1] Seldom do we seek to God, and trust in him, when God and the creature are yoked together in a work that we are much bent upon, as in wars, in a reformation, yea, in a journey, that the spirit is intent upon; but, in trusting on God, we interpose a folding, and a ply of the creature, between our soul-confidence and the Lord, just as a pillow is put between the man's shoulder, and a pressing burden, for fear the burden crush a bone. We are afraid we give God too much to do, or more than he is able to bear. When we sail, we seem to betrust ourselves to the Lord and the sea; but the truth is, often we trust more to the strong ship, than to the sea or the Lord. Our confidence shifteth itself from under the Lord, on upon the creature and the arm of flesh; so we walk often in the strength of the Lord, as some walk upon ice—they walk softly and timorously upon it, fearing it should break under them; they put no faith upon cracking and weak ice. We are not daring and venturous in casting ourselves and our "burdens on the Lord."

So in judgments, David's choice fell upon the pestilence, rather than the sword. Why? God's hand is sweeter and softer than the devil's, than the malignant's hard hand. Samuel is one of the best children, because he is given of God, and is a child of many

[1] En tautois isthi.—*Rutherford.*

prayers. Isaac, the joyful child,—why? No thanks to nature, or to Sarah's dead womb for him; he is the son of an immediate promise. Free-grace is rather Isaac's father and mother, than Abraham and Sarah. In ordinances a man speaketh, but if Christ himself would speak, oh, his spikenard, oh, his own perfume, oh, his own lips drop honey! Oh, his own Lebanon-like countenance! Alas, we think Christ is not Christ, except the king help him; religion is not religion, except worldly thrones bear it up. The gospel is a very immediate thing; the "lily amongst the thorns," is Christ's lily; the church stands more immediately by Christ, than any worldly thing doth. God maketh the earth to bud and bring forth her fruits; but the sun, the soil, the season of the year, and nature, are his under-servants; God watereth the earth, but by clouds. Kings are indigent, and very mediate and dependent creatures; they need armies, multitude, navies, prelates, Babylon, Ireland, France, Spain, Denmark, Holland, money, friends, parliaments;—but grace and the gospel are more immediate, and less needy. The gospel can live without all these.

SERMON XXVI.

"BE *it unto thee as thou wilt.*"—We see what power Christ hath over the devils: Christ sent him an invisible summons, 'Let Satan be gone,' and he must be gone. It is a proper work of Christ to oppose Satan. "He took part of flesh and blood," that he might make Satan unprofitable, and idle, and fruitless, (Heb., ii, 14,) as the word is used,[1] 'Why doth this fruitless tree keep the ground sapless and barren?' (Luke, xiii, 7.) So is the word taken, 'to make a thing of no effect,' (Rom., iii, 3). Things that make sport to children, as nuts, feathers, toys, are called, 'Things of infants to be put away,' (1 Cor., xiii, 11). So hath Christ taken bones, and sap, and strength, from the devil, and made him as fruitless as the feathers that serve to sport children, (1 John, iii, 8). "For this purpose the Son of God was manifested, *(ina lyse)* that he might dissolve the works of the devil." The word in Scripture is ascribed to the casting down of a house, (John, ii, 19,) to the breaking of a ship, (Acts, xxvii, 41,) to the loosing any out of chains, (Acts, xxii, 30). The truth is, Satan's works of sin and hell, in the which he had involved the redeemed world, was a prison house, and a castle of strength, and a strong war-ship, and many strong chains of sin and misery. Christ was manifested to break down and dissolve the house, to break his war-ship, and to set the captives at liberty, (Isa., lxi, 1, 2; John, xiv, 30). "And now cometh the prince of this world, and hath nothing in me." He had much in Christ, he had all his redeemed ones by reason of sin; but Christ took all from him. Since Christ came in the play, and was master of the fields, Satan never did prosper. And consider how easily Christ doth it, with a mere word, "Let it be." How was this? Christ sent an immediate mandate of dominion; he hath an immediate operation upon these invisible spirits of darkness: it is no matter how Christ do it, so it be done. Christ-God

[1] Ina katargese.

is a spirit, and how a spirit acts upon a spirit, is to be believed, rather than searched; but Christ hath these relations to Satan: 1. As God to all creatures, and thus, Satan is the workmanship of God, as he is a spirit; so whatever partaketh of being, is the adequate and consummate effect of Omnipotency—I mean, being either possible or actual; and so the motions of angels from place to place, and of devils, must be under a chain of Omnipotency, as all other things, motions, and actions of the creature are: let Satan go whither he please, Christ traceth him. 2. Christ hath the relation of a judge to Satan, and so he is tied in an invisible chain of justice: and as malefactors that are permitted to go abroad, but always with attendance, so do devils trail about with them everlasting chains of blackness of darkness, (Jude, verse 6). Whithersoever the devil go, Christ hath a keeper at his back. 3. Christ hath the relation of a conqueror to Satan, and Satan is his taken captive, (Col., ii, 15); he cannot be loosed from under Christ, either by ransom, or change of prisoner with prisoner. 4. Christ, as "the heir of all things, beareth up all by his mighty word," (Heb., i, 2, 3,) and is he in whom "all things consist," (Col., i, 17;) and so, by reason that the world, by a new gift of redemption, is subjected to Jesus Christ, there is a special and particular providence of Christ upon Satan. It concerneth the redeemed not a little, that Christ keep a strong and watchful guard upon the black camp out of which he hath redeemed us, and that "the seven eyes that are before the throne," take special notice of hell, who come in, and come out, for there is deep counsel there against us. In this consideration, Christ numbers all the footsteps of devils. Satan hath not a general warrant to tempt the saints;

but to every new act against Job, (chap. i, 12, and Job, ii, 6,) against Peter, ere he can put him upon one single blast, to cast him but once through his sieve, (Luke, xxii, 31,) yea, against one sow, or a bristle of a sow, (Mat., viii, 31, 32,) he must have a new signed commission. Christ's general pass, that Satan be suffered, as any other subject, to pass through Christ's bounds and kingdom, is not enough.

USE 1.—It is much for our faith and comfort, that our Mediator is a God of gods, a God above the "god of this world," a prince more mighty than "the prince of the air, who ruleth in the children of disobedience." Yea, now we have a greater victory over Satan, than we know: Satan is so totally routed, put off the fields, and Christ so strong, that the weakest of saints is stronger than the world, and the spirit Satan that dwelleth in the world. Christ's strength of faith, is stronger than Adam's strength of innocency, (1 John, ii, 13, 14; 1 John, v, 5); the weakest measure of saving grace, is stronger than the highest measure of malice in all hell. When Satan tempteth you, fear him not, resist him in the faith; but be watchful, for he hath a pass from Christ, else he could not come so far as the court of guard, to dally with the senses, to hold out an apple to Eve, a world of kingdoms and glory to Christ. Satan hath a warrant to bid, when he cannot buy; his pass will bear him to go to the more inner works than the senses, even to the chamber of the fancy, to send a trumpeter to the understanding: 1. Yea, to work mediately upon the will and the heart of a Judas, and to act, but in a way of distance, upon David to number the people. But a counterfeit pass with a false subscription, cannot permit Satan to go on in real motions against the will: the chain holdeth him back; there is a restraining link that all the powers in hell cannot break. A moral tie and link of the law of nature in the breast of devils, Satan can, and doth daily break, "because he sinned from the beginning;" but the other link of real acting against the dominion of Providence, is impossible to the strongest of devils or of creatures. 2. We ourselves may put in execution a conditional pass of the devil; for certain it is, Satan could but knock at Eve's door, and play the orator and sophist, to delude mind and affections; but he could not make the king's keys (as we say) and violently break up the door, or force the will, but upon condition that Eve should consent to eat the forbidden fruit: by necessity of divine justice, she must turn the first and oldest devil in the flesh that ever was, to tempt Adam to sin, and to eat; and therefore, if we be not careful to resist, we may sign the devil's pass of Providence with our moral consent. Yield once to Satan's first demand of the treaty, and you shall see you are ensnared by a necessity of God's spotless justice, who punisheth sin by sin, because you go one mile with the devil, to go with him two miles.

USE 2. If Christ at a nod have such a dominion over devils, we are under Satan's power in being tempted, more than we need. Certain it is, we improve not Christ's power of dominion over Satan to the utmost. "Christ can save to the utmost;" (Heb., vii, 25,) then he can sanctify "to the utmost," for Christ is a Saviour, not only by merit, but also by efficacy, as our divines hold, against Socinians and Arminians; and therefore he should give actual strength against temptations, if we should not so carelessly improve that power Christ hath over Satan. I do not mean, as Arminians do that free-will, by order of nature, beginneth, first, to resist Satan, and then God's grace followeth, as a handmaid; but I intend this, that because Peter is self-strong, and his flesh saith to Christ, that Christ is mistaken, and looketh beside the spirit of prophecy;—for Matt., xxvi, 35, he saith, "Though I should die with thee, yet will I not deny thee;"—belike, if he had been diffident of his own strength, and watched, and trusted in the strength of an Intercessor, he should not have been deserted, so as to deny his Lord. We put not Christ to it, to put forth his omnipotency in every act, to save us that we yield not. I deny not, but there is a necessity in regard of God's wise providence, that the saints must sin, and that they be passive vessels to carry the lustre, and hold forth the rays and beams of pardoning grace. Yet certain it is, there be hypothetical connections of supernatural providence in God's eternal decree, never put forth in action, because of our laziness: (As if God shall suffer Job to be tempted, and he by grace sin not; (as Job, i, 22,) the Lord shall also strengthen him when he is tempted the second time, not to sin: and if Abraham be tempted to offer up his only son for God, and if he yield obedience, God shall surely bless him with the blessing 'of sanctification, promised in the covenant;' as is clear, Gen., xxii, 16, 17; Heb., vi, 12–14, for we see these connections sometimes put forth in acts. But other connections are not put forth in acts, (Matt., xi, 21; Luke, xvi, 31; 1 Sam., xxiii, 12,) such as these; if David be tempted by Satan, he shall not resist, but shall number the people: if Peter be tempted, he shall not stand out in confessing his master. Certain it is, that as we come short of these comforts of a communion with God, which we might enjoy, by our loose walking; so, upon the same reason, we fall short of many victories over Satan, which we might have, if we should improve the dominion and kingly power of Christ over that restless spirit.

"*As thou wilt.*"—As thou desirest. God maketh of his free dispensation, a sanctified will and affection in prayer, the measure of his gifts to us. A word, then, 1. Of a sanctified will and affections; 2. How these are the measure of God's goodness towards us, in these positions,

POSIT. 1. The soul is never renewed, till the will be renewed; for the will is the heart of the heart, and the new heart is the new man, (Ezek., xxxvi, 26; Deut., xxx, 6). For the heart is the king and sovereign of obedience, (Deut., xxx, 19).

POSIT. 2. All sanctified affections are threaded upon the will; saving grace can lodge no where but in the centre of the heart, and that is the renewed will, presupposing new light in the mind: grace taketh this first castle.

POSIT. 3. Hence, how many grains of sanctified will, as many grains of new obedience; so love is the fire of our obedience, and willingness the fat of obedience, which is set on fire by love.

POSIT. 4. A civil will, is not a sanctified will; in some men, the will is more moral, less raging, the motions of it being less tumultuous; as in some carnal spirits, the wheels go with less noise. All rivers make not a like action and stirring on their banks; but that taketh nothing from either their nature or deepness, or occasional overswelling.

POSIT. 5. The special mark of a sanctified will, is, that it is a broken thing, as it were fallen in the midst in two pieces, and yielding to God and saving light.

There was a sea of grace and saving light in Christ: no created will stooped to the light of a revealed decree in such a submissive measure, in a hell of fear, sorrow, and anguish for an evil of punishment more than any creature was able to bear, as he did; "*Nevertheless, not my will, but thy will be done:*" far more in other things of less pain should we suffer. Especially in these, the will is to stoop: 1. In opposing our lusts, as we would testify, that the proudest piece in us, the will, hath felt the influence of Christ's death on it, "That we no longer should live the rest of our time to the lusts of men," (1 Pet., iv, 2,) "but to the will of God," (1 Pet., ii, 24; Rom., vi, 6). The dominion of will, is the dominion of sin. 2. In that the soul speaketh out of the dust, and is put to silence before God, and sitteth alone, as melancholics do, (Lam., iii, 28, 29). A tamed man is broken in his will, in which the pride of opposing God consisteth: then, "The wolf dwelleth with the lamb." (Isa., xi, 6.) 3. The subordination of the will to God, is a great sign of a subdued spirit: nothing affecteth independency more, than the vain will; "Rest on the Lord," (Psal. xxxvii, 7).[1] "Be quiet, repine not as disobedient, neither answer again," Christ is sent to bind up those that are broken in will or heart, (Isa., lxi, 1); the Hebrew will include both, "He that hearkeneth to reproof, getteth a heart, possesseth his heart," (Prov., xvi, 31); so Vatablus. The meek spirit, which in obedience submitteth to rebukes, possesseth his heart, and possesseth his own will: now, the contrary must be in the undaunted man; his will and heart must have dominion over him, and his will must possess him, as Prov., xvii, 18. The unconverted man, is a

[1] Hebrew, "Be silent toward the Lord."—*Vatablus.*

man wanting a heart and a will: a will not broken to God is as good as no will, and no heart at all. The broken heart is the heart to God, and the broken will, the will.

Posit. 6. The affections in their naturals being corrupt, grace alone maketh them pure; and when they are purest, they are strongest. It is most of the element of the earth, that is all earth, and wanteth all mixture of other elements; that is most fire, that hath least of earth in it; that is finest gold, that hath in it least of other metals, least dross, least ore. When affections are most steeled with grace, they have the least mixture in them; love, having much of grace, hath least of lust; zeal, with much grace, hath least of the wild-fire of carnal wrath: and these are known by the swiftness of their motion toward their kindly objects. The more of earth in the body, the swifter is the motion downward toward the earth. Fire worketh most as fire, when it carrieth up in the air nothing but itself, or fire-sparks like itself; but when it ascendeth, and carrieth up with it houses, mountains, and great loads of earth, the motion is the slower. Grace being essential to gracious affections, they run and move kindly and swiftly; therefore is supernatural love, "strong as death, hard as the grave." In the martyrs it was stronger than burning quick, than the wheels, racks, and the most exquisite torments; and Christ's love was stronger than hell. Of all loves, that is the strongest that bringeth sickness, swooning, and death. Gracious love produceth love-sickness, (Cant., ii, 5,) swooning, (Cant., v, 6). The martyrs have died to enjoy him, and refused to accept of life, because of the love of a union with him, (Heb., xi, 37). How many deserted souls come to this, 'I die if I enjoy not Christ.'

POSIT. 7. It is good that the affections be balanced and loaden with heavenly and spiritual light. Lower vaults and under houses, send up smoke to the fair pictures that are in the higher houses; lust's dominion over light, maketh a misty and unbelieving mind. So, when the light is carnal, and nothing but worldly policy, it is like the highest house, which, if ruinous and rainy, sendeth down rain, and continual droppings on the lower house. Mind and affections vitiate and corrupt one another: grace in either, contributes much to the spirituality of the actions one of another. So the mockers of eternity and judgment are ignorant, because they will be ignorant, (2 Pet., iii, 5); and Eli's sons will be abominably lustful in their affections, because they know not the Lord, and are ignorant of God, (1 Sam., ii, 12). Matthew heareth and seeth Jesus, and he followeth him, (Matt., ix, 9). The more that Mary Magdalene followeth and loveth, the more she knoweth and seeth the excellency of Christ, (John, xx, 1–14, compared with verses 17, 18).

POSIT. 8. When the desires are natural, then heavenly objects are desired and sorrowed for in a natural way. Balaam desires to die the death of the righteous, but Esau weepeth for the blessing in a carnal way. When the desires are spiritual, earthly objects are desired in a spiritual way—even bread, as it savoureth of Christ, (Matt., vi, 9, compared with verses 11, 12). And so the woman seeketh deliverance to her daughter, spiritually, and with a great faith.

POSIT. 9. The believer saith, 'If the creature will go along with me to my Father's house, welcome; if not, what then? There I must lodge, though gold refuse to go with me.'

See how God in a manner resigneth his own freedom in giving, and transferreth this honour on the woman's desire. God keeps pace with a sanctified will in satisfying, when the will keeps pace with God in acting, longing, and desiring. 1. He putteth heaven upon the choice of a sanctified heart: "Choose life, that both thou and thy seed may live." (Deut., xxx, 19.) "Whosoever will, let him take of the waters of life freely." (Rev., xxii, 17.) "Ho! every one that thirsteth, come ye to the waters." (Isaiah, lv, 1.) 2. Heaven is put upon the quality of the will, and what it desires; "If thou knewest the gift of God, and who it is that says to thee, give me to drink, thou wouldst have asked of him, and he should have given thee water of life." (John, iv, 10.) "I will give unto him that thirsteth, of the fountain of the water of life freely." (Rev., xxi, 6.) There is an edge upon the word "fountain;" for the fountain and first spring of the water of life is above the streams; and this is promised to him that hath a heavenly and spiritual thirst for Christ. 3. God putteth himself, and the measure or compass of heaven, upon the measure and compass of the bent and pitch of heavenly desires: "If thou criest after knowledge, and liftest up thy voice for understanding; if thou seekest her as silver, and searchest for her as for hid treasures, then shalt thou understand the fear of the Lord, and find the knowledge of God." (Prov., ii, 3–5.) There be four words here to express the bent of the will and desire: we are to "cry for wisdom." The Chaldee reads the other part of the verse, "If thou call understanding thy mother;" that the cry spoken of in the former part, may be such a high cry, as children use when they weep and cry after their mother. The other word is, 'To give the voice to wisdom.'

The other two words do note sweating, digging in the bowels of the earth, casting up much earth to find a treasure of silver or gold: "Open thy mouth wide, and I will fill it," (Psalm lxxxi, 10); Vatablus, "Seek what thou wilt, and I will grant it." It is a doubt, if any man, by enlarged desires, can put God's giving goodness to the utmost extent. 4. God maketh his fulness in giving, far beyond our narrowness in seeking: "He is able to do, "(this is as much as "he is willing to do," Rom., xi, 23; Jude, 24,) "exceeding abundantly above all that we ask or think, according to the power that worketh in us." (Eph., iii, 20.) This is considerable, that when Christ shall put the crown of incomparable glory on the head of the glorified soul, there shall be thousand millions of more diamonds, rubies, and jewels of glory on that diadem, than ever your thoughts or imaginations could reach; and more weight of sweetness, delight, joy, and glory in a sight of God, than the seeing eye, the hearing ear, yea, the vast understanding and heart, which can multiply and add to former thoughts, can be able to fathom, (1 Cor., ii, 9). When ye seek and ask Christ from the Father, you know not his weight and worth: when you shall enjoy Christ immediately up at the well-head, this shall much fill the soul with admiration: 'I believed to see much in Christ, having some twilight and afternoon, or moonlight glances of him down in the earth; but, oh! blind I, narrow I, could never have faith, opinion, thought, or imagination, to fathom the thousandth thousandth part of the worth, and incomparable excellency I now see in him.' You may over-think and over-praise Paradise, Rome, Naples, the isles where there be two summers in one year; but you cannot over-think, or in your thoughts reach Christ and the invisible things of God; only glorified thoughts, not thoughts graced only, are comprehensive in any due measure, of God—of heaven. The glorified soul shall be a far wider and more capacious circle, the diameter of it in length, many thousand cubits larger in mind, thoughts, glorified reason, will, heart, desires, love, joy, reverence, than it is now. We would, in seeking, asking, praying, in adoring God in Christ, enlarge our own desires, heart, will, and affections, broad and deep, that we may take in more of Christ. Broad prayers flow from broad desires, narrow prayers from niggard and narrow hearts. We may collect the bigness of a ship, from the proportion and quantity of its bottom, in its new framing. If the bottom draw but to the proportion of a small vessel which can endure no more but a pair of oars, the vessel cannot be five hundred tons, or be able to bear sixty pieces of ordnance: Prayer bottomed on deep and broad hunger, and extreme pain of love-sickness for Christ, and great pinching poverty of spirit, must be in proportion wide and deep. Oh! but our vessels are narrow, and our affections ebb and low, the balance that weigheth Christ weak; it is as if we should labour to cast three or four great mountains in a scale of a merchant's ordinary balance. We are proportioned in our spiritual capacities but for drops of grace: Christ is disposed to give grace as a river. It is too little to seek corn, wine, and oil from God; he is more willing to give great things than small things. To ask a feather, a penny, from a mighty prince, when he saith, "Ask what thou wilt, to the half of my kingdom, and it shall be granted to thee," is the undervaluing of the greatness of his royal magnificence. "Ask what you will," saith Christ, "of my Father in my name, and it shall be granted." Men's desires run upon removal of the sword, peace, protection, plenty, trafficking, peaceable seas, liberties of parliament, subjects, peers, cities: little are men's desires employed in seeking Christ to dwell in the land, and that the temple of the Lord be builded. All these suits are below both the goodness of the Lord, and spiritual capacity of sanctified affections; and God giveth to carnal men that which their soul lusteth after, but in his wrath.

SERMON XXVII.

"*And when she was come to her house, she found the devil gone out and her daughter laid upon the bed.*"—MARK, vii, 30.

BECAUSE I haste to an end, and shall not now refute the dream of Papists, from this collecting the lawfulness of their bastard confirmation, and of confirming children by the unhallowed blessing of the prelate; only observe the case of the child. Mark saith,[1] Cast, in a violent manner, in a bed: for this is not to be a bed of rest and security, as some Papists collect, but to express how violent Satan is in his last farewell, as when he is to be cast out; "When the possessed child is brought to Jesus, and when he saw him, straightway the spirit tare him, and he fell on the ground, and wallowed, foaming." (Mark, ix, 20.) The devil and the unclean spirits are not thrown out of a person, or land, but they must rage and foam.

1. The Lord saith, "I will cut off the names of

[1] Beblemenen epi tes klines.

idols out of the land, and they shall be no more remembered; and I will cause the prophets, and the unclean spirits, to pass out of the land;" (Zech., xiii, 2;) but this cannot be done but with great violence; the father and the mother shall thrust through "with a sword the false prophet," even their own son, before he be put out of the land, (Ver. 3.) The devil will not be removed without blood, sweating, and great violence. When the unclean spirits of men given to curious arts, and the idol, Diana, are preached down in Ephesus, "That whole great city was full of wrath, and they cry out, Great is Diana of the Ephesians! And the whole city was filled with confusion." (Acts, xix, 18, 19.) When Christ cometh to the crown and the throne, Jews and Gentiles, the kings and rulers of the earth, Herod and Pilate, with the Gentiles and the people of Israel, are gathered together, (Acts, iv, 25–27). The word, Psalm ii, 1, (*Rageshu,*) it is, to make a great tumult, as a furious multitude gathered together, that maketh a noise as the noise of a troubled sea. Therefore some, not without reason, say, the sons of Zebedeus are called *Benairegesci*, Sons of Thunder. Luke, (Acts, ii,) useth the word after the seventy *ephryaxan* which Budeus expoundeth of fierce and wild horses. And certainly Christ is crowned upon Mount Zion, with garments rolled in blood; this is a spoiling of, and a triumphing over principalities and powers. Christ dyed the black cross with red blood, when he performed this noble act of redemption, (Col., ii, 14, 15). So, when Christ entereth in any soul to dwell, there he must first bind the devil, and then spoil his house, (Matt., xii, 29). What wonder is it, that multitudes of heresies and sects, and many blasphemous and false ways arise now, when the Lord is to build up

Zion? Satan, when Christ is to sail, and his kingdom a coming kingdom, (as we pray,) raiseth up storms and winds in the broad lake of brimstone, to drown the church of God. Christ hath not fair weather when he goeth to sea, (Matt., viii, 23, 24,) yet his journey is lawful. When Christ is upon acts of his priesthood, and standeth at the great high altar, with his censer of gold, to offer up the prayers of the saints to God, he casteth fire with the same censer down upon the earth, and there be then thunderings, lightnings, and earthquakes; and hence followeth terrible judgments upon the earth, as hail, fire mingled with blood, and a mountain burning with fire, and the third part of the sea becomes blood; and a clear burning star, like a lamp, called Wormwood, making the third part of the waters bitter, doth fall from heaven, which is as much as, when Christ is upon acts of mercy toward his people, pestilent heresies of the popish clergy, and others, darken the third part of the sun and moon, that is, of the light of the gospel, (Rev., viii, 1–12). Even as when our Lord Jesus standeth to intercede for the people, and to pray for fallen Jerusalem, which is as a fire-brand plucked out of the fire, Satan standeth at his right hand, his working hand, to hinder him, (Zech., ii, 1–3).

2. This resolveth to many their state. Many are free of the devil. 'I thank God,' saith one, 'I know not Satan, nor any of his works: I have peace; Satan did never tear me, nor cause me to fall to the earth, nor doth he torment me.' But this is a fearful condition: 1. It is an argument of a false peace. When the strong man is within, the house is in peace. Not to be tempted of the devil, is the greatest temptation out of hell; and if there be any choice of devils, a

raging and a roaring devil, is better than the calm and sleeping devil. When the devil is within, he sleepeth and is silent, and the house or soul he is in is silent, and there is a covenant with Death and Hell, (Isaiah, xxviii, 15). Now, hell keepeth true to a natural man for a time; cessation of arms between the soul and Satan, is security for a time, but it is not peace. The devil's war is better than the devil's peace. Carnal hypocrisy is a dumb and silent thing, but it is terrible to be carried to hell without any noise of feet. The wheels of Satan's chariot are oiled with carnal rest, and they go without rattling and noise. The devil carrieth few to hell with shouting and crying; suspect dumb holiness: when the dog is kept out of doors he howls to be in again. The covenant of Satan to Eve, ("sin and you shall not die,") standeth with all men by nature, till Jesus Christ break peace between us and Satan. 2. Contraries meeting, such as hot and dry fire, and cold and moist water, they conflict one with another; and where Satan findeth a sanctified heart, he tempteth with much importunity; as at one time, Christ findeth three mighty temptations, and he departed from him only for a little time, (Luke, iv, 13). Where there is most of God and of Christ, there, there are strong injections and firebrands cast in at the windows, so as some of much faith have been tempted to doubt, "Is there a Deity that ruleth all; and where is he? We see him not." Another is often assaulted with this, Is there a heaven for saints? Is there a hell for devils and wicked men? We never spoke with a messenger come from any of these two countries." A third is troubled with this, "Such a business I have expeded whether God will or not." The flower of the soul, the high lamp of the light of the mind, is frequently darkened with foggy and misty spirits coming up from the bottomless pit, and darkening any beams and irradiations of light that come from the Sun of Righteousness. Faith is more assaulted than any other grace: Satan shaketh other graces; but this is winnowed between heaven and earth, (Luke, xxii, 31, 32). Satan's first arrow shot at Christ, laboureth to put a terrible *if* upon his light; "If thou be the Son of God." It is as much as, if God be God, if the Son of God be the Son of God. It is not the evidence and certainty of fundamentals, nor the strength of grace, that privilegeth souls from Satan's shafts. Strength of saving light putteth the saints often under the gunshot of Satan, that he may find a shot at them: there is only law-surety against temptations, up in heaven, when you are over score out of time, within eternity's lists; never till then.

3. Not to be troubled thus, argueth a house not watched. The gates are open night and day, as the gates of hell, that want key and lock; and the soul so secure, that the person seeth not what devils come in, what go out. But the watch set by God's fear, examineth all messengers that come in, all motions, all suggestions, all angels white and black: all rises, falls, ebbings and flowings of love, joy, desire, fear, sorrow, come under search and scrutiny; "Whence come ye? from heaven or hell?" It is time of war with the saints in this life; and then, all cities keep watch, and strangers without a pass are examined, searched, and tried, what correspondence they have with the enemy.

4. God's way of hardening by Satan, is often mysterious, silent, dumb, and speaketh not. "For judg-

ment I came into this world," (John, ix, 39); but what a judgment!—such as walketh in the dark, and killeth in a midnight sleep, that "they that see may be made blind." This judgment speaketh not. Oh, terrible! God hath put out the man's two eyes; but how, or when, he cannot tell. The nerves and eye-strings of the man's soul are broken; but there was not a crack, nor any noise heard, when God snapped them in two pieces. Christ came when the man was sleeping, and his serjeant, the devil, with him, and put his hand on his heart, and gave the lock, the sprents, and wards of the heart a thraw and a crook, and all the keys in heaven and earth cannot shut or open his heart. And this was done without noise or pain;—the man was never put to his bed for the business; the conveyance of the business was spiritual, but invisible. Oh, sleeping world! awake out of your rotten and false peace. Oh, the Lord bindeth men, and they cry not! and the devil bindeth many and they cry not. Pharaoh knew not when his heart was hardened; the conscience saw it not; even as a stone groweth in the bladder without our sense of it: the business was transacted without one cry, or any witness. Carnal hellish security is dumb-born. 'Let my child sleep,' saith the devil, 'and awake him not till the heat of the furnace of hell melt away his false peace.' Why? But men may die deluded, having no bands in their death, as they lived deluded. Wrath and justice are moving to many souls sleeping in death, without noise of feet; the sword of God is crying to souls without any voice; the wheels of the fiery chariots of God's indignation are moving over slain men in Scotland and England, without the rattling or prancing of the horses. O pity!—a tempest, a devil comes, and steals away the man's soul and his conscience out of him in the night, and he knoweth not. Christ saith, 'Silence, waken him not, till he be over ears in the lake;' and Satan saith, 'Waken him not, till I be sure of him!' A dumb judgment is twice a judgment.

SOME OTHER BANNER OF TRUTH TITLES

LETTERS OF
SAMUEL RUTHERFORD

A collection of sixty-nine of the famous *Letters*, in whic Rutherford scales the heights of sanctified eloquence t set forth the praises of his 'royal and princely King Jesus'. As pastor separated from his flock, he also gives advice on a wid range of matters and sympathizes with his correspondents i their trials and afflictions. This edition contains brief notes o Rutherford's correspondents, an outline of Rutherford's lif and footnotes giving the meaning of words not in common us today.

'The most remarkable series of devotional letters that th literature of the Reformed churches can show.'

ISBN 0 85151 163 5
208 pp. Paperback

SAMUEL RUTHERFORD
AND HIS FRIENDS

Faith Cook

ascinating biographical sketches of Rutherford himself and some twenty of his friends and correspondents. The main m is to cast additional light on Rutherford's genius as a faith-l counsellor and spiritual guide.

We are also introduced to the beauty of his *Letters* and the ›nsolation afforded to his hearers and correspondents by his ıstoral ministry.

'A fine piece of writing; easy to read and good for the soul. I holeheartedly recommend this book to all Christians.'

PRESYTERIAN BANNER

ISBN 0 85151 635 1
168 pp. Paperback

GRACE IN WINTER
Rutherford in Verse

Faith Cook

Faith Cook has sensitively rendered some of the sayings c Samuel Rutherford into verse, with the hope that, by th means, 'Rutherford may again bring the consolations of God t Christian men and women facing the temptations and trials c life'. Brief accounts of some of Rutherford's correspondents a included. The title is taken from his words to Lady Culross, see grace groweth best in winter.'

'This book is beautifully produced and with the inclusion coloured photographs it is an ideal gift.'

VOX REFORMA

ISBN 0 85151 555 X
96 pp. Clothbound. Illustrated.

For free illustrated catalogue please write to
THE BANNER OF TRUTH TRUST

3 Murrayfield Road,
Edinburgh EH12 6EL
UK

P O Box 621, Carlisle,
Philadelphia 17013,
USA